STAKHANOVISM AND THE POLITICS OF PRODUCTIVITY IN THE USSR, 1935–1941

For other titles in this series, turn to page 326.

STAKHANOVISM AND THE POLITICS OF PRODUCTIVITY IN THE USSR, 1935–1941

LEWIS H. SIEGELBAUM

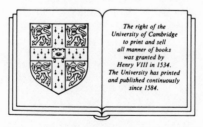

The right of the
University of Cambridge
to print and sell
all manner of books
was granted by
Henry VIII in 1534.
The University has printed
and published continuously
since 1584.

CAMBRIDGE UNIVERSITY PRESS

CAMBRIDGE

NEW YORK   NEW ROCHELLE   MELBOURNE   SYDNEY

Published by the Press Syndicate of the University of Cambridge
The Pitt Building, Trumpington Street, Cambridge CB2 1RP
32 East 57th Street, New York, NY 10022, USA
10 Stamford Road, Oakleigh, Melbourne 3166, Australia

First published 1988

Printed in the United States of America

Library of Congress Cataloging-in-Publication Data
Siegelbaum, Lewis H.
Stakhanovism and the politics of productivity in the
USSR, 1935–1941.
(Soviet and East European studies)
Bibliography: p.
Includes index.
1. Stakhanov movement – History.   2. Industrial
productivity – Soviet Union.   3. Industrial relations –
Soviet Union – History.   4. Soviet Union – Economic
policy – 1938–1942.   I. Title.   II. Series.
HC340.S6S515   1988   331.11'8'0947   87-25605

British Library Cataloguing in Publication Data
Siegelbaum, Lewis H.
Stakhanovism and the politics of
productivity in the USSR, 1935–1941
(Soviet and East European studies).
1. Industrial productivity – Political
aspects – Soviet Union – History – 20th
century   2. Soviet Union – Industries –
Political aspects – History – 20th century
I. Title   II. Series
338'.06'0947   HC340.I52

ISBN 0 521 34548 0

FOR SAMI AND SASU

Contents

Tables

Preface

This book is about work and politics during a discrete and important phase of the Soviet Union's history. "Work" here refers to industrial production as performed by manual workers and as organized and supervised by managerial and technical personnel. "Politics" is defined in the broad sense of the ways in which workers and their bosses as well as party and trade union functionaries at the enterprise and higher levels participate in and thereby help to reproduce production relations. Given the weakness of market forces in the Soviet system, the methods and tempo of production as well as the system of incentives are determined to a large extent administratively. But the execution of administrative orders inevitably entails a considerable degree of maneuvering and manipulation. Hence, one may speak of a peculiar kind of politics of production, or in the case analyzed here the politics of productivity.

Although raising labor productivity has been a nearly constant aim of the Soviet leadership, at no time in Soviet history did that aim assume such importance as in the latter half of the 1930s. Stakhanovism was an expression of this aim and, as such, intruded into the lives of most Soviet citizens. How they responded to the challenge of raising productivity is as much a part of this story as the challenge itself. Thus, culture as well as ideology, the politics of the shop floor as well as the formulation of policy at the highest levels of the political system, resistance to Stakhanovism as well as the mobility of Stakhanovites within the emerging system of industrial relations – all have a legitimate place in our analysis.

Stakhanovism is merely one of many Soviet phenomena of the 1930s that have been in need of closer examination by historians.

This book seeks not only to assess and make more intelligible that phenomenon, but to contribute to a fuller understanding of a period long dominated in Western historiography by the personality of Stalin and the Great Purges. While acknowledging the critical role of state coercion, I have tried to demonstrate that the relations between state and society in the industrial sphere were far more complex and their boundaries more fluid than is commonly recognized. That Stakhanovism was both a state policy and a social phenomenon and that the one aspect can be properly understood only in the light of the other illustrates this general point.

I embarked on this study while living and teaching in Australia. I carried out my research and writing on three continents over a period of eight years, in the course of which I was assisted by many institutions and individuals. A grant from the Vice-Chancellor's Development Fund at La Trobe University made possible at an early stage in the project the purchase of microfilm copies of many key Soviet journals. The International Research and Exchanges Board supported research trips to Britain, Finland, and the Soviet Union, for which I am particularly grateful. I also wish to express my gratitude to Carolyn Rogers for expediting my application to be affiliated with the Institute of History of the USSR in Leningrad during my visit in 1986.

Earlier in my research, I was fortunate to be the recipient of a short-term grant from the Kennan Institute at the Woodrow Wilson Center in Washington, D.C. This enabled me to exploit the Library of Congress's valuable collection of Soviet materials and work in the National Archives. I also received a grant-in-aid from the American Council of Learned Societies that made possible research at Harvard University's Russian Research Center, the repository of that university's Interview Project on the Soviet Social System. Support from the Russian and East European Studies Program at Michigan State University and the Russian and East European Studies Center at the University of Illinois is also gratefully acknowledged.

Being married to a librarian, I am acutely aware of the contributions that librarians make to scholarly research. Several assisted me and deserve my gratitude. They are John Horacek and others on the staff of the Borchardt Library at La Trobe

University, the Slavic Reference Service at the University of Illinois, the librarians at the Biblioteka Akademii Nauk in Leningrad, and, especially, the wonderfully efficient and cooperative staff of the Helsinki University Library's Slavic Division. Finally, for her encouragement and advice, for her willingness to put up with Stakhanovites when I was around and the burdens of being a single parent when I was not, I owe special thanks to Leena Siegelbaum.

Numerous individuals read drafts of chapters, made suggestions about improving them, allowed me to see their own work in progress, and in other ways contributed to this book. Diane Koenker did all of these things and provided encouragement when it was most needed; Hiroaki Kuromiya shared his immense bibliographic knowledge and, by example, set the highest standards for doing labor history; Ron Suny helped me to see the broader picture and was the best of comrades. I am extremely grateful to Sheila Fitzpatrick for answering my odd queries and for inviting me to participate in the series of highly stimulating workshops she organized in 1985–6 and to Kendall Bailes, whose book on the technical intelligentsia was an inspiration and a model. I also thank Barry Carr, Steve Niblo, Gabor Rittersporn, J. Arch Getty, Robert Thurston, Don Filtzer, Henry Norr, R. W. Davies, Richard Stites, John Ackerman, William McCagg, Gordon Stewart, Anne Meyering, and Morton Siegelbaum (my sternest critic) for listening to me ramble on about Stakhanovism and in their own ways challenging me to do the best I could. None should bear any responsibility for my errors, oversights, or malapropisms.

Russian terms and abbreviations

aktiv selected participant in party-sponsored activities

artel traditional peasant-derived work collective

brak spoilage, wastage

brigadir head of work brigade

dekada ten-day period

edinonachalie principle of one-person managerial responsibility

funktsionalka the functional principle of administration and division of labor

glavk main administration (of a branch of industry)

gorkom city committee (of party, trade union, etc.)

Gosplan State Planning Commission

kolkhoz collective farm

Komsomol All-Union Leninist Communist League of Youth

kul'turnost' quality of being cultured according to authorized standards

LP Leningradskaia pravda

Mash. Mashinostroenie

Narkomtiazhprom People's Commissariat of Heavy Industry

NFI Na fronte industrializatsii

obezlichka lack of personal responsibility

obkom regional committee (of party, trade union, etc.)

oblast' administrative region

ORS   Department of Workers' Supply

otlichniki   workers honored for high quality of output

partorg   party organizer dispatched by Central Committee

PI   Puti industrializatsii

praktik   professional lacking educational qualifications

progressivka   progressive (i.e., accelerated) piece-rate wage system

PS   Partiinoe stroitel'stvo

raikom   district committee

raion   administrative district

RP   Ratsionalizatsiia proizvodstva

RSFSR   Russian Soviet Federated Socialist Republic

SD   Sotsialisticheskii Donbass

SIu   Sovetskaia iustitsiia

Sovnarkom   Council of People's Commissars

SZ   Sovetskaia zakonnost'

TsIK   Central Executive Committee (of All-Union Congress of Soviets)

udarnik   shock worker

uravnilovka   leveling; petty bourgeois egalitarianism

Vesenkha   Supreme Council of the National Economy

VTsSPS   All-Union Central Council of Trade Unions

vydvizhentsy   working-class promotees

ZI   Za industrializatsiiu

Introduction

"The Russian is a bad worker compared with the advanced peoples," wrote Lenin in 1918. "The task the Soviet government must set the people in all its scope is – learn to work."[1] Coming six months after the Bolsheviks had assumed power, Lenin's injunction was a nearly desperate response to the revolutionary disintegration of industry that had begun before the October Revolution. But it also expressed a fundamental tenet of Bolshevik ideology: The qualities required to overthrow tsarism and the rule of capital – qualities the Russian proletariat had displayed in abundance in 1917 – were not the same as those necessary to construct the socialist order.[2] Wresting control of the means of production from the capitalists and the state that served their interests required cadres who could channel the masses' antipathy into insurrectionary action; building socialism was an altogether different – and far more complex – task.

Socialism, Lenin asserted, could be built only on the foundations of large-scale machine industry. What distinguished the "advanced peoples," what had made them advanced, was their achievement of a high productivity of labor in the context of large-scale industrial production. Learning to work meant just this – introducing and adapting techniques of organization,

[1] V. I. Lenin, "Ocherednye zadachi sovetskoi vlasti," in *Polnoe sobranie sochinenii*, 5th ed. (hereafter *PSS*) 55 vols. (Moscow: Partizdat, 1959–65), 34:187.

[2] This point has been made by Philip Corrigan, Harvie Ramsay, and Derek Sayer, *Socialist Construction and Marxist Theory: Bolshevism and Its Critique* (New York: Monthly Review Press, 1978), 27–47. Also Carmen Sirianni, *Workers Control and Socialist Democracy: The Soviet Experience* (London: Verso, 1982), chap. 4.

1

administration, and production that were pioneered in the most advanced capitalist countries. Having captured state power and expropriated the expropriators, the proletariat would have to learn how to beat capitalism at its own game. Just as capitalism had superseded the feudal mode of production by generating higher levels of productivity, so "capitalism ... will be decisively beaten when socialism creates a new much higher productivity of labor."[3]

For nearly seventy years, the Soviet government has pursued this goal with unfailing commitment. In the course of this time, quite a few models of organizing work and stimulating production have been advanced. This book is about one of them.

Half a century ago, in the midst of the long, drawn-out Great Depression that gripped the capitalist world, news came from the Soviet Union of astonishing feats of labor productivity. First in coal mining and then in other fields, Soviet workers reportedly were achieving remarkable results by applying new techniques of their own invention. The extensive publicity accorded to these feats spawned a nationwide effort to emulate them, an effort that was to involve virtually every industrial enterprise and extend beyond industry. This was Stakhanovism,[4] named after the miner Aleksei Stakhanov, who on the night of August 30–1, 1935, hewed 102 tons of coal, or fourteen times his quota.

Stakhanovism was most obviously about productivity, about making the most of working time to achieve the maximum output with available technology. This, the economic aspect of Stakhanovism, attracted immediate attention in the West. Correspondents such as the *New York Times*'s Walter Duranty described Stakhanovism as "a new speed-up system," "what is known in American industry as 'rationalization,' based on the principle of specialization."[5] The French daily *Le peuple* noted that it "is not anything other than what is already known under the name of rationalization," something that "capitalism has already endowed us ... to perfection."[6] And according to another

[3] Lenin, *PSS*, 34:189–90; also "Velikii pochin," in ibid., 39:21.
[4] The term "Stakhanovism" is used throughout this study in preference to "Stakhanovite movement" because the phenomenon was more diffuse, and contradictory, than its movement aspects.
[5] *New York Times*, Nov. 10, 1935.
[6] *Le peuple*, Jan. 7–8, 1936.

Times correspondent, Stakhanovism was supplying the "steady pushing" that the average Russian worker, "lazy and inefficient" by American standards, required.[7]

Such initial condescension notwithstanding, Western assessments of Stakhanovism's economic effectiveness generally have been positive. Alexander Baykov, a pioneer of Soviet studies in Britain, wrote in his general survey of the Soviet economic system that "the records of Stakhanov workers were not due to any increased physical effort, but to a thorough understanding of a production process by experienced, highly skilled, imaginative and enterprising workers." Their achievements were based on "a new approach to the division of labor and the utilization of working time" that "sharply raised the production results per unit of labour and time employed."[8] This view was echoed by other British scholars, such as Geoffrey Barker, Maurice Dobb, and Rudolf Schlesinger.[9] More recently, Alec Nove has characterized Stakhanovism as a "means of dramatizing and publicizing a necessary change" – that is, the raising of production quotas or norms – which "no doubt . . . had a positive effect on productivity."[10]

However, there have been exceptions. Joseph Berliner, writing in the mid–1950s, took an agnostic position, arguing that "A clear demonstration of the net positive and negative results of that dramatic movement has not yet been presented by western students, and perhaps never will be because of its numerous peripheral effects."[11] Far more negative was the assessment of Solomon Schwarz, who contributed several articles on Stakhanovism to the emigré Menshevik journal *Sotsialisticheskii vestnik* (The Socialist Herald). Noting the excessive haste and waste

[7] *New York Times*, March 8, 1936.
[8] Alexander Baykov, *The Development of the Soviet Economic System* (Cambridge University Press, 1948), 337.
[9] See G. R. Barker, *Some Problems of Incentives and Labour Productivity in Soviet Industry* (Oxford: Blackwell, n.d.), 76–84; Maurice Dobb, *Soviet Economic Development Since 1917* (London: Routledge & Kegan Paul, 1966), 467–78; and Rudolf Schlesinger, *The Spirit of Post-War Russia* (London: Dobson, 1947), 19, 23.
[10] Alec Nove, *An Economic History of the USSR* (London: Lane, 1969), 232–3.
[11] Joseph Berliner, *Factory and Manager in the USSR* (Cambridge, Mass.: Harvard University Press, 1957), 273.

induced by Stakhanovite periods, Schwarz concluded that Stakhanovism exacerbated the lack of proportionality among different enterprises and sectors of the economy, thus intensifying the planlessness of the entire system. "Stakhanovism," he wrote in his classic study, *Labor in the Soviet Union*, "soon became a euphemism for the utter straining of every bit of energy" that "brought the internal organization of work in the plants to a virtual state of crisis" in 1936–7.[12]

A more elaborate critique of Stakhanovism along these lines can be found in Donald Filtzer's analysis of Soviet production relations in the 1930s. Filtzer argues that Stakhanovism led to serious disruptions of production, a deterioration in quality, an overtaxing of machinery, and increased stoppages and breakdowns. Whatever "benefits" resulted from the speedup and greater intensity of labor were negated by Stakhanovism's disruptive effects. Increases in productivity that others had attributed to the movement were rather the result of the "thoroughgoing modernization" of Soviet plant that had occurred previously and that "brought in its wake further improvements in the technical organization of production."[13]

If Stakhanovism had such a negative impact on productivity and overall economic performance, why, it could be asked, did Soviet authorities promote it with such vigor? Filtzer asserts that Stakhanovism served an important political function. Like shock work, the characteristic mode of labor mobilization during the First Five-Year Plan (1928–32), only to a greater extent, Stakhanovism "allowed the regime to create a privileged caste of industrial workers."[14] This argument has a long lineage. It goes back to Trotsky's *Revolution Betrayed*, which was published in 1937. For Trotsky, Stakhanovites comprised a labor aristocracy whose high wages and privileges were a constant source of irritation to the mass of Soviet workers. "In scope of inequality in

[12] Solomon Schwarz, *Labor in the Soviet Union* (New York: Praeger, 1952), 193–7.
[13] Donald Filtzer, *Soviet Workers and Stalinist Industrialization: The Formation of Modern Soviet Production Relations, 1928–1941* (Armonk, N.Y.: Sharpe, 1986), chap. 7.
[14] Ibid., 205.

the payment of labor," he wrote, "the Soviet Union has not only caught up to, but far surpassed, the capitalist countries."[15]

Essentially the same point was made by Albert Pasquier in his dissertation on Stakhanovism, which was also published in 1937. "The principal aspect of the Stakhanovite movement," he wrote, "is not so much technical as social," that is, "the creation of a privileged category of workers."[16] The means of fostering such a category was the progressive piece-rate system of wages, according to which the amount a worker received for each item (piece) rose once the standard output level or norm was superseded. A subject of considerable discussion and experimentation during the First Five-Year Plan, the *progressivka* flourished in the second half of the 1930s, when some 40 percent of all workers on piece rates were subjected to it. More than a decade later, Isaac Deutscher saw the expansion of progressive piece rates and the abolition of food rationing in 1934–5 as responsible for "inequality inside the working class...much greater than in any other country." Stakhanovism, in which "the piece wage has achieved its supreme triumph,...made Russia an almost classical country of a labour aristocracy."[17]

But why was the "regime" intent on doing this? Trotsky assumed it was a case of "a troubled conscience." "Local ruling groups" shared privileges with Stakhanovites in order to "escape from their isolation." Stakhanovites thus became part of the "reserve for the replenishment of the bureaucracy."[18] Another motive has been imputed by Robert Conquest. In his view, "the probable ulterior purpose was to prevent the development of working class solidarity."[19] This was the same strategy, according to Reinhard Bendix, that Communist authorities pursued in East

---

[15] Leon Trotsky, *The Revolution Betrayed* (New York: Merit, 1965), 124–5.

[16] Albert Pasquier, *Le Stakhanovisme: L'Organisation du travail en URSS* (Caen: Robert, 1937), 109.

[17] Isaac Deutscher, *Soviet Trade Unions: Their Place in Soviet Labour Policy* (London: Royal Institute of International Affairs, 1950), 107–9, 113–14.

[18] Trotsky, *Revolution Betrayed*, 125.

[19] Robert Conquest, *Industrial Workers in the USSR* (New York: Praeger, 1966), 54.

6 *Stakhanovism and the politics of productivity*

Germany during the early 1950s. Such a strategy was "characteristic of Communist rule," constituting "the fulcrum of its managerial practice and ideology."[20]

This brief survey of the ways Stakhanovism has been understood in the West reveals that, despite the variety of interpretations and emphases (as well as the ideological perspectives that informed them), a common core of assumptions has existed. Summarily stated, they are as follows:

1. Stakhanovism was the product of a strategy developed by the "regime," which had a clear idea of what it wanted to do and proceeded to do it.
2. Stakhanovism was directed primarily if not solely at workers and represented the apogee of Soviet Taylorism and a corresponding emphasis on material at the expense of moral incentives.
3. Stakhanovites were a clearly defined stratum of the working class, analogous to Western labor aristocracies.

In the course of my research, I found that each of these assumptions lacked empirical support. I discovered that Stakhanovism was far more complex than it has been portrayed in both Soviet and Western literature. Far from being merely a device – part of "Stalin's totalitarian formula for industrialization," as Merle Fainsod's highly influential text described it[21] – it was an amalgam of practices that both impinged on and were subjected to appropriation by different groups and institutions. It did consist of efforts by central political authorities to extract greater productivity from workers, but this was only part of what Stakhanovism entailed. It was also aimed at disciplining managerial and engineering-technical personnel who had become adept at ignoring, circumventing, or interpreting in their own self-serving ways instructions from above. In this respect alone, Stakhanovism was fundamentally different from Taylorism, which sought to increase managers' powers. If anything, managerial authority was *inversely* proportional to the emphasis given to Stakhanovism by higher authorities. Finally, and most suggestive of the dynamics of Stakhanovism, it involved the varied re-

20 Reinhard Bendix, *Work and Authority in Industry: Ideologies of Management in the Course of Industrialization* (New York: Harper & Row, 1963), 351–433.
21 Merle Fainsod, *How Russia Is Ruled*, rev. ed. (Cambridge, Mass.: Harvard University Press 1965), 109.

sponses of both workers and their immediate bosses to these state initiatives.

In other words, Stakhanovism was not exactly what it was supposed to be. As initiatives came down from above, they were transformed such that Stakhanovism came to be something less and also something more than was originally foreseen or officially sanctioned. It was not that the writ of the "regime" stopped at the factory gates, but that what went on beyond them had a profound effect on the formulation and modification of that writ. The raising of labor productivity to a first-order priority – itself a response to ongoing socioeconomic processes – evoked not only enthusiasm and resistance, as Soviet and Western historians respectively assert. Maneuvering and accommodation were at least as much present. These responses inflected Stakhanovism and may be said to have constituted the politics of productivity. If productivity is defined as output per fixed unit of working time, then the struggles over the means of raising output and the ways of deflecting or minimizing the burdens associated with this effort were its politics.

This conceptualization of Stakhanovism owes as much to labor historians and sociologists working outside the Soviet field as it does to recent developments within it. In particular, I have been impressed by the approach to labor history that sees it not merely as the history of a single class, but in relational terms. I take as axiomatic that work itself simultaneously involves several dimensions – economic, political, ideological, and cultural – and that its performance is subject to contestation, negotiation, and accommodation.

This is not to suggest that an identity or even family resemblance can be established between the politics of productivity in the USSR and in advanced capitalist countries. If such politics can be found in virtually every postfeudal society, each has played by different rules. Most obviously, in capitalist societies, the polity and economics are separated, as are the state and individual corporate apparatuses. Of course, productivity is often a vital concern of the state, but its involvement typically takes the form of intervention and adjudication within a formally autonomous civil sphere. In the Soviet Union (and other state socialist countries), politics at the point of production necessarily involves the state. Not only is the state effectively the only employer, but since profit is not the driving force for increasing productivity, it is the state that must introduce or at least choose mechanisms that will achieve this end. Moreover, the absence of legally constituted independent representation among workers and managers delimits and shapes politics at the point of production. But as this study will show, it does not eliminate such politics altogether.

These general considerations hardly begin to address the specificities of the party/state under Stalin and its relation to the working class, in whose name it claimed to rule. Previously, Western historiography conceived of the Stalinist state in essentially mechanistic terms – as a system of apparatuses, transmission belts, and control levers constructed on the authoritarian foundations of Bolshevism and designed to atomize the Soviet population and exercise total control over it. While still current, this totalitarian model has been subjected to much criticism in the past two decades. In scrutinizing the genealogy of the Stalinist system, both Moshe Lewin and Stephen Cohen have concluded that there was no straight line connecting it to Bolshevism. Rather, they have emphasized the decisive break that occurred in the late 1920s and that involved the suppression of much that had been part of Bolshevism's discourse.[22] Sheila Fitzpatrick has been instrumental in contextualizing Stalin's revolution from above by placing on the historical agenda the Cultural Revolution and the opportunities it provided for workers' upward social mobility. Her work on the First Five-Year Plan period and that of other social historians has seriously undermined "the idea of untrammeled political voluntarism" and the perspective whereby "the society–state relationship is seen entirely in 'we–they' terms – as an inert and unsuspecting society subjected ... by ruthless men who have gained unrestricted control of the political apparatus."[23]

[22] Moshe Lewin, *Russian Peasants and Soviet Power: A Study of Collectivization* (Evanston, Ill.: Northwestern University Press, 1968); idem, *Political Undercurrents in Soviet Economic Debates* (Princeton, N.J.: Princeton University Press, 1974); and Stephen F. Cohen, "Bolshevism and Stalinism," in *Stalinism: Essays in Historical Interpretation*, ed. Robert C. Tucker (New York: Norton, 1977), 3–29, reprinted in idem, *Rethinking the Soviet Experience: Politics and History Since 1917* (New York: Oxford University Press, 1985), 38–70.
[23] Sheila Fitzpatrick, "Editor's Introduction," in *Cultural Revolution in*

If society was less passive than the totalitarian model implies, the party/state was less monolithic and efficient. In his dissection of the "Soviet technostructure," Kendall Bailes demonstrated the persistence throughout the 1930s of tensions between production specialists and political authorities as well as divisions within each camp.[24] J. Arch Getty, relying heavily on the Smolensk Party Archive, has documented the chaotic state of party and governmental affairs in the Western Region. He interprets this chaos as both a cause and a constituent part of a center–periphery struggle, which he has termed "the politics of implementation."[25] These themes figure prominently as well in the work of Gabor Rittersporn.[26]

But if not the totalitarian model, then what? Certainly not the free play of social forces within a public sphere secure from state repression by the rule of law. As one critic of the revisionist trend within Soviet historiography has asserted: "Totalitarianism did capture a definite aspect of Stalinist society, namely, the 'total claim' of the regime on its population, sanctioned by coercive forms of rule and accompanied by a distinctive repertoire of political demands." Even if the claim often could not be cashed in, "the *aspiration* was in itself fundamentally important."[27]

This point has been most fully developed by Moshe Lewin. For him, what emerged in the course of the First Five-Year Plan was an authoritarian state that became "the sole initiator of action and controller of all important spheres of life." Society as a whole

---

Russia, 1928–1931, ed. Sheila Fitzpatrick (Bloomington: Indiana University Press, 1978), 7; and Jerry Hough, "The Cultural Revolution and Western Understanding of the Soviet System," in ibid., 244. See also essays by Fitzpatrick, Gail Lapidus, and Susan Solomon in the same volume.

24 Kendall E. Bailes, *Technology and Society under Lenin and Stalin: Origins of the Soviet Technical Intelligentsia, 1917–1941* (Princeton, N.J.: Princeton University Press, 1978).

25 J. Arch Getty, *Origins of the Great Purges: The Soviet Communist Party Reconsidered, 1933–1938* (Cambridge University Press, 1985). For the "politics of implementation," see p. 199.

26 See especially, Gabor T. Rittersporn, "L'Etat en lutte contre lui-même: Tensions sociales et conflits politiques en URSS, 1936–1938," *Libre*, no. 4 (1978): 3–38; idem, "Société et appareil d'état sovietiques (1936–1938): Contradictions et interferences," *Annales E.S.C.*, 34, no. 4 (1979): 843–67.

27 Geoff Eley, "History with the Politics Left Out – Again?" *Russian Review* 45 (1986): 385–94. Emphasis in the original.

became etatized. At the same time, however, the low level of Russian cultural and material life continued to have a strong influence on – indeed, "contaminated" – the state. "The 'crusaders' themselves got trapped in some of the least modern, most orthodox and nationalistic elements of their tradition." The cities, swollen with peasant immigrants, became "ruralized"; the party, assuming direction over the administration of the economy, became "economized"; the intelligentsia, swamped by the graduates of crash courses and the epigones of a simplified and dogmatized Marxism, became "less intelligent"; workers, more than doubling in number in the space of five years, became less skilled.[28]

It is this dialectical appreciation of the state–society relationship that informs the present study. However, in place of "contamination," which seems too pejorative, we might substitute a military metaphor (in keeping with Soviet political discourse), that of interpenetration. The state penetrated society by incorporating virtually every initiative and organization within the regime. In the sphere most relevant to our concerns, the traditional, peasant-derived work unit, the *artel*, was replaced by brigades; brigade leaders, vested with administrative powers, substituted themselves for artel elders; production-comrades courts, worker and peasant correspondents, and auxiliary organs of the police and courts functioned as disciplinary bodies; trade-union-sponsored clubs and dramatic societies and classes organized by engineers' and managers' wives saw to workers' cultural needs. At the same time, by being incorporated into the state, by participating in its procedures, the masses in some sense defined what that state was. They may not have made the rules, but they often were in a position to interpret them and necessitate their remaking. They certainly were not in a position to exercise freedom of expression, but they could be outspoken. They were not the ones screaming for efficiency, but they could

---

[28] Moshe Lewin, *The Making of the Soviet System: Essays in the Social History of Interwar Russia* (New York: Pantheon, 1985). The two key essays are "Society, State and Ideology During the First Five-year Plan" (pp. 209–40) and "The Social Background of Stalinism" (pp. 258–85), both of which have been published previously. See also the fascinating introduction, "Social Crises and Political Structures in the USSR."

"withdraw their efficiency" or, alternatively, demand that its canons be observed so that they would not unduly suffer when their pay packets were distributed.

Hence, the central issue that this study addresses is not whether or to what extent Stakhanovism increased productivity, but how the issue of raising productivity was handled. This question is treated multidimensionally. In addition to the circumstances within which Stakhanovism emerged and its early development (Chapters 1 and 2), this study explores the involvement of and impact upon managers and production specialists at the height of Stakhanovism's importance (Chapter 3); the sociological dimensions of Stakhanovism (Chapters 4 and 5); the ideological underpinnings of the "movement" in terms of its fostering of a certain culture of work and consumption (Chapter 6); and, finally, the fate of Stakhanovism and Stakhanovites during and after the Great Purges (Chapter 7).

Conceiving of Stakhanovism in these terms, this study makes no pretense of comprehensiveness. Though Stakhanovites could be found in agriculture, the service sector, and transportation, within the professions, among clerical workers, and even within the armed forces and the labor camps of the GULAG, much less space is devoted to these areas than to the sphere of industrial production. This is not only because of the constraints of space and source material, but more essentially because Stakhanovism was generated and always had its greatest resonance within industry. Moreover, although Stakhanovism persisted until shortly after the death of Stalin in 1953, the focus here is on its first years, when the politics of productivity was at its most intense.

Even within these confines, the book addresses several major issues that transcend the particularities of Stakhanovism. One has to do with what is the optimum combination of incentives – collective and individual, moral and material, positive and negative – to raise labor productivity in the context of the demand for labor generally exceeding its supply. A second is the hierarchy among, and division of labor between, managers and managed and particularly the sphere of competence and rewards allocated to foremen, brigade leaders, adjusters, and other intermediary groups. Both issues existed before Stakhanovism, and they have remained very real up to the present. But because of the prodigious overfulfillment of output norms by "outstanding" Stakhanovites and the phenomenal wages many of them received, at no time in Soviet history have they been posed so starkly.

A related issue, the conceptualization and evaluation of work in the context of mass assembly-line production, arises in connection with the comparisons that are frequently made between Stakhanovism and Taylorism, or "scientific management." It is quite true that Aleksei Gastev, the preeminent Soviet Taylorist and visionary director of the Central Institute of Labor, wrote enthusiastically about Stakhanovism. Yet in an important respect, the advent of Stakhanovism symbolized the official rejection of Gastev's technicistically tinged utopia. Even if only at the rhetorical level, the governing principle of Stakhanovism was not that of Taylorism. The latter turned on a clear distinction between managers' conceptualization of work tasks and workers' execution of them; the thrust of Stakhanovism was to abolish the distinction between these two functions.

Social mobility, a theme that has been treated extensively for the First Five-Year Plan period, also emerges in connection with Stakhanovism. The question here relates to the extent of mobility both within and out of the industrial work force and its implications for workers' solidarity. The usefulness of conceiving of Stakhanovites as an aristocracy of labor or an identifiable stratum in any sense is important in this respect and has obvious implications for the question of class and class consciousness. Western Sovietology has been obsessed with the "regime" for so long that scholars are only beginning to address the question of what kind of working class could exist in the absence of a property-owning bourgeoisie.[29] Marx's famous distinction between a class in itself and a class for itself may be a useful starting point, though what the consciousness and behavior of a working class for itself would – or ought to – be in "actually existing" state socialist societies is by no means clear.

Finally, what can Stakhanovism tell us about the evolution of

---

[29] Donald Filtzer, *Soviet Workers*, 7, 254–5, 272–3, broaches this question, as do papers by Patrick Dale, Walter Süss, and Jacques Sapir presented at the University of Birmingham Conference on the Soviet Working Class in the Inter-War Period (June 1981).

Soviet society in the 1930s? Did it revive the revolutionary upheavals that commenced with the Great Turn in 1929 or cap
what Nicholas Timasheff called "the Great Retreat" toward stability on the basis of traditional values?[30] Was it the logical consequence, indeed the apotheosis, of the "productivist" strain in
Bolshevism or rather, as Trotsky insisted, part and parcel of the
betrayal of the Bolshevik revolution? Did it, in short, constitute
a deformity or aberration specific to the period of the "cult of
personality," reinforcing that cult by the glorification of the *praktik*, or did it consolidate Soviet industrial relations, setting them
on a course from which they have not deviated since?

One would be hard-pressed to find an explicit discussion of
these issues in Soviet accounts. With rare exception, Stakhanovism has been lauded by Soviet historians, who have accorded
it an honorable place in the unfolding of Soviet socialism.[31] The
"victories" attributed to it on "the labor front" have been portrayed as analogous to, and preconditions for, the victory
achieved in the Great Patriotic War. And just as the wartime
heroism of Soviet soldiers and partisans has continued to serve
as a means of inculcating the appropriate martial spirit among
succeeding generations, so in a time of relative economic stagnation, veteran Stakhanovites have been held up as models for
emulation.[32]

Yet half a century later, there is something quaint and contradictory about those worker-innovators. On the one hand,
compared with the mundane realities of the present, these Soviet
Hercules seem almost mythological, larger than life, and therefore not quite real. On the other, their production techniques
appear primitive compared with what has been achieved in the
age of the "scientific-technological revolution." How appropriate

---

[30] Nicholas Timasheff, *The Great Retreat: The Growth and Decline of Communism in Russia* (New York: Dutton, 1946).

[31] See, e.g., I. I. Kuz'minov, *Stakhanovskoe dvizhenie – vysshii etap sotsialisticheskogo sorevnovaniia* (Moscow: Sotsekgiz, 1940), and R. Ia. Khabibulina, *Leningradskie   kommunisty-organizatory   stakhanovskogo
dvizheniia (1935–1937 gg.)* (Leningrad: LGU, 1961). For a more recent and circumspect rendition, see V. A. Sakharov, *Zarozhdenie i
razvitie stakhanovskogo dvizheniia (na materialakh po avtotraktornoi promyshlennosti)* (Moscow: MGU, 1985).

[32] See the Conclusion for more discussion of this.

are such symbols from the hoary past for solving the economic problems confronting the USSR today is a question that unfortunately cannot be explored here. But the very fact that Stakhanovism is being invoked on a considerable scale to spur party and people in the building of a "communist society" gives a scholarly analysis of the phenomenon an additional dimension of importance.

Finally, a few remarks about sources are in order. There is no shortage of material on Stakhanovism, but quality, meaning primacy, is another matter. The difficulties of making one's way through the mythological labyrinth to get at what really happened cannot be overestimated. Yet as a growing number of studies of the Stalin period have demonstrated, such difficulties need not freeze historical research in a position of self-abnegation.

The approach to sources adopted here is catholic but not undiscriminating. Essentially three kinds of sources are used. The main category consists of official sources, including the central and regional press; popular, economic, and technical publications; documentary collections; stenographic reports of conferences; and the Smolensk Party Archive. A close reading of these sources confirms what many Western scholars have recently emphasized, namely the confusion, frustration, and even fragmentation within the leadership and considerable deviation from prescribed policies at the regional and enterprise levels. Of course, they should not be treated as a mirror of reality, but rather as providing valuable clues to both the political leaders' perceptions of problems and the "ideal reality" they wished to impose.

This is also the case with Stakhanovites' autobiographies and biographical accounts, some of which were published in the 1930s and others more recently. Iconographic as they tend to be, they nonetheless furnish some basis for sociological and cultural analysis. These personal accounts are supplemented by those of engineers (both Soviet and Western) who worked in Soviet industry and the array of former Soviet citizens interviewed by the Harvard Interview Project on the Soviet Social System. The atypicality of each of these samples is certainly a problem, but that problem can be minimized when they are used in conjunction with other sources.

And for the analysis of the labor process in Soviet industry, studies of technology and its application at the point of production in capitalist societies have provided a useful comparative perspective. In particular, David Noble's emphasis on the social determinants of technological development and the conceptual creativity and rigor displayed in Michael Burawoy's works have proved inspirational.[33] Ultimately, however, Stakhanovism and the politics of productivity it exhibited must be approached and understood in terms of the USSR's own historical evolution, rather than of models derived from capitalism and the class analysis appropriate to it. This is what the present study sets out to do.

[33] David F. Noble, *America by Design: Science, Technology and the Rise of Corporate Capitalism* (New York: Knopf, 1982), and his *Forces of Production: A Social History of Industrial Automation* (New York: Knopf, 1984). The quotation from Lewis Mumford's *Technics and Civilization*, cited epigraphically in *America by Design*, applies equally to the present work. Burawoy's works include *Manufacturing Consent: Changes in the Labor Process under Monopoly Capitalism* (University of Chicago Press, 1979); "Piece Rates, Hungarian Style," *Socialist Review*, no. 79 (1985): 43–85; and *The Politics of Production* (London: Verso, 1985). I would be remiss in not citing a few other works from which I also learned a great deal: Hilde Behrend, "The Effort Bargain," *Industrial and Labour Relations Review*, 10 (1957): 503–15; Robert A. Brady, *The Rationalization Movement in German Industry* (New York: Fertig, 1974 reprint of 1933 edition); Harry Braverman, *Labor and Monopoly Capital: The Degradation of Work in the Twentieth Century* (New York: Monthly Review Press, 1974); Yannick Maignien, *La division du travail manuel et intellectuel, et sa suppression dans le passage au communisme chez Marx et ses successeurs* (Paris: Maspero, 1975); Claus Offe, *Industry and Inequality: The Achievement Principle in Work and Social Status* (London: Arnold, 1976); Donald Roy, "Efficiency and 'the Fix': Informal Intergroup Relations in a Piecework Machine Shop," *American Journal of Sociology*, 60 (1955): 255–66; and Peter Stearns, *Lives of Labour: Work in a Maturing Industrial Society* (London: Croom Helm, 1975).

1

Preconditions and precursors: industrial relations, 1929–1935

The emergence of Stakhanovism in the autumn of 1935 can be understood only against the broad backdrop of rapid industrialization and forced collectivization that had commenced some seven years earlier. The transformations in the material and social bases of the USSR that resulted from these initiatives were as intense and profound as they were exhilarating and painful. Many of the changes can be attributed to state policy, but this is not to say that Soviet society was putty in the hands of state officials. Nor is it to suggest that state policy was consistent or executed in a manner consistent with the aims of party leaders.

After presenting a brief overview of state industrialization policy and its achievements, this chapter examines the evolving relationship between higher party and state organs, on the one hand, and enterprise managerial and technical personnel, on the other, the mobilization of workers for production via socialist competition and the "handling" of this initiative by workers and management at the shop floor level, and, finally, technological and organizational developments in one of the most critical sectors of the economy, the coal-mining industry. The primary aim throughout is to delineate those processes that help to explain why Stakhanovism emerged when it did and in what ways it was a departure from the preexisting pattern of industrial relations.

I

The First Five-Year Plan, which was officially confirmed by the Sixteenth Party Conference in April 1929, was the product of bitter struggles within the party, between the State Planning

Commission (Gosplan), on the one hand, and the Supreme Council of the National Economy (Vesenkha), on the other, and within each of those bodies between nonparty specialists (who were in some cases former Mensheviks) and party planners. The final version reflected the defeat of the more cautious nonparty specialists and those elements within the party who were labeled Right deviationists by the dominant Stalinist faction.[1] The result was that what initially had been considered optimal soon came to be interpreted as minimally achievable.

The party leadership, emboldened by its political triumph, pressed forward on all fronts. Encouraged by the genuine enthusiasm that the plan evoked among many rank-and-file party activists and successes achieved in industry during 1928–9, it seems to have adopted the view that the laws of "bourgeois" economics were inapplicable to the USSR and that there really were "no fortresses that the Bolsheviks could not take." Optimism, in Alec Nove's piquant phrase, "ran riot."[2] By the end of 1929, Nikolai Bukharin, the most articulate spokesman for a more moderate pace of economic development, had been expelled from the Politburo; Mikhail Tomskii had been replaced as chairman of the All-Union Central Council of Trade Unions (VTsSPS) and an extensive purge of industrial unions was underway; the drive for complete (*sploshnaia*) collectivization had begun; and a conference of shock workers was calling for the completion of the Five-Year Plan in four years.

Over the next two years, investment and output targets frequently were revised upward. Some targets were raised in response to unanticipated crises. Such was the case with tractor production, which was stepped up in the wake of the widespread slaughter of livestock by peasants resisting collectivization. Others were based on guesswork and gross overestimation of productive capacity. Though, in most respects, actual output did not keep pace even with the relatively modest projections of the original plan, and though there was undoubtedly some statistical exaggeration, the results in industry were impressive. Gross pro-

[1] E. H. Carr and R. W. Davies, *Foundations of a Planned Economy, 1926–1929*, 3 vols. (Harmondsworth: Penguin, 1971–4), 3:893–949.
[2] Alec Nove, *An Economic History of the USSR* (London: Lane, 1969), 186.

duction in large-scale industry as measured in 1926–7 prices was reported as 30.7 percent greater in 1930 than in 1929 and 23.3 percent greater in 1931 than in the previous year.[3] The fact that the only two indices that were consistently overfulfilled were the size of the industrial labor force and costs of production suggests, in part, how such gains were achieved.

But, in fact, the Five-Year Plan was not so much about turning out goods as it was about constructing the means to do so. The construction of gigantic industrial plants and power stations, assisted by Western technology, advisers, and skilled workers, was perhaps the characteristic feature of the plan. The number of workers employed in large-scale industry increased twofold between 1928 and 1932, and those employed in construction jumped from some 625,000 to 3.1 million, or five times.[4] Given the appalling living conditions at most construction sites and many mines, labor turnover among these two groups of workers was extremely high.[5] For this reason, as well as the shortage of tools, parts, and other equipment, productivity remained well below the control figures. Consequently, by the end of the Five-Year Plan, many projects were still incomplete.

The vast majority of workers in mining and construction were peasants, "freed" from the village thanks to collectivization. Indeed, some 9 million peasants moved to the cities and industrial areas during the First Five-Year Plan. This, plus increased state procurement of grain, was collectivization's contribution to industry. But so heavy were the reverse costs in terms of both capital and cadres, that it is debatable whether collectivization did provide the primary accumulation fund for industrialization, as was intended.[6]

One historian has likened the social transformations that occurred during the late 1920s and early 1930s to a game of musical

[3] *Sotsialisticheskoe stroitel'stvo SSSR* (Moscow: TsUNKhU, 1935), 3.
[4] Nove, *Economic History*, 195.
[5] John Barber, "Labour Discipline in Soviet Industry, 1928–1941" (paper presented at the Twelfth AAASS Convention, Philadelphia, November 1980), Table A; Nobuaki Shiokawa, "Labor Turnover in the USSR, 1929–33: A Sectoral Analysis," *Annals of the Institute of Social Science* (Tokyo), no. 23 (1982):65–94.
[6] James R. Millar and Alec Nove, "Was Stalin Really Necessary? A Debate on Collectivization," *Problems of Communism*, 25 (1976):49–66.

chairs. It was "a gigantic turnover of positions" whereby "the bulk of the population changed their social positions and roles, switched into a new class, a new job, or a new way of doing the same."[7] Peasants became workers and officials or were transformed into *kolkhozniki*. If identified as *kulaks* or *kulak* sympathizers, they were likely to be sent to labor camps, performed corrective labor in construction and industry, or were resettled on generally infertile land. Workers became full-time party and state officials or were sent to technical schools, from which they could graduate directly into technical or managerial positions. And the "bourgeois" specialists had either been arrested or tried as best they could to weather the storms that were raging around them.

By 1932, those storms were subsiding, although they were to have a delayed impact in the countryside, where famine claimed millions of victims in the course of the next two years. Labor policy was reoriented toward stabilization and hierarchical organization. The expansion of piece rates and the widening of differentials between skill categories, the phasing out of the uninterrupted work week in favor of a somewhat more traditional five-day week, and the contract system that gave plant management the right to hire *kolkhozniki* directly or through their *kolkhoz* administrations ramified the new labor policy.

Although the annual plan for 1932 was still wildly optimistic, there were signs already in 1931 and during 1932 that pressure was mounting for lower growth targets. As Eugene Zaleski has noted, the proposed increase in output of large-scale industry was only (!) 36.8 percent, compared with 45 percent for 1931.[8] With a growing body of evidence of underfulfillment and overstrain before them, some Soviet officials were calling for much lower levels in the Second Five-Year Plan. Delivering his report to the Seventeenth Party Conference in February 1932, G. K.

---

[7] Moshe Lewin, "The Social Background of Stalinism," in *Stalinism: Essays in Historical Interpretation* ed. Robert C. Tucker (New York: Norton, 1977), 118; republished in Moshe Lewin, *The Making of the Soviet System: Essays in the History of Interwar Russia* (New York: Pantheon, 1985), 265.

[8] Eugene Zaleski, *Planning for Economic Growth in the Soviet Union, 1918–1932* (Chapel Hill: University of North Carolina Press, 1971), 198–204.

Ordzhonikidze, people's commissar of heavy industry, noted that some officials had the "attitude of people who panic." Ordzhonikidze characterized this attitude as "alien to us," but by October he was referring to "all kinds of chatter" that "we have failed, this didn't work, we spread ourselves too thinly, we must retreat and so forth." Again, he dismissed this view as "not ours."[9] Nevertheless, moderation prevailed. In January 1933, a plenary session of the party's Central Committee heard Stalin ask in typically rhetorical fashion whether "exactly the same policy of accelerating development to the utmost must be pursued in the period of the Second Five-Year Plan." Stalin argued for "less speedy rates" of growth, in the order of minimal average annual increases of 13 to 14 percent. Compared with the (claimed) 22 percent annual growth rates for the First Five-Year Plan period, this was a sizable reduction indeed.[10]

The year 1933 has been characterized as "a compulsory breathing space occasioned by 'leap forward' overstrain."[11] Gross industrial production rose by only 4.8 percent (compared with a projected 16.5 percent), but this modest growth was achieved with some 130,000 fewer workers than in 1932. Coal production rose from 64 million to 76.3 million tons, pig iron from 6.2 million to 7.1 million tons, and steel from 5.9 million to 6.9 million tons.[12] The state was able to accumulate funds for further investment by maintaining agricultural procurement prices at their 1928–9 levels, while keeping the rise in wage levels well below official ration prices and those of the "commercial fund," which made goods available without ration coupons but at higher

[9] G. K. Ordzhonikidze, *Stat'i i rechi*, 2 vols. (Moscow: Gospolizdat, 1956–7), 2:389, 393.
[10] J. V. Stalin, *Works*, 13 vols. (Moscow: FLPH, 1952–5), 13:187–9. Perhaps too sizable: Even during the Seventeenth Party Congress (January 1934), V. M. Molotov, chairman of the Council of People's Commissars, was arguing for annual growth rates of 19%. The officially approved figure, proposed by Ordzhonikidze, was 16.5%. See *XVII s"ezd Vsesoiuznoi kommunisticheskoi partii (bol'shevikov), 27 ianvaria – 10 fevralia 1934 g. Stenograficheskii otchet* [hereafter *XVII s"ezd VKP(b)*] (Moscow: Partizdat, 1934), 354, 435–6, 648–9.
[11] Nove, *Economic History*, 225.
[12] Roger A. Clarke, *Soviet Economic Facts, 1917–1970* (New York: Macmillan, 1972), 8, 53, 59, 60; *Trud v SSSR, Statisticheskii sbornik* (Moscow: TsUNKhU, 1936), 11.

prices.[13] Since prices in the peasant markets that existed in most urban areas were even higher than those of the state's commercial fund, the decline in real wages was even greater than what a few Soviet historians have acknowledged.[14] It should be added, however, that the continued expansion of female employment, enterprise cafeterias, private plots on the outskirts of towns, and favorable comparisons with conditions in the countryside somewhat compensated.

This was also the year in which the "passion for new construction" was replaced as the party's watchwords by the "passion for assimilating new technology." "This is now the main task," Stalin announced at the January session of the Central Committee.[15] It was the task of workers to acquire the skills that would enable them to "master" technology and thereby help the USSR to catch up to and overtake the advanced capitalist countries. During the First Five-Year Plan, some 450,000 workers and peasants graduated from the (normally) four-year factory training schools (FZU).[16] But of these, many went on to higher technical institutions or directly to administrative and technical positions, leaving a dearth of skilled workers. The reintroduction of general secondary schools in 1932–3 cut into the pool of potential FZU students, and within a year, the number enrolled dropped from 958,900 to 400,000.[17] Those entering the FZUs in September 1933 found a curriculum that was much more narrowly vocational in substance and a period of study that was reduced in length to six to ten months. Upon graduation, students could expect to be assigned to one of the "mass" occupations for three years, but were exempted from the technical minimum courses

[13] Nove, *Economic History*, 201–6. *Itogi vypolneniia pervogo piatiletnogo plana razvitiia narodnogo khoziaistva soiuza SSR*, 2d ed. (Moscow: Gosplan, 1934), 105. Average wages for all workers and employees in industry rose from 1,427 rubles in 1932 to 1,571 rubles in 1933.

[14] See, e.g., A. N. Malafeev, *Istoriia tsenoobrazovaniia v SSSR* (Moscow: Mysl', 1964), 174.

[15] Stalin, *Works*, 13:189.

[16] Marcel Anstett, *La formation de la main-oeuvre qualifée en Union Sovietique de 1917 à 1954* (Paris: Riviere, 1958), 106; Sheila Fitzpatrick, *Education and Social Mobility in the Soviet Union, 1921–1934* (Cambridge University Press, 1979), 203–10.

[17] A. G. Rashin, "Rost kul'turno-tekhnicheskogo urovnia rabochego klassa SSSR v 1917–1958 gg.," *Istoriia SSSR*, no. 2 (1961):18.

required of all other workers employed in 255 specially designated "leading" occupations.

The technical minimum courses, introduced by the Council of Labor and Defense (STO) on June 30, 1932, replaced various on-the-job training schemes, of which the production-polytechnical courses (PPK) and the workers' technical schools (RTSh) were the most widespread. As with the FZU, the technical minimum program was more narrowly conceived and shorter than those it replaced, lasting six to ten months rather than one to three years.[18] Along with programs sponsored by the Central Institute of Labor and more informal training by foremen and brigade leaders, these courses were to provide the means for rapid skill acquisition in the context of the rapidly changing technology.

By the time the Second Five-Year Plan was confirmed, most of the steelmaking plants, power stations, and automobile and tractor factories built during the First Five-Year Plan had come "on line," vastly increasing the Soviet Union's industrial capacity. The year 1934 marked the first of what Naum Jasny called the "Three Good Years" of Soviet industrialization.[19] Most output figures showed substantial increases. According to Gosplan's review of the year's results, gross industrial production was up 20.2 percent over that of 1933. Increases were considerably higher for iron ore (32.6 percent), pig iron (31.8 percent), and steel production (28.9 percent).[20] It was also the first year since the collectivization drive had begun that gross agricultural production had not declined. Reducing the gap between ration and free-market prices (mainly by sharply raising the former), the authorities set the stage for the abolition of food rationing, which began with bread on January 1, 1935.

Hence, by the middle of the 1930s, the worst seemed to be over. The frantic all-out push for capital accumulation and con-

---

[18] Anstett, *La formation*, 122–3; G. I. Zelenko, "Podgotovka kvalifitsi-rovannoi rabochei sily," in *Voprosy truda v SSSR*, ed. G. A. Prudenskii (Moscow: Gospolizdat, 1958), 93–5.

[19] Naum Jasny, *Soviet Industrialization, 1928–1952* (University of Chicago Press, 1961), chap. 6.

[20] *Industrializatsiia SSSR, 1933–1937 gg. Dokumenty i materialy* (Moscow: Nauka, 1971), 273. Percent increases calculated on the basis of Clarke, *Soviet Economic Facts*, 58–60.

struction and the struggles and sacrifices inherent in those processes had given way to more sober planning, sustained growth,
and greater social stability. After 1933, the industrial labor force
started to grow again, as an increasing number of urban women
found jobs in industry and many peasant youths, having obtained some technical training in the *kolkhozy*, sought to escape
the fate of their parents. Opportunities for workers to be
"pushed up" into managerial and technical positions were not
as great as they had been in the late 1920s and early 1930s, but
possibilities for advancement from unskilled to semiskilled status
and thence to the ranks of skilled workers were more extensive,
and the corresponding material benefits could be substantial. All
this, plus the inconceivability of overt resistance, were powerful
inducements for accommodation to a system of labor relations
built around the principles of hierarchy and discipline. Yet as
we shall see, the industrial hierarchy was far less entrenched and
labor discipline far more difficult to impose than has generally
been assumed. The accommodation of workers was paralleled
and facilitated by the accommodation of their bosses.

II

Between those who formulated and officially interpreted the
results of industrial policy and the masses of shop floor workers
stood a complex hierarchy of managerial and engineering-
technical personnel. This hierarchy extended all the way from
the "commanding staff" of industry, which consisted of the heads
of commissariat departments, *glavki* and their constituent trusts,
down through enterprise directors, chief engineers, technical
directors, shop supervisors, and other middle-echelon cadres, to
those who in conformity with the prevailing military jargon of
the time could be characterized as the NCOs of industry, that
is, foremen.[21] Along with research personnel and staff workers,
the number of these industrial cadres soared during the early
1930s (Table 1.1). Their growth, in fact, outpaced that of industrial workers. Whereas in 1930 there were 3.8 specialists in

---

[21] For such a characterization, see Lewin, *Making of the Soviet System*,
243–4.

Table 1.1. *Number of industrial cadres, 1930 and 1933*

Category	April 1930	November 1933	Increase (%)
Directors and assistants	8,507	16,926	198.9
Shop and section heads and staff personnel	56,385	197,569	347.6
Scientific-technical institute personnel	4,605	13,714	297.8
Foremen, subforemen	20,814	83,846	402.8
Total	90,761	312,055	343.8

Source: A. E. Beilin, *Kadry spetsialistov SSSR, ikh formirovanie i rost* (Moscow: TsUNKhU Gosplana SSSR, 1935), 216.

industry for every 100 workers, by 1933 the proportion had risen to 8 per 100.[22]

The chief responsibilities of the industrial cadres were the transmission of information concerning the fulfillment of various criteria contained in sectoral and enterprise plans and the execution of whatever directives and decrees had been issued from above, theoretically, on the basis of information supplied. Being in these senses intermediaries, managerial and engineering-technical personnel occupied inherently insecure positions. This insecurity was at its greatest during the First Five-Year Plan period, when it was reinforced by several factors.

First, the impossibly high targets imposed on enterprises and the desperate shortages of supplies, equipment, and skilled workers created a situation of continual emergency. Making up fifty or a hundred years in ten was the way Stalin justified the "Bolshevik tempo" of industrialization in his famous speech to industrial executives in February 1931.[23] Translated into more immediate and concrete terms, this meant that merely fulfilling quarterly and annual plans was not good enough, for operating

[22] *Industrializatsiia SSSR, 1933–1937*, 426.
[23] Stalin, *Works*, 13:41–3. Something of the strain induced by this tempo is conveyed in the First Five-Year Plan "production novels." See, e.g., V. P. Kataev, "Vremia vpered!" in *Sobranie sochinenii* (Moscow: Goslitizdat, 1956), 1:197–520, and Fedor Gladkov, "Energiia," in *Sobranie sochinenii* (Moscow: Goslitizdat, 1958), 3. Stalin's speech is cited twice in Kataev's novel.

in accordance with procedures specified by law was not going to fulfill the demands of higher authorities.

Second, enterprise personnel were subjected to various forms of "control." These ranged from the "flying visits" and "light cavalry raids" of brigades dispatched by the Workers' and Peasants' Inspectorate to periodic press exposés and more regular supervision by party, police, and trade union organs. Although the Central Committee's resolution of September 1929, which invoked the principle of *edinonachalie* (one-person responsibility), certainly tipped the balance in favor of managers, the resolution should not be seen as an open invitation to management to exercise unfettered authority. As higher officials were at pains to point out, responsibility did not mean power.[24] The main function of control was to ensure that management exercised *edinonachalie* in accordance with party policy.[25]

This explains the official displeasure with trade union and party officials who colluded with managerial personnel in avoiding responsibility or violating labor regulations. Mention should be made here as well of pressure from below in the form of worker correspondents (*rabkory*) and letters to the press, proposals submitted to the Bureaus for Rationalization and Inventions (BRIZy) within enterprises, production conferences, and less formal initiatives to be discussed below.[26]

Third, the interrelated issues of technical competence and appropriate sociopolitical backgrounds made life very difficult for those who lacked one or the other. These, of course, were not new issues. Almost immediately after seizing political power, the Bolsheviks were confronted with the question of what to do about "bourgeois" specialists, given the latter's antipathy toward

---

[24] See the statement by I. Kraval' of Vesenkha in *Trud*, Mar. 6, 1929, and *Pravda*, Oct. 8, 1929.

[25] This is one of the main points in Hiroaki Kuromiya, "Edinonachalie and the Soviet Industrial Manager, 1928–1937," *Soviet Studies*, 36 (1984):185–204.

[26] *Ratsionalizatsiia proizvodstva* (hereafter *RP*), no. 3 (1932):35; no. 1 (1933):30–1; no. 6 (1933):4, 26. On the attitude of specialists toward "so-called inventors," see John D. Littlepage and Demeree Bess, *In Search of Soviet Gold* (New York: Harcourt, Brace, 1938), 211, and Kendall E. Bailes, *Technology and Society under Lenin and Stalin* (Princeton, N.J.: Princeton University Press, 1978), 361–5.

the new regime and the distrust of rank-and-file workers toward them. Lenin, notably in "The Immediate Tasks of the Soviet Government" (March 1918), had argued for the necessity of paying "tribute" for their services in the form of high salaries.[27] Although defended by Lenin as a temporary compromise, the relatively privileged position of technical specialists became entrenched, thanks to the disintegration of the proletariat during the civil war and then the emphasis of the New Economic Policy (NEP) on cost accounting.

Tensions, however, persisted, and in the spring of 1928, after the arrest and trial of the Shakhty engineers, they exploded.[28] Bourgeois specialists were subjected to intense persecution by party organizations and the police and widespread "*spets* baiting" by workers. Such pressure continued for several years. By 1931, approximately half of all engineers and technical personnel working in the Donbass at the time of the Shakhty trial had been placed under arrest.[29] Most of the autonomous technical societies, which had preserved a certain castelike identity among their members, were disbanded.

Naked coercion was not the only method of ensuring loyalty among specialists. VMBIT (the All-Union Intersectional Bureau of Engineers and Technicians) and VARNITSO (the All-Union Association of Scientific and Technical Workers for Socialist Construction) emphasized the positive contributions of their members to industrialization while attempting to persuade them to take a more active role in socialist competition and shock work campaigns.[30] For its part, Vesenkha frequently condemned *spets* baiting as "hooliganism" and noted that unjust accusations against engineers had lowered loyal cadres' morale and labor discipline.[31]

If the bourgeois specialists were vulnerable to charges of po-

---

[27] V. I. Lenin, *Polnoe sobranie sochinenii*, 5th ed. (Moscow: Partizdat, 1959–65), 36:178–81.

[28] For an excellent account of the trial and its implications, see Bailes, *Technology and Society*, chap. 3.

[29] Ibid., 150, and Nicholas Lampert, *The Technical Intelligentsia and the Soviet State: A Study of Soviet Managers and Technicians, 1928–1935* (New York: Macmillan, 1979), 92.

[30] Bailes, *Technology and Society*, 128–40.

[31] See, e.g., *Za industrializatsiiu* (hereafter *ZI*), Apr. 18, June 4, 1930.

litical disloyalty, enterprise directors, especially the "Red directors" appointed during the 1920s, often lacked technical competence. As of 1929, less than 10 percent had a degree from a higher educational institution.[32] Lack of technical expertise was a serious obstacle to the application of *edinonachalie*. Rather than assuming full responsibility for the affairs of their enterprises, directors tended to rely on their chief engineers or technical directors, complain about "interference" by the abovementioned control agencies, and blame lower-echelon personnel for their own failure to exercise leadership.

At the same time, the party, the government, and the trade unions embarked on the program of *vydvizhenie* in response to the prodigious expansion of white-collar positions and Stalin's injunction that the proletariat required its own technical intelligentsia. The program consisted of promoting adult workers from the bench into the managerial and technical professions, either by crash courses or via vocational secondary schools (technicums) and higher educational institutions (VUZy and VTUZy). Although most of those who took the second route did not assume positions in industry until the latter half of the 1930s, workers promoted directly from the factory bench during the First Five-Year Plan comprised 105,440 of a total of 483,676 industrial administrators and specialists as of November 1933.[33]

Not surprisingly, these exogenous forces produced both intergenerational and interclass tensions among industrial cadres. Although enterprise directors and young *praktiki* had a certain affinity based on common class backgrounds and lack of formal training, neither was particularly enamored of degree-holding *vydvizhentsy*. The latter, encouraged by central authorities, exuded a cockiness that, in the opinion of many foreign engineers, was out of keeping with their narrow training and lack of experience.[34]

On June 10, 1931, the Central Committee addressed this problem by instructing enterprise directors, party, and trade union organs to "enhance the authority of the engineering and tech-

[32] *RP*, no. 9–10 (1930):48–50.
[33] Fitzpatrick, *Education and Social Mobility*, 240.
[34] See citations from U.S. State Department Decimal File, National Archives, in Bailes, *Technology and Society*, 308–9.

nical personnel," especially young specialists. Their inventiveness, energy, and initiative were to be rewarded through bonuses and publicity, and their mistakes were "to be subject to technical and economic analysis by leaders of factories and units only." As for the specialists previously tried and sentenced to forced labor, those "who have proven by their work devotion to the cause of socialist construction" were to have their sentences annulled and entries about such infractions stricken from their work papers.[35]

The reinstatement of the bourgeois specialists and the enhancement of the position of younger engineers figured prominently in Stalin's speech to industrial executives on June 23, 1931. Now that, according to Stalin, the working class had its own technical intelligentsia and the old bourgeois specialists had seen the errors of their ways, industrial cadres could be entrusted with greater powers. Over the next several years, the government passed a number of decrees that did just that. The most notorious was the law of November 15, 1932, which empowered management to dismiss workers for a single day's unjustified absence.[36] The following month saw a decree transferring the issuance of ration books and coupons for workers from the consumers' societies to enterprise administrations.[37] And from the beginning of 1933, piece rates and output norms were to be determined solely by management without confirmation from the Rates and Conflict Commissions (RKK), which contained trade union representatives.[38]

All the while, the status of industrial cadres was rising. This was reflected in the law of August 1, 1931, which provided them with additional living space, in the introduction of restricted shops and eating facilities for their benefit, and in the differential

---

[35] Quoted in Merle Fainsod, *Smolensk under Soviet Rule* (New York: Vintage, 1958), 319.

[36] *Sobranie zakonov i rasporiazhenii raboche-krest'ianskogo pravitel'stva SSSR,* no. 78 (1932):475. Previously regarded by Western historians as the archetypically repressive decree to instill labor discipline, the law of November 15 has been interpreted in a radically different light by Robert Beattie, "A 'Great Turn' That Never Happened? A Reconsideration of the Soviet Decree on Labor Discipline of November 1932," *Russian History/Histoire russe* (forthcoming).

[37] *Sobranie zakonov,* no. 80 (1932):781–7.

[38] *Trud,* May 9, 1933.

between their salaries and workers' wages, which reached a peak in 1933 and remained well above the ratio prevailing during the First Five-Year Plan.[39] Of course, these developments were not experienced uniformly by all managerial and engineering-technical personnel. First of all, there were considerable differences in the stature of personnel from one branch of industry to another, that is, between high- and low-priority sectors. For example, as one veteran journalist later recalled:

It was during those years that the names of metallurgical factory directors became known, not only to a narrow circle of economic officials, but broad sections of the Soviet public. For their work, for their successes, the country celebrated them as in the days of war it had followed the successes of military leaders.[40]

But the same hardly could be said of directors of food-processing factories, glassworks, or textile mills.

Second, norm setters, timekeepers, foremen, and subforemen did not enjoy the status or many of the perquisites of their white-collar colleagues. In September 1933, the government issued a decree stipulating that graduates of higher and secondary educational institutions do a stint at these lower levels of enterprise administration.[41] However, the decree seems to have been honored in the breach.[42] The vast majority of foremen continued to be drawn from the ranks of workers who had no specialized education. Indeed, as reported in early 1935, many of them "still

---

[39] On housing, see *Sbornik vazhneishikh zakonov i postanovlenii o trude* (Moscow: Profizdat, 1958), 126, and *ZI*, Mar. 26, 1932; on special shops, *ZI*, Oct. 18, 30, 1931; and on salaries, Murray Yanowitch, "Trends in Differentials between Salaried Personnel and Wage Workers in Soviet Industry," *Soviet Studies*, 11 (1960):229–46.

[40] I. S. Peshkin, "Stanovlenie sovetskoi metallurgii," in *Byli industrial'nye: Ocherki i vospominaniia* (Moscow: Gospolizdat, 1970), 195.

[41] *Sbornik vazhneishikh zakonov*, 123.

[42] According to the director of Krivorozhstroi, "The decision of the government to turn young engineers into foremen has not been realized. I at least have not seen such foremen." *Sovet pri narodnom komissare tiazheloi promyshlennosti SSSR. Pervyi plenum, 10–12 maia 1935 g.* (Moscow–Leningrad: NKTP, 1935), 252. See also V. M. Kulagina, *Leningradskie kommunisty v bor'be za osvoenie novoi tekhniki (1933–1935 gg.)* (Leningrad: LGU, 1962), 41–2.

lack the most elementary literacy."[43] As for norm setters, one
speaker at a conference of industrial executives in September
1934 defined their status as that of "second- or third-class employees," unlike in the United States, where, he reported, "as a
rule, the norm setter stands above the foreman."[44]

Nevertheless, for many cadres and particularly those in heavy
industry, the years from 1933 to 1935 represented a period of
unprecedented power on the shop floor and autonomy vis-à-vis
central authorities. For this, they were in no small way indebted
to G. K. Ordzhonikidze, known affectionately as "Sergo" and
apparently regarded with genuine affection by many production
specialists. Having assumed the chairmanship of Vesenkha in
the autumn of 1930 and, after its dissolution in 1932, the Commissariat of Heavy Industry (Narkomtiazhprom), Ordzhonikidze presided over the stabilization of industrial relations and
the improvement in the working and living conditions of his
subordinates. In doing so, he seems to have been guided by the
principle that those who could get the job done should be employed irrespective of their past political affiliations and that, to
get the job done, a modicum of security and respect was
required.[45]

But precisely because the most difficult and, for production
specialists, insecure period was over, there was apprehension
among top officials that complacency was setting in, that the
commanders of enterprises were becoming too comfortable, too
independent of controls. This concern was expressed in two
kinds of criticism, each of which invoked the principle of *edi-*

[43] A. Khavin, "O mastere," *ZI*, Jan. 11, 1935. As of November 1933,
77% of all foremen were former workers promoted during the First
Five-Year Plan. Only 2.1% had higher education, and 5.8% had
graduated from secondary schools.

[44] *Soveshchanie khoziaistvennikov, inzhenerov, tekhnikov, partiinykh i profsoiuznykh rabotnikov tiazheloi promyshlennosti, 20–22 sentiabria 1934 g.,
Stenograficheskii otchet* (Moscow–Leningrad: NKTP, 1935), 116.

[45] For a penetrating analysis of Ordzhonikidze's role in the bureaucratic
politics of Vesenkha, see Sheila Fitzpatrick, "Politics of Soviet Industrialization: Vesenkha and Its Relationship with Rabkrin, 1929–
1930," Occasional Paper no. 167 (Washington, D.C.: Kennan Institute for Advanced Russian Studies, 1983). For Ordzhonikidze as
"patron" of the specialists, see Bailes, *Technology and Society*, 144–51,
270–80.

nonachalie. On the one hand, *Pravda* alleged that "many managers" were exercising "petty tyranny" in their enterprises, as if they were presiding over their own "principalities."[46] These were the "bigwigs" who, according to Stalin, behaved as if "party decisions and Soviet laws are not written for them, but for fools." Past services notwithstanding, "those conceited bigwig bureaucrats" had to be brought down a peg or two and be "put... in their proper place," Stalin told the party's Seventeenth Congress.[47]

The other type of manager who deviated from *edinonachalie* were the honest but incompetent "windbags." They were "masters in the art of demonstrating their loyalty to Party and Government decisions in words, and pigeon-holing them in deed." They, too, had to be removed from operative work, Stalin asserted, for otherwise "they are capable of drowning every live undertaking in a flood of watery and endless speeches."[48]

What Stalin and other party leaders wanted above all from the industrial cadres was responsibility and accountability. Lack of personal responsibility (*obezlichka*) had been a bugbear of the authorities for many years. The problem was to find the right combination of pressures and institutional frameworks to curtail it. Pinning the blame on bureaucratic types (bigwigs, windbags, deceivers, etc.) was the simplest way of treating the problem, but it was not the only one.

In his "New Conditions, New Tasks" speech of June 1931, Stalin had linked *obezlichka* with the uninterrupted work week. This was a system that had been introduced in 1929 to keep industrial enterprises in continuous operation as well as to eliminate Sundays as a day of rest and religious observance. In principle, four-fifths of the work force was to be on the job and one-fifth off at any one time, each worker having a different rest day every week. In practice, management made frequent adjustments to accommodate the needs of families and more highly skilled workers. This may have made for smoother industrial relations, but was often done at the expense of fulfilling at least one of the system's aims, namely continuous operations. Not long

---

[46] *Pravda*, Jan. 2, 1934.
[47] Stalin, *Works*, 13:378.
[48] Ibid., 378–9.

after Stalin denounced such "distortions," the entire system was phased out.[49]

By 1934, another revolutionary innovation of the First Five-Year Plan was under attack for encouraging *obezlichka*. This was the functional system of management (*funktsionalka*) championed by the premier Soviet disciple of Taylorism, Aleksei Gastev. Functional management, an extension of Taylor's system of functional foremanship, divided managerial tasks among a multiplicity of departments. Although it promoted expertise in particular areas of administration – planning, scheduling, routing, purchasing, and the like – the system permitted the evasion of responsibility for overall operations. This at least was the charge made by both Stalin and L. M. Kaganovich in their speeches to the Seventeenth Congress.[50]

The abandonment of the uninterrupted work week and official disillusionment with *funktsionalka* demonstrate the highly provisional nature of Soviet managerial philosophy. The categorical manner in which innovations were at first defended and then, when complications arose, denounced could not conceal the uncertainty prevailing in the Kremlin. This uncertainty, we may surmise, existed not only because of the experimental nature of the entire Soviet industrialization project, but because no one model of management or labor organization was without its drawbacks. Keeping checks on management and at the same time relying on managers to keep workers in line, mobilizing workers to overfulfill production tasks while making disparate production plans compatible, urging initiative and innovation while suppressing "distortions" – the political authorities found

---

[49] Ibid., 62–7. For more on the uninterrupted work week, see Solomon Schwarz, "The Continuous Work Week in Soviet Russia," *International Labour Review*, no. 2 (1931):157–80; and Lewis H. Siegelbaum and William Chase, "Worktime and Industrialization in the USSR, 1917–1941," in *Worktime and Industrialization: An International History*, ed. Gary Cross (forthcoming).

[50] See Stalin, *Works*, 13:376, and *XVII s"ezd VKP(b)*, 532–7. For other attacks on *funktsionalka*, see Z. Grishin, "Voprosy likvidatsii funktsionalki i obezlichki v organizatsii truda," *Voprosy profdvizheniia*, no. 8–9 (1934):48–56, and A. Gastev, "Organizatsionnye idei XVII s"ezda i raboty TsIT (ot funktsional'nogo upravleniia k lineinomu)," *Organizatsiia truda*, no. 2 (1934):3–8. *Funktsionalka* also reared its head in party offices and was likewise condemned by Stalin.

themselves trying to square a number of circles and wondering why the task was proving so difficult.

Not all the leadership's frustration was directed at managers. Frequently, the control agencies, charged with responsibility for supervising the execution of decisions and the probity of executives, were the targets. If, as Stalin claimed, there were managers who had "sabotaged" party decisions and Soviet laws, "we can say with certainty that nine-tenths of our defects and failures are due to the lack of a properly organized check of the fulfillment of decisions."[51] In other words, party organs and other control agencies were colluding with management. Consequently, the Seventeenth Congress resolved to reorganize the control apparatus. The Workers' and Peasants' Inspectorate and the Party's Central Control Commission were to be replaced by respective state and party control commissions, each with representatives in the localities who were supposed to be independent of local authority.[52]

Like many other organizational shake-ups of the 1920s and 1930s, the palliative effects of this one were temporary at best. Emissaries of central organs though they were, party organizers (*partorgy*), political section (*politotdel*) heads, and even officers of the NKVD had a tendency to ally themselves with the local interests they were supposed to supervise. This was particuarly the case when local authorities pleaded for more funds and equipment and emphasized the special circumstances of their enterprises. For Stalin and other party leaders, the politics of cadres was assuming dangerously intractable proportions.

The mounting tensions between central officials and economic functionaries were reflected in successive conferences organized by Narkomtiazhprom in September 1934 and May 1935. The difference in tone and substance between these two meetings is significant. The first was one large buck-passing exercise. Directors of machine-building enterprises complained about poor-quality steel; metallurgical trust officials blamed irregular transport and low-quality coal; coal-trust heads claimed that the fault lay with the factories producing cutting and drilling machines.

[51] Stalin, *Works*, 13:381.
[52] *KPSS v rezoliutsiiakh i resheniiakh s"ezdov, konferentsii i plenumov TsK*, 8th ed. (Moscow: Gospolitizdat, 1971), 5:159–60.

Oil executives, who had more to apologize for than most, pointed the finger at their suppliers, who had failed to deliver measuring devices or who did deliver third-class pipes that were too heavy, too easily cracked, or of variable widths.[53]

The same unwillingness to accept responsibility was apparent in connection with the lack of wage and labor discipline. As K. Ots, director of the Red Putilov Factory, admitted, "an extremely dangerous situation" had been created by directors who hired workers dismissed from other plants for absenteeism and other infractions. The danger was that, by lining up jobs in advance, workers were escaping any punishment and encouraging others to emulate their negative example. "There has to be a general front among directors," Ots insisted, thereby ducking the question of his own lack of "purity."[54]

Other officials urged directors to make use of the authority they already had. M. M. Kaganovich, for example, criticized those who wanted "to play the 'liberal,' to be a 'brother,' to occupy [themselves] with persuasion.... The ground must shake when the director goes around the factory.... A director who has become a liberal isn't worth half a kopeck. Workers do not like such a director. They like a powerful leader." The head of the commissariat's Labor Section, Figatner, applied this message to output norms. "All forms of lowering norms because of a desire not to spoil relations with backward groups of workers must cease," he asserted.[55]

Finally, and not without its own irony, G. D. Veinberg, an official of the Central Council of Trade Unions, suggested that the powers of directors, shop supervisors, and foreman be expanded in administering the wage fund. Where the number of workers employed was less than what the enterprise plan provided, Veinberg argued, "the director should have the right to maneuver the wage fund by, say, three to five percent."[56]

Thus, the proferred solution to the problems encountered by enterprise management was to enhance its authority, if not its

---

[53] *Soveshchanie khoziaistvennikov 1934 g.*, 20–58.
[54] Ibid., 192.
[55] Ibid., 212–13, 227.
[56] Ibid., 297.

autonomy from central controls. This, however, was no solution at all. The real problem lay neither in the lack of formal authority nor in its evasion, but in the structural constraints on the effective exercise of that authority. As far as relations with superordinate and supply organs were concerned, the biggest constraints were "taut" planning and the irregularity of supply deliveries. It was the combination of the two, rather than personal idiosyncrasies or political deviance, that accounted for misinformation, the intentional concealment of production capacity, the covert building up of stocks, and other forms of deception.[57]

With respect to the implementation of labor policy, enterprise management was constrained by the shortage of skilled workers and the limits of the wage–effort relationship. Shaking the ground may or may not have alleviated these problems, but other stratagems were required as well. Among these, according to newspaper extracts sent to district committee (*raikom*) secretaries in the Western Region, were "widespread" instances of piece rates being raised to compensate workers for norm increases, the absence of quality control during the (inevitable) storming sessions at the end of the month or quarterly plan period, forced overtime work masquerading as shock work, and "family nests" feathered by the mutual interest of managers and party officials in perpetuating such practices.[58]

The fact of the matter was that managers, down to the level of foremen, were sometimes compelled to act as "bigwigs" and at other times to play liberals, covering their indulgence by professions of loyalty and claims to have fulfilled their responsibilities. This peculiar managerial style emerged in the course of force-paced industrialization. It was markedly different from

[57] Such practices, of course, were not peculiar to the early 1930s but persisted throughout that decade and to some extent to the present day. See David Granick, *Management of the Industrial Firm in the USSR: A Study in Soviet Economic Planning* (New York: Columbia University Press, 1954), 74–5, 161, 168. See also the resolution of the Council of People's Commissars of April 5, 1940, which condemned "the artificial swelling of operation by buying up materials, the illegal supply of individual enterprises with capital stock, leading to the squandering of deficit materials," in *Industrializatsiia SSSR, 1938–1941 gg. Dokumenty i materialy* (Moscow: Nauka, 1973), 119.

[58] Smolensk Party Archive, 1917–41, WKP-189, pp. 12–13, 38–41.

the behavior of the typical *chinovnik* of tsarist times, who was a tyrant to his subordinates but a slave of those of superior rank, and it seems to have had little to do with the social origins or educational backgrounds of its practitioners. In fact, its newness and uniqueness were precisely what confused and rankled party leaders.

The second conference, in May 1935, raised several new issues in addition to those from the previous conference that remained unresolved. Foremost among them was the business of norm determination, that is, the methods of establishing the rated capacities (technical norms) of each machine as indicated on an attached card or "passport" and, on this basis, of fixing the output standards for each task or job (technically based output norms). Technical norms were supposed to be determined either by reference to manuals – many of them derived from Western manufacturers' specifications – or via tests conducted in specialized laboratories and institutes; the officially approved method of determining output norms was time and motion study of instructors' or shock workers' performances.[59] However, these "scientific" procedures not only were complicated and time-consuming, but threatened to disrupt the tacit understandings that foremen and other line managers had with workers.[60] As a result, technical norms tended to remain in force long after modifications were made to technical processes, and the inevitably lower "experiential" output norms (i.e., those based on foremen's observations of existing output levels) everywhere predominated over those determined by chronometric readings.[61] Even in cases where more difficult, technically based output norms existed, management was able to compensate workers by

[59] These methods were derived from the work of F. W. Taylor and Frank Gilbreth. For more on the origins and development of norm determination in the USSR, see Lewis H. Siegelbaum, "Soviet Norm Determination in Theory and Practice, 1917–1941," *Soviet Studies*, 36 (1984):45–68.

[60] In the Commissariat of Transport alone, there were some 2.5 million output norms to calculate in 1933. *Trud*, May 28, 1933. For evidence of such understandings, see *Voprosy truda*, no. 3–4 (1931):32; *Udarnik*, no. 2 (1932):15–16.

[61] *Voprosy truda*, no. 11–12 (1931):43–6; *RP*, no. 3 (1932):15; *Bol'shevik*, no. 3 (1933):47–67.

shifting them around and applying progressively increasing piece-rate scales within (i.e., below) the norms.[62]

What made the discussion of this issue at the conference so highly charged was the dissatisfaction of Ordzhonikidze and other Narkomtiazhprom officials with the revision of output norms that had just been concluded.[63] Against the assertion of enterprise directors and *glavki* heads that output norms could not be raised any further without some violation of technical standards, the commissar and his deputy, G. L. Piatakov, unloaded a barrage of counterarguments. "Neither in America, nor in Germany, nor in England is technical norm-setting so fetishized as it is here," remarked Piatakov. "Progressive piece rates overturn all technically based output norms. What seemed to be a limit turns out to be minimal," he added.[64] "How many times in the past two years, calculating that machines cannot be overworked, have you actually proven this?" Ordzhonikidze asked one unfortunate *glavk* head. When the latter began to hedge on his definition of a technical norm, the commissar interjected with the "heretical thought that the technical norm determination to which we are accustomed is not fit for the devil. It only hinders our development."[65]

Such acerbity was evident in the discussion of other issues as well. To the complaint of the Khar'kov Tractor Factory's director that limitations on wage and production expenses jeopardized fulfillment of the enterprise's plan, Ordzhonikidze snapped, "Let us agree: You will give us so many tractors, and we will pay so many rubles. And nothing more."[66] Yet at least some managers refused to be cowed. In responding to Ordzhonikidze's unflattering comparisons with Ford, I. A. Likhachev, director of the Stalin Automobile Factory, flatly asserted that "at Ford the entire

---

[62] *Udarnik*, no. 2 (1932):15–16; *Voprosy profdvizheniia*, no. 1–2 (1933):83–4.

[63] According to a joint resolution of the party's Central Committee and the Council of People's Commissars of March 10, "outdated" and "incorrect" norms were to be revised by May 1, 1935. For detailed instructions to this effect, see *Industrializatsiia SSSR, 1933–1937*, 284–5; Smolensk Party Archive, WKP-189, p. 26.

[64] *Sovet pri narodnom komissare*, 230, 235.

[65] Ibid., 172–4.

[66] Ibid., 111.

process is automated assembly line.... You can't force an increase in machine time on every machine." Several other directors demanded that enterprise subsidies for childcare, schools, clubs, and newspapers be transferred to local Soviets in order to reduce their own levels of expenditure.[67]

If the outcome of the May conference was no different from that of its predecessor, there was soon to be pressure from another direction. On May 4, 1935, Stalin delivered a speech to graduating Red Army cadets in which he asserted that "technology without people mastering technology is dead. Technology directed by people mastering technology can and must create miracles." That is why, he added, the old slogan of "technology decides everything" must be replaced by a new one, namely "cadres decide everything."[68]

Just what Stalin meant by this is not at all clear. His reference to "the small" and "the great" who ought to be encouraged and promoted, but who "in a whole series of cases" were being treated in a "heartless bureaucratic" manner, did not shed much light on whether he meant engineering-technical personnel, party cadres, and/or cadre (i.e., experienced) workers.[69] It is possible that he was referring to the same problem that Ordzhonikidze and Piatakov would address, namely the invocation by management of technical limits. There was surely something ironic if this were the case. Previously, technical capacities and the "scientific" methods used to determine them had been invoked by central authorities to curb management's tendency to minimize the capacities of their enterprises. Far from capitulating to this pressure, management fought back by appropriating science for its own purposes, which remained essentially unaltered. Thus, by replacing "technology" with "cadres," Stalin may well have been signaling that a new round in this battle had commenced.

If this was the message, it was lost on many cadres. Materials in the Smolensk Archive illustrate the confusion that reigned among party committees, which were charged with realizing the slogan. Coming in the midst of a review of party documents,

[67] Ibid., 108, 112, 142.
[68] I.V. Stalin, *Sochineniia*, ed. Robert H. McNeal (Stanford, Calif.: Hoover Institution, 1967), 1 (XIV), pp. 56–64.
[69] See reference by Molotov to "cadre managers, ITR, and skilled workers," in *XVII s"ezd VKP(b)*, 364–5.

this task was interpreted by some as a call to exercise more discretion in determining which party members deserved to be promoted.[70] It was also seen as a warning to enterprise directors to curb their abuses of authority and improve conditions for their subordinates. According to one report, "Directors say that the speech is brilliant, that it opens up a new epoch, but in reality, they have not done and are not doing anything about applying it."[71]

Among some directors, however, Stalin's injunction had an effect that he surely could not have intended. This was to make them even less willing to exercise the disciplinary powers they had for fear of being accused of "bureaucratic" behavior. Such laxness provoked the Smolensk city committee (*gorkom*) secretary to make an unintentionally revealing analogy:

In a school, where all the children are permitted to take liberties and are paid no heed, they will be educated poorly. On the other hand, if discipline is established and teachers react correctly to every instance of mischievousness and naughtiness, then education will go well.[72]

It thus would appear that, by the middle of 1935, official industrial policy had yet to achieve the breakthroughs – the "miracles" – that Stalin, Ordzhonikidze, and others insisted were possible. Over the past several years, they had used a variety of carrots and sticks to improve discipline and raise productivity in industry, and not without some success. But the industrial cadres on whom they relied were not donkeys, nor were they, any more than the workers they supervised, children. Somehow, some-where, there was still a missing ingredient. This, Stakhanov was to supply. But before dealing with Stakhanov and his record, we must retrace our steps and pursue two processes that were intricately connected with industrial relations and with the mak-ing of Stakhanov's record. These were socialist competition and the technological and organizational changes in the coal-mining industry.

[70] Smolensk Party Archive, WKP-184, pp. 98–9, 198–9.
[71] Ibid., WKP-84, p. 33. That cadres themselves were capable of inter-preting Stalin's message in a self-interested way is suggested by an-other report indicating that "several employees ask why, instead of two weeks, they can't be given a month's vacation, since Stalin said that the condition of employees must improve" (p. 95).
[72] Ibid., 102.

III

The shift in official strategy outlined in the preceding section – from breakneck industrialization to consolidation, from construction to assimilation of the means of production – was reflected in the party's mass mobilization techniques. Mobilization meant not merely the recruitment of workers and the allocation of tasks to be fulfilled, but the cultivation of certain attitudes toward these tasks, or what could be characterized as a new, specifically Soviet work culture. Shock work and socialist competition were the rubrics under which such mobilization occurred, and this section is devoted to analyzing the trajectories and limitations of these phenomena. As would be the case with Stakhanovism, and for many of the same reasons, the actuality of shock work and socialist competition often bore little resemblance to what authorities intended. The culture of work that emerged in the course of the First Five-Year Plan was tainted by the accommodations and adjustments that took place at all levels of the industrial hierarchy.

"Shock work" (*udarnichestvo*) is a term that originated during the civil war period to denote the performance of particularly arduous or urgent tasks. It acquired new meaning in 1927–8 when isolated groups of workers, primarily members of the Komsomol, organized brigades to fulfill obligations over and above their work assignments.[73] These ranged from cutting down on absences and abstaining from alcohol to overfulfilling output norms and reducing the per unit cost of production.

Socialist competition represented the expansion and systematization of such efforts, usually in the form of open letters, resolutions, and challenges to emulate or outdo the examples of pioneering shock workers.[74] A critical factor in the populariza-

---

[73] See my entry on shock work in *The Modern Encyclopedia of Russian and Soviet History*, ed. Joseph L. Wieczynski (Gulf Breeze, Fla.: Academic International Press, 1983), 35:23–7.

[74] The theoretical literature on socialist competition is enormous and growing. For an interesting debate on the "lawfulness" of the phenomenon and the role of the "subjective factor," see L. A. Beilin, *Ekonomicheskie osnovy sotsialisticheskogo sorevnovaniia* (Moscow, 1975), 36–61, and the remarks of I. I. Kuz'minov in *Sorevnovanie i ego rol'*

tion of socialist competition was the appearance in *Pravda* on January 29, 1929, of Lenin's previously unpublished article "How to Organize Competition." Composed in December 1917, the article placed great emphasis on "the fight against the old habit of regarding the measure of labor ... from the point of view of the man in subjection," of treating "the *people's* factory ... in the old way, with the sole end in view of 'getting as much as possible and clearing out.'" To succeed in this fight, it was necessary to "develop th[e] independent initiative of workers ... as widely as possible in creative *organizational* work" and, in organizing competition among them, to avoid "stereotyped forms and uniformity imposed from above."

Lenin's contrast between old and new work cultures may well have inspired and guided the party, Komsomol, and trade union activists who were charged with stimulating socialist competition. But circumstances in 1929 and subsequent years were very different from what they had been in 1917–18. Then, in the wake of the political defeat and expropriation of large-scale capital, the entire wage system and division of labor lacked definition. Lenin's appeal was essentially to Bolshevik workers who were already engaged in the restitution of authority and discipline through the factory committee and trade union movements.[75] By the late 1920s, the division of labor between managers and managed had become much more clear cut. Moreover, there were not two, but at least three work cultures competing on the shop floor.[76]

First, the peasants who migrated to the factories in such large numbers in the late 1920s and early 1930s brought with them a work culture that most closely approximated Lenin's "man of

v usloviiakh razvitogo sotsializma (Moscow: Mysl', 1977), 15–18. Western scholars have tended to treat both the phenomenon and the theorizing about it in a dismissive manner, but see Isaac Deutscher, *Heretics and Renegades and Other Essays* (London: Cape, 1969), 131–50, and my own "Socialist Competition and Socialist Construction in the USSR: The Experience of the First Five-Year Plan (1928–1932)," *Thesis Eleven*, no. 4 (1982):48–67.

[75] See William Rosenberg, "Russian Labor and Bolshevik Power After October," *Slavic Review*, 44, no. 2 (1985):213–38, especially 225–6.

[76] My analysis of work cultures closely follows that of Hiroaki Kuromiya, "The Crisis of Proletarian Identity in the Soviet Factory, 1928–1929," *Slavic Review*, 44 no. 2 (1985):280–97.

subjection." For the most part unskilled, politically illiterate, and disoriented by the radical change in their situation, they posed a real challenge to organizers. Many attempted to negotiate the transition by clinging to their artels, village-based work units that elected "elders," rotated jobs, and provided room and board for their members out of their common wage fund. But since 1926, the artel had been under assault for sustaining peasants' "petty bourgeois property instincts."[77] Treated with scorn by more experienced workers and their bosses, they reacted in kind, arriving late (or not at all) to work, deliberately smashing machinery, "flitting" from one place of work to another, and engaging in "hooligan" attacks against both managers and shock workers.

The authorities may have been predisposed to attribute resistance to socialist competition to peasants' political "backwardness." But the existence of such opposition is not to be denied.[78] Yet it was often the same peasants who, in pursuit of higher wages, worked overtime at the most physically demanding jobs. Eventually, from their midst would emerge the largest number of Stakhanovites.

Second, skilled workers, many with production experience (*stazh*) extending back before the 1917 revolution, were the repositories of another work culture. This was the culture of worker, or rather trade, solidarity, of jealously guarded craft knowledge, and of numerous rites that accompanied the initiation into, and celebration of, craft practices. Such workers were

accustomed to close ranks and stand firm against the foreman, against the boss. The[y] ... disliked upstarts and bootlickers, those who sought to "curry favor" and beat down the piece rates, those who whispered to the foreman about fellow workers' idleness, and so on and so forth.[79]

It was they who, having been the party's solid base of support, experienced "the crisis of proletarian identity," about which Hiroaki Kuromiya has written so insightfully. Besieged by the tide of peasant migrants, they were threatened as well by increased

[77] Hiroaki Kuromiya, "The Artel and Social Relations in Soviet Industry in the 1920s" (paper presented at a colloquium, "The Social History of the Soviet Union in the NEP Period," Bloomington, Ind., Oct. 2, 1986).
[78] See, e.g., *Bol'shevik*, no. 17 (1930):46; *IX Vsesoiuznyi s"ezd VLKSM, Stenograficheskii otchet* (Moscow: Molodaia gvardiia, 1931), 16.
[79] G. Lebedev, "Vziat' novyi kurs," *Molodaia gvardiia*, no. 16 (1929):52.

mechanization and rationalization measures. The introduction of "Fordist" assembly-line production, which increased the demand for semiskilled operatives, heightened older skilled workers' anxiety and provoked their opposition.

Finally, there was the emerging culture embodied by younger skilled and semiskilled graduates of the factory apprentice schools and Komsomol activists. Inspired by the militant rhetoric that pervaded party discourse, they provided the initial recruits for the shock troops of socialist competition. It was not uncommon for such workers to forego their days off; to work without a lunch break or on two successive shifts; to formulate "counterplans" that were higher than those worked out by management; to increase "voluntarily" their output norms or cut their rates; and to participate in "storming" sessions to remove bottlenecks, avert disasters, and complete construction projects.[80]

However enthusiastically these workers assumed such tasks, neither management nor the central political authorities wished to leave the organization of competition to their "independent initative." At first, specially constituted troikas, staffs, and commissions, usually containing party, Komsomol, and trade union representatives, were vested with this responsibility. But, apparently, this arrangement did not provide sufficient guarantees against "localist" distortions.[81] On May 9, 1929, the party's Central Committee, citing the necessity of mobilizing "the conscious and active part of the masses" as well as the most active specialists, resolved to turn over the organization of competition to the trade unions. The resolution went on to define the "concrete tasks" of competition (fulfillment and overfulfillment of industrial-financial plans, fulfillment and overfulfillment of norms for rais-

---

[80] For some examples, see *IX s"ezd VLKSM*, 16–17, 116, 146; I. N. Mikhailovskii, *Komsomol Ukrainy v bor'be za postroenie sotsializma v SSSR (1925–1937 gg.)* (L'vov:izdatel'stvo L'vovskogo universiteta, 1966), 104, 107–9; and A. B. Slutskii, *Rabochii klass Ukrainy v bor'be za sozdanie fundamenta sotsialisticheskoi ekonomiki (1926–1932 gg.)* (Kiev: Naukova Dumka, 1963), 200, 211.

[81] V. Ol'khov, *Za zhivoe rukovodstvo sotssorevnovaniem* (Moscow: VTsSPS, 1930), 16; A. Kapustin and N. Trifonov, *Sotsialisticheskoe sorevnovanie v massy* (Moscow–Leningrad: Gosizdat, 1929), 40–1; I. P. Ostapenko, *Uchastie rabochego klassa SSSR v upravlenii proizvodstvom (Proizvodstvennye soveshchaniia v promyshlennosti v 1921–1932 gg.)* (Moscow: Nauka, 1964), 139–40; *Trud*, May 3, June 1, 1929.

ing the quality of goods, etc.) and to call on Vesenkha and VTsSPS to administer a special bonus fund for the most successful competitors.[82] Four months later, the Council of People's Commissars (Sovnarkom) supplemented this resolution by linking the amount of bonuses to the savings achieved via socialist competition.[83] Further decrees in 1930 and 1931 gave shock workers and their families privileged access to housing, "deficit" goods, educational institutions, and sanatoria.[84]

"Bureaucratism" is a term that is perhaps a trifle overused in discussions of the Stalinist system. However, there is no better word to describe what became of socialist competition after 1929. Not all initiatives to improve the performance of industry were dictated from above. But only those deemed appropriate by central authorities became the objects of socialist competition campaigns. Under the guise of *glasnost'* (here, publicity), the press orchestrated such campaigns, stipulating what targets were to be met and how. Since monetary and other material incentives were now involved, questions of who qualified as a shock worker and the methodology for calculating savings that could be attributed to competition assumed considerable importance. Still, no matter how many articles were written about these questions and no matter how many commissions were appointed to resolve them, in practice, it was enterprise management and trade union and party committees that determined them on the spot.[85]

If trade unions were supposed to organize competition and register its results, management was to facilitate and party organs supervise the process. Thus was forged a triple alliance, the main objective of which was to exaggerate the extent of and success achieved by shock work and competition. Despite the party's admonition against turning competition into "sham proclamations without the real participation of the masses," that is exactly what these organs did.[86] They did so because of pressure from

[82] *Politicheskii i trudovoi pod"em rabochego klassa SSSR (1928–1929 gg.), Sbornik dokumentov* (Moscow: Akademiia nauk SSSR, 1956), 257–9.
[83] *Sobranie zakonov,* no. 58 (1929), cols. 1145–7.
[84] *Za promyshlennye kadry,* no. 2–3 (1931):89–90.
[85] For examples, see *Na planovom fronte,* no. 7 (1930):15–23; *Voprosy truda,* no. 7–8 (1930):14–29; no. 10–11 (1930):47–53, *ZI,* June 28, 1930.
[86] *Politicheskii i trudovoi pod"em,* 258.

above to expand competition and pressure from below to ame-
liorate its disruptive effects. The best example of this was the
Leninist enrollment campaign of January–March 1930.
Launched around the slogan "Not one party/Komsomol worker
outside the shock brigades," the campaign involved quotas set
by trade union and party organizations for each region and
industry. When it was all over, some 1.5 million workers had
been added to the shock worker rolls.[87] Although many organizations subsequently were chastised for "chasing after numbers" and encouraging "phony shock work" (*lzheudarnichestvo*),
the proportion of workers reportedly engaged in socialist competition and shock work continued to be an important criterion
of activeness for party and trade union officials.[88] For management, socialist competition could be something of a nuisance –
in effect, another form of control. But when supplies arrived
unexpectedly or when the end of a plan period approached, it
could also be a convenient device for getting around the legal
prohibition against mandatory overtime.

The new work culture that emerged during the First Five-
Year Plan thus conformed less to the leadership's dictates than
to the logic of what Moshe Lewin has called the "contamination
effect." That is, "the quicker you break and change, the more
of the old you recreate. Institutions and methods which seemed
to be entirely new, after deeper insight show the often quite
astonishing reemergence of many old traits and forms."[89] Put
another way, the transformation of shock work into a mass phenomenon was achieved via compromise. In exchange for extending to undeserving workers the title of shock workers – and
the access to privileges that went along with it – factory committees and party organizations achieved consent to socialist
competition as an integral – and permanent – feature of Soviet
industrial culture. Nominalism went a long way in those chaotic

---

[87] *Pravda*, Apr. 29, 1930; G. Ia. Ponomarenko, *Vo glave trudovogo
pod"ema: Kommunisty Donbassa-organizatory sotsialisticheskogo sorevnovaniia rabochego klassa v pervoi piatiletki* (Kiev: Vishche shkola, 1971),
102, 104.

[88] Ponomarenko, *Vo glave*, 115; *Na fronte industrializatsii* (hereafter *NFI*),
no. 8 (1930):40–2; no. 9 (1930):7–10; *Rezoliutsiia IX s"ezda profsoiuzov*
(Moscow: Profizdat, 1932), 7, 11.

[89] Lewin, "Social Background," 126.

times, and the inclusion of workers who failed to fulfill their competition agreements or who had never been party to such an agreement strongly suggests that quantity was achieved at the expense of quality.

The compromise, however, had its limits. On the one hand, resistance to shock work and socialist competition did not cease. Verbal harassment of and physical attacks against shock workers reached such proportions that the Supreme Court of the RSFSR issued special instructions to judicial authorities on the prosecution of such "criminal" acts.[90] On the other hand, not all forms of socialist competition received official approval. The fate of production collectives and communes is instructive here.

These work units were organized in most branches of industry but were most numerous in the metalworks and textile factories of the older industrial regions. Their membership was drawn mainly from existing shock brigades, and the proportion of party members among them was considerably higher than the national average. Komsomol membership was not, reflecting the fact that 70 percent of collectivists and communards were twenty-five years of age or older. As of April 1931, collectives and communes contained 134,000 (7.19 percent) of approximately 1.8 million workers surveyed.[91]

Typically, collectives pooled wages among workers of the same skill grade or divided them on the basis of different grades (rather than individual performance); communes consisted of workers who shared their wages on an equal basis or according to family need, irrespective of skill levels or output. Both types of organization elected their own leaders ("elders"), drew up

[90] Donald Filtzer, *Soviet Workers and Stalinist Industrilization: The Formation of Soviet Production Relations, 1928–1941* (Armonk, NY: Sharpe, 1986), 79, citing *Sudebnaia praktika RSFSR*, no. 13 (1931):2. For a discussion of such instances, see Filtzer, 76–81.

[91] For statistics on production collectives and communes, see G. S. Polliak, S. I. Batsfen, and A. R. Semenina, "Proizvodstvennye kollektivy i kommuny," in *Sotsialisticheskoe sorevnovanie v promyshlennosti SSSR, Sbornik statei*, ed. Ia. M. Bineman (Moscow: Plankhozgiz, 1930), 90–103, and *Trud v SSSR, 1931 g.* (Moscow: Gosekgiz, 1932), 123. For an elaboration of the argument presented here, see Lewis H. Siegelbaum, "Production Collectives and Communes and the 'Imperatives' of Soviet Industrialization, 1929–1931," *Slavic Review*, 45, no. 1 (1986):65–84.

their own statutes, introduced rationalization measures, rotated jobs among their members, and imposed fines on those who violated the statutes.

Many labor economists and regional party and trade union organizations praised these new forms for encouraging a higher level of consciousness and work culture than shock brigades. Throughout 1930 and into 1931, the press extolled their productivity.[92] Yet unlike shock brigades, they never received unequivocal endorsement from central party and state organs, and eventually, by 1932, they were suppressed. Why? Essentially because they were too self-contained (or "syndicalist") and, strange as it may seem, too egalitarian. That is, not only did they implicitly – and in some instances, explicitly – challenge the rationale for the division of labor between managers and managed, but they also ran counter to the assumption that higher productivity could be achieved via the specialization of labor and corresponding incentive schemes.

Speaking to a conference of business executives on June 23, 1931, Stalin listed six conditions he considered necessary for the continuation of the industrialization drive. Among these were the abolition of *obezlichka*, to which we have already made reference, and the curtailment of "petty bourgeois egalitarianism" (*uravnilovka*). The equalization of wages, he argued, had nothing in common with Marxism, did nothing to encourage unskilled workers to acquire skills, and only served to promote a parasitic mentality among them.[93] Stalin did not mention collectives and communes in this connection, but others soon did. They cited examples of skilled workers withdrawing from communes ostensibly because their wages were being dragged down by free-loading members.[94]

---

[92] See, e.g., I. Zaromskii, "Proizvodstvennye kollektivy – novaia forma organizatsii truda," *Voprosy truda*, no. 4 (1930):19–20; P. M. Dubner and M. Kozyrev, *Kollektivy i kommuny v bor'be za kommunisticheskoi formy truda* (Moscow–Leningrad: Gosizdat, 1930); Iu. A. Kalistratov, *Za udarnyi proizvodstvennyi kollektiv*, 2d ed. (Moscow: VTsSPS, 1931); *Trud*, Apr. 9, 1930; *ZI*, May 30, 1930; St. Samueli, "Raboty proizvodstvennykh kommun i kollektivov – na novye rel'sy," *Partiinoe stroitel'stvo* (hereafter *PS*), no. 15–16 (1931):12–18.

[93] Stalin, *Works*, 13:58–67.

[94] Stalin did refer to communes in his speech to the Seventeenth Party Congress. See the epigraph to Siegelbaum, "Productive Collectives,"

Production collectives and communes were not formally abolished, but official policy created conditions that were highly unfavorable to their survival. Throughout the summer of 1931, Gosplan was hard at work drawing up new pay scales that were announced for most major branches of industry in September and succeeding months.[95] These differed from the previous system in three respects: Differentials between the highest and lowest skill grades were widened; the proportion of workers on individual piece rates was increased; and the *progressivka*, according to which rates would rise once the norm had been reached, was introduced. Collective or brigade piece rates, critical to the functioning of production collectives and communes, were now condemned as inimical to the development of material incentives and as a source of *obezlichka*.[96]

There are several ironies here. First, collectivists and communards frequently expressed support for industrialization and the collectivization of agriculture, even while creatively defending themselves from the depredations caused by those policies. Second, they were at least as productivist in their orientation as the party itself. But while dedicating themselves to the establishment of "communist" relations of production, they actually reproduced many of the features of the traditional pre-Soviet artels.[97] Perhaps the greatest irony, however, was that ultimately they were sacrificed on the altar of managerial authority and incentive schemes reminiscent of capitalist labor policies.

Stripped of its collectivist impulses, socialist competition continued to involve an increasing proportion of the labor force. At least as reported by the trade unions, the percentage of workers participating in competition agreements rose from 29 at the beginning of 1930 to 65 by January 1931, 68 in 1932, and 71

65. For criticisms of these forms, voiced in the wake of Stalin's speech, see *Trud*, July 16, 1931, and Ia. Leibman, "Aktual'nye problemy truda na sovremennom etape," *Bol'shevik*, no. 12 (1931):15–17.

[95] *Trud*, Sept. 23, 1931; *Industrializatsiia SSSR, 1929–1932 gg. Dokumenty i materialy* (Moscow: Nauka, 1970), 266–70.

[96] A. Rozanov, "Forsirovat' perestroiku sistemy zarabotnoi platy," *NFI*, no. 19–20 (1931):34.

[97] This was occasionally acknowledged by communards themselves. See, e.g., S. Zarkhii, *Kommuna v tsekhe* (Moscow–Leningrad: Molodaia gvardiia, 1930), 50; and Kalistratov, *Za udarnyi*, 15.

in 1933.[98] The forms that competition took during these years also expanded. Generally, they represented a differentiation of goals previously subsumed under shock work, reflecting the party's increased emphasis after mid-1931 on cost accounting, the assimilation of technology, and individual piece rates – hence, the emergence of cost-accounting brigades, planning-operative groups, shift counterplanning brigades, brigades to "catch up to and overtake" advanced capitalist countries (so-called DiP brigades, from *dogniat' i peregnat'*), and periodic competitions for the "best shock worker" in particular branches of industry as measured by output norm overfulfillment.

A thorough analysis of these forms lies outside the present study. It is important to note, however, that their contamination by older practices continued to occur. Despite explicit instructions to the contrary, cost-accounting brigade leaders frequently were elected and exercised powers very much along the lines of traditional, and ostensibly liquidated, artel elders. Like artels, such brigades traded a degree of autonomy for bearing material responsibility (in the form of wage deductions) when they surpassed their estimated costs of production.[99] Then again, accounting procedures were so imprecise that management could sometimes lavish bonuses on favored workers while denying them to brigades that *had* fulfilled their obligations.[100] In the case of counterplanning, it was not difficult for management to adjust downward its original program, according to the principle "Better to overfulfill a small plan than underfulfill a great one."[101]

The problem of phony shock work did not abate, despite continued pressure from above to curb the arbitrariness responsible for it. Among the charges laid by the party's Central Committee against the party organization at the Petrovskii Metallurgical Factory in May 1933 was its "formal relationship to socialist competition and shock work." By virtue of the fact that the number of shock workers was carried over from one period to the next

[98] *Trud*, Apr. 29, 1935.

[99] *RP*, no. 2 (1932):5–6; *Istoriia industrializatsii nizhegorodskogo-Gor'kovskogo kraia (1926–1941 gg.)* (Gor'kii: Volgo-Viatskoe khizhnoe izdatel'stvo, 1968), 170–8.

[100] *NFI*, no. 3–4 (1932):6–12; *RP*, no. 8 (1933): 8–11.

[101] *Puti industrializatsii* (hereafter *PI*), no. 19 (1930):22.

and that agreements to compete were automatically renewed, shock workers outnumbered the total labor force in the foundry section.[102] This may have been the most extreme case, but reports of the formal quantitative approach to socialist competition were commonplace. Higher officials often ridiculed the inflationary practice, but were unable – or unwilling – to put a stop to it.[103] The privileges formally extended to shock workers were increased during this period. In addition to those already mentioned, they included a shorter qualifying period of employment to receive full pay in case of incapacitation and maternity leave, a supplement to the pension of 3 percent for every year of shock work, and supplementary rations.[104] Perhaps most important of all, preferential servicing of shock workers on the shop floor, previously attacked as inviting "justifiable censure from backward, non-shock workers," was now considered to be "of huge significance for the successful development of socialist forms of labor."[105]

Here, however, was the paradox. If upward of 40 percent of all workers were listed as shock workers, how privileged could they be? Was not statistical inflation threatening to devalue the status of shock workers? The answer is yes, but there were some countervailing tendencies. One was the arbitrary power of management and the enterprise party and trade union organizations in the distribution of those privileges to which all shock workers were ostensibly entitled. Some privileges, such as special flower-laden tables in factory canteens, were easier to provide than others. Obviously, not all shock workers could be assigned to the *best* machines or receive the most prompt technical assistance. That is, in the shop floor pecking order, distinctions among shock workers had to be made. And they were. The Komsomol committee in Ivanovo, reporting on an All-Union contest for

[102] See resolution in *KPSS v rezoliutsiiakh*, 5:104–7.
[103] *VII Vsesoiuznaia konferentsiia VLKSM, Stenograficheskii otchet* (Moscow: Molodaia gvardiia, 1933), 32–7, 51, 63–4, 79, 83; and the speech by L. M. Kaganovich in *Pravda*, Dec. 28, 1935.
[104] *Sbornik vazhneishikh zakonov*, 235–6; *Trud*, Oct. 27, 1933; *NFI*, no. 3–4 (1933):59–60.
[105] A. I. Kapustin, *Udarniki: praktika raboty udarnykh brigad* (Moscow: Moskovskii rabochii, 1930), 59; *Voprosy profdvizheniia*, no. 1 (1934): 48. See also *VII Vsesoiuznaia konferentsiia VLKSM*, 59.

the best weaver in 1932–3, could not find any other term to describe the winners than "the best of the best," since the "best shock workers" were those who had not only competed but performed well.[106] During 1933, such terms as "worker-shock heroes" and "especially outstanding advanced shock workers" were used to refer to a more select group.[107] Even among the latter, there were those who had been awarded medals (Order of the Red Banner of Labor, Order of Lenin).

How workers achieved such relatively exalted status is a complicated question. Consistent fulfillment or overfulfillment of output norms and participation in socialist competition were prerequisites, but meeting them also entailed preconditions. Obtaining and maintaining preferential treatment on and off the shop floor involved compromises that not all workers were willing, or in a position, to make. Participation in production-comrades courts, assistance groups affiliated with technical norm bureaus, and the performance of other self-policing functions expected of shock workers may have secured preferential treatment from management but strained relations with fellow workers.[108] According to Andrew Smith, an American worker employed at Moscow's Elektrozavod, shock workers were "the smoothest bootlickers...who wandered about aimlessly doing nothing" and who, being "technically incompetent,...sought this method of gaining favor."[109] Although not universally ap-

[106] *Komsomol'tsy i molodezh Ivanovskoi oblasti v gody stroitel'stva sotsializma (1921–1940 gg.), Sbornik dokumentov i materialov* (Ivanovo: Ivanovskii oblastnoi komitet VLKSM, 1967), 141.

[107] See, e.g., *Voprosy profdvizheniia*, no. 1–2 (1933):46–7; no. 6 (1933):38–43.

[108] In 232 enterprises surveyed by VTsSPS, 83.5% of the 9,540 members of production-comrades courts were shock workers, as of May 1933. See *Industrializatsiia SSSR, 1933–1937*, 523. For the role of assistance groups, see *NFI*, no. 19–20 (1932): 41–2.

[109] Andrew Smith, *I Was a Soviet Worker* (London: Hale, 1937), 61. In the view of an American drilling superintendent who had worked in Baku, "Shock brigades are composed largely of...publicity seekers. Ordinary workers resent what they consider to be the unfairness of the *udarniks'* claim to superiority and hypocrisy of the whole shock brigade movement." J. C. Wiley to Secretary of State, concerning experiences of Mr. August Tross, State Department Decimal File, NA, 861.5017/771, Nov. 3, 1934.

plicable, such a characterization does imply that occupational expertise may not always have been of paramount importance.

In sum, then, the enjoyment of privileges derived from shock worker status – if not the category itself – was dependent on a number of variables, of which the performance of certain not very pleasant duties was no less important than any productive criteria. This was the inevitable consequence of the flexibility enjoyed by management in the period 1931–4.

During 1934 and into 1935, some of the forms of socialist competition generated in the previous period were phased out, while new ones emerged. Among the former were cost-accounting brigades. Whereas a reported 35 percent of all workers belonged to such brigades in 1933, only 27 percent were involved in 1934, and by 1935 the proportion was down to 22 percent.[110] According to one contemporary account, the reasons for the decline were the continued failure of management to pay bonuses, the passivity of the trade unions, and the rising popularity of technical-industrial planning by brigades.[111] Another sort of explanation was contained in a "discussion article," which appeared in Narkomtiazhprom's organ, *Za industrializatsiiu,* in January 1935. Entitled "What Is to Be Done with Brigade Cost Accounting," the article was a thinly veiled critique of the entire brigade system. "Where tasks have been individualized and payment is according to individual piece rate," it asserted, "the brigade leader becomes superfluous, as does the brigade. . . . Where workers service one apparatus, brigades are necessary. But to characterize brigade work as the highest form of the organization of labor would be incorrect for a majority of branches of industry."[112] The radical implications of this position probably account for its status as a discussion article. Yet there is no doubt that during 1934–5 the thrust of socialist competition was toward the individuation of production tasks and accounting procedures. Hence, the emergence of *otlichnichestvo* (the movement for excellence), which involved the distribution of bonuses to individual workers with the lowest proportion of defective ar-

---

[110] M. Eskin, *Osnovnye puti razvitiia sotsialisticheskikh form truda,* 2d ed. (Leningrad: Sotsekgiz, 1936), 196–7.
[111] Ibid., 87.
[112] *ZI,* Jan. 18, 1935.

ticles. As with earlier forms of socialist competition, the criteria and the means for measuring them were far from standard. The accounting procedures necessary to distinguish "excellent" from "good" or "satisfactory" work were beyond most enterprises. In Leningrad, there were only some 15,500 *otlichniki* by June 1935, that is, nearly eighteen months after the movement had begun. By July, only 2.8 percent of all workers and 6.7 percent of shock workers in the USSR were *otlichniki*, although half of all enterprises were said to contain at least one.[113] All the same, *otlichnichestvo* did highlight the regime's efforts to combat *obezlichka* with respect to the quality of goods produced.

On a broader scale, competition was sustained by frequent contests (*konkursy*) for the best worker in particular branches of industry, by the publicity given to norm overfulfillment and even world records, and by meetings of outstanding shock workers at the regional and All-Union levels. None of this, however, resolved the problem of the devaluation of shock worker status or, to cite a Leningrad Party Bureau resolution, "a whole series of deficiencies and distortions of party directives concerning socialist competition and shock work."[114] "It is no secret," editorialized *Za industrializatsiiu* in January 1935, "that the title of shock worker these days has become less substantial."[115] Bodgers and machine smashers continued to be designated as shock workers even after VTsSPS had issued instructions to enterprise production conferences to review the lists.[116] After six years of organized socialist competition, the problem of "deficiencies and distortions" appeared irremediable. Still, there were genuinely outstanding workers whose achievements did not go unnoticed.

IV

"The Best Pickman and the Best Machinist of the Donbass – Bolshevik Record Holders," read the headline in *Pravda*, not in the aftermath of Stakhanov's record shift of August 30–1, 1935,

---

[113] *Trud*, June 5, 1935, p. 2; *Industrializatsiia SSSR, 1933–1937*, 548.
[114] Eskin, *Osnovnye puti*, 82.
[115] *ZI*, Jan, 9, 1935.
[116] *Trud*, Jan. 18, 1935.

but more than three years earlier, in May 1932.[117] The machinist, who was producing 12,000 tons of coal per month at the Bagitskii mine, was A. Minaev. The pickman, a ten-year veteran at Gorlovka no. 1 (with two years out for military service), was Nikita Izotov. Of the two, Izotov was the real find. Described by the *Pravda* journalist who discovered him as "the model for a sculpture called 'Cutter,' " he had an average rate of norm fulfillment of 474 percent for the first three months of 1932. Minaev's "story" was included "for political and technical balance," and subsequently nothing was heard of him.[118] The publicity surrounding Izotov, however, was sufficient to generate "Izotov schools," that is, training sessions in which Izotovites instructed novices in their skills. Izotovites existed not only in the Donbass, but in other coal-mining centers and in other branches of industry.

In these respects, Izotovism was a precursor of Stakhanovism. Why it did not blossom into what Stakhanovism became is an important question, a consideration of which can help to clarify the historical specificity of the latter phenomenon. To some extent, the question has already been answered. In 1932–3, the theme of assimilating and mastering technology was only beginning to be stressed. It competed for the party's attention with the consequences of the famine, with stabilizing and disciplining the industrial work force through legal compulsion, and with completing the gigantic construction projects by whatever means possible. Finally, and perhaps most important, the party was committed to restoring the authority of technical experts and expanding that of management, which, as we shall see, was not the case after 1935. With the revision of the rate scales and the introduction of progressive piece rates, the incentives offered to workers had taken a turn toward material rewards. Not until 1935, however, when rationing was phased out, could monetary wages be translated easily into purchasing power.

These general considerations must be supplemented by those specific to the coal-mining industry and the Donbass in particular. At the outset of the First Five-Year Plan, coal mining, like

---

[117] *Pravda*, May 11, 1932.
[118] S. R. Gershberg, *Rabota u nas takaia: Zapisi zhurnalista – pravdista tridtsatykh godov* (Moscow: Gospolit, 1971), 107–12. The analogies with Andrej Wajda's film, "Man of Marble," are striking.

many branches of Soviet industry, only perhaps more so, was backward relative to that in the advanced capitalist countries. Less than 20 percent of all coal produced in the USSR in 1928 was cut by mechanical means.[119] In the United States, approximately three-quarters of all coal produced in the mid-1920s was cut by mechanical devices, primarily the chain-breast cutting machine. In France, Germany, and Belgium, the proportions were, if anything, higher, though owing to the predominance of irregular, steeply inclined, and relatively soft seams, the hand-held mechanical pick was the preferred device.[120] Britain was the exception. There, owing mainly, it would seem, to the small-scale nature of most mining enterprises and the relative cheapness of labor power, mechanization was retarded. As of 1924, only 19 percent of output was cut by mechanical means, and by 1930 it was still a relatively modest 31 percent.[121]

According to this criterion alone, by the end of the First Five-Year Plan, the USSR had nearly caught up to the United States and western Europe. In 1932, 62.6 percent of all coal produced in the country was mined by mechanical means, and in the Donbass the proportion was greater than 70 percent. Whereas at the end of 1928, Soviet mines were supplied with some 800 heavy and light cutting machines and fewer than 100 pneumatic picks – all or nearly all of them foreign-produced – by December 1932 the corresponding numbers were 1,800 and 9,000. Moreover, of all cutting machines supplied to the mines in 1932, those produced within the USSR outnumbered imported models for the first time.[122]

---

[119] *Tekhnika gornogo dela i metallurgii* (Moscow: Nauka, 1968), 90.

[120] V. P. Nemchinov, *Razvitie tekhniki dobychi uglia* (Moscow: Nauka, 1965), 102–4; Harold Berger and S. H. Schurr, *The Mining Industries, 1899–1939: A Study of Output, Employment and Productivity* (New York: National Bureau of Economic Research, 1944), 174.

[121] A. J. Taylor, "Labour Productivity and Technological Innovation in the British Coal Industry, 1850–1914," *Economic History Review*, 14 (1961–2):58–63; Derek Aldcroft and Harry Richardson, *The British Economy, 1870–1939* (New York: Humanities Press, 1970), 146; A. R. Griffin, *The British Coalmining Industry: Retrospect and Prospect* (London: Moreland, Buxton, 1977), 173.

[122] *Tekhnika gornogo dela*, 90; *Trud v SSSR, 1931*, 106; A. Zvorykin, *Ocherki po istorii sovetskoi gornoi tekhniki* (Moscow: AN SSSR, 1950), 186.

Much of the credit for bringing about this technological revolution in coal mining must go to the party. It was the party's Central Committee that kept up a steady stream of resolutions on the shortcomings of the Donbass and other coal-mining areas, ordered the removal of high officials who were alleged to harbor "anti-mechanizing attitudes," dispatched Molotov on a much publicized troubleshooting mission in September 1930, and after his return declared "forced mechanization" to be the order of the day.[123] By making mechanization such a high priority, by compelling mining administrators to install mechanical devices, the party hastened a process that took far longer to achieve elsewhere.

In this light, Izotov, a manual pickman, might seem an odd choice for heroic treatment, even if his fellow workers referred to him – perhaps not entirely with admiration – as a "human cutting machine."[124] In fact, the choice was highly appropriate. Even as late as March 1932, the vast majority of miners employed in underground work – some 71.1 percent in the Donbass – were manual laborers.[125] This was essentially because mechanization had proceeded so unevenly. Among the four basic steps in coal mining – hewing, loading, conveying to the pit head, and hauling – only the third had kept pace with the first in terms of mechanization, and even in this case, a large number of workers were used to disassemble and move the mechanical conveyors and scrapers. As far as haulage was concerned, by 1932 electric-powered trains had only begun to replace horses. In the case of loading as well as such ancillary operations as clearing, laying tracks, and timbering, human power was used exclusively.

Mechanization proceeded unevenly in other countries, too. But what made the Soviet experience unique was that mechanization was imposed at a time when the labor force was still in part migratory and expanding rapidly. Already in the nineteenth century, a pattern of seasonal migration had been established between the overpopulated central Russian provinces and the Donbass coal fields. Each spring, usually around Easter, tens of

---

[123] *Trud*, Jan. 18, 1929; Oct. 5, 10, 1930; July 8, 1931; *ZI*, Sept. 28, Oct. 1, 14, 1930; *Pravda*, Sept. 25, 1932.

[124] *Pravda*, May 11, 1932.

[125] B. Sukharevskii, "Zavershenie tekhnicheskoi rekonstruktsii i voprosy mekhanizatsii promyshlennosti," *Problemy ekonomiki*, no. 1 (1934):87.

thousands of mine workers, both skilled and unskilled, left the Donbass for their native villages, returning after the summer harvest. This pattern persisted (or rather was reestablished after the hiatus of the civil war years) into the 1920s and accounts in large part for the high rates of labor turnover in the industry.[126]

Collectivization, which in the long run would vitiate the cycle of arrivals and departures, had the opposite effect in the shorter term, once again illustrating the contamination effect. As the number of mine workers increased, from 266,000 in January 1929 to 407,400 just three years later, labor turnover intensified. Whereas for every mine worker employed in 1928, 1.4 workers began a new job and 1.3 left one, in 1929 the corresponding figures were 2.0 and 1.9, in 1930 an incredible 3.0 and 2.9, and in 1931, 2.3 and 2.1.[127]

Recruited from newly formed *kolkhozy* or arriving of their own accord, the mine workers were housed in barracks that, judging from numerous reports, were overcrowded, bug-infested, and lacking in the most basic amenities.[128] The number of square meters of living space in the Donbass mining area, which had been a meager 4.91 per person in October 1928, dropped to 3.7 by the end of 1930.[129] Despite the party's efforts to encourage voluntary settlement (*samozakreplenie*), many miners drifted back to their villages, "flitted" from one mine to another, or sought employment in another industry. Not surprisingly, the proportion of party members, shock workers, and participants in socialist competition among coal miners was significantly lower than in most other branches of industry.[130]

Faced with such a fluid labor force, mining management demanded and won the right to recruit more extensively, thereby often taking on more workers than could be accommodated or employed at any one time. Although this led to acute deprivation

[126] Barber, "Labour Discipline," Table A.
[127] Ibid., Shiokawa, "Labor Turnover," 66–7.
[128] See, e.g., *ZI*, July 11, Oct. 6, 1930; *Pravda*, Aug. 18, 1932.
[129] *Trud*, Jan. 9, 1929; *PI*, no. 8 (1931):26.
[130] Slutskii, *Rabochii klass Ukrainy*, 140–1; S. A. Kheinman, "Sotsialisticheskoe sorevnovanie v promyshlennosti SSSR," in *Sotsialisticheskoe sorevnovanie v promyshlennosti SSSR* (1930), 11; I. I. Kuz'minov, *Stakhanovskoe dvizhenie – vysshii etap sotsialisticheskogo sorevnovaniia* (Moscow: Sotsekgizd., 1940), 40–1.

among miners, it suited the needs of management for a labor
force that could be thrown into the breach when the frequently
unreliable and "barbarically" treated machines malfunctioned or
when the "coal debt" reached intolerable proportions. To determine which workers would work a given shift and where,
management relied on the traditional roster (*nariad*) system
whereby shift assignments were made on the basis of whoever
showed up. The system was condemned repeatedly in the press
as backward, as encouraging turnover, and as a particularly vir-
ulent form of *obezlichka*.[131] According to a Central Committee
resolution of July 5, 1931, it was to have been replaced by production brigades, which would receive monthly assignments. Yet
well into 1932, shift rostering was described as being in use at
a majority of mines, and *Pravda*'s recommendation later that
year that the *nariad* be turned into a "flying production conference" suggests the party's grudging capitulation.[132]

The increasing proportion of coal that was mechanically cut
and conveyed is not, therefore, a very reliable indicator of
whether backwardness had been overcome. Another, output per
worker, actually showed a decline between 1930 and 1932. When
engineers and administrative personnel (whose number more
than doubled between 1929 and 1932) are included, the decline
was even steeper. While the average monthly output of cutting
machines rose, that of pneumatic picks remained constant.[133] A
system whereby cutting machines could be used in all three shifts
instead of two was developed in 1930 and received strong official
backing. So, too, did a method for the undercutting of seams
that could double the number of productive "cycles." But because both innovations required a degree of preparation and
coordination among different groups of miners that was difficult
to achieve, they failed to gain wide application.[134]

One of the reasons for the difficulty of coordinating work was
the acute degree of specialization among miners. In the United
States, the typical division of labor at the coal face was between

[131] *ZI*, Feb. 3, Apr. 19, 1931.
[132] *Trud*, July 7, 1931; June 26, 1932; *Pravda*, Aug. 18, 1932.
[133] *Trud v SSSR, 1931*, 106; N. P. Lakoza, "Razvitie mekhanizatsii sov-
etskikh ugol'nykh basseinov za 1930–1934 gody," *Ugol'*, no. 112
(1935):25–32.
[134] *ZI*, Feb. 11, 1931; *Pravda*, Apr. 27, 1931.

machine men and loaders. The former traveled from one panel to another to cut into the seam; the latter drilled shot holes, laid explosive charges, extended the length of track, and installed props, sometimes also loading loose coal onto conveyors or into pit cars. Attempts by owners to introduce special teams of shot firers and timbermen were strongly resisted by miners, and it was not until the advent of mechanical loading devices in the late 1930s that the miner's "craft" was further subdivided.[135]

In the USSR, the occupational profile of miners' work was already much narrower in the late 1920s and early 1930s. That is, working at the coal face were shot drillers, firers, conveyor operators and movers, timbermen, loaders, roofers, and rubble removers, each performing a separate task in sequence.[136] This was not a survival of old ways, but rather the consequence of the campaign to liquidate the traditional artel, whose members performed several different tasks in the course of a shift.[137] Aside from eliminating the artel elder as an intermediary between foremen and workers, the new system had the advantages of lending itself to individual piece-work payment and a relatively short period of training.

However, there were several drawbacks. The chief one was the small amount of working time in which each category of worker was actually engaged. Chronometric studies conducted at the Donugol' trust's mines in 1927–8 revealed that the actual working time in a seven-hour shift was two hours and fifty-five minutes for a manual pickman, two hours and thirty-nine minutes for loaders, two hours and nine minutes for shot drillers, two hours and fifty-six minutes for ponymen, and two hours

[135] Carter Goodrich, *The Miner's Freedom: A Study of the Working Life in a Changing Industry* (Boston: Jones, 1925), 130–3; William E. Hotchkiss et al., *Mechanization, Employment and Output per Man in Bituminous Coal Mining*, 2 vols. (Philadelphia: WPA National Research Project, 1939), 1:12.

[136] See list in *Trudy pervoi Vsesoiuznoi konferentsii po mekhanizatsii kamennougol'noi promyshlennosti* (Khar'kov: Ugol', 1931), 304.

[137] The campaign appears to have begun in 1926–7. See *Resheniia II plenuma Tsentral'nogo komiteta Soiuza gornorabochikh SSSR, Shestogo sozyva (20–26 sentiabria, 1928 goda)* (Moscow, 1928), 83; and P. B. Zil'bergleit, *Proizvoditel'nost' truda v kamennougol'noi promyshlennosti* (Khar'kov, 1930), 33, 39, 79. See also note 77.

and thirty-three minutes for rubble removers.[138] Another study at the Artem mines in August 1929 found that, in a six-hour shift, the cutting machine was idle for three hours and thirty-five minutes.[139] There is no indication that either working or machine time substantially increased in the course of the First Five-Year Plan. On the contrary, *Pravda* reported in August 1932 that at the Kadievka Proletarian mine, cutting machines operated for two hours per shift, and Ordzhonikidze, addressing a group of shock workers in November 1933, referred to another mine where the work day was "in reality" three hours and, for cutting machines, a mere thirty-nine minutes per shift.[140]

The obvious alternative was to combine skills or operations (*sovmeshchat' operatsii*). This was advocated as early as May 1930 in a report to the First All-Union Conference on Mechanizing the Coal Industry. The rapporteur, while declaring himself in favor of differentiating production processes into their constituent elements, argued that this cardinal principle of the "scientific organization of labor" (abbreviated *NOT*) had been carried to extreme and counterproductive lengths in the case of coal mining. He referred to German and American experience, asserting that their practice "does not contradict the political and social conditions of our Soviet construction," and illustrated how, by its adoption, costs could be reduced and output raised. Anticipating objections that this would only revive the artel, he stressed that individual rates for each task would provide an incentive that was lacking in the artel, where wages were divided among members irrespective of individual performance. Still, one delegate doubted that "a machinist would agree to work at the rate that a loader, taken from the plow, receives," and others seemed to share the conventional wisdom that, the simpler the task, the more efficiently it could be performed.[141]

But the story does not end here. Minaev, the soon to be forgotten machinist, may only have cut coal, but Izotov was more a generalist. In addition to wielding his pick, he did the prop-

[138] *Trud*, Jan. 12, 1929, p. 2.
[139] *Trudy pervoi Vsesoiuznoi konferentsii po mekhanizatsii*, 192.
[140] *Pravda*, Aug. 18, 1932; Ordzhonikidze, *Stat'i i rechi* 2:506. Comparable instances are reported in *Trud*, May 17, 1933, and *ZI*, Feb. 11, 1935.
[141] *Trudy pervoi Vsesoiuznoi konferentsii po mekhanizatsii*, 101–4, 304, 308.

ping, and, as he put it, "When I see that I need wood, I would rather spend a half hour fetching it than one to two waiting for the timber getter."[142] How much attention was paid to this aspect of Izotov's "method" is not clear. Coincidentally, the very month that Izotov's story appeared in *Pravda*, experiments conducted at an iron ore mine near Briansk appeared to demonstrate the advantages of *dividing* work between hewer and timberer. Then again, at least one coal trust (Sevkavugol') included provisions for combining operations into its collective agreement.[143]

In any case, when coal mining once again came under close party scrutiny in the spring of 1933, it was not the organization or division of labor that was deemed to be deficient. Responding to the fact that output in the first quarter was less than that in the same period in 1932, the party blamed the decline on the "outdated, thoroughly bankrupted, bureaucratic method of leadership... beginning with the mines and ending with the Main Fuel Administration of Narkomtiazhprom." In a joint resolution of April 8, 1933, the Central Committee and the Council of People's Commissars ordered a reorganization of the administration at the top, the transfer of the bulk of engineering-technical personnel out of trust offices and into the mines, the maximization of party members employed in underground work, the enforcement of the law of November 15, 1932, to combat "flitting" and absenteeism, and the dispatch of party organizers reporting directly to the Orgburo of the Central Committee.[144]

Despite the lack of central direction, or perhaps because no one method was being prescribed from above, experimentation with combining operations proceeded on several fronts. By 1934, it could be claimed that "the experience of a number of mines has shown the effectiveness of combining such occupations as hewer and loader (on soft seams), cutter and timberer (on steeply sloping seams), cutting machinist and hewer (in preparatory work), etc." Indeed, the "extensive application" of combining

---

[142] *Pravda*, May 11, 1932.
[143] *Novyi gorniak*, no. 18 (1932):5; O. A. Ermanskii, *Teoriia i praktika ratsionalizatsii*, 5th ed. (Moscow: ONTI, 1933), 305–8.
[144] *Industrializatsiia SSSR 1933–1937*, 242–7. For the law of November 15, see note 36.

hewing and loading at the Stalinugol' trust's mines was said to
have raised productivity by 15 to 35 percent.[145]

As fears of reviving the artel receded and as the Central Institute of Labor came under attack for promoting an excessive
division of labor in the textile industry, the combination of occupations in coal mining gained respectability. For example, in
January 1935, an article in *Za industrializatsiiu* flatly asserted that
"the labor of the miner in our country is too differentiated."[146]
No less an authority than V. M. Bazhanov, the chairman of Glavugol' (Main Coal Administration), called for the combination
of occupations as part of the technical plan for 1935, and to his
voice was added that of another Glavugol' official.[147]

Their case was strengthened by a series of experiments that
tested an innovation attributed to S. A. Sviridov. Sviridov, a
miner at the Artem no. 10 mine, had doubled the length of the
step or ledge on a steeply sloping seam. It was found that this
increased productivity, measured in the number of square meters of coal mined, by 45 percent. However, when hewer and
timberer combined their functions, productivity was greater still.
Sviridov himself, using this method, had managed to produce
40 tons of coal in a single shift, compared with an average shift
output per hewer of 6.7 tons in the first half of 1935. At least
two other pick operators had surpassed Sviridov's mark, the
highest figure of 85 tons being recorded by P. M. Grishin at the
Kadievka trust's Central Irmino mine.[148]

These and other individual achievements were noted by Ordzhonikidze in his speech to the Seventh All-Union Congress of
Soviets as evidence that the mere fulfillment of the 1934 plan
for coal output was far from what could be achieved. But the
results obtained in the first half of 1935 were far from brilliant.
Investigating the situation in the Donbass, Narkomtiazhprom
reported a worsening of labor discipline and an increase in labor
turnover. Among the measures it called for was a revision of
rates that would favor manual pick operators.[149] By the end of

[145] Sukharevskii, "Zavershenie," 89–90.
[146] *ZI*, Jan. 3, 1935.
[147] *Ugol'*, no. 112 (1935):12, 72.
[148] *Novyi gorniak*, no. 9–10 (1935):7–9; *Ugol'*, no. 113–14 (1935):8–31;
    Novatory, Sbornik (Moscow: Molodaia gvardiia, 1972), 100.
[149] *ZI*, July 14, 1935.

Aleksei G. Stakhanov. From E. V. Nikolaeva, *Iskusstvo i rabochii klass* (Leningrad: Khudozhnik RSFSR, 1983).

August, output was still 2.5 million tons below the plan. The number of workers had fallen, owing to seasonal migration, from 314,000 to 285,000, and mining officials were pressing for mass recruitment to make up the difference.[150]

Then, in early September, came news of Stakhanov's record. Using his Soviet-produced pneumatic pick, the thirty-year-old miner, with eight years' experience at the Central Irmino mine, had cut 102 tons of coal, or fourteen times his shift norm. The somewhat special circumstances in which this record was made and its immediate impact will be discussed in the next chapter. Here, it is important to stress the method that was used. Stakhanov worked on ledges that had not been lengthened, but the fact that there were no other pick operators working that shift

[150] *Ugol'*, no. 120 (1935):1.

enabled him to cut on all eight ledges instead of only one.[151] The absence of other pneumatic picks also ensured adequate pressure for the entire shift. But the most significant departure from normal, the thing that according to Stakhanov was new and guaranteed his success, was the division of labor. "Throughout nearly the entire six hours, I hewed while two timberers put in props behind me."[152]

In short, the innovation attributed to Stakhanov was nothing more than a return to a method that previously, though not traditionally, had been standard. Those who had led the movement toward combining the two functions, hewing and timbering, found themselves in a rather awkward position. By the time they had absorbed the shock, the Stakhanovite movement had been born. Bazhanov hailed the new movement as guaranteeing the fulfillment of the Donbass's annual plan, but apparently hoping to limit its effects, he pointed out that "such great changes in technical processes are not applicable to gently sloping seams" and criticized officials whose first response was to divide labor "come what may."[153] Nevertheless, Bazhanov could not have been very happy to be reminded by the Donetsk regional (*obkom*) secretary that, before the advent of Stakhanovism, "some officials" had advocated an approach that was now once again in disrepute.[154]

The zigzag policy that was pursued with respect to the division of labor in coal mining between the late 1920s and the mid-1930s and its culmination in Stakhanov's method have some important implications. First, contrary to Stakhanov's assertion and what generally has been claimed, there was little that was new in the method of dividing labor between hewer and timberer, and the extent to which his record output could be attributed to the method itself was grossly exaggerated. Second, what was at stake was not simply a *division* of labor, but its hierarchical status and differential remuneration. As we shall see, in all the fuss made about Stakhanov's record, the contribution

[151] *Novyi gorniak*, no. 13 (1935):3–6.
[152] A. G. Stakhanov, *Rasskaz o moei zhizni* (Moscow: Gossotsizd., 1937), 25. This point is stressed in O. A. Ermanskii, *Stakhanovskoe dvizhenie i stakhanovskie metody raboty* (Moscow: Sotsekgiz, 1940), 25.
[153] *Ugol'*, no. 120 (1935):1–3.
[154] *PS*, no. 22–3 (1935):34.

of the two timberers, not to mention those who arranged for the special shift, was all but forgotten. This as well as the earlier assaults against the artel and production communes, and the individuation of piece rates and socialist competition, indicate that social as well as economic objectives were involved. Finally, more than the dimensions of Stakhanov's record or the method used to achieve it, it would appear that the growing impatience of higher officials with managerial freedom and the impasse that socialist competition had reached as an effective means for the mobilization of workers endowed Stakhanov's feat with that miraculous quality that Stalin had invoked earlier.

2

From Stakhanov to Stakhanovism

The relationship between Stakhanov's record and the phenomenon that bore his name has been interpreted in one of two ways. On the one hand, many historians have tended to stress the role of the party in taking up Stakhanov's method and applying it to other branches of industry.[1] On the other, we have Stalin's assertion, subsequently repeated in many accounts, that "this movement began somehow of itself, almost spontaneously, from below ... like a hurricane." Mixing his metaphors, Stalin went on to say that "if ... the match thrown by Stakhanov and Busygin was sufficient to start a conflagration, it means that the Stakhanov movement is absolutely ripe."[2]

Neither the view that Stakhanovism was the product of the party's actions nor the attempt to portray it as "almost spontaneous" is satisfactory. One assumes that the party operated as a unitary body, molding Stakhanovism to suit "its" purposes; the other treats the first Stakhanovites as free, albeit primed, agents. Both imply automaticity, thereby obscuring elements of contingency and struggle that were present. To resort to yet another metaphor, if Stakhanov's record was the prologue to a drama subsequently entitled "Stakhanovism," it was performed without knowledge of what was to come, and what did follow was the

[1] See, e.g., Alec Nove, *An Economic History of the USSR* (London: Lane, 1969), 233, and the introduction to the present volume.

[2] I. V. Stalin, *Sochineniia*, ed. Robert H. McNeal (Stanford, Calif.: Hoover Institution, 1967), 1 (XIV), 89–90. See O. A. Ermanskii, *Stakhanovskoe dvizhenie i stakhanovskie metody* (Moscow: Sotsekgiz, 1940), 5–6, where the metaphor of the "wave" is employed, and N. B. Lebedeva and O. I. Shkaratan, *Ocherki istorii sotsialisticheskogo sorevnovaniia* (Leningrad: Lenizdat, 1966), 133–8.

product of much improvisation, notwithstanding attempts by several individuals to serve as directors.

I

We shall begin with Stakhanov's record shift. In the previous chapter, it was implied that the initiative for reorganizing production techniques did not come from Stakhanov himself and that, in any case, the new – or, rather, revived – division of labor was at best only one factor in the making of the record. Who, then, provided the initiative, and what other factors were responsible for the record?

Much of the credit can go to the twenty-seven-year-old party organizer (*partorg*) at Central Irmino, Konstantin Petrov. Of proletarian background, Petrov had been trained as a fitter at the Lugansk Technical School. On his nineteenth birthday in 1929, he was admitted to the party just in time to be sent to the countryside to take "the most direct part in the collectivization drive." On his return to the Golubovka mine, where he previously worked, he became secretary of the party cell, but in 1933, shortly after the institution of party organizer was created, he was dispatched by the Central Committee to the Central Irmino mine. There, he found matters in some disarray and endeavored to find a means to increase output. Among other things, he saw to it that letters were sent to some 600 miners asking why in their opinion work was going badly. In response to complaints about time wasted on line at the mine's store, he arranged for the delivery of supplies to 210 of the best shock workers. He also directed agitational work, which was carried out before each shift as miners waited for their assignments. In the Nikanor-East section, where Stakhanov was employed, three party members and seven candidates harangued the 117 mine workers with excerpts from speeches by party leaders, including Stalin's address to Red Army cadets.[3]

[3] A. G. Stakhanov, *Rasskaz o moei zhizni* (Moscow: Gossotsizd., 1937), 18–19; S. R. Gershberg, *Rukovodstvo kommunisticheskoi partii dvizheniem novatorov v promyshlennosti (1935–1941)* (Moscow: Gospolitizdat, 1956), 42–5; K. G. Petrov, *Zhivye sily* (Donetsk, 1971), 20–5. For a biograph-

For all these efforts, Central Irmino still lagged behind its plan. Assigned a daily output quota of 1,000 to 1,100 tons, the enterprise's seven faces were averaging only 900 to 950 in the first half of 1935. On August 23, 1935, the party committee decided to initiate a contest for the best hewer as a means of overcoming the lag and fulfilling the annual plan one month early. Petrov, at least, was to claim later that this decision was more "historic" than Stakhanov's record shift.[4] In fact, there was nothing uncommon about a party committee launching such a campaign. Even the decision to mark International Youth Day (September 1) with a special labor achievement appears to have been something of a tradition in the Donbass.[5] In any case, it was toward these ends that Petrov, accompanied by N. I. Mashurov, the supervisor of the Nikanor-East section, visited the home of Stakhanov on the night of August 29.

Stakhanov was no Frederick Winslow Taylor. He had not been experimenting with different organizational or production techniques. Then again, neither did he resemble "Schmidt," Taylor's good-natured guinea pig.[6] Having left his native village in Orel province for Irmino in the spring of 1927, Stakhanov worked his way up from brakeman on a pony train to ponydriver, manual pickman, and, by 1934, pneumatic pick operator. After he had completed a four-month course for the state technical minimum examination, his average productivity was around 10 tons per shift, well above his norm of 6.5 tons. Married and a father, he had long ago abandoned his earlier desire to earn just enough to buy a horse and gear and return to Orel Province. It is not clear how much if any formal education he had, or to what extent he had been involved in party-sponsored activities. He makes frequent mention in his autobiography of the positive influence

ical profile of Petrov, see I. Tikhomirov, "Svetit' vsegda," *Pravda*, Aug. 30. 1984.
[4] *Stakhanovets*, no. 1 (1936):10.
[5] S. R. Gershberg, *Rabota u nas takaia: Zapisi zhurnalista-pravdista tridtsatykh godov* (Moscow: Gospolit, 1971), 322.
[6] On Taylor's selection of the man "we will call Schmidt," see Frederick W. Taylor, *The Principles of Scientific Management* (New York: Norton, 1967), 41–7. For a critical commentary on Taylor's famous experiment, see Harry Braverman, *Labor and Monopoly Capital: The Degradation of Work in the Twentieth Century* (New York: Monthly Review Press, 1974), 102–8.

of Miron Diukanov, who was six years Stakhanov's senior, a hewer, and party secretary of the Nikanor-East section.[7] Many years later, Stakhanov still had not worked out why Petrov had chosen him. "Other miners could have achieved the record, but Kostia apparently took into account that I had obtained good results even before the competition for the best hewer and systematically gave high productivity."[8] It is likely that, as a steady and productive worker, Stakhanov previously had come to the attention of the party committee. On the night of Petrov and Mashurov's visit, after Stakhanov had spoken his mind about the crowded conditions in the mine, interruptions in the supply of compressed air, and other factors inhibiting production, the two guests indicated that they could arrange ideal conditions for a special shift. "There will be air, there will be wood," Mashurov is reported to have said. "How much you squeeze out, we will see. I guarantee over a hundred tons. It will be a record." Stakhanov accepted the challenge.[9]

Throughout the following day, preparations were made for the special shift that would begin at 10:00 P.M. According to Stakhanov, the night shift was chosen so as to avoid interference by "kulaks," who were known for their wrecking activities.[10] It is more likely that, because this shift was ordinarily devoted to preparatory and repair work, the special arrangements would cause less disruption. These called for timber getters to deliver their loads during the previous shift, fitters and other repair workers to appear at 5:00 A.M., and haulers, who normally worked the day shifts, to be on duty during the night. Other than Stakhanov and two handpicked propers, the only ones present at the coal face were Petrov, who (symbolically) held a battery-powered lamp, Mashurov, and the editor of the mine's newspaper.

[7] Stakhanov, *Rasskaz*, 10–17; V. K. Diunin and V. Proskura, *Shagni pervym* (Moscow: Gospolit, 1972), 15.
[8] A. G. Stakhanov, *Zhizn' shakhterskaia* (Kiev: Politizdat Ukrainy, 1975), 54. According to a recent account by two Soviet historians, it was not "Kostia" at all, but Mashurov, who picked Stakhanov. See A. V. Mitrofanova and L. S. Rogachevskaia, "Stakhanovskoe dvizhenie: Istoriia i istoriografiia," *Voprosy istorii*, no. 8 (1985):3–20.
[9] Stakhanov, *Rasskaz*, 20–1.
[10] Ibid., 21.

Stakhanov at the coal face. From Semen Gershberg, *Stakhanov i stak-hanovtsy* (Moscow: Politizdat, 1985), p. 19.

Stakhanov then set to work cutting coal. For the next five hours and forty-five minutes, he worked uninterruptedly. On making his way back to the main drift, he was greeted by Mashurov, who shook his hand and congratulated him. "By my calculation," he is quoted as telling Stakhanov, "there are more than one hundred tons of coal." There were, in fact, 102 tons, earning Stakhanov 200 rubles instead of the 23 to 30 he normally received.[11]

Putting Stakhanov's achievement into perspective, it will be recalled that normally eight miners worked the face that Stakhanov cut alone. Assuming that each fulfilled his norm of 6.5 tons, that would mean 52 tons per shift.[12] Stakhanov alone had

---

[11] Ibid., 25.
[12] According to A. Zvorykin, "Metod Stakhanova," *Pravda*, Sept. 24, 1935, average output per shift was 120 to 150 tons, or more than twice the sum of individual norms.

nearly doubled this amount, but then Stakhanov was not entirely alone. Since pick operators normally did their own prop work, we must include the two propers who followed Stakhanov throughout the shift. Thus, three accomplished nearly twice what eight were expected to produce. Output per man was 5.23 times the norm. The extent to which this increase was due to the continual supply of compressed air and wood as opposed to the division of labor to which Stakhanov attributed his success cannot be measured. It is also impossible to calculate the savings in wages by the employment of fewer workers, as opposed to the bonus payments distributed to Stakhanov in accordance with the progressive piece-rate system and the advantages of using only one pneumatic pick as against its additional wear and tear.

Although in the long term such considerations of cost effectiveness would be crucial, in the immediate circumstances they were quite beside the point. In the view of the party committee, which was assembled by Petrov for an extraordinary meeting at 6:00 A.M., Stakhanov had established a world record for productivity, the significance of which was characterized as "political." "Here is the correct path that leads to the fulfillment of comrade Stalin's instructions about cadres and unquestionably guarantees the fulfillment of the annual plan ahead of schedule," the committee's resolution read.[13]

The rest of the resolution called for measures that illustrated the importance the committee attached to what had taken place. Stakhanov's name was to be prominently displayed on the mine's honor board; he was to be given a bonus equal to one month's wage; an apartment among those reserved for technical personnel was to be made available to him and his family, and it was to be equipped with a telephone and "all necessary and comfortable furniture"; the miners' union was to provide Stakhanov and his wife with passes to the cinema and live performances at the local workers' club, and places at a resort. A special meeting for hewers, with obligatory attendance by sectional party, union, and managerial leaders, was to be addressed by Stakhanov, and sectional competitions for the best emulator were to follow. Finally, "all those who try to slander Stakhanov and his record"

---

[13] Stakhanov, *Rasskaz*, 26.

were warned that "they will be considered by the party committee as the most vile enemies of the people." This resolution was dispatched to the regional party committee in Donetsk.

The immediate response among hewers at Central Irmino seems to have been just what the party committee had intended. Several, including Diukanov, demanded that their supervisors arrange shifts so that they could surpass Stakhanov's record. This was achieved by Diukanov on September 3–4 and by Kontsedalov on September 5.

But what about the propers, formerly part-time hewers themselves, who had made these new records possible? Presumably, they worked at the rate for prop work, which was lower than that for cutting coal.[14] And what of the timber getters, who would have to deliver more wood, and the ponydrivers, who would have to drive more wagons per shift in order to keep pace with the increased output of coal? There is no indication in the available sources of any protest against such a speedup. However, the party committee's decision to extend the *progressivka* to these categories of workers may well have resulted from its recognition that, without such an incentive, the entire initiative could be sabotaged.[15]

In the meantime, news of the record was spreading. *Sotsialis- ticheskii Donbass*, the organ of the Donetsk party *obkom*, reported it on September 1. The next day, *Pravda* carried a small item on its back page, indicating that Stakhanov had set a new All-Union (but not world?) record, surpassing such masters of the pneumatic pick as Grishin and Sviridov. More elaborate information was provided on September 6, this time on page 1 under the headline " 'Soviet Hercules,' Records of the Donbass Hewers Diukanov and Stakhanov." Then, on the seventh, came news of new records: Terekhin had dug 119 tons at the Karl Marx mine, and Kontsedalov had produced 125 tons.

Quite clearly, something extraordinary was happening.

[14] The average daily wage of hewers in September 1935 was 16.54 rubles, compared with only 10.35 for propers. Whereas 95.4% of the former were paid according to the progressive piece-rate system, this was the case with only 48.7 percent of the latter. *Trud v SSSR, 1935 g.* (Moscow: TsUNKhU, 1936), 112. Figures are derived from nine Donbass coal trusts.

[15] Gershberg, *Rukovodstvo*, 52.

Pravda's initial terse report was fairly standard as far as the announcement of records in production was concerned. It was, in fact, strikingly similar to one printed on September 5 about a record amount of steel produced in an open-hearth furnace.[16] The fact that it was Stakhanov's record rather than that of steel founder Alimov, which became the focal point of a national campaign, cannot be attributed to *Pravda*. According to the memoirs of the *Pravda* journalist S. R. Gershberg, the impetus came from none other than People's Commissar for Heavy Industry Ordzhonikidze. Even before Stakhanov's record, Ordzhonikidze had urged *Pravda*'s economics department to find "new people" among the working class and make heroes of them. "In capitalist countries, nothing can compare with the popularity of gangsters like Al Capone," he is quoted as saying. "In our country, under socialism, heroes of labor, our Izotovites, must become the most famous." Gershberg claims that when Ordzhonikidze, then on vacation in Kislovodsk, realized that Stakhanov's record had been given no significance – indeed, had not been reported by *Za industrializatsiiu* until September 4– he was "beside himself." It was allegedly his telephone calls to the commissariat and Glavugol' that galvanized *Pravda* into action.[17]

On September 8, *Pravda* began calling for a mass movement among Donbass miners under the banner "From competition of individuals to mass competition." On the ninth, a large photograph of Stakhanov and Diukanov graced the front page. Two days later, *Pravda* used the term "Stakhanovite movement" for the first time, thus honoring Stakhanov in a manner previously reserved only for Izotov. Coincidentally, on this very day, *Pravda* announced that Izotov, while on furlough from the Red Army, had cut 240 tons of coal in a six-hour shift.

Up to this point, the movement was confined to pneumatic pick operators. Even within these limits, however, certain themes that would subsequently become characteristic of Stakhanovism were being articulated. In an interview with *Pravda*, S. Sarkisov, the Donetsk *obkom* secretary, claimed that the new movement

[16] *Pravda*, Sept. 5, 1935.
[17] Gershberg, *Rabota u nas*, 320–2. Gershberg had been instrumental in discovering and publicizing the achievements of Izotov in 1932, would serve as Stakhanov's ghostwriter, and later still, chronicler of Stakhanovism.

demonstrated the baselessness of management's complaints of a shortage of workers. Only the remnants of old conservative traditions and the antimechanizers, he asserted, would now deny that the plan could be fulfilled.[18]

Sarkisov's point anticipated Ordzhonikidze's first public statement on Stakhanovism. This took the form of an open letter to Sarkisov and Bazhanov, the chairman of Glavugol', which was published on September 14. The significance of Stakhanovism, he pointed out, was to demonstrate "how far behind life lag those pseudoleaders who seek objective reasons to justify their bad work, their bad leadership." Although Ordzhonikidze expressed confidence that managerial and engineering-technical personnel would "head up and organize" the movement, he did not "conceal the fact that I am deeply afraid that some backward leaders will regard this movement with vulgar skepticism, which in reality will mean sabotage." And, he added, "such pseudoleaders must be removed immediately."[19]

What exactly did heading up and organizing the movement mean? According to Ordzhonikidze, it meant generalizing the advances in productivity both geographically (i.e., to the entire Donbass and other coal basins) and to other categories of mine workers. An order to this effect was issued several days after the publication of the open letter. It called for an output of 20 million tons of coal from the Donbass alone in the fourth quarter of 1935 and required Glavugol' and its constituent trusts to extend the Stakhanovite method to all mines during September and October.[20]

This was in line with *Pravda*'s earlier injunction "not to chase after new individual records" but "to achieve an increase in labor

---

[18] *Pravda*, Sept. 8, 1935.
[19] Ibid., Sept. 14, 1935. This is consistent with the remark attributed to Ordzhonikidze by Gershberg that "the Stakhanovite movement was born from below in the Donbass in spite of the trust leaders [*trestoviki*] and without them. Now, some of them want to wreak revenge on us and slow down the Stakhanovite movement. It started without us, they say, nothing will come of it. These are rotten people. We need to forewarn them that we will replace them with Stakhanovites." Gershberg, *Rabota u nas*, 377. The remark was alleged to have been made at conference (unspecified) in Narkomtiazhprom.
[20] Stakhanov, *Rasskaz*, 39; *ZI*, Sept. 21, 1935.

productivity on all mechanisms."[21] Yet the pages of *Pravda* and other newspapers continued to carry news of new individual records, only a few of which were not achieved by pick operators or machine cutters. This undoubtedly reflected the fact that it was much easier to arrange for a special stint by a skillful and ambitious individual than to sustain the same level of production over a period of time. The latter presupposed

the entire reorganization of the mine both in advance of and behind the point of extraction. It meant that the extraction of galleries would have to be accelerated, that the coal chipped from the face would have to be removed in sequence, and that for this to happen, the galleries would have to be cleared of rubble and lengthened, locomotives would have to be kept in good order and the coal cars would have to operate on a tighter schedule.[22]

These tasks required Herculean efforts, which mining enterprise management was often unwilling or unable to make, and in September and October there were already widespread reports of resistance among foremen, section heads, chief engineers, and directors to the general application of Stakhanov's method.[23]

As we shall see, the contradictions between individual record stints and the systematic, generalized increase in productivity – and the tensions arising therefrom – were to become embedded in the framework of Stakhanovism. But at this early juncture, it was not at all clear how seriously and in what ways Stakhanovism would impinge on enterprise management and the organization of production. Directives from above to adopt innovations were nothing new. We have seen that dispensing with the practice of rostering, introducing three-shift production, and other organizational and technical changes had been urged upon management but without much success. Even the demotion and dismissal of several administrative and technical personnel, announced in Ordzhonikidze's order, were not unusual, since there had been several shake-ups of mining officials in the past. Could it not

[21] *Pravda*, Sept. 11, 1935.
[22] J. P. Depretto, "Le record de Stakhanov," in *L'Industrialisation de l'URSS dans les années trente*, ed. Charles Bettelheim (Paris: Ecole des hautes études en sciences sociales, 1982), 139.
[23] See, e.g., *Pravda*, Sept. 20, 21, 24; Oct. 2, 13, 1935.

have been assumed that this campaign, as yet still limited to coal mining, would blow over like others before it?

If such expectations existed, they were given a severe jolt by the extension of Stakhanovism to other branches of industry via an avalanche of individual records. On September 19, Aleksandr Busygin was credited with forging a record number of crankshafts at the Molotov Automobile Works in Gor'kii. Given a shift norm of 675, Busygin had managed to turn out 966. Two days later, Nikolai Smetanin lasted 1,400 pairs of shoes at the Skorokhod Shoe Factory in Leningrad. Then, from the Donbass, it was reported that Petr Krivonos, an engine driver on the Slaviansk–Lozovaia line, raised his average speed to more than forty kilometers per hour; from the Nogin Mill in Vychuga, word went out that Mariia and Evdokiia Vinogradova, working in two different shifts, had each managed to supervise the operation of 94 and a few days later 100 Northrupp automatic weaving machines; Mariia Demchenko brought in 523 centners of sugar beet per hectare; Ivan Gudov set a record for machine milling; Musinskii sawed 221 cubic meters of wood, far above his norm of 95; and so forth.

All the while, the initial records were being superseded. Faustov, Velikzhanin, and Busygin outdid one another in forging crankshafts, hubcaps, and pinions; Fillippov of Moscow's Burevestnik Shoe Factory surpassed Smetanin's record, only to have Morozov, Sidorov, and Smetanin beat him. The weaver T. I. Odintseva vied with the Vinogradovas over the number of looms each could tend; other railwaymen disproved the "reactionary" proverb "more haste, less speed" by driving their goods trains faster and faster.

II

Recordmania (*rekordmenstvo*) swept the country. Characteristic of the first three months of Stakhanovism, indeed defining its essence, this phenomenon has retained its almost legendary quality. Its dimensions are astounding. By December 1935, the records achieved in heavy industry alone filled two volumes.[24]

---

[24] *Khronika stakhanovskogo dvizheniia v tiazheloi promyshlennosti*, 2 vols.

The second, covering the month of November, contained 647 entries from the national, regional, and local or factory press. Many entries merely refer to the percentage by which an individual or brigade fulfilled their shift norms. Very few appear to have constituted national or world records, but rather were intended to represent particularly noteworthy achievements. The distribution across different branches of heavy industry and occupations was uneven (Table 2.1). This probably reflected both real differences in opportunities and the extent to which press organs and the compilers of the volume were predisposed toward concentrating on some rather than others.

It bears emphasizing that this list is very partial. It covers only one month's records in heavy industry and, even then, not all occupations falling within that general category. Similar compilations covering October and including light industry, transport, and agriculture as well as heavy industry would undoubtedly swell the list to several thousand. But how are we to assess the significance of all these records? Were the USSR's productive forces suddenly unleashed, and if so, how?

We can find part of the answer by examining the careers of the initial record holders and the nature of their records. It is remarkable how many had made a name for themselves within their respective enterprises before achieving national acclaim. Their notoriety was of two sorts. Whereas Smetanin was a brigade leader and known throughout Skorokhod as one of a handful of outstanding shock workers – an Izotovite, in fact – Busygin had run into trouble with lower management for his objections to being transferred from one job to another and had been dismissed temporarily in 1934.[25] Krivonos had been a party member since 1929, was among a delegation of the best railroad

(Moscow: Tsentral'nyi institut tekhniko-ekonomicheskoi informatsii, 1935).

[25] V. N. Bobrov, "Obuvnaia fabrika 'Skorokhod' im. Iak. Kalinina," in *K godovshchine I Vsesoiuznogo soveshchaniia stakhanovtsev. Sbornik statei direktorov leningradskikh predpriiatii legkoi promyshlennosti* (Moscow–Leningrad: Gizlegprom, 1936), 26–9; E. A. Ershova et al., *Istoriia Leningradskoi Gosudarstvennoi Ordena Lenina i Ordena Trudovogo Krasnogo Znameni obuvnoi fabrike Skorokhod imeni Ia. Kalinina* (Leningrad: Lenizdat, 1969), 353–4; A. Kh. Busygin, *Sversheniia* (Moscow: Profizdat, 1972), 56–9; *Novatory, Sbornik* (Moscow: Molodaia gvardiia, 1972), 143.

Table 2.1. *Reported records of Stakhanovites (November 1935)*

Occupational group	Number of entries	% of total
Pick operators	63	9.74
Machine cutters	20	3.09
Drill borers	18	2.78
Manual hewers and loaders	4	0.62
Haulers	11	1.70
Total miners	116	17.93
Total smiths	108	16.69
Fitters	31	4.79
Turners	68	10.51
Millers	28	4.33
Turret lathe operators	8	1.24
Planers	11	1.70
Borers	11	1.70
Mortisers	5	0.77
Grinding machine operators	13	2.01
Press operators	5	0.77
Platers	9	1.39
Riveters	8	1.24
Welders	29	4.48
Casters	6	0.93
Chippers and fettlers	16	2.47
Molders	30	4.64
Total metal machinists	278	42.97
Steel founders	54	8.35
Rolling mill operators	45	6.95
Total ferrous metallurgists	99	15.30
Total chemicals workers	10	1.55
Assemblers/mounters	19	2.94
Plasterers	3	0.46
Carpenters	3	0.46
Masons	5	0.77
Concrete pourers	6	0.93
Total construction workers	36	5.56
Total all workers	647	100.00

Source: Khronika stakhanovskogo dvizheniia v tiazheloi promyshlennosti (Moscow: Tsentral'nyi institut tekhno-ekonomicheskoi informatsii, 1935), vol. 2.

workers that was received in the Kremlin on July 30, 1935, and was awarded an Order of Lenin on August 6.[26] In contrast, Gudov had been fined for experimenting with, and apparently damaging, a milling machine during the night shift.[27] Demchenko, a delegate to the First Shock Workers of Agriculture Conference in February 1935, had promised Stalin that her brigade would harvest 500 centners; but A. V. Dushenkov, a turner at the Lenin Works in Leningrad, had had his rate cut because he had overfulfilled his norm by what the rate setter considered an excessive amount.[28]

Of course, it would be surprising if these outstanding Stakhanovites had been relatively unskilled workers with little or no previous record of achievement. However, it was not skill that necessarily set these workers apart. Rather, it was the opportunity to apply their skills, either by having attained a relatively privileged position on the shop floor – as brigade leaders, instructors, or medal winners – or by rebelling against output-restrictive rules and traditions, thereby gaining a certain visibility.

In a sense, the difference in career patterns and positions within their respective enterprises has been overdrawn. Despite having had his rate clipped, Dushenkov soon was appointed an instructor for imported machinery, an indication of managerial respect for his skill. Despite Busygin's troubles with his section head, the shop supervisor asked him to return and he was placed in charge of a brigade. Then again, Krivonos had violated rules governing the "technical speed" of his locomotive engine and had gone public with a letter to a newspaper asking, "How is it possible to remain silent when the locomotive is only used at three-quarters of its capacity?"[29]

The records in most cases were not individual feats but, like Stakhanov's, the result of collective efforts, those of brigades. In the case of Smetanin, the number of brigade members was actually increased from eleven to thirteen, the leader (Smetanin) thus being freed from a task that could be performed by a worker

[26] *Novatory*, 177–9.
[27] I. I. Gudov, *Sud'ba rabochego* (Moscow: Politizdat, 1970), 33–4.
[28] *Pervoe Vsesoiuznoe soveshchanie rabochikh i rabotnits-stakhanovtsev, 14–17 noiabria 1935. Stenograficheskii otchet* (Moscow: Partizdat, 1935), 88.
[29] Busygin, *Sversheniia*, 60; *Novatory*, 173, 175.

of a lower skill category. At the same time, four instead of three workers were assigned to mounting the heel, a manual operation. Comparing figures for September 15 (i.e., before the new method was employed) with those for November 1, we find that output per worker did increase by 34.5 percent, but this was not nearly as dramatic as the 56.4 percent increase achieved by Smetanin.[30] Busygin set his record principally by rearranging the schedules of his brigade members such that he would not have to wait for the metal to be heated or brought to his steam hammer.[31] And the Vinogradovas were able to increase the number of machines tended by having an increasing number of weavers relegated to auxiliary functions such as delivering yarn, loading the machines, and cleaning scraps. Thus, whereas there was something like a ninefold increase in output per *weaver* between 1933 and October 1935, the increase in output per worker was a far more modest 20 to 28 percent.[32]

None of this is to deny that these first Stakhanovites did make innovations in their work methods. Gudov was able to mill parts in record quantities by increasing the cutting speed of his machine and operating several machines simultaneously; Busygin combined two operations – engaging his steam hammer by depressing a foot pedal and positioning the piece to be punched – which previously were performed in sequence; the Vinogradovas devised a route that eliminated return trips past the machines they tended; and so forth.[33] Nevertheless, none of these innovations would have been possible without changes in the division of labor, and for such changes to be made, the permission and/or active involvement of technical-managerial personnel usually was required. According to O. A. Ermanskii, who was more explicit about such matters than other Soviet commentators, Gudov was able to turn out parts at the rate of 1,900 percent of his norm only with the assistance of two engineers, a tech-

---

[30] M. Eskin, *Osnovnye puti razvitiia sotsialisticheskikh form truda*, 2d ed. (Leningrad: Sotsekgiz, 1936), 129–30.

[31] *Organizatsiia truda v stakhanovskom dvizhenii, Sbornik TsIT* (Moscow–Leningrad: TsIT NKTP SSSR, 1936), 53–4.

[32] Albert Pasquier, *Le Stakhanovisme: L'Organisation du travail en URSS* (Caen: Robert, 1937), 33.

[33] Ermanskii, *Stakhanovskoe dvizhenie*, 64, 74–5, 163–4.

nician, the shop supervisor, other engineering-technical personnel, and at least three workers.[34]

Why then, it may be asked, were the records misleadingly celebrated as individual accomplishments, and more specifically, why were they frequently expressed as percentages of individual output norms? In part it was a way of demonstrating to workers what they could do if they mastered technology. But as far as Narkomtiazhprom was concerned, there was another target, namely the so-called technically based norms and those who had sanctioned them. As indicated in Chapter 1, the question of norm determination had been a sore point for years. By May 1935, Ordzhonikidze had become so frustrated with managerial prevarication that he uttered the "heretical thought" that "the technical norming that we now have is not even fit for the devil." This and the remark by Piatakov that "in all the world such norms are superseded" may have carried the weight of authority, but they still lacked that of example.[35]

Narkomtiazhprom was thus quick to exploit Stakhanovites' records in its struggle against recalcitrant officials. As the commissariat's organ asserted in an editorial, "The blow of Stakhanov's hammer was a signal to all heavy industry to step over antiquated norms, to cast out the bugbear of projected production capacities."[36] Or to put it another way, if Stakhanov was able to fulfill his norm by 1,400 percent, what had the norm setters been doing? "It is perfectly obvious," wrote a correspondent for *Za industrializatsiiu,* "that their calculations are but the product of clerical-bureaucratic activity... the mechanical recording of chronometric readings, and the working out of some kind of average norm based on insufficiently verified literature, doubtful calculations and even more doubtful experiments and observations."[37]

There were bigger fish to fry than norm setters. After all, responsibility for norm determination lay squarely with the technical director or chief engineer of an enterprise, and ultimately

[34] Ibid., 75.
[35] *Sovet pri narodnom komissare tiazheloi promyshlennosti SSSR, Pervyi plenum, 10–12 maia 1935 g.* (Moscow–Leningrad: NKTP, 1935), 174.
[36] *ZI,* Oct. 21, 1935.
[37] Ibid., Oct. 11, 1935.

with its director.[38] Why had they routinely accepted such "doubtful" calculations in the past and were even now persisting in
their old ways? Addressing a meeting of *glavki* heads and chief
engineers on October 20, Piatakov described four types of "bad
bureacrats": slaves of routine, those who were offended because
their expertise had been called into question, the lazy, and young
engineers who relied exclusively on theoretical literature.[39]

Notably absent from this rogues' gallery were "saboteurs,"
about whom Ordzhonikidze had earlier expressed his fears. At
a time when the press was screaming about alleged acts of sabotage against Stakhanovites, such an omission is puzzling. Then
again, it is consistent with other statements emanating from Narkomtiazhprom. In an editorial of October 16, that is, four days
before Piatakov's speech, *Za industrializatsiiu* characterized the
Stakhanovite movement as "a fiery protest of the most advanced
elements of our proletariat against routines, inertia and technical
stagnation." "When," it asked, "will the fire of this hatred ignite
the hearts of all our engineers?"[40] In other words, those industrial cadres who previously had been guilty of inertia and stagnation were not to be punished as saboteurs, but offered a chance
to redeem themselves, indeed, as the headline above the tran-
script of Piatakov's speech proclaimed, "to organize the Stakhanovite movement and stand at its head." Essentially the same
message was conveyed by Ordzhonikidze in his address to the
First All-Union Conference of Stakhanovite Workers in mid-
November. There were, he asserted, economic leaders who displayed a "downright hooligan attitude" toward Stakhanovites,
and they should be removed from their commanding positions.
But there were also a "vast number" of executives and engineers
who "will assume the lead of the Stakhanovite movement and
organize it."[41]

[38] See the joint decree of VTsSPS and Narkomtiazhprom in *ZI*, July
14, 1932.
[39] Ibid., Oct. 24, 1935.
[40] Ibid., Oct. 16, 1935. See also Bazhanov's characterization of the opponents of Stakhanovism as "routiners, the lazy and the offended"
in ibid., Oct. 21, 1935.
[41] *Pravda*, Nov. 18, 1935. A reprint of the speech appears in G. K.
Ordzhonikidze, *Stat'i i rechi*, 2 vols. (Moscow: Pollitizdat, 1956–7),
2:696–711.

Even more remarkable in this respect was Ordzhonikidze's speech to a plenum of the All-Union Intersectional Bureau of Engineers and Technicians (VMBIT) on November 22, 1935. Assembled to discuss the role of specialists in the Stakhanovite movement, the delegates heard Ordzhonikidze repeatedly profess his affinity for, and confidence in, the technical intelligentsia. "It would be sad," he noted,

> if we begin to doubt that the engineers will know how to take charge of the movement. It would be a shame for both you and us. These young engineers, raised by us, are our children, our brothers. How can we doubt that they will put themselves at the head of our movement? Whoever wavers, we will straighten them out.

As for the "curses" and condemnation to which they had been subjected, the commissar insisted that this was merely a means of educating them so that they could "lead the people" and "go forward together with the party."[42]

Such conciliatory remarks differed from those of other party leaders, notably A. A. Zhdanov, Leningrad party secretary and a candidate member of the Politburo. Speaking at a reception for Stakhanovites in late October, Zhdanov offered his threefold typology of their opponents: those who "consider that all they have to do is organize supplies for the Stakhanovite movement to develop"; those who are afraid that Stakhanovism will mean revising the industrial-financial plan of one or another enterprise, "as if that were a bad thing"; and a third group that "slanders Stakhanovites as self-seekers who grab for the last ruble." Such people, Zhdandov stated, "are enemies of the working class and the party."[43]

Did the Leningrad party secretary mean that all three groups were "enemies," or only the last? If his audience was in some doubt, another gathering of Stakhanovites a few days later could not have been. "All saboteurs, routiners, and bureaucrats,"

[42] "Neopublikovannoe vystuplenie G. K. Ordzhonikidze," *Voprosy istorii*, no. 8 (1978):94–7. It is also remarkable that this speech was not published until 1978 and then only in an edited version.

[43] *Leningradskaia pravda* (hereafter *LP*), Oct. 22, 1935. For similar typologies by L. M. Kaganovich and N. S. Khrushchev, see D. Berdnikova, "Ot kommunisticheskikh subbotnikov k stakhanovskomu dvizheniiu," *Uchenye zapiski Leningradskogo universiteta*, no. 1 (1940):159; *PS*, no. 22–3 (1935):26–7.

Zhdandov predicted, "will be swept away by the victorious march of the Stakhanovites. . . . Who does not lead this movement, this initiative, will be cast out as leaders."[44]

Thus, although Stakhanovism presented the central authorities with a powerful weapon to wield against undisciplined managerial and technical personnel, there were signs of disagreement or at least differing emphases over the way in which the weapon was to be used. Lacking further evidence, one might speculate that the differences were as much institutional as personal. More than any other Politburo member, Ordzhonikidze was closely connected in his daily work with the "commanding staff" of industry. Zhdanov, in contrast, presided over the most proletarianized constituency in the country. It is true that the former had initiated the harsh rhetoric against his subordinates, but his subsequent remarks suggest that he was less than enthusiastic about unleashing an all-out attack, preferring rather to "forewarn" them. The latter, however, may have seen some advantage in an alliance with Stakhanovites that would be directed against an intermediary level of enterprise bureaucrats.

Before proceeding, we might pause to consider whether Ordzhonikidze's confidence was misplaced. That is, what was the prevailing attitude of enterprise personnel toward Stakhanovism? Was their failure to head up the new movement the result of their own incompetence, their antipathy to Stakhanovism, or some other factor? There is no doubt that many enterprise employees lacked the skills that were demanded of them. The vast majority of rate and norm setters had no formal technical education. Foremen were no better in this respect, and some lacked even basic literacy.[45] Many of the young engineers toward whom Ordzhonikidze was so solicitous had just graduated from technical schools and were still acclimating themselves to practical experience, whereas others had been promoted directly from the bench without formal training. In the words of John Scott, an American specialist who worked at Magnitogorsk, "Whereas most of the workers in the mills were fairly well trained by 1935, . . . most of the administrators were far from having mastered

---

[44] *Pravda*, Oct. 27, 1935.
[45] See Chapter 1, Section II, and A. Khavin, "O mastere," *ZI*, Jan. 11, 1935.

their jobs. They had not one quarter the practical experience of men occupying similar positions in industry in America or Western Europe."[46]

Somewhat short on expertise, Soviet managers and engineers generally did not evince an enthusiasm for, or commitment to, Stakhanovism that might have compensated in the eyes of the central authorities. For every Mashurov, there appeared to be three or four section heads and shop supervisors who were reprimanded or dismissed for asserting that Stakhanov's method was inappropriate to their fields, or for otherwise failing to apply it.[47] By the middle of December, criminal charges had been brought against three mine supervisors, six chief engineers, twenty-eight section heads, and nineteen foremen in the Donbass alone.[48]

Was this simply persecution, a means of finding "enemies" where none existed, or did Stakhanovism encounter genuine opposition? It would seem that both were the case. The refusal of lower managerial personnel to provide the wherewithal for Stakhanovites to set new records or maintain their high rates of productivity – a frequent charge – may have reflected resentment against these "upstart" workers whose wages far outstripped their own salaries. For years, engineers had been besieged by "worker-inventors" who were encouraged by the party to bring forward their rationalization proposals. Apparently, the trick was to accept formally but file in the wastebasket schemes considered unworkable.[49] But Stakhanovism clearly made this strategy more dangerous, and some "bureaucrats" may

---

[46] John Scott, *Behind the Urals: An American Worker in Russia's City of Steel* (Bloomington: Indiana University Press, 1973), 175. See also Kendall E. Bailes, *Technology and Society under Lenin and Stalin* (Princeton, N.J.: Princeton University Press, 1978), 308–12.

[47] Stakhanov, *Rasskaz*, 38–9; *Pravda*, Oct. 15, 1935; *PS*, no. 21 (1935):24; R. Ia. Khabibulina, *Leningradskie kommunisty-organizatory stakhanovskogo dvizheniia (1935–1937 gg.)* (Leningrad: LGU, 1961), 60; *Industrializatsiia SSSR, 1933–1937 gg. Dokumenty i materialy* (Moscow: Nauka, 1971), 568.

[48] *PS*, no. 22–3 (1935):18.

[49] See Joseph Berliner, *Factory and Manager in the USSR* (Cambridge, Mass.: Harvard University Press, 1957), 273; John D. Littlepage and Demaree Bess, *In Search of Soviet Gold* (New York: Harcourt, Brace, 1938), 211–12.

well have paid a high price for past slights. It is possible, though, that opposition to Stakhanovites' innovations stemmed from genuine concern for safety, not wanting to disrupt production schedules, and a sense of fairness toward other workers.

As far as directors and other high-ranking enterprise personnel were concerned, few were as rash as one mine head who allegedly called Stakhanovism "nonsense" on the grounds that "the worker gives 200 percent of the coal yield today and tomorrow his hands are sore and he gives nothing."[50] Once they sensed which way the wind was blowing, most hailed the new movement and seemed proud of "their" Stakhanovites. However, as Ordzhonikidze noted, "Our directors are great supporters of the Stakhanovite movement, applaud it, but do not like one question – if the Stakhanovite movement is a good thing, then can the [enterprise's] program be increased?"[51]

In the final analysis, the predominant form that Stakhanovism assumed in its early months – the creation of conditions for a handful of workers in each enterprise to set records – presented all of enterprise management and engineering-technical personnel with a cruel dilemma. On the one hand, without proper enterprise and, indeed, industrywide rescheduling of assortments, deliveries, repairs, and work routines, increased output by a few individuals or brigades was bound to lead to backlogs, bottlenecks, and eventual shutdowns. "For the first half of the month," complained a worker at the Kirov Factory in Leningrad, "we worked in a Stakhanovite manner on brake fittings. But in the second half we had stoppages, since we were not supplied with materials."[52] On the other hand, to reject Stakhanovites' pressure, backed in many cases by party committee secretaries and the inertia of recordmania, was to go against the grain of the movement and risk denunciation as a "conservative," "routiner," or worse. How cruel the dilemma could be is illustrated by the case of six engineering-technical personnel who let a group of Stakhanovite miners work a gallery that had not been

---

[50] *Izvestiia*, Oct. 2, 1935.

[51] Quoted in *Novatory*, 114.

[52] *Industrializatsiia severo-zapadnogo raiona v gody vtoroi i tret'ei piatiletok, 1933–1941 gg. Dokumenty i materialy* (Leningrad: LGU, 1969), 348. See similar comments by F. N. Artiukhov, a Stakhanovite miner, in *Pervoe Vsesoiuznoe soveshchanie*, 44–5.

adequately prepared. After ten of the workers were killed in a cave-in, one of the engineers was sentenced to be shot and the others received prison terms ranging from one to ten years. Not wishing to take any more risks, mining officials banned the use of explosives in the Cheliabinsk region where the cave-in had occurred. For this, they were labeled "conservatives" and "routiners."[53]

Aside from how management and technical specialists were coping with Stakhanovism and how their shortcomings were being regarded, the question of what to do about the "outdated" output norms caused considerable confusion in the autumn of 1935. Some enterprise officials drew the logical conclusion that, if norms were outdated, they should be revised. At least five enterprises in Leningrad were reported to have attempted to raise Stakhanovites' norms in October.[54] At an enterprise in Dne-propetrovsk, the head of the Department of Planning and Labor ordered that all norms be raised after two Stakhanovites had substantially overfulfilled theirs. However, this decision was attacked as "anti-Stakhanovite" by the editor of the factory's newspaper.[55] Who was right?

As strenuously as they condemned existing norms, the central authorities were at pains to prevent any increases. "Again and again," proclaimed an editorial of October 16 in *Za industriali-zatsiiu,* "it is necessary to slap the hands of those who are trying to revise the norms, who do not realize that a revision of the norms *at present* is a blow against the new movement." When, at the aforementioned meeting of *glavki* heads, Rataichek, the chairman of the Chemicals Industry Administration, questioned this position, he was told by Piatakov, "If you want to wreck the Stakhanovite movement, revise the norms. It is forbidden to revise the norms."[56] On this point at least, Zhdanov was at one with Narkomtiazhprom. In his speech to Leningrad Stakhan-ovites, he cited the commissariat's decree of March 1, 1935, which stipulated that norms were to be frozen for a period of one year

---

[53] *Pravda,* Nov. 4, 1935; *New York Times,* Nov. 5, 1935; *Pravda,* Dec. 18, 1935.
[54] *Industrializatsiia severo-zapadnogo raiona,* 350.
[55] I am indebted to Donald Filtzer for providing this information based on his access to *Zvezda,* the factory's newspaper.
[56] *ZI,* Oct. 21, 1935. Emphasis mine.

(actually, until May 1, 1936).[57] A joint plenary session of the Leningrad *obkom* and *gorkom* reiterated this point on October 26.[58]

Not until Stalin, who hitherto had remained publicly silent about the issue and indeed Stakhanovism in general, addressed the First All-Union Conference of Stakhanovite Workers was this line breached. "We need output norms that are somewhere midway between the present norms and those achieved by people like Stakhanov and Busygin," he affirmed.[59] But neither Stalin nor anyone else indicated how and when the norms would be revised. Thus, returning to Gor'kii after the conference, Busygin could tell his fellow workers that, according to Ordzhonikidze, "it is not necessary to review norms now."[60]

III

Why, then, were party leaders so reluctant to come out in favor of raising output norms? It will be recalled that output norms had been revised in the spring of 1935. The extent of the revisions and the procedures used to arrive at the new norms remain shadowy. It would appear that they conformed to previous practice in that norm setters at each constituent enterprise provided the data used by respective *glavki* to fix the new norms and that the increase was in the range of 3 to 7 percent.[61] However, the revisions were not set in concrete. Norm setters had the authority to adjust norms to suit local circumstances or whenever a technical process was altered, and as indicated in Chapter 1, there was considerable pressure from both foremen and workers to adjust norms downward, or at least to limit the extent of upward revisions. Informal pressure was also exerted on rate setters (*tarifikatory*) to adjust rates upwardly, which, in terms of *wages*, would have amounted to the same thing.

---

[57] Ibid., Oct. 23, 1935. The decree was republished, with the clause about freezing the revised norms in bold face, in ibid., Oct. 11, 1935.

[58] Khabibulina, *Leningradskie kommunisty*, 63.

[59] Stalin, *Sochineniia*, 1 (XIV), 95–6.

[60] *Pravda*, Nov. 23, 1935.

[61] A. Vinnikov, "K peresmotru norm vyrabotki v promyshlennosti," *Plan*, no. 8 (1936):37.

In the wake of the Stakhanovites' records, party leaders were faced with a dilemma. On the one hand, insofar as the records were supposed to encourage workers to emulate Stakhanovites' examples and put pressure on enterprise officials to provide them with the means of doing so, it would not do to diminish their impact. Raising norms not only would make the records seem less impressive in terms of percentage of overfulfillment, but would reduce the multiplier effect of the progressive piece-rate system and hence the wages received for such record shifts. On the other hand, the fantastic sums earned by some Stakhanovites and the prospect of their examples being repeated by tens of thousands of other workers threatened to deplete the wage funds allocated to individual enterprises by the State Bank. Even if enterprise management could temporarily cover the additional wage costs by transferring funds from its working capital supply, this was not a long-term solution.

This problem was more serious in some branches of industry than in others. In the textile industry, the payment of progressive piece rates beginning at 80 percent of the norm was a standard practice. Several categories of mine workers were paid double their base rates for all production in excess of the output norm up to 10 percent and triple rates for the entire output above the norm if the norm were exceeded by more than 10 percent. In contrast, workers who produced up to 10 percent above the norm in the assembly and other "cold" shops of tractor factories received a relatively modest 25 percent in excess of the base level, and only when the norm was overfulfilled by more than 20 percent did they receive double pay.[62]

Although only some 30 percent of all workers were paid according to progressive piece rates, norm overfulfillment by a substantial proportion of them could, and apparently did, lead to significant overexpenditures of the industrial wage fund in the fourth quarter of 1935. At Central Irmino, wage costs rose

---

[62] E. Loshkin, "Formy zarplaty na sovremennom etape," *Problemy Ekonomiki*, no. 3 (1936):110, 112–13. For other schedules see Scott, *Behind the Urals*, 149, and Jerzy Glicksman, "Conditions of Industrial Labor in the USSR: A Study of the Incentive System in Soviet Industry," Harvard Interview Project on the Soviet Social System, manuscript (1954), in Russian Research Center Library, Harvard University, pp. 28–32.

from 340,000 rubles in September to 500,000 in December, representing an increase in miners' average monthly earnings from 235 to 320 rubles. According to Scott, the average wage at Magnitogorsk shot up from 308 rubles in September to 407 in October.[63]

The problem of wage overexpenditure was compounded by the fact that, irrespective of the branch of industry where they were applied, "steep" progressive piece rates generally were linked to the supposedly more difficult technically based norms – that is, those formulated on the basis of the projected capacities of technical equipment rather than the less "scientific" statistical or observational output norms. Hence, in agricultural machine production enterprises, the same scale prevailing among coal miners was applied to jobs with technical norms, whereas in work in which statistical norms were used, overfulfillment of from 1 to 20 percent increased the rate by only 50 percent.[64] So long as workers only barely overfulfilled technically based norms, enterprises could remain within or close to their projected wage bills. Once Stakhanovites began to apply new methods, "financial discipline" was severely strained. Given that Narkomtiazhprom had long been advocating technically based norms as a panacea to the problem of correlating labor productivity to wages, its sense of betrayal was quite real and may explain in part the ferocity of the attacks against the norm-setting apparatus, as cited earlier.

If wage fund overexpenditures constituted a compelling reason for raising norms, there was still, however, one consideration that constrained Soviet leaders from taking this step too precipitously. Stakhanovites' records had already engendered considerable opposition from rank-and-file workers as well as foremen precisely because such records seemed to presage norm increases. Since for years the official procedure for determining norms had been to base them on the performance of "workers

---

[63]   *Trud*, Jan. 20, 1936; Scott *Behind the Urals*, 277. As Scott points out, the administration could afford to pay premiums because "the fixed charges were so much greater than the labor cost, that the actual wages paid out were covered by the increased production obtained from the same fixed costs" (pp. 149–50).

[64]   Glicksman, "Conditions of Industrial Labor," 30.

demonstrating an intense tempo, that is shock workers,"[65] it could reasonably be assumed that Stakhanovites would now fulfill this function. That is, at least some Stakhanovites were perceived by their fellow workers to be rate busters.

Rate busting and the antagonisms it aroused were by no means new phenomena in Russia. The former Red Guard Eduard Dune recalled that in the chemical dye factory where he worked before the First World War there were novices who "arrived on the job long before the whistle blew" and were "ready to work overtime until the middle of the night." In such cases, if warnings by other workers were to no avail,

it was usually enough to pour graphite or talc on the transmission belt of his machine, in order to reduce the number of revolutions it made, or to supply him with raw materials and semifinished materials of poor quality, in order to bring his output down to the norm, if not less than that of others.[66]

A social revolution, a civil war, and the establishment of Soviet power did not alter attitudes toward rate busting. The official argument that all would benefit by higher productivity and that higher norms were a mark of the Soviet Union's maturity as an industrial society only went so far or so deep. There is no shortage of examples from the Soviet press, legal journals, and other sources of workers' opposition during the autumn of 1935.[67]

At one factory in Rostov-on-Don, a Stakhanovite found a dirty broom on her machine with the following message attached: "Comrade Beloi is hereby presented with a bouquet of flowers for fulfilling three norms." At another, in Moscow, two workers, a father and son, reportedly told the Stakhanovite Solovin that, "because of his work, the rates would be lowered." They then enjoined two other workers to light a piece of paper that had been placed between Solovin's legs while he slept, resulting in

---

[65] The statement was issued by the Council of Technical Norms in 1930. See L. H. Siegelbaum, "Soviet Norm Determination in Theory and Practice, 1917–1941," *Soviet Studies*, 36, no. 1 (1984):54.

[66] Eduard Dune, "Zapiski krasnogvardeitsa," manuscript in the Nicolaevsky Archive, Hoover Institution, Stanford, Calif., pp. 6–7. I am indebted for this source to Diane Koenker, whose translation this is.

[67] A more extensive analysis of workers' responses to Stakhanovism is presented in Chapter 5.

Stakhanov emerges triumphant. From *Labour in the Land of Socialism, Stakhanovites in Conference* (Moscow: Co-op Pub. Society of Foreign Workers in the USSR, 1936), p. 127.

"serious burns."[68] Outstanding Stakhanovites were by no means immune to such actions. Stakhanov reported that several older workers (*starichki*), whom he characterized as politically unconscious, began whispering that his records were in vain because wages would be lowered.[69] The locomotive operated by Krivonos was smeared with dirt and partially dismantled in his absence. This sabotage was attributed by the authorities to Shchukin, a machinist, who "openly swore that he would carry out a 'St. Bartholomew's Night' against the Krivonos family."[70] G. I. Likhoradov, a young turner at the Uritskii Works in Briansk, told the All-Union Conference of Stakhanovites that, "when I turned out seven tires, there was such commotion in the shop that the backward workers were almost ready to tear me to pieces." One such worker, Sviridov, allegedly organized a group, which damaged several machines. He then spread the rumor that Likhor-

[68] *Trud*, Nov. 1, 1935; *Izvestiia*, Oct. 28, 1935, as cited in N. Markin, "Stakhanovskoe dvizhenie," *Biulleten' oppozitsii*, no. 47 (1936):46–7.
[69] Stakhanov, *Rasskaz*, 60.
[70] *Sovetskaia zakonnost'* (hereafter *SZ*), no. 1 (1936):50.

adov was responsible and that he "attributes to himself the work of others."[71]

This claim is interesting because it suggests yet another source of antagonism to Stakhanovites' records, one that had less to do with expectations of norm increases and strategies for preventing them. The source was the principle endemic to the functioning of the artel and other traditional forms of collective work that no worker should take or be given credit for someone else's labor. Whether the accusations leveled at Likhoradov referred to the elaborate preparations that preceeded the setting of many records or the usually unacknowledged assistance of workers performing auxiliary tasks cannot be determined. It may have been the result of a personal grudge or a misunderstanding, but it could also have stemmed from Sviridov's awareness that the calculation of Likhoradov's output masked the contribution of others and hence violated this principle.

The question of setting norms and how and when to raise them was thus complex and vexed. We will probably never know the substance of the deliberations among party leaders at this time and cannot be sure that a definite strategy with respect to norms emerged from them. There seems little reason to doubt the reports that individual normers took it upon themselves to revise Stakhanovites' norms upwardly, particularly since some of these reports were confidential. But the public condemnation of these initiatives and, later, the prosecution of some of these low-level officials may well have been a demogogic maneuver designed to encourage workers to emulate Stakhanovites. The extent to which it worked is open to question. Pasquier's assertion that "naïve workers applauded the impressive records" before the norms were revised does not get us very far, because the term "naïve" is clearly tendentious. The claim by Scott that the norm increases at Magnitogorsk in the fall (*sic*) of 1936 "created a restlessness among many workers who had received the impression that all improvements in production would reflect themselves in direct wage increases, and that the norms would never be changed" seems itself naïve and does not get us any farther.[72]

[71] *Pervoe Vsesoiuznoe soveshchanie*, 178; *Sovetskaia iustitsiia* (hereafter *SIu*), no. 3 (1936):5.
[72] Pasquier, *Le Stakhanovisme*, 88; Scott, *Behind the Urals*, 163.

One thing is clear. If norms were to fulfill their function as an incentive for raising productivity (not to mention for determining enterprise plans and delineating the wages of individual workers), they would have to be fixed at a level that workers believed could be fulfilled. The discrediting of the old norms (and those responsible for setting them) and the proliferation of Stakhanovite record holders must have gone some way toward achieving this end. Bearing in mind the output-restrictive practices of both workers and their immediate bosses, it should also be pointed out that, whatever the extent of resistance to revising the norms, workers knew that the norms were below what could be achieved, irrespective of Stakhanovites or their new methods.

On December 21, 1935, the party's Central Committee convened in plenary session. Five weeks had passed since Stalin announced that norms should be raised, and during that time the initial production records were dwarfed. I. A. Borisov, a hewer at the Eikhe mine in the Kuznets Basin of western Siberia, produced 778 tons of coal in his shift, surpassing his norm by 46 times; in Kiev, Gomul'ko, a shoe laster, got through 2,582 pairs in six hours; Faustov, continuing his competition with other automobile workers, turned out 1,360 crankshafts.[73] As Stalin had, *Pravda* noted that "the record achievements of the best masters cannot immediately become the law for all." "But," it added, "they are that lighthouse which clearly illuminates the way for all the masses, driving them forward. This is why," the editorial continued, flatly contradicting one that had appeared in September, "the struggle for high records must be developed in all branches of production."[74]

Citing the achievements of the leading Stakhanovites, the speakers at the plenary session condemned existing norms as backward and demanded that they be increased. Back in November, when Stakhanovites had announced to the All-Union conference how much they were earning, they were met with applause from their colleagues and, according to one delegate, "satisfaction, smiles, and joy on our leaders' faces."[75] But when,

[73] *Pravda*, Nov. 19, 23, 30, 1935.
[74] Ibid., Nov. 19, 1935. For the earlier editorial, see note 21.
[75] Ibid., Nov. 18, 1935.

by way of demonstrating the absurdity of existing norms, Ordzhonikidze told the Central Committee about a seventeen-year-old metalworker who had earned 900 rubles in one shift, there was "laughter [and] animation in the hall."[76] Sarkisov, the Donetsk party secretary, was so impatient for output norms to be raised that he suggested they take effect in January rather than April or May. And the commissar of light industry, Liubimov, went so far as to advocate that the new norms be equated as soon as possible to those of the best Stakhanovites.[77] In the end, the plenum resolved that branch conferences be convened in the early part of 1936 to determine the extent of output norm increases and the timing of their introduction. Attending these conferences would be enterprise directors, chief engineers, shop heads, foremen, and "the best Stakhanovites," but not trade union officials.[78]

Aside from reviewing output norms, the more than ninety conferences were to revise the technical standards for machinery and the capacities of enterprises "based on the verified experience of the best Stakhanovites." All those who commented on this matter were in agreement that the levels previously assigned reflected the pernicious "theory of limits" and that Stakhanovites had exploded the theory. A. A. Andreev, for example, asserted that the manuals according to which technical capacities were determined should be "thrown out like garbage," to which Ordzhonikidze added, "They should be burned."[79]

Some speakers went farther, attacking not only the theory of limits, but those who propounded it and those who acquiesced in its application. Labeling the authors of manuals used by railway officials as "reactionary professors," L. M. Kaganovich, commissar of transport, contended that no group of professors "would have dared in 1935 to put forward such a platform of

---

[76] Ibid., Dec. 27, 1935.

[77] Ibid.

[78] *Kommunisticheskaia partiia sovetskogo soiuza v rezoliutsiiakh i resheniiakh s"ezdov, konferentsii i plenumov TsK*, 9th ed. (Moscow: Politizdat, 1984), 5:236, 6:289. However, it was stipulated that the revision of norms in light industry be completed in time for the compilation of the production plans for 1937 (p. 290).

[79] *ZI*, Dec. 29, 1935.

«Новый» —
Гулливер» —
карикатура В.
1935 год

"The New Gulliver." The Lilliputian bureaucrat holds up a sign proclaiming "technically based norm of 7 tons." From Semen Gershberg,
Stakhanov i stakhanovtsy (Moscow: Politizdat, 1985), p. 112.

naked sabotage, unless they considered that there would be sympathizers among the commanders."[80] Although Kaganovich was
referring to the railways before the shake-up he had supervised
earlier in the year, the implications of his remarks for all of
industry were obvious. Zhdanov turned his wrath on other targets – norm setters, among whom were "not a few Menshevik
elements and opportunists"; trade unionists who had also op-
portunistically taken the path of least resistance by defending
old technical norms; and party members whose membership
cards were in order but who, because they were not participating
in the Stakhanovite movement and were even in some cases
opposing it, did not deserve the high calling of belonging to the
party.[81]

   Such verbal sallies are not reflected in the Central Committee's
resolution on Stakhanovism. Indeed, what is so striking about
the resolution is how little it departed from existing practice.
Two examples will suffice: In his report to the plenum, Liubimov

[80] *Pravda*, Dec. 28, 1935.
[81] Ibid., Jan. 18, 1936.

referred to the different forms that Stakhanovism had taken in light industry. In textiles it was the increase in the number of looms and spindles supervised and the corresponding liberation of the skilled worker from auxiliary tasks; in shoe manufacturing, a more rational division of labor and the reorganization of the work place. This, he suggested, was not only what had occurred, but what ought to be done on an ever wider scale. Not so, argued Andreev. The guiding principle of Stakhanovism as enunciated by Stalin in November was "to extract the maximum from technology," and in the case of textiles this principle was being violated. "The pursuit of a great number of machines... by weavers and spinners is leading to a failure to fulfill the norm for the use of the machines," he asserted. Why else was it that in the Iakovlev Combinat there were more than one thousand Vinogradovites, and yet the combinat's annual plan had been fulfilled by only 66 percent as of the end of November? Nevertheless, the resolution as it applied to light industry avoided any criticism of the way Stakhanovism had proceeded, merely indicating that "when Stakhanovites take on a large number of machines, a further increase in the productivity of machinery should be ensured."[82]

The second example has to do with the role of managers and engineers. It appears that the original draft of the resolution did not go beyond the assertion that "it is necessary to smash all remaining opposition to the Stakhanovite movement by the conservative part of management and engineering-technical personnel." Left by itself, this statement would have reflected the harsh line advocated by Zhdanov and already practiced by Kaganovich. But the final version of the resolution included another "necessity": "to assist in every way the assumption of the direction of the Stakhanovite movement by the executives, engineers, and technicians who welcomed but have still not managed to lead it." As revealed by Ordzhonikidze several months later, it was none other than Stalin who had had the latter phrase inserted, thereby restoring the balance that had existed for several months already.[83]

We cannot be sure about Stalin's motives in taking this intiative.

[82] Ibid., Dec. 27, 1935; *Kommunisticheskaia partiia*, 6:286.
[83] Ordzhonikidze, *Stat'i i rechi*, 2:770.

He may simply have been trying to placate Ordzhonikidze and others who were fearful of the consequences of relying exclusively on intimidation. Then again, it is possible that his intervention had a more sinister objective, that is, to hold managers and engineering-technical personnel responsible for the leadership of the movement, only later to punish them – and their patrons – for their shortcomings.

Whatever the motivations involved, it is clear that the plenary session's resolutions established Stakhanovism as a major concern of the party and the commanders of production. This, however, was no guarantee that the balance that had been achieved would last or that the path charted for Stakhanovism during 1936, the "Stakhanovite year," would remain smooth.

3

Managers and specialists in the Stakhanovite year

The first phase of Stakhanovism, extending from September 1935 to the Central Committee's plenary session in late December, contained much ambiguity about the meaning and long-term implications of the phenomenon. At the root of this ambiguity were differing assessments among Soviet leaders concerning the means by which Stakhanovism could be used to raise productivity and, more specifically, to implement the innovations attributed to the outstanding Stakhanovites. Since such implementation involved both enterprise managerial and technical personnel and workers, the problem boiled down to deciding on whom to lean and how.

As implied by Ordzhonikidze's open letter of September 14, some degree of coercion over and above that imposed routinely if arbitrarily would be administered against the most flagrant opponents of Stakhanovite methods of work. And throughout the autumn of 1935, scores of engineers, section heads, foremen, and ordinary workers were demoted, dismissed, or subjected to criminal prosecution. Two things must be noted about this repression. First, it was indiscriminate. That is, no one group or stratum in the industrial hierarchy was singled out. Saboteurs were saboteurs whether they happened to be salaried personnel or "backward" workers.[1] Second, it was counterbalanced by a combination of appeals, cajolery, and flattery emphasizing the maturity, skills, and resourcefulness of managerial-technical personnel and by concessions to workers in the form of opportun-

[1] Such a lack of discrimination was in marked contrast to the policy advocated by the Commissariat of Justice in 1936. For a discussion of this policy, see Chapter 4.

ities to increase wages via the extension of the progressive piece-rate system and a freeze on rates and norms.

Already by late October, impatience with such indulgence could be discerned in Zhdanov's strong attacks on industrial officials and in high-level questioning of the policy on output norms. Not until the Central Committee plenum, however, did the party formally commit itself to the adjustment of norms (but not rates), and as for other questions raised by Stakhanovism, the discussion and resolutions merely perpetuated the ambiguities.

What follows is an analysis of how in the course of 1936 Stakhanovism impinged on managers and specialists and how they reacted to and had an impact on Stakhanovism. It will be argued that Stakhanovism did impose new burdens on these middle-level industrial cadres but that it did not resolve the problems it was supposed to overcome and, to some extent, made them worse. The failure of Stakhanovism to realize its assigned task, already apparent in the early months of 1936, was to have serious, indeed fatal, consequences for many who had been called upon to lead the movement. It also led to the deemphasis and eventual marginalization of Stakhanovism itself.

I

Recordmania, characteristic of Stakhanovism's first phase, peaked in November 1935. Having demonstrated the possibilities of new methods of production and having attracted worldwide attention, it had also revealed several tendencies that were counterproductive to the aims of the Soviet leadership. Though individual achievements continued to receive publicity, only a handful of innovators and record breakers were to attain the prestige enjoyed by the original cohort of outstanding Stakhanovites. Thus, even before the Central Committee met in plenary session to chart the future of the movement, it was undergoing a transition.

As had been the case at the outset, Stakhanovism's second phase began in the Donbass coal-mining industry. Reportedly at the insistence of Komsomol Stakhanovites but quite possibly owing to the direct intervention of Sarkisov, the district party secretary, the Dzerzhinskii mine (Artemugol' trust) organized a "Stakhanovite shift" on November 30, 1935. The aim was to fulfill the mine's annual program with one month to spare. Stakhanovites from the other two shifts were recruited, and in the end nearly twice the shift's quota of coal was brought to the surface.[2]

Within a matter of days, other mines in the Artemugol' trust and then farther afield began to imitate this example, extending it to all three shifts such as to comprise "Stakhanovite days" (*sutki*). By the middle of December, Sarkisov was proclaiming Stakhanovite shifts and days "excellent organizational forms for drawing the masses of workers into the Stakhanovite movement."[3] In his speech to the Central Committee's plenary session, Ordzhonikidze warmly endorsed what the Donbassites had done, though he stopped just short of recommending the new forms to other branches of industry.[4] The fact that the plenum's resolution made no mention of them suggests that there was still some hesitation among the party leadership about their viability. In any case, Narkomtiazhprom was quick to give its imprimatur. Its organ, *Za industrializatsiiu*, greeted the Stakhanovite year by encouraging enterprises in all branches of industry to organize Stakhanovite days and extend them into Stakhanovite ten-day periods (*dekady*) and Stakhanovite months.[5]

Throughout the first months of 1936, not a day passed without a report in the national press about a Stakhanovite period (*polosa*) at one enterprise or another. Preparations – or the lack thereof – execution, and results were scrutinized and assessed in considerable detail. It is from such material as well as memoir accounts and those in the emigré press that something of the frenzy associated with this phase of Stakhanovism can be reconstructed and analyzed.

Initially, however, we must examine what the Stakhanovite periods were intended to accomplish. Four aims were evident.

---

[2] O. A. Ermanskii, *Stakhanovskoe dvizhenie i stakhanovskie metody* (Moscow: Sotsekgiz, 1940), 25. Sarkisov seems to have taken credit for the initiative, using the first person plural to describe it, in *ZI*, Dec. 29, 1935.

[3] *Pravda*, Dec. 14, 1935.

[4] Ibid., Dec. 27, 1935.

[5] *ZI*, Jan. 1, 1936.

First, as Sarkisov's comment indicates, they could transform Stakhanovism into a mass phenomenon.[6] Whereas, previously, Stakhanovite status had been awarded to the relatively small number of workers who had the wherewithal to apply innovative techniques, Stakhanovite periods involved, or were supposed to involve, all workers. By focusing attention and effort on a short-term goal, these stints could promote collective activity and a sense of accomplishment, which Stakhanovism had not emphasized earlier. Those who successfully coped with the intensified pace of work, usually measured in terms of individual output above the norm, were now enrolled as Stakhanovites. This democratization of the category "Stakhanovite" had the obvious advantage of reducing tensions between those so designated and the shrinking majority of non-Stakhanovite workers.

Second, Stakhanovite periods were designed to overcome a problem that had plagued Soviet industry for many years. This was the problem of stoppages to the flow of production. During the 1920s, stoppages were masked to some extent by the generally slack pace of production, officially sponsored campaigns against worker indiscipline, and the recourse of management to temporary layoffs in the event of shutdowns. As with so many other phenomena, the First Five-Year Plan both highlighted and exacerbated the problem. To be sure, the inadequate training of workers and the persistence of indiscipline was one factor in the alarming frequency of breakdowns and stoppages. This was particularly evident at the newly constructed and reconverted plants where conveyor systems had been installed. Seen by some as a panacea, assembly lines actually magnified the problem – the absence or incapacitation of a few workers could shut down production throughout the line.

It must also be recognized that the planning system itself made a major contribution to stoppages. It was – and remains – beyond the capacity of planners in the USSR to make the multitude of elements that comprise the plan cohere. Especially under the regime of scarcity that prevailed throughout the 1930s, there

---

[6] On Jan. 8, 1936, the party organization of the Western *oblast'* trade union council (*oblprofkom*) resolved to develop Stakhanovite days and five-day periods "in order to multiply the ranks of Stakhanovites." See Smolensk Party Archive, microfilm copy, WKP- 96, p. 1.

was no way that the frequent revisions of output targets and production batches could be correlated precisely with changes in supply schedules, financial or wage plans.[7] Delays in the completion of steel complexes, poor-quality machines and parts, and irregular deliveries could cripple an enterprise's production program and in some cases led to plant shutdowns.[8]

There were various ways in which management tried to overcome the problem. These included the exaggeration of supply needs in the hope of obtaining requisite amounts, the building up of reserve stocks, the use of expediters (*tolkachi*), and informal bargaining and bartering with other enterprises.[9] A series of decrees issued by the Commissariat of Labor in 1932 attacked the problem from another angle. Previously, workers who were subjected to stoppages could obtain a "running empty" ticket from the foreman and were paid for the period of their inactivity according to their average output or time rate. The decrees, however, stipulated that workers would receive one-half their rate (two-thirds in the case of metallurgical and mine workers) for stoppage time that was not their fault and no wage at all if the fault was attributed to them.[10] But since responsibility was often difficult to establish, its determination – like so much else that occurred on the shop floor – was the subject of negotiation and the exchange of favors between foremen and workers.

That the problem of stoppages persisted is made abundantly clear by figures breaking down the working day of skilled work-

[7] For an analysis of these structural constraints, which persist to the present, see Alec Nove, *The Soviet Economic System* (London: Allen & Unwin, 1977), 99–108.

[8] The temporary closures of the Khar'kov, Cheliabinsk, and Stalingrad Tractor Factories and the Molotov Automobile Works in Nizhni-Novgorod were reported by Felix Cole (July 11, 1932), U.S. State Department Decimal File, National Archives, 861.50/785.

[9] V. M. Kulagina, *Leningradskie kommunisty v bor'be za osvoenie novoi tekhniki (1933–1935 gg.)* (Leningrad: LGU, 1962), 38. These strategies have become endemic to the Soviet system. See David Granick, *Management of the Industrial Firm in the USSR* (New York: Columbia University Press, 1954), 74–5, 168, 182; and Nove, *Soviet Economic System*, 100–1.

[10] *Sbornik vazhneishikh zakonov i postanovlenii o trude* (Moscow: Profizdat, 1958), 73, 133. For the impact of these decrees at the Red Putilov plant, see Lili Körber, *Life in a Soviet Factory*, trans. Claud W. Sykes (London: Head, 1933), 102.

ers during the first nine months of 1935. These showed that
between 30 and 50 percent of the working day in the tractor
industry and 32 percent in the oil industry was taken up by
stoppages.[11] This was still largely before the emergence of Stakhanovism. Although equivalent figures for the last quarter of
1935 are not available, there is some evidence that the encouragement of individual records only made the problem worse.
Reviewing the performance of enterprises in the Gor'kii Region,
the party committee (*kraikom*) found that between August and
November stoppages as a percentage of working time nearly
doubled in the diesel section of one engineering plant, whereas
in the same plant's machine shop, the increase was fivefold. According to the committee's report, stoppages increased at many
factories in the region largely because although "the Stakhanovite movement has raised labor productivity markedly, the supply and planning apparatuses have not managed to adjust
themselves to service the increased demand ... nor have the
preparatory sections and shop supervisors managed to organize
the rapid transfer of materials to the work place."[12]

In other words, the high productivity of Stakhanovites increased imbalances among and within sections and shops to the
detriment of the entire enterprise. Either Stakhanovism would
have to involve all phases of the production process, or it would
discredit itself. This is one reason why Ordzhonikidze, among
others, found Stakhanovite shifts and days so promising. "The
Donbassites have achieved a new level of organization," he told
the Central Committee. "Previously, the hewer dug so much coal,
but all other sections – removal, construction, timbering, raising
coal to the surface – were not coordinated, and often got in the
way of each other."[13]

Coordination within and among sections was therefore the
key to the success of Stakhanovite periods. But coordination
presupposed a much more active involvement of managers and
engineers than had been the case. Here, indeed, was another
advantage of the Stakhanovite periods. They could serve as a

[11] *ZI*, Jan. 1, 1936. See also S. Shvarts (Solomon Schwarz), "Pod flagom
ratsionalizatsii," *Sotsialisticheskii vestnik*, no. 6–7 (1936):16.
[12] *Istoriia industrializatsii nizhegorodskogo-Gor'kovskogo kraia (1926–1941
gg.)* (Gor'kii: Volgo-Viatskoe knizhnoe izdatel'stvo, 1968), 316.
[13] *Pravda*, Dec. 27, 1935.

test of the commitment of production specialists to Stakhanovism, which the arrangement of individual records had not provided. As Sarkisov put it, "The qualitative difference is that this
form gives engineers and technicians a vital role in the organization of work." The necessity for organization and coordination
would compel the "commanders" and "specialists" to "move to
the head of this movement or stand openly against it."[14] Ordzhonikidze expressed the same idea somewhat differently. "I am
your great friend," he told the "comrade metallurgists" in March
1936, "and I must in a friendly manner warn you that if you do
not take hold of this work as you must, in a new, Stakhanovite
way, ... you will lose priority."[15]

Finally, the progression from Stakhanovite shifts to days, to
five- and ten- day periods, and then to months suggests that
what began as a departure from ordinary, routine procedures
was intended to become the routine. In this sense, Stakhanovite
periods can be seen as an assault or series of blows, gradually
increasing in duration, against preexisting shop floor practices.
Ultimately, Stakhanovite periods would crowd out the hiatuses
between them; every worker would be a Stakhanovite; imbalances, bottlenecks, and shutdowns would be eliminated; and the
cadres would come to accept their responsibility to organize and
coordinate production as their normal function.

Of these four aims, only the first and third were fulfilled.
Stakhanovism did become a mass phenomenon, although, as will
be discussed in the next chapter, the phenomenon existed more
on paper than in reality; and Stakhanovite periods did provide
a test for managers and specialists, but one that most failed. The
reasons for this failure are what we must seek.

Some enterprises and even whole branches of industry did
improve their performance during the months when Stakhanovite periods occurred.[16] A comparison between output per
worker in the first five months of 1936 and the corresponding
period in 1935 shows significant increases in ferrous metallurgy,

---

[14]   Ibid., Dec. 14, 29, 1935. See also statement by R. Khitarov, Magni-
    togorsk district party secretary, in ibid., Mar. 4, 1936.
[15]   Ibid., Dec. 27, 1935.
[16]   See, e.g., ibid., Mar. 25, Apr. 8, 25, 1936; *Industrializatsiia SSSR,
    1933–1937 gg. Dokumenty i materialy* (Moscow: Nauka, 1971), 578.

chemicals, and machine construction.[17] To cite another measure of industrial performance, the two key indices for steel production – the coefficient of utilization of useful capacity of blast furnaces and the output in metric tons per square meter of floor space in open-hearth furnaces – were on their way to being the best for any year of the prewar period.[18] How much Stakhanovite periods were responsible for these and other achievements is impossible to determine, but at least it does not appear that they held the productive forces back. Still, the problems that emerged in connection with the new forms, precisely because they were so common, must be considered to have been endemic, even if the political leadership thought otherwise.

Lack of adequate preparation was one such difficulty. This included the absence of sufficient quantities of supplies or fuel to sustain increased output, failure to integrate production and delivery schedules, and inadequate attention to the preparation of workers, psychologically and otherwise. To some extent, management was able to use the shortage of supplies to deflect criticism of its own shortcomings. Reporting on the first, largely successful Stakhanovite day at the Petrovskii Metallurgical Factory in Dnepropetrovsk, S. Birman, the plant's director, claimed that results would have been even better had there been more coke, limestone, and coking gas on hand.[19] Radiator fittings, ball bearings, and frame girders were what the Kirov Works lacked to achieve its target of seventy-five tractors per day during its Stakhanovite *dekada*, whereas at the Leningrad Elektrosila plant, it was a question not only of the late delivery of supplies, but of their alleged poor quality.[20]

---

[17] G. N. Evstaf'ev, *Sotsialisticheskoe sorevnovanie – zakonomernost' i dvizhushchaia sila ekonomicheskogo razvitiia sovetskogo obshchestva* (Moscow: Gospolitizdat, 1952), 146.

[18] M. Gardner Clark, *The Economics of Soviet Steel* (Cambridge, Mass: Harvard University Press, 1956), 254; *Industrializatsiia SSSR, 1933–1937*, 312.

[19] *ZI*, Jan. 4, 1936.

[20] *NFI*, no. 2 (1936):9, 25. At least some of these complaints were no doubt genuine. As a Urals cryolite factory committee chairman argued in a letter to the party *raikom* bureau, "If we immediately go over to a mass Stakhanovite movement, there inevitably will be a shortage of raw material." See A. V. Bakunin, *Vozniknovenie i razvitie*

Since coordinating the supply programs of their constituent enterprises was the responsibility of trusts and *glavki*, Narkomtiazhprom was able to use such complaints as ammunition for criticizing these organs.[21] However, the buck could not always be passed so easily. Commenting on the five-day campaign in machine construction, *Za industrializatsiiu* wondered whether complaints about poor supplies were justified. "Directors of some factories," it asserted, "in the chase after record figures, fed their shops not with parts that were needed for assembly, but rather to store them up." It also claimed that shops concentrated on the production of profitable lines at the expense of those that were most needed.[22]

As far as the preparation of workers was concerned, the party and trade union committees bore the brunt of responsibility. If management was expected to devise an appropriate schedule (*grafik*) of work and clearly define targets, the role of the other two corners of the enterprise triangle was to ensure that maximum effort was exerted to carry through the campaign. In cases where workers did not learn of the existence of a Stakhanovite period until the day before it was to commence, or when the output of party members was below their norms, the party organization could expect to be held accountable.[23] Occasionally, as in the aftermath of the disappointing *dekada* (February 13–22) in the oil industry, the party *obkom* absorbed the blame.[24] Trade union committees found themselves under attack for their "passivity," a catchall term that connoted everything from the failure to hold meetings and/or ensure a large turnout to slowness in taking up the grievances of Stakhanovites against unfriendly foremen or fellow workers.

Of course, neither management nor party and trade union

stakhanovskogo dvizheniia na Urale (Sverdlovsk: AN SSSR Ural, 1985), 35.

[21] See the editorial statement in *ZI*, Jan. 16, 1936: "We must unfortunately assert that *glavki* weakly prepared themselves for the Stakhanovite five-day period."

[22] *ZI*, Jan. 24, 26, Feb. 1, 1936.

[23] Smolensk Party Archive, WKP-96, p. 20; *Bol'shevik*, no. 7 (1936):144–54.

[24] *Pravda*, Apr. 19, 1936; S. R. Gershberg, *Rukovodstvo kommunisticheskoi partii dvizheniem novatorov v promyshlennosti (1935–1941)* (Moscow: Gospolitizdat, 1956), 161.

organizations had an entirely free hand in the timing of a Stakhanovite period. The vagaries of supply deliveries, the impending arrival of an inspection team from district party headquarters, a challenge from another enterprise, the decision of trust officials, or simply the realization that something had to be done to demonstrate a commitment to Stakhanovism could dictate when a period of intense activity should occur. In the case of coal mining, the introduction of revised output norms on February 1 sparked numerous five- and ten-day periods. Progress was monitored closely, and when, despite previous declarations of readiness, several mines were found to be under-fulfilling their targets, Narkomtiazhprom ordered that they cease to participate. Even so, of the 279 mines that completed the *dekada*, only 51 had fulfilled their plans.[25] No less embarrassing was the five-day period commencing on April 1 at the Paris Commune mine (Kadievka trust). Before the first shift, the mine director and several engineers promised the assembled workers that all was in readiness and that not one minute would be lost in stoppages. The workers in their turn committed themselves to producing a record amount of coal. Accompanied by music, the miners descended into the pits, only to discover that "all the promises were lies." Thanks to a five-hour delay in one of the sections, only seventy-seven tons were produced.[26]

Unpreparedness was not the only or even the main problem. The very temporariness of Stakhanovite periods invited "storming," a characteristic feature of the First Five-Year Plan that by 1936 was considered a sign of backwardness. The problem with storming was that it caused extraordinary wear and tear on both machinery and human beings, which was manifested in rising rates of mechanical failures and accidents and which was usually followed by a slump in output back to previous levels or worse. This pattern is illustrated by average daily output data from before, during, and after the first All-Union Stakhanovite five-day period (January 20–24), which was extended to a *dekada* (Table 3.1).

Thus, having been geared up for a Stakhanovite five-day pe-

---

[25] Ermanskii, *Stakhanovskoe dvizhenie*, 264.

[26] Ibid., 264–5. In this case, the head of the trust was threatened with dismissal.

Table 3.1. *Average daily output before, during, and after All-Union Stakhanovite dekada, January 20–9, 1936*
(in tons)

Date	Pig iron		Steel		Rolled iron		Coal (Donbass)	
	Plan	Output	Plan	Output	Plan	Output	Plan	Output
Dec. 1–31	—	37,340	—	38,891	—	32,445	—	230,239
Jan. 15–19	39,000	36,862	43,000	38,581	34,000	29,419	229,874	219,164
Jan. 20–4	39,000	41,247	43,000	48,361	34,000	42,648	232,010	235,016
Jan. 25–9	39,000	40,047	43,000	44,007	34,000	38,913	232,010	223,778
Jan. 20–9	39,000	40,647	43,000	46,184	34,000	40,773	232,010	228,772
Feb. 1–15	40,000	36,674	46,000	39,297	36,000	31,195	232,010	215,476[a]

[a]Average for Jan. 30–1.
Source: *Za industrializatsiiu*, Jan.–Feb. 1936.

riod, the metallurgical and coal-mining industries superseded their output programs, the former rather more impressively than the latter. Over the next five days, however, production declined, and in the case of mining fell well below the plan.[27] Declines were even steeper in pig iron, steel, and rolled iron production during the first five days of February. Meanwhile, the Donbass coal mines cut back on production, perhaps to catch up on repair and clearing operations before a new Stakhanovite five-day period commenced on February 1. Much the same pattern was to be observed during the next Stakhanovite *dekada* in mid-February.[28]

How were Stakhanovite periods organized and experienced? According to a Stakhanovite milling machine operator at the Molotov Automobile Works:

Before the *dekada*, everything is prepared energetically. Foremen, engineers, and technicians run around like mad, sometimes senselessly. The servicing of work places improves and productivity is increased. But as soon as the *dekada* is over, they forget about servicing us. Everything is as it was before. Productivity... falls sharply.[29]

The same impression of chaotic exertion emerges from a report on the Moscow Stalin Automobile Factory's *dekada* – "commanders" spending twelve to fourteen hours on the shop floor, foremen and shift engineers chasing after parts, hundreds of overtime hours interspersed with shutdowns.[30]

But it is to S. Birman, director of the Petrovskii metallurgical complex, that we owe the most vivid contemporary account of a Stakhanovite period. On January 2, 1936, the enterprise conducted its first Stakhanovite day. Three days later, the director met with shop supervisors to begin planning for another twenty-four-hour stint, this to be held on January 9. The account reads like a compressed version of the Soviet production novel.[31] It is a tale of sacrifice and struggle – of extraordinary preparations

---

[27] Production slumped on the sixth day (Jan. 25) and, in the case of steel, was below the figure set by the plan.

[28] *ZI*, Feb. 20, 1936.

[29] Quoted in Ermanskii, *Stakhanovskoe dvizhenie*, 265.

[30] *ZI*, Jan. 30, 1936.

[31] For a rendition of the "master plot" of this subgenre, see Katerina Clark, *The Soviet Novel: History as Ritual* (University of Chicago Press, 1981), 256–60.

("In essence, the Stakhanovite day ... commences on the morning of January 8"), of emergencies, wavering confidence, redoubled effort ("How the people have grown! What a sense of responsibility!"), and ultimate triumph, as represented by the following figures:

	Jan. 2 (actual)	Jan. 9	
		Target	Actual
Pig iron (tons)	2,905	3,050	3,075
Steel (tons)	3,112	3,400	3,416
Rolled iron (tons)	3,232	3,300	3,385

However, the moral of the tale is not as singular or simple as might have been expected. To be sure, Birman mentions the "enormous capabilities" revealed by the twenty-four-hour period, and as in his report on the first Stakhanovite day, there is a plea for more and better-quality coke and ore. But he also refers to the "extraordinary vigilance, the concentration of attention, and the straining of all powers" that was required and adds:

All this is achieved as a result of such strain that cannot possibly be maintained indefinitely. Not all shop supervisors can stay on duty day and night. The entire leadership of the factory cannot be in the shops day and night. It is impossible to expect each brigade willingly to come to work several hours before its shift and stay there several hours after the shift ends.... The cost is literally mad strain accompanied by unbelievable bustle.[32]

This was a remarkably frank admission. What is even more remarkable is that it was published two days before the beginning of the first All-Union Stakhanovite five-day period. However, we should not rush to conclude that Narkomtiazphrom was advocating the abandonment of Stakhanovite periods. As Birman put it: "Our task is to prepare ourselves for the next Stakhanovite day in order to give at least the same results, but without such strain, without extraordinary measures, to give them in normal 'humdrum' circumstances."[33] As suggested by the figures in Table 3.1, this is precisely what enterprises could not do.

[32] *Pravda*, Jan 18, 1936.
[33] Ibid.

II

It would be wrong to assume that the problems discussed here were peculiar to Stakhanovite periods. Failure to coordinate production schedules and achieve a balanced production mix, storming sessions in which machines and those tending them were pushed well beyond their normal limits, the emphasis on quantitative indices at the expense of repair work and the quality of the finished product were all well-known features of the Soviet industrialization drive from its inception, and they continue to plague the USSR even in its putatively mature socialist stage. The fact that they have been so widespread and persistent has inspired periodic attempts at reform, most of which have involved a greater degree of enterprise autonomy and emphasis on profitability than was permitted under Stalin.

What distinguished the Stakhanovite periods of early 1936 was neither the nature nor the magnitude of the problems associated with them. Rather, it was the extent to which the periods and the publicity surrounding them highlighted such problems and their political consequences. Having invested so much prestige in these forms and Stakhanovism as a whole, the industrial commissariats were compelled to press forward, all the while pinning shortcomings and failures on overworked and hapless cadres. Something of the pressure felt by them at this time is conveyed by Victor Kravchenko, who worked as an engineer at a Nikopol' pipe-making plant:

Politics, flying the banners of efficiency, had the right of way. Communist and police officials often had the final word as against the engineer and manager, even on purely technical problems. We were in the midst of an era of anarchy and civil strife in industry. I was caught between instructions from Moscow and suspicion from below, between tougher tasks and declining discipline. Nervousness and strain became almost my normal condition.[34]

Defying local party and NKVD officials who were on the lookout for saboteurs, Kravchenko saw to the fulfillment of a number of urgent orders and thereafter was able to rely on the protection

---

[34] Victor Kravchenko, *I Chose Freedom* (New York: Scribner's, 1946), 192.

of Ordzhonikidze. But not all "commanders" were so brave or fortunate. They had to resort to other strategies to cope with the pressure. Obtaining maximum publicity for the achievements of outstanding Stakhanovites and rewarding workers and technical personnel with bonuses from the director's fund were among the ways of keeping "suspicion from below" at tolerable levels; maneuvering between enterprise and shop plans, juggling orders measured in terms of value and those expressed in weight or units produced, and simply "cooking" the books were techniques for keeping superordinate organs at bay.[35]

Obviously, the choice and success of any one strategy depended on a number of factors – relationships with local party and police officials as well as those in charge of trusts and *glavki*, geographical location and national importance of the enterprise, and so forth. In this light, the performance of the Kaganovich Ball Bearings Factory (Sharikopodpishnik no. 1) in Moscow and the fate of its director, Bodrov, is instructive. Built at a cost of 116 million rubles and containing some five thousand imported machines, the enterprise was one of the giant projects of the First Five-Year Plan.[36] It was also one of the most essential, assigned the task of supplying all necessary bearings to the automobile and tractor industries. By 1933, the plant was turning out approximately fifty types of ball and roller bearings, but it did not come close to fulfilling its program. Moreover, in 1934, nearly one-fifth of its output, valued at 12.8 million rubles, was defective.[37]

Shoddy construction and/or poor maintenance of the plant might have contributed to the high proportion of *brak*. After visiting the factory in July 1934, a U.S. embassy official described the floors as being "in very bad shape." More than a year later, when Walter Citrine, the British Trades Union Council's general

---

[35] For examples drawn from Leningrad alone, see M. Ben', "Planirovat' po-Stakhanovski," *NFI*, no. 6 (1936):37–9.

[36] Anthony C. Sutton, *Western Technology and Soviet Economic Development, 1930 to 1945* (Stanford, Calif.: Hoover Institution, 1971), 145.

[37] Ibid., 148–9; *Sovet pri narodnom kommissare tiazheloi promyshlennosti SSSR, Pervyi plenum, 10–12 maia 1935 g.* (Moscow–Leningrad: NKTP, 1935), 95–6. It should be noted, however, that specifications and tolerances were unusually rigorous.

secretary, was shown the plant, he found that "not a single door fitted properly, the concrete floor was full of holes and rolled up and down like the waves of the sea."[38] Scheduled to produce 24 million bearings in 1935, Sharikopodpishnik no. 1 averaged just 1.1 million per month in the first half of the year. Hard on the heels of management's request for an additional one thousand machines – a request that was evidently turned down – Stakhanovism arrived in the plant. The first and most famous Stakhanovite in the factory was Ia. S. Iusim, an engineer who, working as a foreman in the forge shop, developed a new technique for turning out ball races.[39] Instead of the 28,000 provided by the norm, Iusim managed to produce 42,000 in a single shift.

At the All-Union Conference of Stakhanovites, the technical director of the plant, I. I. Melamed, confessed that this was a totally unforeseen event. "It is astonishing how much we failed to see what was under our noses," he remarked. "In every section, wherever we began to probe, we found opportunities for utilizing things . . . in order to increase output." On the basis of this new way of looking at things, Melamed promised to raise output to 27 million bearings in 1936. This, however, did not satisfy Ordzhonikidze, who called for 36 million. "I think that this level of production – 36 million bearings per year, three million per month – we will be able to achieve by the second half of 1936," Melamed replied.[40]

The factory got off to an inauspicious start. Already on January 11, Melamed was quoted in *Pravda* as admitting that its Stakhanovite shifts and five-day period "were not free from the element of storming." In an editorial published just as the All-Union five-day campaign was getting under way, *Za industrializatsiiu* singled out the enterprise for lagging behind and implied that Bodrov was more fond of playing billiards than of exercising

---

[38] "Visit of Hanson to Kaganovich Ball-Bearing Plant" (July 12, 1934), U.S. State Dept. Decimal File, NA, 861.6511/30; Sir Walter M. Citrine, *I Search for the Truth in Russia* (London: Routledge, 1936), 85.

[39] *Pervoe Vsesoiuznoe soveshchanie rabochikh i rabotnits stakhanovtsev, 14–17 noiabria 1935. Stenograficheskii otchet.* (Moscow: Partizdat, 1935), 82–3; *Pravda*, Nov. 13, 1935.

[40] *Pervoe Vsesoiuznoe soveshchanie*, 84–5.

his responsibilities as director.[41] In all probability, Bodrov's fate had already been decided, but the enterprise's performance in the campaign sealed it. Cutting down on the variety of bearings did not help. Instead of the 120,000 per day prescribed by the "Stakhanovite plan," or even the 86,000 that had been approved earlier, Sharikopodpishnik no. 1 could manage only 70,000 to 75,000. Aside from storming and other "outrageous" occurrences, it was reported that the prize-winning Stakhanovite, Iusim, went in tears to the Komsomol committee to complain about the "ham-fistedness" of the administration.[42] On January 28, *Pravda* announced that Bodrov had been relieved of his duties as director and replaced by Melamed.

Throughout the following months, the cycle of mobilization, disappointing results, and recrimination, illustrated in the case of the Kaganovich Ball Bearings Factory, was repeated in many other enterprises. Insofar as past disappointments raised the level of tension, one may speak of a vicious cycle. Moreover, what had begun as a test for managers and specialists at the enterprise level eventually spiraled upward.

It has already been mentioned that Narkomtiazhprom was not averse to publicizing complaints of enterprise directors about inadequate supplies, even going so far as to name individual trust and *glavki* heads who were responsible. But by mid-February, *Pravda* was aiming higher. Taking up an idea expressed by Molotov, it urged the commissariats to transform themselves into "production-technical staffs" in order to place all reserves of production at the disposal of Stakhanovites.[43] The model in this respect was L. M. Kaganovich's Commissariat of Transport; the antitheses, the Commissariats of Forestry Products and Light Industry.

The Commissariat of Light Industry bore the brunt of criticism for permitting "the most evil storming," which included the reduction of rest periods and the lengthening of the work day at many enterprises. Its textile division was subjected to a series

---

[41] *ZI*, Jan. 20, 1936. A cartoon depicting Bodrov in this manner was published on Jan. 21.
[42] Ibid., Jan. 26, 1936.
[43] *Pravda*, Feb. 21, 1936.

of withering attacks. Many "bureaucrats" were said to have "lost their taste" for Stakhanovism. Indicative of their attempt to "bury" the movement was the failure of many textile workers to fulfill their new output norms and a decline in the number of Stakhanovites.[44] One might otherwise conclude that this was because the norms had been set too high, but evidently Sovnarkom and the party's Central Committee viewed the problem in a different way. On April 2, it was announced that they had ordered the dissolution of the commissariat's Institute of Labor because it had underestimated the technical capacities of semi-automatic weaving machines and water frames.[45]

The campaign against the Commissariat of Light Industry culminated in a curious incident. On April 17, an article appeared in *Pravda* by A. Gracheva, a Stakhanovite weaver at the Moscow Red Rosa Mill. Gracheva complained about the disrepair of many machines and the disorganization in the piece-rate system, both of which, she alleged, depressed earnings. Such articles were not uncommon, and there was nothing particularly scandalous about the complaints. Yet *Pravda* considered them sufficiently serious to demand an explanation from none other than the commissar, I. E. Liubimov.

What appeared instead was an account by Gracheva of her confrontation with Liubimov after he had summoned her to his office. The account could not have revealed the commissar in a worse light. "How is *Pravda* going to help you?" he is quoted as saying. "Before you write to *Pravda*, you should see your director, and if she doesn't help, come to the *glavk* office." Besides, he added, "you should check your facts. . . . In what is written under your name there is much that is untrue."[46] True or not, *Pravda* printed in the same issue the testimony of two of Gracheva's fellow workers, which confirmed her complaints and indicated that she had returned from her encounter with Liubimov in a "downcast" state.

---

[44] Ibid., Feb. 27, Mar. 22, 25, 1936.
[45] Ibid., Apr. 2, 1936.
[46] Ibid., Apr. 17, 18, 1936. It is impossible to convey in English the flavor of Liubimov's remarks. His use of the familiar form of "you" is in marked contrast to the harshness of his tone and Gracheva's use of the more polite "Vyi." Gracheva had just been awarded an Order of the Red Banner of Labor.

All the while, the campaign against managers and specialists continued. "Smash Sabotage of Stakhanovite Methods of Work," "Fire on the Saboteurs of the Stakhanovite Movement," screamed *Pravda*'s headlines. "We must open fire on the saboteurs and drive them out of the ranks of heavy industry," thundered an editorial in *Za industrializatsiiu*.[47] "Boldly looking truth in the eye," Zhdanov told a conference in Leningrad, "criticizing from below, you can help us correct mistakes and unmask the saboteurs and brakemen of the Stakhanovite movement."[48]

From March 22, a column appearing regularly in *Pravda* under the headline "Tribune of the Stakhanovite" did just that. Here, Stakhanovites, many of whom had attended the All-Union conference, engaged in "criticism from below." Detailing cases of negligence, rudeness, and the liquidation of Stakhanovite methods by shop personnel and attempts by directors to buy off leading Stakhanovites, the columns had a distinctly antibureaucratic flavor, one that may well have been to the taste of many ordinary workers.

III

Thus, in the midst of the mobilizations for Stakhanovite periods, or rather as a consequence of their shortcomings, another mobilization was launched, one that threatened to develop into an all-out purge of managers and specialists. This was nowhere so evident as in the Donbass, where both Stakhanovism and the Stakhanovite periods had originated and where the coal industry was going from bad to worse. Exposé followed upon exposé. From the Central Irmino mine, Stakhanov reported that horses and pipes were in short supply and timber was the wrong size, but the mine's administration was "stewing in its own juice."[49] Gershberg, the *Pravda* journalist who had discovered Izotov in 1932 and was to ghostwrite Stakhanov's autobiography in 1937, discovered that the 19,000 inhabitants of Irmino had to walk

---

[47] Ibid., Mar. 22, 26, 1936, *ZI*, Mar. 16, 1936.
[48] Quoted in R. Ia. Khabibulina, *Leningradskie kommunisty – organizatory stakhanovskogo dvizheniia (1935–1937 gg.)* (Leningrad: LGU, 1961), 131.
[49] *Pravda*, Feb. 6, 1936.

Stakhanov explains his method to fellow miners. From Semen Gershberg, *Stakhanov i stakhanovtsy* (Moscow: Politizdat, 1985), p. 95.

four kilometers over unpaved roads to obtain consumer goods.[50] Nor was the picture any brighter at other mines. Returning from vacation in Sochi, L. Dolgopolov, a machine cutter at the Shcheglovka no. 1 mine, found that "all proceeds as if there were no such thing as a Stakhanovite movement."[51] Daily output in the Donbass, which had averaged 230,500 tons in December, fell to 222,600 in January, 220,200 in February, 210,000 in March, and only 201,300 tons in April. As in the case of textiles, many workers were not fulfilling their output norms and the number of Stakhanovites was dwindling.[52]

All this caused considerable consternation to Sarkisov, the Donetsk party secretary and the first prominent leader to champion

[50] Ibid., Feb. 4, 1936.
[51] Ibid., Apr. 4, 1936. See also *Stakhanovets*, no. 7 (1936):2–3.
[52] *ZI*, June 5, 1936. For slightly different figures, see *Pravda*, Apr. 29, May 21, 1936.

Stakhanovite periods. Already in January, he had written that sabotage of the periods was less open but no less real than it had been during Stakhanovism's first phase. By late March, he issued in the name of the Donetsk *obkom* bureau a warning to several coal trust heads to liquidate sabotage within one month or lose their jobs.[53] The extent to which the threat was carried out is difficult to determine. Articles critical of mining management continued to appear in the regional and national press.[54] But it was not until June 2, when a speech by the Ukrainian party secretary, P. P. Postyshev, was published, that any information on the party organizations' activities became available.

Postyshev congratulated the Donetsk comrades for removing several specialists who had been engaging in the sabotage of Stakhanovism. He also asserted that the struggle against "genuine conservatives and saboteurs" must go on. But after reminding his audience that Stalin had emphasized "persuasion, patient persuasion" with respect to engineering-technical personnel, he condemned the indiscriminate harassment, the character assassination, and "political hooliganism" that had been directed against "good men," communist engineers. This could only play into the hands of the real saboteurs, he argued. Already it had led to a decline in labor discipline, demoralization, and an increase in the turnover rate among the staff of the Donbass mines.[55]

Not only did *Pravda* publish the speech in full, but a few days later, in an editorial entitled "The Lesson of the Donbass," it took a less equivocal line. "If the Donetsk press and many speeches at meetings are to be believed, the majority of engineering-technical personnel consists of saboteurs and conservatives," it stated. This was "nonsense." "In the Donbass are

[53] *Pravda*, Jan. 27, Mar. 22, 1936.
[54] Ibid., Apr. 4, 15, 25, 29, 1936. See also the condemnation by R. I. Eikhe, western Siberian party *obkom* secretary, of those who employed the "rotten theory" that the Kuzbass was no worse than the Donbass and his demand that saboteurs be given a "strong knock." Ibid., May 27, 1936.
[55] On Postyshev, who enjoyed the reputation of being "fair-minded," see Robert Conquest, *The Great Terror: Stalin's Purges of the Thirties* (New York: Collier, 1973), 226–9, 267–9, 347. See also Lev Kopelev, *The Education of a True Believer* (New York: Harper & Row, 1980), 274–80.

many good specialists who need patient assistance to free themselves from conservative attitudes. But instead they are cursed
and 'worked over.' " The persecution of production specialists
must stop, the editorial affirmed. Party organs must cease in-
terfering in the management of industrial enterprises.[56]

Aside from suggesting the degree of persecution to which
specialists were subjected, Postyshev's speech and the coverage
it was given by *Pravda* are noteworthy in another respect. Together they marked a decisive shift at the top in the treatment
of specialists. Similar to the official rehabilitation of the old bourgeois technical intelligentsia in 1931, the end of the campaign
against production specialists five years later did not come as a
bolt out of the blue. For one thing, the Stakhanovite periods all
but expired by May. It is impossible to tell whether this was
because they clearly had not fulfilled their mission to overcome
stoppages and other disruptions in production – indeed, had
exacerbated such problems in many cases – or had succeeded
only too well in exposing the lack of enthusiasm among "commanders" of production for taking charge of the movement.
One should note, in any case, the coincidence of their cessation
with the assimilation of the revised output norms, the emphasis
on the need for technical education of Stakhanovites, and the
rediscovery of the category of shock worker, all of which suggest
a deemphasis of Stakhanovism's more conflictual aspects.

Second, a number of developments outside the sphere of material production and the relations stemming therefrom suggest
that, for the Soviet leadership, social stability had become a paramount aim. These developments included the law banning
abortions and the inculcation of the family and parental responsibilities, the publicity given to the philanthropic activities
of wives of executives and engineering-technical personnel, the
completion of the draft for a new constitution and the extensive
propaganda surrounding its provisions for full civil equality, and
the corresponding claim that, with the arrival of socialism, an-
tagonistic class relations had ceased to exist in the USSR. Given
the close proximity of these developments to the first of the Great
Show Trials and the onset of the Great Purges, it is tempting to
try to establish causal links. Was it a case of lulling the population

[56] *Pravda*, June 7, 1936. See also editorial in *Izvestiia*, July 4, 1936.

– including industrial cadres – into a false sense of security, of promoting reconciliation and civil peace, before unleashing the full force of repression? Or on the contrary, should we see the two processes as products of distinctly different, if not antithetical, tendencies within the Soviet leadership?

Assuming that the party purges of 1933–6 and the mass arrests and executions carried out by Ezhov's NKVD in 1936–8 were one and the same process, or at least could be explained in the same functionalist terms, most Western scholars seem to have overlooked or treated as epiphenomenal the above-mentioned developments, which do not fit neatly into such schemes. An alternative approach by J. Arch Getty posits a "struggle between provincial party cliques and the Central Committee Secretariat," which "erupted" into the Ezhovshchina and the destruction of "the bureaucracy." The merit of this perspective is that it delineates the "ups and downs" of the central-regional struggle and distinguishes them from the "traditional landmarks of the Great Purges."[57] It also parallels our discussion of tensions among the different levels of the economic apparatus, and insofar as the center was determined to destroy the "family nests" that enterprise personnel and local party officials had so assiduously feathered, the two approaches could be said to intersect. However, as one of Getty's critics has pointed out: "His reconstruction of the Great Terror as the violent resolution of a central-regional conflict ... encounters the objection that the terror of 1937–38 was directed as much against the central institutions of the party-state as against the regional leadership."[58]

Hence, one is drawn to the center and the hypothesis that rival strategies within it account for the zigs and zags in official policy toward managers and specialists. Earlier it was noted that the spectrum of strategies ran from flattery and persuasion to instigation among Stakhanovites and threats against "bureaucrats, conservatives, and saboteurs." The association of Ordzhonikidze with the former and Zhdanov and Kaganovich with the latter was tentatively made. For the months of January to May 1936, it is more difficult to discern differences within the Politburo.

[57] J. Arch Getty, "Party and Purge in Smolensk: 1933–1937," *Slavic Review* 42 (1983):60–79, esp. 77–8.
[58] Robert C. Tucker, "Problems of Interpretation," in ibid., 84.

Yes, they are all applauding. From left to right: Andreev, Ordzhoni-kidze, Kaganovich, Voroshilov, Stalin, and (in rear) Zhdanov at the All-Union Conference of Stakhanovites, November 1935. From *Sputnik agitatora*, no. 26 (1935).

Factions may have existed, and the failure of Ordzhonikidze's subordinates to "take charge" of Stakhanovism certainly suggests that the political balance was swinging in the direction of those advocating a harsher line.

Yet one need not assume factional squabbling or, for that matter, political (im)balance at the center to explain the perse-cution of industrial cadres in early 1936, the brief period of reconciliation, and then the onset of the Great Purges. The fact that it was Ordzhonikidze who initially promoted Stakhano-vism as a means of leaning on enterprise management and engineering-technical personnel, that it was he who first drew attention to the likelihood of sabotage against Stakhanovism, and that his commissariat's newspaper joined in the denunciation of "saboteurs" provokes another explanation. This is that improv-isation was the prevailing mode of operation, that within the framework of the state's monopolization of political power and its grand design for the industrialization of the country, all man-ner of techniques were admissible and many were tried. Some techniques proved to be more successful than others, but none was free from distortion (and/or various forms of passive re-sistance) by functionaries assigned to execute them and the rest of society subjected to them.

Analyzing the 1930s in terms of the "longue durée" of Soviet history, Gabor Rittersporn has come to much the same conclusion:

The takeover of the national economy and the annihilation of one of the last bases of resistance, the small peasant propriety, concluded a long process of integrating within one sole apparatus the management of practically all activities that could influence the system's reproduction and guaranteed the primacy of the Party-State's initiatives in almost all important areas of social life. Far from making the regime's functioning predictable and controllable, the political monopoly and the need to guard it tended to make uncontrollable both those who were supposed to represent and defend it, and the relations which the latter were supposed to maintain with the rest of society.[59]

Within the leadership itself, Stalin undoubtedly had the greatest flexibility and was least touched by the inefficacies of any one technique. Obviously, without any information on the policy-making process, it is impossible to ascertain whose policies Stalin could take credit for and subsequently abandon. Nevertheless, it is reasonable to assume that calls for vigilance were bound to strengthen the hand of some, whereas criticisms of "political hooliganism" – which in substance could refer to the same thing – gave more power to others.

Improvisation with respect to Stakhanovism caused it to be pulled now in this direction, now in that, and at times simultaneously in several directions. Though recordmania had subsided, individual production records continued to receive publicity in 1936 (and beyond); after a hiatus of several months, Stakhanovite periods reemerged, though with less fanfare, in the autumn, while in the meantime new organizational forms, also labeled Stakhanovite, were developed. These were the Stakhanovite brigades, integrated (*skvoznye*) brigades, and Stakhanovite schools.

Actually, none of these was entirely new. As had been the case with their First Five-Year Plan antecedents, they represented correctives to the evolving hierarchy of industrial relations. And repeating earlier experience, their existence was precarious,

---

[59] Gabor Rittersporn, "The 1930s in the Longue Durée of Soviet History," *Telos*, no. 53 (1982):115. Rittersporn elaborates on this view in his "Rethinking Stalinism" (paper presented at the Annual Conference of the British National Association for Soviet and East European Studies, Cambridge, England, 1983).

124   *Stakhanovism and the politics of productivity*

being contingent on higher authorities' tolerance for forms that permitted some autonomy. Their various fates thus suggest both the possibilities for, and limits of, officially sanctioned improvisation.

The Stakhanovite brigades, assembled from among workers who had already distinguished themselves, closely resembled the shock brigades of the late 1920s. They were particularly numerous in the automobile industry – the Stalin Automobile Factory contained 210 of them by mid-February 1936 – but despite their allegedly good production results, they were short- lived.[60] Most were disbanded by 1937, although there was a revival of the form later that year and into 1938.[61] The problem with the Stakhanovite brigades was identical to that experienced during Stakhanovism's first phase. Dependent on the non-Stakhanovite work of other brigades, their work was constantly disrupted. Moreover, the lack of direct ties between different occupational groups, each comprising a Stakhanovite brigade, tended to increase the lack of complementarity in their work schedules and production mixes.

This was what the Stakhanovite integrated brigades were supposed to overcome. The first such unit was organized at the Kalinin Spinning Mill, located in the city of Kalinin, in April 1936. It appears to have been an almost exact replica of the similarly titled (minus, of course, the Stakhanovite sobriquet) brigades pioneered during the construction of the Rostov-on-Don Agricultural Machinery Plant (Sel'mashstroi) in mid–1930.

The principle of both First and Second Five-Year Plan versions was to combine workers from various stages of the production process into one large brigade. Instead of the average of ten to fifteen brigade members, integrated brigades usually contained upward of fifty. The only substantial difference between the two versions was that, whereas the earlier one provided a staff (*shtab*) drawn from brigade members and a *nachal'nik* who was relieved of production duties, the latter contained a *brigadir* and assis-

[60] V. A. Sakharov, "Zarozhdenie i razvitie stakhanovskogo dvizheniia v avto-traktornoi promyshlennosti v gody vtoroi piatiletki" (kandidatskaia dissertatsiia, Moskovskii oblastnoi pedagogicheskii institut im. N. K. Krupskoi, 1979), 149, 285.
[61] I. O. Okuneva, *O rezervakh povysheniia proizvoditel'nosti truda* (Moscow: Profizdat, 1940), 40.

tants, all of whom continued to work at their production tasks.[62] The *brigadir*, defined in one instance as a "public-spirited organizer" (*organizator-obshchestvennik*), had the right to check up on the technological process, order deliveries from the dispatcher's office, and contact administrative personnel up to and including the enterprise director when trouble arose.[63] The process of selecting brigade leaders, in both earlier and later versions, remains somewhat obscure. Consistent with contemporary practices of production collectives, communes, and many cost-accounting brigades, it is quite likely that *nachal'niki* and their staffs were elected by brigade members. In the case of Stakhanovite version, the picture is not as clear. According to the director of the Red Weaver Mill in Leningrad, "the *brigadir* is chosen from the best people, the best record setters. They are the most popular Stakhanovites of their brigades."[64] But the use of the passive voice (deliberately?) prevents us from knowing *who* did the choosing, and the characterization of the best Stakhanovites as the "most popular" must be regarded with some skepticism. The statement by the director of Skorokhod that "participants of the integrated brigades chose the shift *brigadir* from among the best stitchers" could still be misconstrued since we do not know the extent of "guidance" from above.[65]

Not out of any respect for democratic principles, but simply to avoid sabotage by workers, management quite possibly permitted genuine elections of *brigadiry* or at least was willing to negotiate about acceptable choices. Elected or not, brigade leaders were exercising powers that infringed on those of foremen. The direct line to the dispatcher's office was a privilege to be envied by leaders of ordinary brigades and must have led to agitation on their part and headaches for dispatchers and fore-

---

[62] On the earlier version, see S. A. Kheinman, "Sotsialisticheskoe sorevnovanie v promyshlennosti SSSR," in *Sostialisticheskoe sorevnovanie v promyshlennosti SSSR, Sbornik statei* (Moscow: Plankhozgiz, 1930), 48–9; *Trud*, July 6, 1930; and L. S. Rogachevskaia, *Sotsialisticheskoe sorevnovanie v SSSR, istoricheskie ocherki, 1917–1970 gg.* (Moscow: Nauka, 1977), 116–19.

[63] *K godovshchine I Vsesoiuznogo soveshchaniia stakhanovtsev, Sbornik statei direktorov leningradskikh predpriiatii legkoi promyshlennosti* (Moscow–Leningrad: Gizlegprom, 1936), 174.

[64] Ibid.

[65] Ibid., 77.

126   *Stakhanovism and the politics of productivity*

men alike.[66] Irrespective of their production performance (generally regarded as impressive)[67] and the fact that directors considered integrated brigades to be "the highest stage of the Stakhanovite movement,"[68] they never encompassed more than a tiny fraction of the labor force in any branch of industry. Among the reasons that one Soviet historian has given for this were the difficulty of organizing them and their "violation" of the cardinal principle of one-person managerial responsibility – *edinonachalie.*[69] Such language is reminiscent of standard explanations for the liquidation of production collectives and communes in the early 1930s. The absence of any reference to productivity is revealing.

As for the Stakhanovite schools, the First Five-Year Plan equivalents were the Izotovite schools and the public-tow (*obshchestvennyi buksir*) movement.[70] The Stakhanovite schools were not formal institutions, but rather brief on-the-job training courses consisting mainly of lectures and demonstrations by leading Stakhanovites, followed by practical application under their supervision as well as that of technical personnel. The first such "school" was established in October 1935 at the Paris Commune Shoe Factory in Moscow.[71]

---

[66] "Must have been" because direct evidence is lacking in available sources. But for complaints from workers about standing in line to receive tools, see *Trud*, Mar. 17, 1936. For tensions arising from differential access to crib attendants at a Chicago machine-tool factory where piece rates prevailed, see Michael Burawoy, *Manufacturing Consent: Changes in the Labor Process under Monopoly Capitalism* (University of Chicago Press, 1979), 52–3, 65–6, 171, 173. The parceling-out of foremen's functions to *brigadiry* contrasted markedly with the Taylorist-inspired procedure of vesting responsibility in more specialized personnel.
[67] For positive evaluations of Stakhanovite integrated brigades, see *ZI*, May 30, June 10, 11, 21, 1936; *Industrializatsiia severo – zapadnogo raiona v gody vtoroi i tret'ei piatiletok (1933–1941 gg.). Dokumenty i materialy* (Leningrad: LGU, 1969), 374–5; *Stakhanovets*, no. 13 (1936):14–17; no. 14 (1936):14–15; no. 16 (1936):12.
[68] For directors' assessments, see *K godovshchine*, 119, 172.
[69] Sakharov, "Zarozhdenie i razvitie," 150–2.
[70] For summaries of these phenomena, see Rogachevskaia, *Sotsialisticheskoe sorevnovanie*, 119–24.
[71] See *Trud*, Nov. 2, 1935; I. I. Kuz'minov, *Stakhanovskoe dvizhenie – vysshii etap sotsialisticheskogo sorevnovaniia* (Moscow: Sotsekgiz, 1940),

Simultaneously, schools for ordinary Stakhanovites who required further education before they could hope to qualify for entrance into technikums and other advanced institutions were established by many enterprises. Intended to take up where the seven-year general educational institutions and the vocational training provided by the technical minimum courses left off, these schools offered two-year programs of study in the natural sciences, mathematics, and the Russian language as well as on-the-job production practice.[72] As such, they were part of the prodigious expansion of part-time training programs for adult workers in the latter half of the 1930s.[73] They survived into the 1940s and, along with the avalanche of brochures and journals devoted to popularizing production techniques, contributed to the spread of technical culture in the USSR.[74] In their unspectacular way, they may have constituted the most successful aspect of Stakhanovism.

IV

To return to the politics of productivity at higher levels, it was becoming increasingly clear toward the middle of the Stakhanovite year that tolerance and reconciliation had once again gained the upper hand over accusation and repression. "Sabotage" had all but disappeared from the vocabulary of the central press. Instead, restoring managers and engineers to the "honored place that befits them as commanders of production" and cultivating experienced cadres – including those of the "old school" – were the tasks assigned to party organizations as "Conditions for the Triumph of the Stakhanovite Movement."[75]

It was at this juncture, in late June, that Narkomtiazhprom convened a session of its council. Formed in April 1935 to replace

129; Marcel Anstett, *La formation de la main-oeuvre qualifée en Union Sovietique de 1917 à 1954.* (Paris: Riviere, 1958), 135.

[72] *Stakhanovets*, no. 5–6 (1936):34–6.

[73] See Sheila Fitzpatrick, *Education and Social Mobility in the Soviet Union, 1921–1934* (Cambridge University Press, 1979), 237–42.

[74] See, e.g., *Stakhanovets*, no. 1 (1940):26; no. 6 (1940), 11; *Industrializatsiia SSSR, 1938–1941 gg. Dokumenty i materialy* (Moscow: Nauka, 1973), 233–6.

[75] *Pravda*, June 23, 1936.

the commissariat's somewhat smaller collegium, the council, was an advisory body consisting of *glavki*, department, and some trust heads, as well as a few enterprise directors.[76] To this elite group of 104 were added 215 individuals in June 1936. Of the new members, slightly more than half (108) had engineering degrees. Sixteen were *glavki* officials, ten served in the commissariat's departments, and thirty-seven were from various trusts and supply organizations. Individual enterprises were represented by seventy-three directors, twenty-two chief engineers and technical directors, twenty-three shop supervisors, five foremen, and twenty-two workers, some of whom were listed as instructors. The remainder belonged to various research institutes, and one was the editor of the commissariat's newspaper. Nearly all of the workers can be identified as outstanding Stakhanovites, recipients of the Orders of Lenin and the Red Banner of Labor, and participants in the All-Union and other conferences. Among them were Stakhanov, Diukanov, Izotov, Busygin, and Likhoradov. Of all 215, there were two women, one a director of a synthetic rubber plant and the other a drill press operator.[77]

In addition to its expanded membership, the council's session was remarkable in a number of respects. Not only was it the last meeting of this body before the division of Narkomtiazhprom into more than a dozen separate commissariats in early 1938, but it also marked the last appearance at any All-Union forum for many of those in attendance. Finally, it provided an opportunity for assessing the impact of Stakhanovism at a time when the fate of that movement hung in the balance.

On the face of it, heavy industry had performed well. The 1936 plan had been fulfilled by a reported 50.3 percent during the first six months. This meant an increase in gross output of some 37.4 percent compared with the same period in 1935. Some branches of industry had done better than others, but as Ordzhonikidze remarked to "stormy applause," heavy industry was on target for fulfilling the Five-Year Plan in four years.[78]

This basically positive assessment was in strange contrast to

[76] For the statute establishing the council and its initial membership, see *ZI*, Apr. 21, 1935.

[77] Ibid., June 11, 1936.

[78] *Stakhanovets*, no. 15 (1936):4.

the frankness with which many speakers admitted to serious deficiencies in their respective branches of industry and individual enterprises. Forward planning was minimal, they confessed, and thus too often workers were left without work schedules (*grafiki*) or proper instructions; production costs had not been reduced; the new norms inspired by individual Stakhanovites' achievements were still out of reach for many workers, and as a result, wage levels had fallen in some cases or at best had remained stagnant. Trade union officials had ceased to care about or even count shock workers; foremen and other low-echelon managerial personnel were discontented because they received less than many rank-and-file workers, to say nothing of the outstanding achievers; labor turnover had crept upward, particularly in the Donbass coal-mining industry, and at least in one coal trust, the rate among engineering-technical personnel was an astonishing 41.2 percent for the first five months of the year.[79]

No one, of course, blamed Stakhanovism for these problems. "They all swear by it," said Ordzhonikidze.[80] And yet it must have been obvious to all present that attention to planning, the less visible phases of the production process, shock and ordinary workers, and the salaries of foremen was being sacrificed to those aspects of production that the Stakhanovite movement had emphasized.

Having devoted themselves to the organization and execution of Stakhanovite periods, production specialists nonetheless were subjected to the antisabotage campaign of the spring, a campaign that several speakers at the council's session characterized as inappropriate and counterproductive. According to the usually outspoken S. Birman, the failure of specialists to advance Stakhanovism was not due to sabotage at all. Rather it had to do with their "technological arrogance," which had been fostered by the educational system and the emphasis that *Za industrializatsiiu* had placed on technical expertise as the sine qua non of competence.[81] L. Ia. Vysotskii, director of the Kadievugol' trust,

<hr>

[79] See speeches by Bazhanov, Vysotskii, Kartashev, and Birman in *ZI*, June 27, 28, July 3, 1936.
[80] *Stakhanovets*, no. 15 (1936):10.
[81] *ZI*, July 3, 1936.

claimed that it was possible to teach old specialists new tricks if only the patience demanded of officials by, among others, Stalin was exercised. But replying to Ordzhonikidze's query about high turnover rates, Vysotskii asserted:

People have to be taught, but to teach how to work is more difficult than to dismiss from work. In a majority of cases, the trusts and mines proceeded according to the old way: dismiss the old people and take on new ones, assuming that new people don't have to be taught.[82]

It was, however, Vysotskii's counterpart at Stalinugol', A. M. Khachatur'iants, who provided the boldest defense of the specialists and, in the process, implicitly questioned whether the introduction of Stakhanovite methods was compatible with increasing output. The mining official couched much of his speech in self-critical terms. "We have committed a big mistake," he admitted, "by extending the instructions of comrades Stalin and Sergo about conservatives and saboteurs to the entire command staff." It was "our mistake" to address accusations of sabotage to any commander who was not able to apply Stakhanovite methods of work. The problems that beset the mining industry could not be attributed to sabotage, he asserted, but rather to

the demands that the Stakhanovites presented to the command staff. These were so great that our engineers and technicians were insufficiently prepared to cope with them. And instead of patiently assisting in the adoption of Stakhanovite methods of work as instructed by comrade Stalin, we declared any mistake or lack of comprehension as sabotage on the part of the command staff.

In this mistake, however, trust officials were not alone. Local organizations and the press were implicated as well. The latter in particular had raised efforts to blame poor performance solely on sabotage "to the second power, to the third and several still higher powers." As for the specialists, they had become so paralyzed by fear, that they could function only by working according to the letter of the law. Many believed that

if I do not give output, do not cut costs and do not fulfill the plan for preparatory work, they will fire me. But if I do not introduce Stakhanovite methods of work, they will not only fire me, but hold me accountable as a saboteur.[83]

[82] Ibid., June 28, 1936.
[83] Ibid.

Thus was Khachatur'iants able to suggest a contradiction that could not otherwise be publicly uttered.

Of course, production specialists and their defenders did not have things entirely their way at the meeting. While acknowledging that the essence of the problem did not lie in sabotage, Piatakov reminded the council that "we did meet sabotage . . . we did and still do meet with inertness." The deputy commissar went on to single out Vysotskii and another mining official as examples, for "I do not know how else to interpret their speeches but as attempts to prove that Stakhanovite methods cannot be considered the basis of our activity."[84]

There was also criticism from below, that is, from the contingent of Stakhanovites. Most critical of all was Busygin, who appears to have made a second career out of publicizing the deficiencies of the Molotov Automobile Works and the lethargy of higher officials.[85] "Two months ago, I wrote in *Trud* that we needed to establish integrated brigades," he complained, but nothing had been done. Sent to Moscow by the factory's director, Busygin had obtained promises from the *glavk* head, Dybets, that steel would be delivered in ten days, but instead it took two months. In the meantime, "we would come to work, walk around the shop, and go home." Wages fell. After an extended vacation, Busygin returned to work only to find the machines in "sad" condition. The shop superintendent, B. Ia. Sokolinskii, had agreed that repairs were necessary "but did nothing" about it.[86]

These were serious charges, and when Sokolinskii rose to speak, Ordzhonikidze made sure he answered them. Wages had not fallen, the superintendent claimed, at least not those of the leading Stakhanovites, Faustov and Velikzhanin. Why had Busygin spent so little time working in the past four or five months? the commissar wanted to know. "As a famous person, he has been chosen to participate in all kinds of delegations and commissions" was the reply. "Why do you allow it?" Ordzhonikidze shot back. "It is impossible not to let him go, when the regional organizations select him, say, to attend Gor'kii's funeral or the

---

[84] Ibid., June 30, 1936. See also note 80, for Ordzhonikidze's comment.

[85] See, e.g., *ZI*, June 4, 9, 1936; and A. Kh. Busygin, *Zhizn' moia i moikh druzei* (Moscow: Profizdat, 1939), 32–7.

[86] *ZI*, July 2, 1936.

May 1 celebrations in Moscow." As for the tardy repair of machinery, Sokolinskii's explanation was characteristic of complaints registered by many speakers. "If previously we were able to repair equipment once in six months, now this interval will not do. . . . Our punches do not last a single shift," Sokolinskii remarked.[87] In other words, the Stakhanovite speedup had placed an unbearable strain on machines and the repair shops.

These exchanges, as well as the discussion on sabotage, reveal that the tensions sparked by Stakhanovism were still very much alive. The council's members, therefore, must have been more than a little anxious for some signal from Ordzhonikidze about how he proposed to resolve them. When the commissar praised Busygin and his workmate, Faustov, for their revelations about the Molotov Automobile Works, the production specialists could not have been very pleased. But then "in order not to be unfair," he mentioned that both the Molotov and Stalin factories were undergoing reconstruction and that "even Ford stops the factory when a new model is being prepared." While chastising management for sending Busygin to Moscow in search of metal and to all kinds of meetings ("What is he – a roving agitator?"), he also spoke of those individuals that Busygin had criticized as "people who in their time had greatly helped comrade Busygin."[88]

In the same vein, Ordzhonikidze discussed engineers' stormy relationship to the Stakhanovite movement. Attempting to lay to rest the charges of sabotage, he reiterated the message of his address to the engineers' Intersectional Bureau:

Some say that engineering-technical personnel are saboteurs. That is nonsense. Some saboteurs! During the nineteen years that Soviet power has existed, we have educated engineers and technicians in our schools and technical colleges, we have turned out over 100,000 engineers and a similar number of technicians. If all of them, and likewise the old engineers whom we reeducated, turned out in 1936 to be saboteurs, then congratulate yourselves on such a success. Some saboteurs! They are not saboteurs, but good people – our sons, our brothers, our comrades who are entirely and completely for Soviet power. They would die on the front for Soviet power, if this were required.[89]

[87] Ibid.
[88] *Stakhanovets*, no. 15 (1936):2, 4.
[89] Ibid., 6.

But having evoked "stormy and prolonged applause," Ordzhonikidze reminded his audience that "a fact remains a fact. You have not headed up the Stakhanovite movement to the extent demanded by our party, by comrade Stalin, who in his own mighty hand wrote that engineers, technicians and managers must head up the Stakhanovite movement."

In his discussion of the reasons for this failure, the commissar focused on the Donbass coal-mining industry, the birthplace of Stakhanovism, and the "peg of our council." By selectively quoting from Khachatur'iants's speech, which he considered "most correctly of all explained what had happened in the Donbass," he was able to support complaints about persecution but also make the most of admissions of complacency. After all, he pointed out, the accusations of conservatism and sabotage came *after* "you, laying on the stove, had made a mess of output."[90]

This was bad enough, but worse still was that the decline in output had led some managers and engineers to adopt a "revisionist attitude" about the efficacy of Stakhanovite methods. Indeed, in February and March the liquidation of Stakhanovite methods had proceeded "quite intensively" in the Donbass. This was quite intolerable and could not be allowed to reoccur.

In short, Ordzhonikidze was reaffirming the inviolability of those practices that were labeled Stakhanovite or that were considered conducive to the movement. Nothing had changed. The original assumption that Stakhanovism could tap the colossal reserves of productivity if only industrial cadres abandoned their lethargy and suspiciousness remained intact. Their reprieve from persecution was not to be misconstrued as a carte blanche. Far from it. Incompetent individuals would still be dismissed. Criticism from above and below would still be encouraged. While acknowledging that labor management had been complicated by the Stakhanovite movement, he dismissed complaints that the burdens were too much to bear. Characteristically sprinkling his remarks with references to the civil war period, he reminded the council of the necessity "to establish iron discipline and order...Bolshevik order," as a means of consolidating Stakhanovism.[91]

[90] Ibid., 6, 9–10.
[91] Ibid., 12.

It was not for managers and specialists to question Stakhanovism, still less to repudiate it. Rather, they had to measure their own performance against its requirements. In one of several passages severely edited in the 1939 edition of Ordzhonikidze's speeches, he held up the Kaganovich Ball Bearings Factory and its director, I. I. Melamed, as an inspirational model. Not only had the director fulfilled his promise to turn out 3 million ball bearings, but he saw to it ahead of schedule. "The way is open to all of you," the commissar proclaimed. "Those who want to lead the mighty Stakhanovite movement" would be "surrounded by concern, a comradely atmosphere, and support of every kind."[92]

In addition to making this grandiose but rather vague promise, Ordzhonikidze pledged something else. All technical personnel in the mines, down to the level of section heads, would be confirmed by the commissar himself, and "without the people's commissar, no one has the right to remove or transfer them." Farther down the line, foremen could be appointed, transferred, and dismissed only by heads of trusts or combines. Intended to curb turnover and raise morale as well, Ordzhonikidze's directive was the only real concession to industrial cadres that emerged from the council's meeting. But it was no small concession. It represented nothing less than a direct slap in the face of regional and local party *apparatchiki* and a challenge to the NKVD, both of which had taken an active part in the antisabotage campaign.

In sum, the signal that Ordzhonikidze sent out was that, so long as managers and specialists did not abandon Stakhanovism, his commissariat would not abandon them. This formula was really no different from that which the commissar had concocted in the autumn of 1935. Despite an abundance of evidence that Stakhanovism had created as many problems as it had resolved, neither the commissar nor his deputies wavered in their public affirmation of the movement. To them and to the party leadership in general, Stakhanovism remained a potentially effective means of combating the "technological arrogance" of engineers and the output-restrictive practices of management and workers

[92] The much abridged version of Ordzhonikidze's speech can be found in G. K. Ordzhonikidze, *Izbrannye stat'i i rechi, 1911–1937* (Moscow: Gosizpollit, 1939), 476–502. The speech as it appeared in *Stakhanovets* was reprinted in G. K. Ordzhonikidze, *Stat'i i rechi*, 2 vols. (Moscow: Pollitizdat, 1956–7), 2:760–99.

alike. It left the party leadership as the sole interpreter of what was objectively possible, and true to the original thrust of the industrialization drive, the leadership tended to interpret the possibilities as almost limitless.

But as suggested by the divergent emphases within the leadership and the "excesses" of the antisabotage campaign, the amount of pressure to be exerted and the mechanisms for doing so were neither unanimously agreed upon nor permanently fixed. Between Stalin's call at the All-Union conference for patience in dealing with recalcitrant specialists and his threat, delivered to the same gathering, of a "light tap on the jaw," there was much room for improvisation. By assuming control over appointments and dismissals and acknowledging the loyalty of the specialists, Ordzhonikidze was, in effect, telling his colleagues that problems arising in connection with Stakhanovism were an affair internal to his commissariat. This message was to have far-reaching and largely unanticipated implications for the politics of productivity.

V

In the months following the council's session, it appeared that Ordzhonikidze's formula was working. Reports from the industrial front continued for some time to sound the same themes that had been articulated by the commissar and his deputies. Individual specialists might be castigated for neglecting their responsibilities, but there was no suggestion that this was intentional sabotage or part of a general pattern. In July, a *Pravda* editorial characterized the charge of sabotage leveled against engineers and technicians as "of course, stupidity."[93] Nearly a month later, the newspaper looked forward to the first anniversary of Stakhanov's record without the slightest hint that the party's line had changed.[94]

In fact, the party's line with respect to managerial-technical personnel had not changed. The secret letter, "On Terrorist Activities of the Trotskyite–Zinovievite Counterrevolutionary

[93] *Pravda*, July 10, 1936.
[94] Ibid., Aug. 5, 1936.

Bloc," that the Central Committee distributed to all higher party organizations on July 29, 1936, referred to conspiracies of a purely political nature among former Oppositionists.[95] None of those convicted and sentenced to death in the first Show Trial had held an industrial post at the time of his arrest. Trotskyism, not conservatism or industrial sabotage, was what distinguished these "enemies of the people," and others, as yet unmasked, were said to be hiding within the ranks of the party rather than the industrial hierarchy.

However, this is not to say that this, the opening round of the Great Purges, left industrial personnel untouched. Once party officials became more "vigilant" as instructed by the Central Committee's letter, they discovered that all manner of people, among them factory directors, had Trotskyite pasts. In cases where such officials had been insufficiently diligent or, being made aware of the existence of "Trotskyite agents," had taken a "rotten liberal" position (i.e., had done nothing), they were reminded of their duty.[96] On top of this, among the former Trotskyists implicated by the defendants in the Zinoviev–Kamenev trial was Piatakov, who not long afterward was placed under arrest.[97]

Still, the industrial cadres as a group were not subjected to the sort of harassment they had experienced in the spring. Criticism from below there was. Busygin was "unable to keep silent about such 'everyday trivia' " as long lines in the factory's cafeteria and the lack of drinking water in the forge shop; numerous other workers explained why they were not yet or no longer Stakhanovites by registering complaints against supervisory personnel.[98] Yet the thrust of such criticism was lack of punctuality or attention to the needs of Stakhanovites and shock workers, not sabotage.

Then, in the midst of preparations for the Eighth Congress of Soviets, which would approve the new constitution, came news of a trial in Novosibirsk. The accused, six engineers employed at the "Central" coal mine in Kemerovo, were charged with ar-

[95] Merle Fainsod, *Smolensk under Soviet Rule* (New York: Vintage, 1958), 233–7.
[96] As, e.g., by *Pravda*, Aug. 6, 1936, and *Stakhanovets*, no. 16 (1936):7.
[97] Conquest, *Great Terror*, 220–2.
[98] *Pravda*, Aug. 3, 4, 1936; *Stakhanovets*, no. 16 (1936):8, 33, 42–4.

ranging an explosion at the behest of the "Trotskyite Center," which allegedly was working with foreign industrialist circles and Gestapo agents to restore capitalism in the USSR. In the explosion, which occurred on September 23, 1936, ten workers were killed and fourteen others were seriously injured. As Robert Conquest has pointed out, by linking Trotskyist and fascist intrigue with industrial sabotage, the Novosibirsk trial set the stage for the second Show Trial, the "Trial of the Seventeen" (January 1937), at which Piatakov was the main defendant.[99]

For us, the significance lies elsewhere. It is that explosions, cave-ins, fires, floods, and other industrial accidents superseded Stakhanovism as a test of the loyalty of industrial cadres. Such mishaps had now become politicized and were publicized in that light. Indeed, the politicization of industrial accidents was made retrospective. In the aftermath of the Novosibirsk trial, A. Vyshinskii, the procurator general, issued a directive to the effect that all criminal cases arising from industrial accidents be reviewed in order to expose the role played by counterrevolutionary sabotage.[100] Correspondingly, at the Piatakov trial, the explosion at the Gorlovka Nitrogen Fertilizer Works that had occurred in November 1935 and the sixty pit fires reported up to the end of 1935 at the Prokopevsk mines in western Siberia were attributed to the "anti-Soviet Trotskyite Center."[101]

It did not matter that both at Gorlovka and at the "Central" mine there were outstanding Stakhanovites who, at least in the latter case, reportedly had been fulfilling their shift norms by 400, 800, and even 1,000 percent.[102] Or rather, it mattered very much that Stakhanovites were among the victims of both explosions. For this seemed only to confirm that these accidents had not been accidental at all. Thus, one of the implications of the

[99] Conquest, *Great Terror*, 222–4. See also Kravchenko, *I Chose Freedom*, 329–30.

[100] *Sovetskoe gosudarstvo i pravo*, no. 3 (1965), cited in Conquest, *Great Terror*, 223.

[101] *Report of the Court Proceedings in the Case of the Anti-Soviet Trotskyite Centre* (Moscow: People's Commissariat of Justice of the USSR, 1937), 256, 481.

[102] See citations in the excellent summary of the trial by S. Schwarz, "Novosibirskii protsess," *Sotsialisticheskii vestnik*, no. 23–4 (1936):13–14. One such report was sent from trust headquarters on the very day of the explosion!

Novosibirsk and Piatakov trials was that the organization of Stakhanovite methods could neither prevent politically motivated sabotage and wrecking nor fulfill its historic mission so long as such counterrevolutionary activity continued. Whether intended as a rebuff to Ordzhonikidze or not, the trials, Vyshinskii's order, and the repression that ensued made his formula null and void.

But what of the movement itself? From late August, the cycle through which Stakhanovism had already passed began to repeat itself in abbreviated fashion. Industrial enterprises geared themselves up for a day of records to coincide with the anniversary of Stakhanov's feat. For several days thereafter, *Za industrializatsiiu* ran banner headlines proclaiming the "New Records of New Stakhanovites."[103] Some older Stakhanovites joined the campaign too. Busygin achieved a new record, turning out 1,657 shafts in a single shift, only to be surpassed by Faustov's 1,774.[104] Stakhanovite *dekady* made their reappearance from mid-September. There followed a much publicized *dvukhdekadnik* (twenty-day period) in the oil industry and another in light industry that was extended into a Stakhanovite *mesiachnik* (month).[105]

Perhaps the most ambitious campaigns of all took place in the metallurgical and Donbass coal-mining industries. The former involved the production of 60,000 tons of steel and 45,000 tons of rolled iron per day by the end of the calendar year; the latter aimed for a target of 250,000 tons of coal in one day. Just how ambitious these targets were can be judged by comparing them with average daily output over the period September 12–16, as shown in Table 3.2.

In both coal mining and ferrous metallurgy as well as the oil industry, the targets were announced and the campaigns launched at meetings attended by trust directors, enterprise managers, regional party secretaries, factory committee chairmen, and outstanding Stakhanovites. However, it is extremely unlikely that the initiative was taken at this level. One possibility is that it came from outside Narkomtiazhprom, perhaps from within the Politburo itself. According to this line of reasoning, the targets were intentionally set at a level that could not be

---

[103] *ZI*, Aug. 30, Sept. 3, 1936.
[104] Ibid., Sept. 4, 15, 1936.
[105] *Pravda*, Oct. 13, 1936; *Stakhanovets*, no. 23 (1936):2.

Table 3.2. *Planned and actual output in comparison with
Stakhanovite campaign targets (September 12–16, 1936)*

Branch of industry	Plan	Actual	Campaign target		
			Amount	% Plan	% Actual
Coal (Donbass)	222,319	199,120	250,000	112.5	125.6
Steel	46,200	45,286	60,000	129.9	132.5
Rolled iron	36,000	33,085	45,000	125.0	136.0

Note: Figures are in average tons per day.
Source: Za industrializatsiiu, Sept. 14–18, 1936.

reached, which would further discredit industrial cadres and
lead to accusations of sabotage and wrecking. Yet we should not
take target figures too literally. Soviet economic targets, like
many laws passed during this period, appear to have been established as orientational guidelines indicative of priorities.[106]
Alternatively, we might see this campaign as a desperate maneuver by Ordzhonikidze who, counting on the normal forth
quarter storming effort, hoped that the commanding staff would
vindicate itself.

Whatever the motives and whosever they were, actual output
did not come close to the targets. In November, whereas steel
output surpassed the plan by a reported 2.8 percent and rolled
iron output was shy of its mark by a similar margin, Donbass
coal mines produced a miserable 218,300 tons per day, or 85.3
percent of the plan. During December, the mines turned out an
average of 221,200 tons, which was 9,300 tons less than the
amount produced in December 1935.[107] As for ferrous metallurgy, a meeting of outstanding Stakhanovites was convened on
December 30 at which it was unanimously agreed to extend the
campaign indefinitely into 1937.[108]

December 30 was also the date of Ordzhonikidze's last major
public address. Speaking to Muscovite administrators and en-

[106] I am indebted to John Barber of Cambridge University for this
insight.
[107] *ZI,* Dec. 8, 1936, and S. Schwarz, "Bezradostnaia godovshchina,"
Sotsialisticheskii vestnik, no. 17–18 (1937):13.
[108] *Pravda,* Jan 3, 1937.

gineers, he drew attention to the "ruptures" that had occurred on the industrial front and then asked what was becoming an increasingly common question: "Who is guilty?" His answer, that "of course, we, dear comrades, the leaders – beginning with your obedient servant, the people's commissar and ending with foremen – all the comrades here are guilty," must have raised a few eyebrows.[109] Within six weeks, "Sergo" would be dead, officially (until 1956) the victim of a heart attack, but almost certainly a suicide case.[110]

Even before Ordzhonikidze's death, the formula he had worked out had become inoperative and the movement he had worked so hard to shape and utilize had been dealt a severe blow. *Pravda* could chide the apparently once again overzealous Donetsk party organization for interpreting every mistake made by industrial cadres as the work of enemies, but it was the failure of party members to expose wreckers that entailed the most severe penalties.[111] The implicit message of the Novosibirsk trial – that Stakhanovism was insufficient as a coercive mechanism – was made explicit by Stalin at the Central Committee's plenary session in March 1937. "It is necessary," he said,

to smash and discard the theory which states that the Stakhanovite movement is the essential means for the liquidation of wrecking.... Isn't it clear that the Stakhanovite movement needs real assistance on our part against any and all machinations of our enemies so that it can move forward and fulfill its great mission? Isn't it clear that the struggle to check wrecking is a precondition for the Stakhanovite movement to flourish in all spheres? I think that the issue is so clear that it does not require further elaboration.[112]

Further elaboration there nonetheless was. The day after Stalin spoke, *Za industrializatsiiu* admitted its error in having advanced the view that Stakhanovism could in and of itself overcome wrecking.[113] This did not, however, prevent *Pravda* from excoriating Narkomtiazhprom's organ and claiming that

---

[109] *ZI*, Feb. 20, 1937.
[110] See the account of his death in Roy Medvedev, *Let History Judge* (London: Spokesman, 1976), 193–6. Conquest, *Great Terror*, 259–65, argues that Ordzhonikidze was murdered.
[111] *Pravda*, Feb. 17, 1937.
[112] *Stakhanovets*, no. 5 (1937):1.
[113] *ZI*, Mar. 4, 1937.

echoes of such a "rotten theory" could still be heard among the commissariat's officials.[114] With Ordzhonikidze gone, a large proportion of his staff in the commissariat, directors of *glavki*, trusts, and enterprises, and many chief engineers were removed from their posts, imprisoned, and in some cases executed in the course of 1937. Others apparently took Ordzhonikidze's path. Those who survived in their jobs did so by showing proper deference to, and otherwise cultivating friendly relations with, NKVD officials who were in charge of the special sections (*spetsotdely*) of the larger industrial plants.[115]

The argument presented here is that Stakhanovism played a significant role in the politics of productivity in Soviet industry in 1936. Essentially, it provided a means of exerting pressure on middle-level industrial cadres to supplement existing mechanisms. The latter included plan targets and the allocation of resources, the mobilizing functions of party organizations, and the investigatory functions of the press and the police. Gross output and plan fulfillment remained important criteria for measuring the performance of industrial enterprises, but they were often unreliable guides to the utilization of production capacity and revealed little if anything about the means by which output figures were reached. Party officials down to the shop committee level took their instructions from higher organs but, in the course of day-to-day contact with managerial-technical personnel, tended to develop a mutuality of interests that blunted their effectiveness. The same was true of trade union activists, who had learned the importance and means of presenting a favorable image of shop floor activity to the press and higher bodies. The police were quick to investigate mishaps, but their limited technical knowledge and pressure from above to find culprits made it difficult for them to get to the bottom of many problems.

The pressure exerted via Stakhanovism took many forms. First, Stakhanovites' production records were interpreted as evi-

[114] *Pravda*, Mar. 6, 1937.
[115] For a detailed account of production specialists in 1937, see Kendall E. Bailes, *Technology and Society under Lenin and Stalin* (Princeton, N.J.: Princeton University Press, 1978), 279–87, 328–31. See also Chapter 7, this volume.

dence of underutilized capacity and were invoked frequently by higher authorities during the norm revision conferences. Second, Stakhanovism provided additional criteria for judging managers' and engineers' mastery of their jobs. These criteria ranged from the implementation of "Stakhanovite" methods of work (division of labor in some cases, combination of tasks in others, lengthening the shelf and the rosterless – *beznariad* – system in coal mining, increasing the speed and feed in machine tool construction, etc.), to the proportion of Stakhanovites in a given shop or plant, to various production indices during and after a Stakhanovite period. Finally, the movement expanded opportunities for, and gave more weight to, criticism from below.

All of this immensely complicated the lives of managers and specialists. It required as much political acumen as administrative and technical skill to know which criteria could be ignored and which had to be observed, whose pressure to bow to and whose to resist, which workers' suggestions could be shelved and which should be approved. Such maneuvering evoked charges of sabotage against the Stakhanovite movement. From another perspective, that which has informed this study, it was part and parcel of Stakhanovism. It was as much a part of the "movement" as the swelling of the ranks of Stakhanovites, the new production records achieved in the autumn of 1936, and other phenomena of which higher authorities approved. This, of course, is not the way that party leaders viewed Stakhanovism, but there is no reason for the historian to limit his or her understanding of this or any other social phenomenon to official definitions and prescriptions.

What to do about the noncompliance of middle-level industrial cadres with directives from above proved to be a politically charged issue throughout the Stakhanovite year. Narkomtiazhprom was not averse to cracking the whip, particularly in connection with the disappointing results of the Stakhanovite periods. But other political forces had weapons too and were anxious to employ them. The antisabotage campaign of the spring, prosecuted most vigorously by the Donetsk party *obkom*, exceeded what Ordzhonikidze and some other party leaders deemed appropriate. However strained were relations between "center" and "periphery" within the industrial sphere, the

June session of Narkomtiazhprom's council demonstrated that in the face of an external threat the two could band together, albeit on the center's terms.

Those terms included the reaffirmation of the criteria associated with Stakhanovism. Though it is not clear what produced the impetus for a new round of recordmania, Stakhanovite periods, and socialist competition in the second half of the year, these phenomena were not incompatible with the alliance forged at the June meeting. But even before the end of the year, these activities were overshadowed by a fresh initiative that had little to do with Stakhanovism and owed its origins to politics outside of the industrial sphere. Once vigilance and the hunt for "enemies of the people" became paramount, it did not matter which criteria industrial personnel violated or fulfilled. In the guise of assisting the Stakhanovite movement, Stalin, Molotov, Kaganovich, and the police apparatus on which they relied were abandoning it as a method of disciplining industrial management. By the time Stalin was equating the slow tempo of capital construction and preparatory work in the Donbass mines with wrecking activity and *Za industrializatsiiu* was reporting that several Stakhanovite steelworkers had burned out a furnace in their attempt to achieve a record, Stakhanovism was well on its way to being marginalized.[116]

We are thus compelled to accept a somewhat paradoxical conclusion: Despite the stresses and strains Stakhanovism had caused, for managers and specialists its essentially economic criteria were preferable to the political criteria that prevailed during 1937–8. Precisely because "heading up" the Stakhanovite movement could mean so many different things, specialists could usually point to some achievement associated with it. But they could not erase some past political association, indiscrete remark, or action, nor could they prove that such behavior would not be repeated in the future. Whether the thinning and then closing of ranks within the upper echelons of the party and state can be attributed to the internal politics of the regime, a response to the gathering storm clouds of European war, or other factors

---

[116] *ZI*, Mar. 10, 1937.

is a question that continues to evoke intense scholarly discussion.[117] It cannot, however, be pursued here.

One qualification must be made with respect to our conclusion, a qualification that may also shed some light on the prosecution of, if not the motivation for, the Great Purges. Criticism from above and below did tend to discredit middle-ranking cadres, creating an image of them as incompetent, dishonest, and unconcerned with the welfare of workers. To that extent, it made subsequent charges of deliberate wrecking and politically motivated sabotage that much more plausible and cast their Narkomtiazhprom taskmasters in the role of protectors. This was an outcome that was not without its cruel irony.

[117] See, e.g., J. Arch Getty, *Origins of the Great Purges: The Soviet Communist Party Reconsidered, 1933–1938* (Cambridge University Press, 1985).

4

The making of Stakhanovites

One of the difficulties of analyzing Stakhanovism is the protean nature of the term "Stakhanovite." It has already been encountered in connection with certain workers, brigades, methods of production, vocational training, output norms, and periods of intense industrial activity varying in length from a single shift to an entire month and, at least in the rhetoric of the times, the entire year of 1936. In practice, some of these terms merely represented updated versions of earlier phenomena. Hence, Stakhanovite brigades resuscitated organizational forms dating back to the late 1920s and early 1930s; Stakhanovite schools were, in effect, Izotovite schools by another name; and Stakhanovite periods frequently resembled the "storming" sessions of the First Five-Year Plan, even though the authorities intended something quite different. It should also be pointed out that parallels with more recent phenomena are appropriate. Stakhanovite through-brigades have had their counterparts in the "complex" and "mixed" brigades of the late 1970s; Stakhanovite schools have given way to various forms of worker patronage (*shefstvo*), and, of course, storming as a by-product of some All-Union or branch competition remains a characteristic of the Soviet industrial system.

What, then, of the noun "Stakhanovite" (*stakhanovets*), as opposed to its adjectival form, *stakhanovskii*? Was this simply a mid-1930s version of the First and early Second Five-Year Plan shock worker, the innovator (*novator*) and front-rank worker (*peredovik proizvodstva*) of the 1950s, and the still more recent shock worker of Communist labor?

To some extent, the answer would have to be affirmative. All of these titles represent official acknowledgment of labor activism and achievement. All have entitled their bearers to certain material benefits and privileges, distinguishing them from their fellow workers to a greater or lesser degree. But the question is precisely to what degree? Can we speak of each of these categories as designating a distinct stratum among manual workers in the same way that, for example, mid-Victorian artisans and skilled craftsmen have been referred to as a labor aristocracy?

There are several issues to sort out here: the relationship of Stakhanovites to categories of workers that preceded and post-dated them; the distinctions between Stakhanovites and non-Stakhanovite workers; and those among Stakhanovites. The first issue can be treated rather succinctly. As stated in Chapter 1, the title of shock worker was originally employed with respect to workers who put out extra effort in response to explicit appeals by the party/state. The model shock worker stayed on an extra shift, agreed to have his or her rates reduced, initiated socialist competition, and took an active part in shop and enterprise production conferences, all in the interests of socialist construction. After 1930, the model was differentiated as workers were called upon to redress some of the more extreme imbalances and dislocations that had developed in the course of the all-out drive for socialist construction. Hence, cost-accounting brigade members, Izotovites, and, later, *otlichniki* were all subsumed under the ever expanding but increasingly meaningless category of shock worker.[1]

Much the same processes of differentiation, expansion, and insignificance occurred with respect to Stakhanovites. By 1939, high-speed workers (*skorostniki*) had made their appearance among metal-machine operators. Then, as the manpower needs of the army began to take precedence, workers were encouraged to perform a variety of jobs, that is, to combine occupations; others were encouraged to operate several machines simultaneously (*mnogostanochniki*); and during the war, such terms as "two hundred," "three hundred," and "one thousand percenters" were applied to workers who had taken over and fulfilled the norms of those inducted into the army. All of these workers

---

[1] By July 1935, this category included 42 percent of the industrial work force, or some 2 million workers. See *Industrializatsiia SSSR, 1933–1937 gg. Dokumenty i materialy* (Moscow: Nauka, 1971), 548.

were included in the ranks of Stakhanovites, whose number reached nearly 3 million (51.1 percent of all industrial workers) by July 1940, dropped to 1.6 million by 1943, and rose again to 3.1 million (34.4 percent of all workers) by 1945.[2]

Quite clearly, shock work, Stakhanovism, and their postwar equivalents were products of essentially the same thrust, to mobilize workers to achieve greater output and, more ambitiously, to integrate them into the officially sanctioned technical and shop floor cultures. Each product appears to have succumbed to the same logic of inflation. However, what distinguishes Stakhanovism – and therefore Stakhanovites – is the extent to which this thrust was ramified by socioeconomic and cultural policies. Neither before 1935 nor since the late 1930s has the party/state invested so much of its prestige in what it defined as a movement.

Certainly, much effort went into establishing shock brigades and organizing competition among them in 1929–30. However, this effort was severely constrained by a number of factors, among which the relatively egalitarian wage structure, the fluidity of labor power, the social chaos, and the collectivization drive were probably the most powerful. In the postwar era and particularly since the death of Stalin, the productionist ethos that suffused the Stalin period has been less prominent; labor heroism, though still officially celebrated, has long since ceased to arouse massive popular adulation; and insofar as feats of production still legitimate the Soviet system, it is the exemplars of the scientific-technical revolution – the technical intelligentsia – that are most closely identified with such successes. As a consequence, socialist competition and the forms it has assumed no longer resonate to the degree that they once did, even and most importantly among manual workers.

This raises the question of what the authorities were trying to achieve by investing so much in Stakhanovism. In the previous two chapters, emphasis was placed on the legitimation of norm increases and the exertion of pressure on enterprise management to execute official policy. Viewed in broader terms, however, Stakhanovism, like the new constitution then being drafted,

---

[2] *Industrializatsiia SSSR, 1938–1941 gg. Dokumenty i materialy* (Moscow: Nauka, 1973), 366; *Profsoiuzy SSSR, Dokumenty i materialy*, 5 vols. (Moscow: Profizdat, 1963–73), 3:372.

was meant to symbolize the USSR's coming of age. In terms of labor productivity, which as Lenin had asserted (and Soviet commentators never tired of repeating) was "in the final analysis, the most important, the main condition for the victory of the new social order,"[3] it indicated that victory was at hand. At a time when record-breaking aviators and athletes had largely replaced explorers and generals as important sources of national pride, the world records of Stakhanovites showed the Soviet Union to be a world leader in this not unimportant field of human endeavor. The USSR had its aeronautical heroes as well, but it is indicative of Stakhanovism's significance that their exploits very rarely eclipsed those of the outstanding labor heroes.[4]

Then again, Stakhanovism consisted of more than the setting of records and their celebration. It, in fact, constituted an important ingredient of the socialization of a largely peasant derived labor force. It offered a model of behavior and a set of values that workers could adopt to negotiate the difficult transition from a largely preindustrial to an industrial society. In this and the next two chapters, we shall examine this model, the values it incorporated, and the way in which workers responded to and helped shape the prescribed behavioral norms.

I

How, then, should one define a Stakhanovite? This question must be addressed on three different levels: the metaphorical, the ideal-typical, and the pragmatic. Each level corresponds to a different function that the definition served and, to some extent, a different audience.

Beginning with the metaphorical, the earliest characterization of Stakhanov (and Diukanov) was that of the *bogatyr'*.[5] Literally translated as Hercules, hero, or athlete, the term had a more significant Russo-specific connotation. This was of the brave,

---

[3] V. I. Lenin, *Polnoe sobranie sochinenii*, 5th ed., 55 vols. (Moscow: Politizdat, 1959–65), 39:21.

[4] Indeed, Soviet pilots were occasionally referred to as "Stakhanovites of the air." See *New York Times*, Feb. 2, 1936, and *Pravda*, May 26, 1936.

[5] *Pravda*, Sept. 6, 1935.

"Forward, the Stalinist tribe of Stakhanovites!" From *Stakhanovets*, no. 9 (1936).

warrior-knight of folk epics (*byliny*). Defenders of the faith, heroes of the people, and symbolic of all that was noble and good, the *bogatyry* of Kievan Rus' were transplanted, in the rhetoric of the times, to the more mundane reality of the Soviet factory. At least initially, the enemies they confronted and triumphed over were not individuals, but rather procedures and attitudes that, so it was claimed, had been holding Soviet society back from its inexorable march toward communism. Among these were the technical norms and the output quotas based on them, the complacency of conservative bureaucrats, the "routinism" of engineers and technicians, and the old, irresponsible attitude toward work of "backward" workers. Stakhanovites did not just overfulfill their norms, they "smashed" them and in the process set "miraculous records"; they did not unthinkingly follow instructions, but on the contrary dared to defy them.

As Katerina Clark has pointed out, Stakhanovite *bogatyry* were "extra-systemic figures" in the sense that they did not belong to the existing bureaucratic or political hierarchies.[6] Their relationship to political leaders was characterized by one of two motifs. The more common was fictive kinship; that is, they were members of "Stalin's tribe." Entry into this exalted group involved being "born again," or at least experiencing a "profound change" in one's life.[7] The blood relationship was frequently emphasized by outstanding Stakhanovites who tended to view Stalin and/or Ordzhonikidze as stern but kindhearted fathers, the former being slightly more distant than the latter. Invited to the Bolshoi Theater to celebrate the anniversary of the October Revolution, Stakhanov saw "for the first time in my life our own (*rodnoi*) comrade Stalin," discovered that "I could not take my eyes off [him]," and "very much wanted to get closer to him."[8] Later, at the All-Union conference, he noticed that Stalin "looked down on us with the eyes of a father and teacher," an image virtually identical to the one used by Gudov.[9] When Busygin was summoned to Moscow in the spring of 1936, he was greeted by Ordzhonikidze "as a father would lovingly look on his grown up children whom he had not seen for a long time." And when, less than a year later, he learned of Sergo's death, he recalled the day his own father had died, adding that "nevertheless, there was no day in my life more bitter than February 19, 1937."[10]

---

[6] Katerina Clark, "Utopian Anthropology as a Context for Stalinist Literature," in *Stalinism: Essays in Historical Interpretation*, ed. Robert C. Tucker (New York: Norton, 1977), 194.

[7] See statements by Krivonos and Demchenko in *Stakhanovtsy* (Moscow: Profizdat, 1935), 36, 91.

[8] A. G. Stakhanov, *Rasskaz o moei zhizni* (Moscow: Gossotsizd., 1937), 45.

[9] Ibid., 59, and I. I. Gudov, *Put' stakhanovtsa* (Moscow: Sotsekgiz, 1938), 59. See also *Pravda*, Nov. 14, 1936, and Aug. 30, 1938. Commemorating the third anniversary of his feat, Stakhanov referred to Stalin as the "father of the Stakhanovite movement" and Stakhanovites as "Stalin's students."

[10] A. Kh. Busygin, *Zhizn' moia i moikh druzei* (Moscow: Profizdat, 1939), 36, 41.

The other motif linking Stakhanovite *bogatyry* to the Soviet authority structure was military. Just as the semimythical warriors of old had faithfully served their princes, so would Stakhanovites follow their commanding officers. For example, after Ordzhonikidze delivered his speech to Narkomtiazhprom's council, Busygin felt "like a soldier of a great army, fighting under the banner of Lenin–Stalin for the construction of a communist society."[11] This army contained no junior officers; *glavki* heads, factory directors, and engineers do not figure in the military motif.

Along with the image of Soviet *bogatyry* was another that in some ways contradicted it. This was that of Stakhanovites as professors, scientists, inventors, or experts who with their own hands proved the academicians and specialists wrong. "They only need to be encouraged a little and they will outdo our 'learned' professors," remarked Voroshilov.[12] Indeed, scientists could be found who affirmed that this was already the case.[13] Here was an obvious case of role reversal. Cast in the role of mentors, Stakhanovites were not fabulistic, but decidedly rationalistic. Their advice was sought at sessions of Narkomtiazhprom's council and at norm revision conferences. They were also people of the future, prototypes of the New Soviet Man, who smoothed out the contradiction between mental and manual labor.[14]

These two images, the one derived from the hoary past, the other pointing to the future, were not prescriptions for concrete action any more than they corresponded to reality. They were rather artifacts of the syncretic culture that was emerging in the mid-1930s, a culture that combined the celebration of the triumphs of Russian national heroes with obeisance to a Marxist–Leninist conceptualization of the transition from socialist to communist society. The reference points of this culture were not limited to workers or material production. Its stress on the con-

---

[11] Ibid., 40.
[12] *Pervoe Vsesoiuznoe soveshchanie rabochikh i rabotnits stakhanovtsev, 14–17 noiabria, Stenograficheskii otchet* (Moscow: Partizdat, 1935), 351.
[13] See, e.g., *ZI*, Nov. 22, 1935, and *Stakhanovets*, no. 1 (1936):13.
[14] Stalin referred to this quality in his speech to the All-Union conference. I. V. Stalin, *Sochineniia*, ed. Robert H. McNeal, (Stanford, Calif.: Hoover Institution, 1967), 1 (XIV), 91. See also V. A. Karpinskii, *Stakhanovskoe dvizhenie* (Moscow: Sotsekgiz, 1936), 42–3.

quest of nature and the compatibility of individual fulfillment and the collective good applied equally to fictional war heroes such as Pavel Korchagin and miracle-working "scientists" such as T. D. Lysenko. What was needed to give workers a model to emulate was a definition of Stakhanovites that incorporated qualities peculiar to *their* work situations. These were to be provided in abundance.

Some of the attributes of the ideal Stakhanovite were established even before the movement had extended beyond the bounds of the coal-mining industry. Addressing a meeting of the Donetsk party *obkom* in September 1935, the party secretary, Sarkisov, defined a Stakhanovite as "a worker who by completely utilizing work time without absences and stoppages achieves highly productive work."[15] These qualities of punctuality, conscientiousness, and skill should not surprise us. They were, after all, the bread and butter of much nineteenth-century self-improvement literature in Britain and the United States, were inculcated by most incentive schemes employed by management, and found their way into the Soviet Union as the antithesis of "Asiatic backwardness." Suitable for emulation, they were nonetheless inadequate in distinguishing what was unique about Stakhanovites.

It was at the All-Union conference in November 1935 that the typology of requisite qualities received its most elaborate treatment. To A. V. Dushenkov, an experienced turner from the Lenin Works in Leningrad, "a Stakhanovite is a person who, working calmly, really gets out of technology all it can give, because he loves his job, loves his machine, and believes in the victory of socialism, the victory of the system which is giving us a better life."[16] Busygin referred to another quality when he remarked that

the real Stakhanovite is one who worries not only about his own records, who thinks not only about his own work, but who is always ready to help his comrade with advice, who rejoices not only over his own success, but over the success of his whole shop and of his whole plant.[17]

The highest authorities of the party and state took their turn at defining Stakhanovites too. V. I. Molotov dealt at length with

[15] *Novyi gorniak*, no. 13 (1935):7.
[16] *Pervoe Vsesoiuznoe soveshchanie*, 90.
[17] Ibid., 26.

the matter, providing thumbnail sketches of several outstanding Stakhanovites. In summing up, he emphasized that what all had in common was an ability to combine "shock work methods and mastery of technique," a combination that, he asserted, every worker could achieve.[18] Knowing and loving their job "as every honest party and non-party Bolshevik should" was the way K. E. Voroshilov, commissar of defense, described the Stakhanovites he had encountered in the Red Army.[19] And in what inevitably was to become the most frequently cited definition, Stalin characterized Stakhanovites as "people with culture and technical knowledge, who show examples of precision and accuracy in work, appreciating the time factor in work and who have learned to count not in minutes, but also in seconds."[20]

Knowledge, mastery of technique, time (as opposed to task) orientation, love of work, pride in one's achievements but also in those of others, and a willingness to share the secret that made such achievements possible – these virtues were emphasized again and again. But no matter how many times they were repeated, none could serve as an accurate yardstick for determining whether a worker deserved the title of Stakhanovite. Unless Stakhanovism was to be confined to a relatively small group of outstanding record breakers, less ambitious and more precise criteria had to be found.

These criteria inevitably revolved around the two questions of "how much" and "how," the former referring to the amount of goods or pieces produced, and the latter, the technique used to achieve a high level of productivity.[21] Logically, the two were inextricably linked. Norms could be overfulfilled by the adoption of new methods of production. In reality, however, this was not necessarily the case. Under the right circumstances, norms could be exceeded by considerable margins. But deprived of a regular supply of goods of sufficient quality and technical assistance, even Stakhanov himself could not fulfill his norm.

The lack of congruence between these criteria caused a great deal of confusion and wrangling throughout the industrial and political hierarchies. We have already encountered one instance

[18] Ibid., 264–6, 277.
[19] Ibid., 348.
[20] Stalin, *Sochineniia*, 1 (XIV):91.
[21] See O. A. Ermanskii, *Stakhanovskoe dvizhenie i stakhanovskie metody* (Moscow: Sotsekgiz, 1940), 15–23.

of disagreement at the Central Committee level over the appropriate criteria for textile workers.[22] In heavy industry, the issue arose even earlier at a meeting of industrial executives presided over by Deputy Commissar Piatakov. Referring to the failure of a particular machine-tool enterprise to generate more than five or six Stakhanovites, the chief engineer of the superordinate *glavk* suggested that greater attention be paid to workers on time rates and technicians, and that corresponding criteria such as quality of output and the introduction of rationalizing measures be applied. "Why are we busying ourselves with defining the concept of 'Stakhanovite'?" was Piatakov's reply. "A Stakhanovite – that's someone who overthrows all our norms."[23]

Although the anachronistic nature of norms was the major theme of Piatakov's speech, it is doubtful that he intended his remark to be taken literally. In any case, it was not long before party organs were voicing criticism of enterprise officials who employed the rate of norm overfulfillment as the sole criterion for determining Stakhanovites.[24] Cases of workers exceeding their norms by as much as 300 percent but in the process damaging their machines appeared in the press from time to time to underline the importance of employing correct technique.[25] Yet as late as 1938, exclusive reliance on norm overfulfillment was still being criticized as "bureaucratic" and "formalistic."[26]

At issue was not simply finding the right balance of incentives, but a fundamental contradiction in bureaucratic priorities. Faced with the task of "heading up" and developing the Stakhanovite movement, enterprise management and the corresponding party and trade union organizations had to ensure that this was not accomplished at the expense of other goals, including enterprise plan fulfillment. In these circumstances, it was easier to

---

[22] See Chapter 2, Section III.

[23] *ZI*, Oct. 22, 1935.

[24] See the overview of the Stakhanovite movement by the Gor'kii *gorkom*, dated December 4, 1935, in *Istoriia industrializatsii nizhegorodskogo-Gor'kovskogo kraia (1926–1941 gg.)* (Gor'kii: Volgo-Viatskoe knizhnoe izd., 1968), 306; and Ermanskii, *Stakhanovskoe dvizhenie*, 16–19.

[25] *ZI*, Mar. 10, 1937. See the example from the same newspaper reproduced in Ermanskii, *Stakhanovskoe dvizhenie*, 19–20; *Industriia*, Dec. 1, 1937; and *Pravda*, Dec. 27, 28, 29, 1937.

[26] A. I. Rotshtein, *Problemy promyshlennoi statistiki*, 3 vols. (Leningrad: Sotsekgiz, 1936–47), 2:303–4.

employ the criterion of "how much" than to introduce on a mass scale new techniques that may or may not have been appropriate to an enterprise's particular conditions. Preference for the former was strengthened by the ability of enterprise officials to manipulate norm fulfillment figures by means of outright falsification, by counting goods already in stock as current output, or by crediting work done on overtime to normal shift hours.[27]

Occasional objections notwithstanding, higher party and state officials generally acquiesced in the use of quantitative indices to designate Stakhanovites. Thus, when in June 1936 Ordzhonikidze was asked to define a Stakhanovite, he stressed that each branch of industry, enterprise, and even machine ought to have its own specifications. But the examples he gave – the achievement of 10 to 15 percent above the norm for blast furnace work; 12.5 to 20 percent for open-hearth production; and 100 percent for coal mining – were all purely quantitative.[28]

Less tolerable was the practice of including among Stakhanovites those who had merely fulfilled their norms and even those who only occasionally did so. Nevertheless, whether because this modest criterion gave the appearance of vitality to the movement or because it smoothed over internal tensions, enterprise officials were reported to have resorted to it on a fairly wide scale.[29] This was particularly the case after new output norms had been introduced and where, as in the textile industry, workers had considerable difficulty in fulfilling them.

II

The arbitrariness of enterprise officials makes the reported number of Stakhanovites an unreliable index of the extent of the movement. During the last quarter of 1935 and into 1936, there

[27] For some examples, see *Trud*, Apr. 27, 1936; *Stakhanovets*, no. 7 (1937):10; Harvard Interview Project on the Soviet Social System, Russian Research Center Library, Harvard University, interview no. 46, p. 3.

[28] *Stakhanovets*, no. 15 (1936):5–6.

[29] *Bol'shevik*, no. 7 (1936):48; A. Vainshtein, *Voprosy stakhanovskogo dvizheniia v leningradskoi promyshlennosti* (Leningrad: Sotsekgiz, 1937), 14; Harvard Project, no. 513, p. 15; no. 1398, p. 11.

was a general trend toward the adoption of liberal criteria, and this was reflected in part by the tremendous expansion in the number of Stakhanovites. For example, in the Ukraine, there were approximately 39,000 in industry as of November 1935, but more than twice that number, or 89,000, by January 1936, and 145,000 by May.[30] Among industrial enterprises in Leningrad, their number grew from 12,534 in October 1935 to 107,313 by January and 163,076 in April 1936.[31] And in Moscow, the percentage of Stakhanovites among workers in twenty-two of the largest industrial enterprises rose as follows: November 1, 1935 – 6.0; January 1, 1936 – 18.9; February 1, 1936 – 26.1; March 1, 1936 – 27.7; April 1, 1936 – 29.7.[32]

However, there was an additional reason for this increase: The old output norms were still in effect and at least in certain industries were being prodigiously overfulfilled. The official statistics, even taking into account some exaggeration, are impressive. They show that, at the Stalin Automobile Factory in December 1935, one of every three workers on piece rates had fulfilled his or her norm by 151 to 200 percent, and 17 per cent had more than doubled their norms.[33] Results in the enterprises comprising the two main steel trusts of the Ukraine were nearly of the same magnitude. Thirty percent of workers on piece rates had rates of fulfillment between 126 and 150, 14.2 percent had fulfilled their norms by 151 to 200 percent, 3 per cent had more than doubled their norms, and only one in ten workers was not fulfilling his or her norms.[34]

Why was this happening? First, many norms were genuinely outdated, either because they presupposed manual processes that had been mechanized or because of organizational improvements, some of which can be attributed to Stakhanovites. This

[30] *Promyshlennost' i rabochii klass Ukrainskoi SSR, 1933–1941 gg.* 2 vols. (Kiev: Naukova Dumka, 1977), 1:384–5.

[31] *Industrializatsiia severo-zapadnogo raiona v gody vtoroi i tret'ei piatiletok, 1933–1941 gg., dokumenty i materialy* (Leningrad: LGU, 1969), 379.

[32] *Dokumenty trudovoi slavy Moskvichei, 1919–1965.* (Moscow: Nauka, 1967), 162.

[33] V. A. Sakharov, "Zarozhdenie i razvitie stakhanovskogo dvizheniia v avtotraktornoi promyshlennosti v gody vtoroi piatiletki" (kandidat-skaia dissertatsiia, Moskovskii oblastnoi pedagogicheskii institut im. N. K. Krupskoi, 1979), 313–16.

[34] *Trud v SSSR, Statisticheskii sbornik* (Moscow: TsUNKhU, 1936), 149.

was particularly the case in machine building and metalworking, where capital investment had been particularly heavy. By contrast, in the relatively labor intensive textile industry, only 11.6 percent of cotton weavers and 3.1 percent of waterframe operators fulfilled their norms by more than 110 percent in December 1935.[35]

Second, the increase in norm overfulfillment was happening because enterprise management in these branches of industry could afford to let it happen. That is, wage costs as a proportion of the total expenditure of these machine-building and metallurgical enterprises were low relative to more labor intensive industries, and thus payments over and above the wage fund could be at least partially met by the transferal of monies assigned for other purposes. Indeed, the practice of buying some extra effort from workers in this manner at the end of a yearly (or shorter) plan period was fast on its way to becoming a tradition.

This would explain why enterprise officials could afford to allow such high rates and perhaps why they encouraged them. The question nonetheless remains why so many piece workers would exceed their norms by such large margins and on the very eve of the branch conferences that were charged with raising norms. Since these workers were no doubt aware that their norms were about to be raised and that the terms of reference for doing so would at least in part be preexisting levels of norm fulfillment, we can safely rule out ignorance and naïveté. Must we therefore assume that they were fired by Stakhanovite zeal, or could it be that they had no choice in the matter?

The question involves not only these workers' attitudes toward Stakhanovism, but the thorny issue of motivation in general. Against some evidence that workers deliberately gave less than they were capable of, appearing to work hard as if they could do no more, was a general acquiescence to the piece-rate system, the desire of some to get ahead and of others simply to avoid the boredom induced by a slow pace of work, as well as the intrinsic satisfaction derived from a job well done and from pitting one's skill against the norm.[36] Known among American

[35] Ibid., 190.
[36] Harvard Project, no. 159, p. 9; no. 338, p. 24; no. 1497, pp. 17–18. It would be interesting to compare rates of norm fulfillment in the

workers as "making out," these incentives lent themselves to manipulation by management and, in the USSR, by the party as well. However, there were limits to this manipulation, just as the incentives were manifested to a greater or lesser degree depending on the kind of work performed and the circumstances in which it was performed. Once it is recognized that Soviet workers' attitudes toward work were neither frozen nor uniform, but rather depended on a number of contingencies, seemingly inexplicable or irrational behavior becomes more understandable. However apprehensive these workers may have been about an increase in their norms, the fear and frustration of not fulfilling existing norms in the winter of 1935–6 were probably greater.

Then, beginning with the coal-mining industry in February 1936 and extending to other industries over the next several months, new technical and output norms were introduced. The extent of output norm increases varied considerably from one occupation to another. For example, in the blast furnace shops of Ukrainian metallurgical plants, increases averaged 14 to 15 percent; in open-hearth sections, the increase was 23 percent; for rolled iron production, it was 27 percent.[37] The figure cited by several sources for coal mining was 22 to 27.5 percent, but this included increases of 37.9 percent for hewers and 35.8 percent for conveyor operators.[38] In the motor and tractor industry, the average increase was 27.5 percent, but at individual enterprises, it varied from a low of 16 percent (Cheliabinsk Tractor Factory) all the way up to 50 percent (Kuibyshev Carborator).[39] Whereas in 1935 only 30 percent of the norms in this industry had been reviewed, in 1936 the branch conference could boast of having altered 90.4 percent of existing norms.[40]

same enterprises over a number of years, but with the exception of 1935–6, such information is not available.

[37] *Promyshlennost'*, 1:368.

[38] Ermanskii, *Stakhanovskoe dvizhenie*, 248; I. I. Kuz'minov, *Stakhanovskoe dvizhenie – vysshii etap sotsialisticheskogo sorevnovaniia* (Moscow: Sotsekgiz, 1940), 106; Z. G. Likholoboda, *Rabochie Donbassa v gody pervykh piatiletok (1928–1937 gg.)* (Donetsk, 1973), 148.

[39] *Industrializatsiia SSSR, 1933–1937*, 302; Sakharov, "Zarozhdenie," 319.

[40] *Industrializatsiia SSSR, 1933–1937*, 303–4.

However, several features of the more than ninety conferences and the norms they issued provoked criticism. The official summary claimed that the essential method for calculating new norms was to factor the indices of Stakhanovites' productivity into the average of what the general mass of workers had achieved.[41] Accounts of individual conferences portrayed a different story.

It was charged, for example, that the conference of the motor and tractor industry based its calculations of manual time on the average level of productivity over the previous two months.[42] This procedure not only would have given lower norms, but appears to have been in direct violation of the Central Committee's instruction to liquidate the "experiential-statistical" approach to norm determination.[43] In the case of coal mining, the new norms were not even close to the average level of fulfillment as recorded for January 1936.[44] Writing several years later, O. A. Ermanskii could not help wondering whether "many members of the conferences (e.g., in coal) really believed in the practicality of the resolution concerning rationalization measures." "If in this industry," he continued, "intentionally low norms were adopted, then weren't among the motives to do so the '*strakhovka*' [insurance]? Didn't they try to insure themselves against the underfulfillment of production plans, given their poor organization of work?"[45]

As low as Ermanskii and others thought the new norms were, many workers had trouble fulfilling them. At the Elektrosila

[41] *Osnovnye itogi otraslevykh konferentsii tiazheloi promyshlennosti* (Moscow: Za industrializatsiiu, 1936), 5. See also *O novykh normakh i stakhanovskoi rabote. Po materialam otraslevykh konferentsii* (Leningrad: Lenolizd., 1936), 21.

[42] G. Patrunov, "Novye moshchnosti i normy v avtotraktornoi promyshlennosti," *Tekhnicheskaia propaganda*, no. 5 (1936):23, cited in Ermanskii, *Stakhanovskoe dvizhenie*, 242.

[43] The instruction was contained in the resolution of Dec. 25, 1935. See *Kommunisticheskaia partiia sovetskogo soiuza v rezoliutsiiakh i resheniiakh s"ezdov, konferentsii i plenumov TsK*, 9th ed. (Moscow: Partizdat, 1984), 6:287.

[44] *Osnovnye itogi*, 24. In the Donbass, norms were raised an average of 26.6% as compared with 50.0–58.0% overfulfillment of norms in Jan. 1936. Corresponding figures for the Kuzbass were 22.0 and 27.5%.

[45] Ermanskii, *Stakhanovskoe dvizhenie*, 245.

plant in Leningrad, 10.4 percent of piece workers were under-fulfilling their norms in November 1935, but by April 1936, after the new norms had been introduced, the proportion rose to 22.1 percent.[46] As of July, when virtually all enterprises were operating under the new regimen, the percentage of workers failing to reach their norms was as follows: electric power, 9.6; ore mining, 9.9; ferrous metallurgy, 29.1; machine construction and metalworks, 22.8; cement, 31.3; chemicals, 23.0; cotton, 59; saw milling, 51.8; paper, 29.2. To be sure, the situation improved thereafter. By the end of the year, the proportion of workers underfulfilling their norms had fallen in every industry except ore mining, cement, and paper, though it was still an astonishing 44.9 percent in cotton manufacturing.[47] This pattern was to repeat itself after another general revision of norms in the spring of 1937.[48]

The new norms were bound to reduce the number of workers who qualified as Stakhanovites unless the quantitative indices were correspondingly adjusted downward. In fact, if the motor and tractor industry is any guide, the adjustments were in the opposition direction (Table 4.1). Even where the rate of fulfillment remained unchanged, as at the Molotov Automobile Works in Gor'kii (GAZ), it would have been more difficult to reach, since the norm itself had been raised. This accounts, at least in part, for the precipitous drop in the number of Stakhanovites, from slightly more than 8,000 in March 1936 to 3,025 by September. An even steeper decline was registered at the Stalin Automobile Factory (ZIS), where there were 6,321 Stakhanovites as of April 1, but only 1,854 six months later.[49] In fact, the decline in the number of Stakhanovites was a nearly universal phenomenon in the summer of 1936. In Leningrad industry, there were

[46] R. Ia. Khabibulina, *Leningradskie kommunisty – organizatory stakhanovskogo dvizheniia (1935–1937 gg.)* (Leningrad: LGU, 1961), 80; Vainshtein, *Voprosy stakhanovskogo dvizheniia*, 26–7.

[47] A. Vinnikov, "K peresmotru norm vyrabotki v promyshlennosti," *Plan*, no. 8 (1937):38.

[48] Sakharov, "Zarozhdenie," 157–9, 313–16; A. Grigor'ev, "Voprosy proizvoditel'nosti truda v promyshlennosti," *Planovoe khoziaistvo*, no. 2 (1938):77.

[49] V. A. Sakharov, *Zarozhdenie i razvitie stakhanovskogo dvizheniia (na materialakh avtotraktornoi promyshlennosti)* (Moscow: MGU, 1985), 115.

Table 4.1. *Minimal norm fulfillment for Stakhanovites before and after 1936 norm revisions*

Enterprise	Before (%)	After (%)
GAZ	125	125
ZIS	125	125–200
Iaroslav Automobile	100	125–150
Stalingrad Tractor	100	?
Cheliabinsk Tractor	175	150

Source: V. A. Sakharov, *Zarozhdenie i razvitie stakhanovskogo dvizheniia* (*na materialakh avtotraktornoi promyshlennosti*) (Moscow: MGU, 1985), 92.

182,560 Stakhanovites (approximately one-third of all workers) in July, but some 60,000 fewer in September. Thereafter, the number began to creep upwards, and by January 1937, stood at 148,500, or 25 percent of all workers.[50]

Juggling rates of fulfillment was not the only way of making Stakhanovite status more difficult to achieve. Another strategy was to alter the basis for calculating norm fulfillment from time actually worked to the statutory work day. Initiated at the Khar'kov Tractor Factory, this practice was consistent with the emphasis on filling up (*uplotnenie*) the work day but probably violated the 1932 law pertaining to compensation for stoppages.[51] The new method was criticized not on these grounds, but because it prevented even the best Stakhanovites from reaching their norms through no fault of their own.[52] Nevertheless, it continued to be employed at a number of enterprises and in the textile industry served as a basis for distinguishing between shock workers (who fulfilled norms during time actually worked) and Stakhanovites.[53]

[50] *Industrializatsiia severo-zapadnogo raiona*, 379.
[51] The law provided for payment of one-half the base rate for stoppage time that was judged not to be the fault of the workers and full payment during periods of assimilation of new techniques. *Sbornik vazhneishikh zakonov i postanovlenii o trude* (Moscow: Profizdat, 1958), 73.
[52] *ZI*, May 16, 30, June 6, 1936.
[53] Ibid., May 21, 1937; *Industriia*, Sept. 5, 1938; Nov. 24, 1939; *K godovshchine I Vsesoiuznogo soveshchaniia stakhanovtsev. Sbornik statei di-*

But why would enterprise authorities choose to stiffen requirements at this time? The answer surely lies in the resuscitation of the category of shock worker, which had all but disappeared since the advent of Stakhanovism. It was no coincidence that, just as new norms were being introduced, *Pravda* was complaining that "the army of shock workers is being forgotten."[54] The complaint was echoed by Ordzhonikidze, who, at the meeting of Narkomtiazhprom's council, referred to shock workers as "the reserve army from which Stakhanovites would be recruited."[55] The insertion of this revived category between Stakhanovites and non-Stakhanovite workers had several advantages. It provided a means of gradating rewards, which satisfied those who distributed them; it partially compensated workers who would otherwise have been registered as Stakhanovites; and it forestalled the debasement of the more honored title, which no doubt pleased those who received it.

It also meant establishing complex and varied formulas for distinguishing between the two. Table 4.2 gives some idea of the permutations.

Inevitably, some enterprise officials got into a tangle over just who was and who was not a Stakhanovite, and others clearly went to excessive lengths to restrict their number. According to the chief norm setter at the Kalinin Wagon Construction Factory, his enterprise contained 2,242 Stakhanovites, but the figure quoted by the planning section was only 1,347, and in a letter to *Pravda*, a worker from the factory put the number at no more than 500.[56] Then there was the infamous case of the Leningrad Kirov Works, where it was decided that only those "who bring forth rationalization suggestions [and] changes in the technological processes" would be considered Stakhanovites. The result was that even workers fulfilling their norms by 200+ percent were not included, a situation that evoked a reprimand from the party *gorkom*.[57] Obviously stung by the negative publicity

rektorov leningradskikh predpriiatii legkoi promyshlennosti (Moscow–Leningrad: Gizlegprom, 1936), 18.
[54] *Pravda*, May 8, 1936; also June 27, 1936.
[55] *Stakhanovets*, no. 15 (1936):6.
[56] *ZI*, Aug. 1, 1936; *Pravda*, Aug. 31, 1936.
[57] *LP*, Dec. 22, 1936. The resolution also cited similar "distortions" at the Stalin and Elektroapparat factories.

Table 4.2. *Minimal criteria for shock workers and Stakhanovites*

Enterprise	% Norm fulfillment for shock worker	% Norm fulfillment for Stakhanovite	Other criteria for Stakhanovite
Berezniki Chemical	100	110–30	Good quality; reduction of costs
Kolomna Machine	110	150	Mastery of technology
Red Sormovo	105–30	130	—
Tagilstroi	100	150	Adopts Stakhanovite methods
Khar'kov Electrotechnical	100	140	—
Red Proletarian	105–20	130–50	One-third output "excellent" quality
Cheliabinsk Tractor	?	150	—

Source: *Za industrializatsiiu*, June 28 and Aug. 5, 1936.

surrounding its policy, the enterprise administration reversed itself. Consequently, between September 1936 and April 1937, the number of Stakhanovites shot up from 1,032 (4.8 percent of all workers) to 8,181 (36.1 percent), whereas shock workers declined from 5,192 to 4,512.[58]

Stakhanovites could thus be made and unmade merely by the alteration of the criteria by which they were distinguished from other workers. However, there was yet another factor in the making of Stakhanovites that requires a slightly different level of analysis. Up to this point, it has been assumed that all workers had an equal opportunity to satisfy the criteria selected by enterprise administrations. But this was never the case, for the simple reason that conditions of production varied from one shop, section, and shift to another and, indeed even on the same shift, between brigades and individual workers. We have already seen how conditions were arranged so that a production record

[58] *Industrializatsiia severo-zapadnogo raiona*, 380.

164   *Stakhanovism and the politics of productivity*

could occur and how, during Stakhanovite periods, engineering-technical personnel exhausted themselves providing requisite materials and service. But even during a normal working day, some workers were assigned to better machines, richer veins of coal, or better places in the forest than others, and this could make all the difference in terms of fulfilling norms or qualifying as a Stakhanovite.

Theoretically, norm and rate setters could take differences in working conditions into account and make appropriate adjustments. However, this required a considerable amount of extra work, and there was always the risk of criminal prosecution if adjustments were judged to be inspired by anti-Stakhanovite motives.[59] Moreover, workers, in the course of a single shift, could be assigned to several different machines or be given a range of tasks, some with tighter norms than others. It would therefore appear that the assignment of workers was a critical variable in the making of Stakhanovites, and this meant that those who made the assignments wielded much power over workers. Those normally vested with this power were the foremen.

Much remains unclear about the role of foremen in the emerging Soviet industrial hierarchy. One reason for this is terminological. *Prorab, desiatnik,* and *master* can all be translated as "foreman," although each term had its specific origin and connotations. Another was that, although they comprised the largest component of managerial personnel, foremen were the orphans of organizational innovation. As of the mid-1930s, such critical questions as whether they should have the right to adjust piece rates, the way in which their functions should be differentiated from those of *brigadiry,* and the basis on which they should be paid had not been resolved in principle and therefore seem to have been left to ad hoc arrangements within each enterprise.[60]

[59] See, e.g., *SIu,* no. 10 (1936):2; *SZ,* no. 3 (1936):47; no. 6 (1936):30.
[60] For discussions of foremen's responsibilities, see *XVII konferentsiia VKP(b), ianv.–fev. 1932 g. Stenograficheskii otchet* (Moscow: Partizdat, 1932), 29; *Soveshchanie khoziaistvennikov, inzhenerov, tekhnikov, partiinykh i profsoiuznykh rabotnikov tiazheloi promyshlennosti, 20–22 sentiabria 1934 g. Stenograficheskii otchet* (Moscow–Leningrad: ONTI NKTP SSSR, 1935), 215; *Voprosy profdvizheniia,* no. 8–9 (1934):48–56. On

Nevertheless, we know that, to facilitate production, foremen performed a wide variety of functions, so wide in fact that the actual supervision of workers was often a luxury. A photographic study of their working day at the Kirov Works showed that foremen spent 90 percent of their time chasing after tools, repair workers, spare parts, and permissions as well as signing papers of one sort or another.[61] This does not appear to have been extraordinary.

The responsibilities of foremen as well as their position at the bottom of the managerial ladder often put them in a precarious position. If stoppages occurred too frequently and targets were not fulfilled, they tended to be the first to be blamed, either by their superiors, a party functionary, or the workers for whom they were responsible. It was to avoid such recrimination that foremen often resorted to trading favors, doctoring results, and other chicanery. "I could raise the value of any particular piece of work," recalled one foreman from a machine-construction factory. "Let's say one piece of repair work costs 10 rubles and I would raise to 15 by adding some artificial cost to the transport of goods which they could not check upon. And so the worker would overfulfill [sic] his norm by 150 percent."[62] Even so, it was undoubtedly the case that, as another Harvard Interview Project respondent claimed, "it is easier to fire a foreman than a worker."[63]

Stakhanovism seems to have compounded the responsibilities of foremen and the dangers to which they were exposed. They now had to ensure that a sufficient proportion of their workers were adequately supplied and given their fair share of easy tasks in order to produce and maintain the section's or shift's contingent of Stakhanovites. "If I had had no Stakhanovites," re-

foremen's pay, see *ZI*, Feb. 6, 1935; *NFI*, no. 11 (1935):147–56; no. 4 (1936):51–3; no. 1 (1937):14–22.
[61] *ZI*, Oct. 4, 1936.
[62] Harvard Project, no. 99, pp. 8–9.
[63] Ibid., no. 415, p. 8. Eugenia Hanfmann and Jacob W. Getzels, "Interpersonal Attitudes of Former Soviet Citizens, as Studied by a Semi-Projective Method," *Psychological Monographs, General and Applied*, 69, no. 4 (1955):14, conclude that fear played a large role in foremen's motivations.

marked a former construction foreman, "I would be guilty as a foreman because I had to organize it. They asked me: Where are your Stakhanovites? Where are your good workers?"[64] The problem was not only to service a given number of workers, but to know which workers to service. This is where foremen had to exercise their judgment and where many ran into trouble. Sometimes it would appear that the choice was made for them. A worker occasionally, even accidentally, overfulfilling the norm for a certain job might thereby be given especially favorable working conditions. In other cases, foremen would promote their favorites or those who had propitiated them with a liter of vodka or sexual favors.[65] In these ways, they could exploit the dependency relationship that has accompanied the piece-rate system wherever it has been applied.[66]

As quite a few foremen found out, however, that dependency could work both ways. If workers were subjected to foremen's whims, foremen were vulnerable to complaints by Stakhanovites and, apparently less often, workers seeking to become Stakhanovites. These complaints concerned shutting down for lack of supplies, being required to fetch one's own tools, having to perform tasks that paid less or could be done by workers in lower skill categories, and being poorly serviced by inexperienced workers.[67]

None of these instances necessarily sprang from foremen's hostility to Stakhanovites or Stakhanovism, even if that was the way they were treated in the press and by the courts. All may simply have been due to forces beyond foremen's control or the impossibility of balancing competing demands. However, there

---

[64] Harvard Project, no. 611, p. 20.

[65] Ibid., no. 119, p. 5; no. 153, p. 17; no. 456, p. 10; no. 640, p. 6; no. 642, p. 56. Among the charges made against A. L. Vasil'chenko, a foreman at Magnitogorsk, was that he created good conditions for his son, whereas the other brigades were serviced poorly. *Magnitogorskii rabochii*, Jan. 30, 1936.

[66] See, e.g., Miklos Haraszti, *A Worker in a Worker's State*, trans. Michael Wright (Harmondsworth: Penguin, 1977), 49–52, 86–94; and Michael Burawoy, *Manufacturing Consent: Changes in the Labor Process under Monopoly Capitalism* (University of Chicago Press, 1979), 60–2.

[67] *Industrializatsiia severo-zapadnogo raiona*, 348–9; *SIu*, no. 1 (1936):5; no. 2 (1936):4; no. 3 (1936):5; no. 4 (1936):1; *Stakhanovets*, no. 21–2 (1936):53.

were cases that involved more than a question of ability. It was one thing for Stakhanov to claim that the foreman Il'chenko (who happened to be the son of a tsarist policeman) "intentionally did not turn up to work and undermined a Stakhanovite shift."[68] It was another when, according to a report by the district procurator, a shop foreman at a factory in Saratov "systematically opposed the Stakhanovite movement mainly by not permitting any worker to earn more than the foreman." He did this by reducing the current to a milling machine on which a worker had been turning out twelve to sixteen parts instead of the normal eight to nine, after allegedly telling the machinist, "We will see how you will produce sixteen parts." He also transferred another worker, who had been applying an (unspecified) Stakhanovite method, from piece rates to time payment.[69]

Another case, that of a foreman in the children's shoe section of Skorokhod, came to light after the section's outstanding Stakhanovite, Rodionov, complained to the factory administration that the foreman was allocating part of Rodionov's wages to an auxiliary worker. An investigation revealed that Golenkov, the foreman in question, had undermined productivity by tricking workers into thinking that their rates were about to be cut, by refusing to permit rationalization measures on the pretext that output would suffer, and by capriciously raising the output norms for workers who employed Stakhanovite methods on a conveyor. He was also accused of forcing female workers to have sex with him, which appears to have been the grounds for his earlier exclusion from the party. As if Golenkov were not in enough trouble, the investigation revealed that his father had owned a bootmaking workshop that had exploited workers. Golenkov received a sentence of ten years' deprivation of freedom.[70]

Several points emerge from these and other trials. First, it is not surprising that foremen would try to cut the wages of Stakhanovites, some of whom earned twice and three times the average foreman's salary.[71] The anomaly of workers, albeit skilled

---

[68] Stakhanov, *Rasskaz*, 79.
[69] *SZ*, no. 9 (1936):44.
[70] Ibid., no. 6 (1936):29.
[71] For some comparisons, see *Pravda*, Apr. 9, 10, 20, 26, 1936; Sept.

workers, earning more than their bosses occasionally provoked comment in the press to the effect that it was bad for morale and served as a disincentive for promotion.[72] It was not until 1940, however, that the problem was officially acknowledged as serious and was, at least on paper, rectified.

Even so, one wonders whether rate cutting or norm raising by foremen sprang primarily from their personal resentment. With reference to the two cases just cited, it is possible that the reduction of current to a machine had a different motive, namely safeguarding the machine from burnout, and paying an auxiliary worker out of the wages of a Stakhanovite could well have reflected the same "moral economy" that impelled workers to accuse Stakhanovites of attributing the work of others to themselves. This is not to exonerate foremen or to attempt to portray them as champions of ordinary workers, although some foremen undoubtedly did what they could for their unskilled and poorly paid charges. It is rather to suggest that the evidence presented by the authorities may be read in more than one way, and to remain sensitive to the specific circumstances prevailing in the thousands of enterprises that comprised Soviet industry, even if those circumstances cannot be reconstructed in their entirety.

We may now return to two issues that were adumbrated earlier, namely whether the process of making Stakhanovites can be interpreted as also creating a distinct stratum and whether that stratum can be considered an aristocracy of labor. The fact that a large number of workers could be sometime or occasional Stakhanovites should itself cast doubt on the notion of Stakhanovism producing stratification. Much less can we consider Stakhanovites *tout court* as constituting an aristocracy of labor, for an aristocracy comprising upward of 25 percent of all industrial workers is no aristocracy at all.

The issue is not merely one of semantics. Even if we eliminate occasional Stakhanovites from consideration, the use of the term "aristocracy of labor" would do violence to its historical origins and would lead to a misunderstanding of the historical specificity

---

4, 1938; B. L. Markus, *Trud v sotsialisticheskom obshchestve* (Moscow: Gosizdpolit, 1939), 244.

[72] See the decree of May 27, 1940, in *Industrializatsiia SSSR, 1938–1941*, 121–3.

of Soviet working-class formation. As much recent research has demonstrated, a labor aristocracy arose in Britain and to a lesser extent in other parts of western Europe on the basis of its unique skills that enhanced its bargaining power vis-à-vis employers. Mechanization, the dilution of the apprentice system, and the emergence of a white-collar work force undermined the power and status of the craft aristocrats in the late nineteenth and early twentieth centuries. As a result they were compelled to open their unions to the unskilled and semiskilled operatives who had been spurned in the past, thus giving rise to the "new unionism" in Britain and the prodigious growth of trade union membership in other countries.[73] Thus, once shorn of the Leninist imputation of false consciousness, the term emerges as a useful analytical category for demarcating labor struggles during the transition to modern industrial capitalism.

As noted in Chapter 1, Soviet industrialization was not without its own tensions among experienced cadre workers, younger workers who had come up through the Komsomol and factory training schools (FZU), and the mass of "backward" peasant workers. However, far from being able to generate craft unions to hold onto the vestiges of privileges, the experienced workers were swamped by the enormous influx of new semiskilled and unskilled workers. The preexisting trade unions that had afforded them a modicum of bargaining power and even craft self-regulation in the 1920s were pulverized by a combination of purging and a multiplication of the number of unions. Finally, it was not from this stratum, but rather the other two, that the shock workers and Stakhanovites of the Second Five-Year Plan emerged.

III

Unlike the English working class, Stakhanovites did "rise like the sun at an appointed time."[74] Their making was a function

---

[73] Eric Hobsbawm, *Workers: Worlds of Labor* (New York: Pantheon, 1984), chaps. 9–14. For a summary of the literature on the labor aristocracy, see esp. pp. 214–26.

[74] The phrase is from E. P. Thompson, *The Making of the English Working Class* (Harmondsworth: Penguin, 1980), 8.

Table 4.3. *Percentage of Stakhanovites among trade union members in August 1936*

Industry	All workers	Women	Youths
Electrical power	42.0	32.1	55.1
Oil extraction	36.4	14.7	33.5
Oil refining	57.7	38.5	57.5
Ore mining	21.6	5.3	19.4
Ferrous metallurgy	26.2	14.1	25.1
Metalworks	27.7	19.4	26.2
Chemicals	26.7	16.5	34.6
Textiles	19.7	21.3	16.1
Leather goods	39.8	40.4	36.9
Meat processing	38.8	32.0	37.6
Confectionary	35.5	39.0	29.5
Saw milling	30.5	26.0	32.5
Paper	25.8	19.2	25.5
Average	32.9	24.5	33.0

Source: Sotsialisticheskoe sorevnovanie v SSSR, 1918–1964 gg. Dokumenty i materialy Profsoiuzov (Moscow: Proifizdat, 1965), 140.

of Soviet labor and cultural policies that themselves owed much to the specific circumstances of the mid-1930s. Moreover, Stakhanovite status was not so much achieved as granted or withdrawn, as the case may be, by enterprise officials who had their own reasons for both expanding and contracting the number of Stakhanovites. Yet not just any worker was chosen. As much as the criteria were manipulated and as arbitrary as foremen were in distributing favors, certain workers stood a better chance of being designated Stakhanovites than others. Let us examine the kinds of workers who became Stakhanovites.

As Table 4.3 indicates, the proportion of female workers who were Stakhanovites was greater than that of all workers in only three of thirteen branches of industry – textiles, leather goods, and confectionary – and in each case marginally so. The percentage of youths (twenty-three years and under) was also greater in only three cases (electrical power, chemicals, and saw milling) but by considerably wider margins, and in those branches where the proportion was lower, the margins tended to be negligible.

Table 4.4. *Women as a percentage of Stakhanovites in Ukraine (May 1936) and of all workers in the USSR (July 1935)*

Branch of industry	% Female Stakhanovites (Ukraine)	% Female workers (USSR)
Coal mining	4.3	24.1
Ore mining	6.2	23.0
Chemicals	10.2	31.8
Ferrous metallurgy	7.9	23.4
Metalworks	12.5	26.2
Confectionary	41.1	63.3

Sources: For Ukraine, *Promyshlennost' i rabochii klass Ukrainskoi SSR, 1933–1941* 2 vols. (Kiev: Naukova Dumka, 1977), 1:386; for USSR, *Trud v SSSR, Statisticheskii sbornik* (Moscow: TsUNKhU, 1936), 74.

The underrepresentation of women among Stakhanovites is even more apparent from a comparison of their percentage among Stakhanovites in the major branches of Ukrainian industry with their percentage among the entire work force in the USSR (Table 4.4). Although the comparison is not a perfect one, the differences are sufficiently large to merit attention.

This imbalance in the sexual composition of Stakhanovites was the product of a number of factors. First, protective legislation barred women from certain strenuous occupations, such as underground mine work and the operation of heavy lathes, or those that brought them into contact with substances thought to be particularly injurious to their health and that of potential offspring.[75] Several of these were among the "leading occupations" in which Stakhanovites were especially plentiful.

Second, as revealed in the trade union census of 1932–3, the average skill level of women was well below that of male workers in heavy industry, generally falling within the range of semi- or even unskilled workers.[76] To what extent this gap was due to

[75] For brief summaries of the legislation, see Susan M. Kingsbury and Mildred Fairchild, *Factory, Family and Woman in the Soviet Union* (New York: Putnam's, 1935), 100–1, 106, 114–15; and Solomon M. Schwarz, *Labor in the Soviet Union* (New York: Praeger, 1952), 74.

[76] VTsSPS Statotdel, *Profsoiuznaia perepis', 1932–1933 g.* (Moscow: Profizdat, 1934), 23.

lower female enrollment in training schools, discrimination on the job, or other sociocultural factors is a question that cannot be pursued here. The abolition of rationing and the concomitant decline in the number of meals served in factory canteens and other communal dining facilities may well have disadvantaged female workers, whose housewifely chores correspondingly increased. Though referring to *kolkhozniki*, the following example suggests other ways in which family chores militated against women becoming Stakhanovites:

> Let's say that I have a mother and wife. My mother is old and cannot work in the *kolkhoz* but she can work around the house and take care of the children. Now, in this case, I and my wife can both work quite easily, put in all the work-days we are supposed to, and thereby become Stakhanovites. But you on the other hand are married, your wife had several children and there is no grandmother in the house to take care of them. Then, your wife cannot work very much.... But my wife, who has an older woman in the house, can be a Stakhanovite and get a little suckling pig.[77]

If women were underrepresented among Stakhanovites, evidence in addition to that presented in Table 4.3 suggests that the reverse was the case with young workers. As of November 1935, 1,483 of the 1,874 Stakhanovites at the Skorokhod Shoe Factory were under thirty and 738 (39 percent) were less than twenty-five years old. This compares with 32.5 percent of all workers in shoe manufacturing who were twenty-three and under.[78] At the Stalin Metalworks Factory, also in Leningrad, 54 percent of all workers but 74 percent of Stakhanovites were under thirty, and at the Voskov Instruments Factory in nearby Sestroretsk, the corresponding figures were 56.3 and 81.1 percent.[79] Overall, throughout Leningrad industry, 53 percent of all Stakhanovites were under thirty years of age in November 1935.[80]

[77] Harvard Project, no. 27, p. 32. See also, no. 394, p. 6.
[78] M. Eskin, *Osnovnye puti razvitiia sotsialisticheskikh form truda*, 2d ed. (Leningrad: Sotsekgiz, 1936), 160; *Industrializatsiia SSSR, 1933–1937*, 440.
[79] Eskin, *Osnovnye puti*, 119.
[80] R. Ia. Khabibulina, "Opyt sravnitel'nogo analiza sostava stakhanovtsev i uchastnikov dvizheniia za kommunisticheskoe otnoshenie k trudu," in *Rabochii klass SSSR na sovremennom etape*, vyp. 9 (Leningrad: LGU, 1982), 82.

Lack of experience (*stazh*) did not necessarily put workers at a disadvantage in becoming Stakhanovites. According to a survey conducted by the Southern Metallurgical Workers Union in January 1936, 67.9 percent of Stakhanovites at the Stalin Factory in Stalino (formerly and subsequently Donetsk) had less than 3 years of production experience, and a further 19 percent had between three and five years.[81] This was far below the average for metallurgical workers, which in 1933 was 6.1 years and presumably would have been even longer three years later.[82]

Even among Stakhanovites singled out by provincial organs for their impressive results, younger, less experienced workers predominated. For example, among twenty-eight such Stakhanovites in the Kursk *oblast'*, eleven were listed as belonging to the Komsomol, being under thirty years of age, or having less than six years' *stazh*. Since information on age or experience is lacking for all but one of the remaining seventeen, it is possible that several of them were also relatively young and inexperienced.[83]

One factor that might account for the overrepresentation of young workers among Stakhanovites was their relatively high rate of literacy. However, this is not to suggest that literacy was a prerequisite for Stakhanovite status, and there is indeed some evidence of illiterate Stakhanovites even in such relatively advanced enterprises as the Hammer and Sickle Steelworks in Moscow.[84] The wider availability of technical training courses during the Second Five-Year Plan period probably played an even greater role. A survey of 7,138 young workers from nine industrial centers indicates that the proportion of those passing the state technical examinations and receiving "excellent" results was significantly higher among Stakhanovites. The same survey,

[81] *Industrializatsiia SSSR, 1933–1937,* 581.
[82] VTsSPS, *Profsoiuznaia perepis',* 16.
[83] The list, entitled "Production Characteristics of Stakhanovites of Kursk *oblast'* Industrial Enterprises," was originally published in *Sotsialisticheskoe stroitel'stvo Kurskoi oblasti* in November 1936 and reprinted in *Istoriia industrializatsii tsentral'no-chernozemnogo raiona (1933–1941 gg.)* (Kursk, 1972), 270–6.
[84] For comparative rates of illiteracy among different age groups, see VTsSPS, *Profsoiuznaia perepis',* 42, 45. For mention of illiteracy among Stakhanovites at the Hammer and Sickle Factory see *ZI,* Mar. 18, 1936. See also *Profsoiuznyi rabotnik,* no. 11 (1936):10–11; *Klub,* no. 1 (1936):31.

however, shows very little difference between Stakhanovites and other workers in terms of level of formal education (Table 4.5). Yet another factor, adduced by Joseph Berliner from his interviews with Soviet emigrés after the Second World War, was that "young workers... 'in order to show themselves a hero... want to make a name for themselves and beat the older workers.' " It was they to whom Berliner attributed the "sporadic Stakhanovite movements from below, within shop or section, often without the advice of more cautious engineers."[85]

Data on the party membership of Stakhanovites are scarce, and the lack of information on the rate of membership among workers in different branches of industry makes it difficult to draw useful comparisons. We do know that, despite frequent appeals to party members working at the bench to become Stakhanovites and the claims by several Harvard project respondents that preference was given to them, by no means did all such workers find a place in the ranks of the Stakhanovites.[86] Roughly half of all Leningrad factory workers who belonged to the party or were candidate members were enrolled as Stakhanovites by the end of 1935.[87] A Gor'kii *obkom* inquiry of early 1938 showed that, at six major enterprises, the proportion of party members and candidates at the bench who were Stakhanovites ranged from 67.5 percent down to 37 percent and that the overall proportion was 59 percent.[88]

Party members certainly did not predominate among Stakhanovites. In the Ukraine, only 6.6 percent of Stakhanovites were listed as party members as of May 1936.[89] This was well below the national figure of 13.6 percent for all workers at the beginning of 1933, though the purge during that year and the verification of party cards in 1935 no doubt seriously cut into working-class membership.[90] The proportion of Leningrad Stak-

---

[85] J. S. Berliner, *Factory and Manager in the USSR* (Cambridge, Mass.: Harvard University Press, 1957), 274. For more on workers' motivations for becoming Stakhanovites, see chapter 5, this volume.

[86] Harvard Project, no. 17, p. 18; no. 470, schedule B4, p. 9.

[87] Khabibulina, "Opyt sravnitel'nogo analiza," 82.

[88] *Istoriia industrializatsii nizhegorodskogo-Gor'kovskogo kraia*, 356.

[89] *Promyshlennost'*, 1:384–5.

[90] A. I. Vdovin and V. Z. Drobizhev, *Rost rabochego klassa SSSR, 1917– 1940 gg.* (Moscow: Mysl', 1976), 179. Party membership declined by

Table 4.5. *Technical training and education of young workers in nine industrial centers as of January 15, 1936*

	Machine building	Metallurgy	Coal mining	Textile	Total	Stakhanovites	Komsomolites
Technical training							
Passing state technical examination	61	42	51	51	54	68	60
Receiving grade of "excellent"	24	21	29	27	25	36	31
Other preparation (FZU, etc.)	10	8	6	6	8	9	11
Total[a]	71	50	57	57	62	77	71
Education							
Illiterate	0.4	1.3	2.4	0.5	1.0	0.5	0.1
Incomplete primary	13.5	21.4	26.3	13.1	20.7	17.7	11.4
Primary school	39.2	40.4	45.6	43.6	41.4	40.6	38.6
Incomplete secondary	43.5	34.5	24.5	40.0	34.6	38.4	46.6
Secondary and higher	3.4	2.4	1.2	2.8	2.3	2.8	3.3

Note: The nine industrial centers are Moscow, Leningrad, Khar'kov, Dnepropetrovsk, the Donbass, Ivanovo, Orekhovo, Gor'kii, and Sverdlovsk. Data are percentages.
[a] Represents those passing and those exempted from examinations by virtue of other preparation.
Source: Molodezh SSSR, Statisticheskii sbornik (Moscow: TsUNKhU, 1936), 224–5, 238–9.

hanovites who were party members was considerably higher and was also greater than the rate of party membership among all workers in that city, though not by a great margin. For metalworkers the respective percentages were 15 and 11.1, for electrotechnical workers, 14 and 11.8, and for chemical workers, 8.9 and 8.6.[91] Thus, Stakhanovites, who were party members proved to be the exception rather than the rule, although once a Stakhanovite, a worker undoubtedly improved her or his chances of being taken into the party.

Finally, it is necessary to consider skill as a factor in the making of Stakhanovites. Given that mastery of technology figured prominently in the ideal-typical definitions of Stakhanovites, one would expect that Stakhanovites were drawn disproportionately from the higher skill grades. The correlation between the relatively low skill of women and their underrepresentation among Stakhanovites, and Stakhanovites' higher examination scores, support this assumption. Nevertheless, data from the Dzerzhinskii Metallurgical Factory indicate that, at least in this one enterprise, the bulk of Stakhanovites came from the semiskilled categories (Table 4.6).

Unfortunately, no corresponding breakdown of the skill levels of non-Stakhanovites is available. Figures pertaining to all ferrous metallurgical workers as of November 1934 suggest that in this branch of industry the average skill grade of Stakhanovites was perhaps only slightly higher than that of other workers:[92]

Unskilled (1–2)	Semiskilled (3–4)	Skilled (5–8)	Total
64,250 (20.2%)	159,989 (50.3%)	93,831 (29.5%)	318,070 (100%)

33% during 1933–4 owing to the purge and voluntary withdrawals, and a further 16% (excluding demotions to candidate status) as a result of the verifications of 1935, according to T. H. Rigby, *Communist Party Membership in the U.S.S.R., 1917–1967* (Princeton, N.J.: Princeton University Press, 1968), 202–4. Rigby claims that "the *chistka* took its main toll among workers and peasants who entered the party during the mass recruitment drive of the collectivization and first Five Year Plan era" and that "rural communists suffered more heavily than urban" (p. 203).

[91] Khabibulina, "Opyt sravnitel'nogo analiza," 82.
[92] *Industrializatsiia SSSR, 1933–1937*, 475–6.

Table 4.6. *Skill levels of Stakhanovites at Dzerzhinskii Metallurgical Factory (Dnepropetrovsk), January 1936*

Shop	Number of Stakhanovites	Skill category								Average skill category
		1	2	3	4	5	6	7	8	
Blast furnace	426	—	1	73	273	71	44	2	12	4.32
Bessemer	192	—	15	56	44	46	23	8	—	4.16
Rolled iron	423	—	98	78	116	44	61	19	7	3.94
Total	1,041	—	114	207	383	161	128	29	19	4.14

Source: Industrializatsiia SSSR, 1933–1937 gg. Dokumenty i materialy (Moscow: Nauka, 1971), 581.

It is dangerous to extrapolate from this one case to Stakhan-ovites in other industries, or even to assume that their complex-ion remained constant within metallurgy. The mix of skilled, semiskilled, and unskilled workers varied considerably from one branch of industry to another. Even within a particular industry, there were variations among enterprises depending on the age and degree of technical sophistication of the enterprise, the sub-jective evaluations of those who compiled the wage–skill hand-books (*tarifno–kvalifikatsionnye spravochniki*), and the frequently arbitrary judgment of foremen about grading individual work-ers. It should also be noted that the majority of workers in coal and ore mining, textiles, and several other industries were graded not by skill but by task or occupation, which did not take account of individual proficiency.

To summarize, the formula for becoming a Stakhanovite that the political authorities had outlined was at best only partially realized. At certain times in certain enterprises, some workers were able to apply production techniques that resulted in sub-stantial overfulfillment of their norms and lower rates of wastage and production costs. These workers tended to be young, male, and, one would imagine, in relatively good health. They also were likely to be working in an occupation designated as "lead-ing" and to possess skills that would enable them to cope with the tasks assigned to them, should conditions permit. To a large extent, however, the provision of such conditions was deter-mined by foremen, and it certainly enhanced a worker's chance of becoming a Stakhanovite to establish good relations with his or her immediate boss.

None of this, however, explains what it meant to be a Stak-hanovite. Was Stakhanovite status something that workers ea-gerly sought, or were the benefits that it entailed so meager as to be outweighed by other considerations? Why would some workers actively oppose Stakhanovism to the point of taking actions that the state considered criminal? It is to these questions that we now turn.

5

Stakhanovites and non-Stakhanovites

In the preceding chapter, our examination of the category of Stakhanovite revealed a variety of meanings, associations, and ways by which workers came to be designated as such. We now consider what sort of advantages Stakhanovism offered to workers, whether at least for some they were not outweighed by other considerations, and how workers responded to the opportunities and pressures associated with Stakhanovism.

I

Being a Stakhanovite meant very different things depending, first of all, on the kind of Stakhanovite one was. Both in official parlance and in reality, a sharp distinction existed between outstanding and ordinary Stakhanovites. We will have occasion to discuss differences among the latter group, but let us concentrate initially on the relatively small stratum of leading Stakhanovites.

These numbered no more than a few hundred and consisted of workers who had introduced significant improvements in production methods. The core of this group contained some 140 "initiators of the Stakhanovite movement" who were awarded either the Red Banner of Labor or the more prestigious Order of Lenin on December 8, 1935.[1] Although it is not possible to construct a complete social profile based on the list of medal recipients, certain characteristics are discernible and can be supported by other evidence.

Once again, but to an even greater extent, males were dis-

---

[1] For the list, see *Pravda*, Dec. 9, 1935.

proportionately represented. Of the 140, only 32 (22.8 percent) were women, among whom 7 (of a total of 43) received the Order of Lenin. The fact that workers from capital goods industries far outnumbered those from consumer goods among medal recipients is relevant here. Whereas throughout the USSR women comprised well over half of the work force in consumer goods industries, only 1 in 4 workers in capital goods production was female.[2] Indeed, of the 32 female medal winners, 25 were in consumer goods production.

The preponderance of medal winners from heavy industry reflected official priorities. So, too, did the occupations of these workers. Very few of the 140 were engaged in what were classified as auxiliary occupations – maintenance, conveyance, repair work, and the like. Thus, to take mining as an example, ten of sixteen medal winners (all of whom were male) were either hewers or cutting machinists, and of the remaining six, only two were engaged in auxiliary operations. In railroad transport, there were twelve engine drivers, but only one conductor, stationmaster, router, switcher, repairer, and greaser. All twelve drivers were men; the router and repairer were women. Virtually all of the steel- and metalworkers were employed in the key sectors of their respective industries – blast or open-hearth furnaces, and automobile or machine building – and the vast majority were men.

Most were in the prime of their working lives, and there is no reason to doubt that they took their work seriously. Though initially subjected to taunting by their fellow workers and even sabotage of their work, these outstanding Stakhanovites soon came to lead a charmed existence. They were not so much a workers' aristocracy as part of the highest strata of general Soviet society. Never before, anywhere, had individual workers been the object of such attention and adulation. Delegations of workers had been received in the Kremlin for years, and it was not unknown for supplicants from humble backgrounds to travel to Moscow in order to beseech some high official to intercede on their behalf. Some shock workers had been subjects of portraits, both artistic and journalistic, and one, Izotov, could be considered to have

[2] *Industrializatsiia SSSR, 1933–1937 gg. Dokumenty i materialy* (Moscow: Nauka, 1971), 410, 608.

From left to right: Busygin, Stakhanov, Diukanov, and Gudov in the Kremlin, November 1935. From Semen Gershberg, *Stakhanov i stakhanovtsy* (Moscow: Politizdat, 1985), p. 148.

reached proto-Stakhanovite status. However, nothing could compare to the treatment accorded to the outstanding Stakhanovites.

Showered with publicity and gifts, granted access to the press and the offices of Soviet leaders, they assumed the mantle of national heroes. The treatment accorded to them must have required immense psychological adjustment. None could have dreamed of attaining such notoriety. Many were from peasant villages and had never been to a large city, much less the capital, before officialdom beckoned. Busygin claims that when he traveled to Moscow to attend the October Revolution celebrations and speak before the All-Union conference, it was the first time that he had been on a train.[3] It is little wonder, then, that he and other outstanding Stakhanovites were awed by their meeting with Stalin and by hearing their names intoned from the rostrum by other Soviet leaders.

For a time, they attended an almost continual round of meetings, conferences, and celebrations. L. Dolgopolov, the first Stakhanovite cutting machinist, went to Kiev four times, as well as Moscow and Sochi – all in the space of five months – before returning to the Shcheglovka mine "with new eyes."[4] Pasha Angelina, the first female tractor brigade leader and, after Mariia Demchenko, the best-known agrarian Stakhanovite, reported that she worked only three days a month and spent the rest of the time on tour.[5] Other outstanding Stakhanovites, including Stakhanov himself, were temporarily promoted to positions as instructors, enabling them to travel from one enterprise to another to demonstrate their technique.[6]

It is not clear whether these Stakhanovites found such peregrinations disorienting or whether their excursions had a destabilizing effect on the enterprises they visited. Whatever the reason, both Stakhanovites and party leaders soon grew weary of this method of advertising Stakhanovite methods. Angelina complained to the Tenth Komsomol Congress that she was often surrounded by a hundred people shaking her hand and pulling at her jacket, and pleaded to be allowed to return to work. Demchenko made the same request.[7] A. V. Kosarev, first secretary of the Komsomol, illustrated the folly of using the best Stakhanovites in this manner by referring to them as "Chekhovian wedding generals," a term derived from the Chekhov short story in which a petty bourgeois hires a general to attend his daughter's marriage, thereby adding luster to the occasion.[8]

---

[3] A. Kh. Busygin, *Zhizn' moia i moikh druzei* (Moscow: Profizdat, 1939), 30.
[4] *Pravda*, Apr. 4, 1936.
[5] *Desiaty s"ezd VLKSM, Stenograficheckii otchet*, 2 vols. (Moscow: Partizdat, 1936), 1:200.
[6] For Stakhanov's "diary" of his experiences as instructor, see A. G. Stakhanov, *Rasskaz o moei zhizni* (Moscow: Gossotsizd., 1937), 71–87.
[7] *Desiaty s"ezd VLKSM*, 200, 258.
[8] Ibid., 65–6.

Nevertheless, few outstanding Stakhanovites remained at the bench for very long. Even if they stayed on the enterprise payroll, they ceased to be workers, becoming instead living icons. Exactly what they symbolized and what their future careers were will be taken up in subsequent chapters.

We may now turn to the much larger group of ordinary Stakhanovites. The first point to make about this group is its lack of homogeneity. So striking were the differences among these Stakhanovites in terms of the circumstances in which they worked and their rewards that one is tempted to subdivide them into at least two categories.

On the one hand, there were leading Stakhanovites in many factories who, because their enterprises were small and/or strategically unimportant, did not achieve national recognition. The names of these workers flit across the pages of the contemporary press and in reports by party and trade union *obkomy*. They were likely to be invited to local celebrations and be sent by their trade union committees to district or regional conferences of Stakhanovites. Their names were well known to other workers in their shops and maybe even outside of them. Their wages were high relative to those of their workmates but could be less than those of more anonymous Stakhanovites or even non-Stakhanovite workers at enterprises of All-Union importance. Perhaps we should also include in the same subcategory Stakhanovites at larger enterprises who systematically overfulfilled their norms through their leverage as *brigadiry*, because they were favorites of foremen, or as a result of their proficiency at their jobs.

On the other hand, there were what might be called occasional or even accidental Stakhanovites, namely workers who sometimes overfulfilled their norms and received bonuses but who were for all intents and purposes anonymous and virtually indistinguishable from non-Stakhanovites. Such a bipartite division among what we have referred to as ordinary Stakhanovites features in Jerzy Glicksman's analysis, "Conditions of Industrial Labor in the USSR," wherein the distinction is made between intermediate and rank-and-file Stakhanovites.[9]

---

[9] Jerzy Glicksman, "Conditions of Industrial Labor in the USSR: A Study of the Incentive System in Soviet Industry," Harvard Interview Project on the Soviet Social System, manuscript (1954), in Russian Research Center Library, Harvard University, chap. 10.

Tempting as it may be to adopt this model, Glicksman's analysis suffers from two serious problems. First, it is extremely difficult to draw the line between intermediate and rank-and-file Stakhanovites. Ultimately, the distinction boils down to one between "genuinely capable" workers and those "skilled and unskilled who were able to overfulfill their work norms mostly by physical exertion."[10] There is simply no way of knowing who was genuinely capable or why skilled workers who exerted themselves were not included among them.

Second, the model is essentially static in that it does not take account of the extraordinary "mobility" – downward as well as upward – within the Stakhanovite rubric. Glicksman himself points out with reference to the intermediate group that "many of them, like those of the top group, will be made Stakhanovites over and over again or transferred to easier work if in difficulties. But others live continuously under the danger of being unable to maintain their own productivity or keep up with rising requirements."[11] Thus, almost anyone but the outstanding Stakhanovites could be relegated to the status of shock worker or ordinary worker thanks to a change in criteria, an increase in norms, or the replacement of a helpful foreman by one who did not yet know the ropes or with whom amicable relations had yet to be established.

Ephemeral as it may have been, Stakhanovite status did provide a number of advantages that were sufficient to make it desirable to many workers. These advantages were both material and nonmaterial. The most obvious material advantage, but in some ways the most difficult to assess, comprised the relatively high wages that Stakhanovites earned. Data on the average earnings of Stakhanovites compared with those of other workers are, perhaps surprisingly, scarce. One survey, conducted by Gosplan, revealed that the average wage of 7,138 young workers from nine industrial centers was 279 rubles in December 1935. Among Stakhanovites it was 325 rubles. The survey also compared the monthly wages of those who had been employed as workers in January 1931 with what they received nearly five years later. Whereas the difference between future Stakhanovites and all

10 Ibid., 282, 290.
11 Ibid., 284.

workers was small in 1931 (87 compared with 83 rubles), the gap as of the later date was considerable, Stakhanovites earning 344 rubles on average and all workers 275.[12] Especially before the norm increases of the spring of 1936, it was not uncommon for Stakhanovites to earn several thousand rubles per month, or as much as ten times the average monthly wage for industrial workers. Even after norms were raised, Stakhanovite cutting machinists were reported to have received upward of 2,000 rubles per month, and as late as December 1937, after another norm increase had gone into effect, monthly wages of between 1,300 and 1,900 rubles were not unusual among metallurgical workers.[13]

It is important to recognize, however, that such wages were a function not of Stakhanovite status, but rather of the progressive piece-rate system. The latter was one component of official wage policy that produced gross wage inequality among workers. A second major component was the skill grade system and the rated differences between each grade. That is to say, ignoring progressive piece rates for norm overfulfillment, the ratio of a highly skilled worker's standard wage to that of an unskilled worker within the same branch of industry could be as much as 4 to 1.[14] Finally, there were significant differences between wage scales in capital goods industries and those prevailing in the lower-priority consumer goods sector.

The combination of these three factors meant that skilled metalworkers and coal miners could earn 600 to 700 rubles per month without too much difficulty and also without being acknowledged as Stakhanovites. In contrast, even relatively wellk-

[12] S. Kheinman, "K voprosu o likvidatsii protivopolozhnosti mezhdu trudom umstvennym i trudom fizicheskim," *Problemy ekonomiki*, no. 4 (1936):78.

[13] The wages of Stakhanovites seem to have fascinated contemporary Western commentators. See in particular Walter Citrine, *I Search for Truth in Russia* (London: Routledge, 1936), 353; Albert Pasquier, *Le Stakhanovisme: L'Organisation du travail en URSS* (Caen: Robert, 1937), 52–5, 63; Georges Friedmann, *De la sainte Russie a l'URSS*, 2d ed. (Paris: Gallimard, 1938), 113. For examples from the Soviet press, see *Pravda*, Sept. 11, 1937; Jan. 12, Feb. 8, 1938.

[14] Robert Conquest, *Industrial Workers in the USSR* (London: Head, 1967), 48. See Solomon Schwarz, *Labor in the Soviet Union* (New York: Praeger, 1952), 148, where a ratio of 1 : 4.5 is given.

nown Stakhanovite textile and food-processing workers were hard-pressed to bring home more than 400 rubles per month.[15]

One other consideration in this connection is the question of what wages could buy. The raising of "standardized" prices on foodstuffs in enterprise outlets and public canteens and the reduction of free-market prices before the abolition of rationing in 1935 were definitely to the disadvantage of workers receiving low wages, notwithstanding a simultaneous wage increase of around 10 percent across the board. By contrast, workers who could afford to buy goods in *kolkhoz* bazaars and other market outlets benefited from the reduction in their cost, which in the case of bread amounted to as much as 37 percent between January and October 1935 and even more after prices were further reduced on October 1.[16]

There is no doubt that the elimination of the ration system and the accompanying price changes significantly heightened the importance of monetary wages. Yet we should be more cautious than Molotov, who, at the All-Union conference of Stakhanovites, remarked that "a simple interest in increasing their earnings" was "the direct impetus to high productivity" among Stakhanovites.[17] Even after 1935, increased wages were only imperfectly translated into increased purchasing power. Many consumer durables were still priced beyond the reach of all but the most highly paid workers, and goods that ostensibly could be purchased were often unavailable through the mechanism of the market.

In short, if not all highly paid workers were Stakhanovites and not all Stakhanovites were highly paid, then neither the wage as such nor what it could buy was necessarily perceived by workers as the main material advantage of being a Stakhanovite; for Stakhanovites also had access to certain goods and services in the form of bonuses. In this respect, the ground had been well prepared for them by legislation enacted during the First Five-Year Plan period. Ever since 1928, enterprise management had had the authority to allocate a portion of what had been saved

[15] Friedmann, *De la sainte Russie*, 115.

[16] Alec Nove, *An Economic History of the USSR* (London: Lane, 1969), 247–8.

[17] *Pervoe Vsesoiuznoe soveshchanie rabochikh i rabotnits-stakhanovtsev, 14–17 noiabria 1935. Stenograficheskii otchet* (Moscow: Partizdat, 1935), 279.

in terms of production costs below initial estimates to improve employment and living conditions. A decree of August 1931 tied such rewards to rationalization measures and also provided for a fund consisting of 0.5 percent of the total wage bill to be distributed to shock workers. Additional disbursements could be made from savings achieved as a result of socialist competition.[18] This decree was in turn revised in April 1936, when a consolidated director's fund was established in each enterprise. The fund consisted of 4 percent of net profits as per the enterprise's financial plan, plus 50 percent of additional profits. Half was to go toward housing construction and improvements, and the other half could be used for individual premiums and benefits to workers and employees alike.[19]

How enterprise directors actually spent their special funds would be extremely revealing if such information were available. According to one source, only 55 million rubles, or 6 percent of funds, were allocated to housing during 1936–7, whereas 117 million went for premiums. The proportion of premiums that went to Stakhanovites as opposed to managerial-technical personnel or other workers was not indicated.[20] However, it is clear that at least some Stakhanovites were well stocked with deficit and luxury goods.

This was especially true during the first phase of Stakhanovism, when some enterprise administrations went to extreme lengths to celebrate the achievements of their outstanding Stakhanovites. Iasha Iusim, the Stakhanovite with an engineering degree, received from the administration of the Kaganovich Ball Bearings Factory a "magnificently furnished apartment" and presents in the form of fruit, wine, and other foodstuffs.[21] Arriving home one day shortly after his record stint, Busygin found a representative from the local department store with a "small present" sent on behalf of the Molotov Automobile Works by

[18] Abram Bergson, *The Structure of Soviet Wages* (Cambridge, Mass.: Harvard University Press, 1944), 138–9; *ILO Bulletin*, 40, no. 4 (1931):113–18.
[19] *Sbornik vazhneishikh zakonov i postanovlenii o trude* (Moscow: Profizdat, 1958), 226–8; Schwarz, *Labor*, 247–8.
[20] G. Poliak, "O fonde direktora promyshlennogo predpriiatiia," *Planovoe khoziaistvo*, no. 4 (1938):66–8.
[21] Pasquier, *Le Stakhanovisme*, 55.

the assistant director. The present contained a box of apples, three kilograms of meat, ten kilograms of flour, and packages of butter, sausage, cured sturgeon, pirogi, and chocolates. Subsequently, he was presented with an M-1 car.[22]

Before 1935 and particularly during the famine years of 1932–3, shock workers were typically rewarded by increased food rations or special dining facilities in enterprise cafeterias. Once the food shortage eased, the most critical deficit item appears to have been housing. Thus, according to the Soviet historian V. A. Sakharov, "In conditions where the housing problem in the country was extremely severe,... all factories [in the motor and tractor industry] reinforced the practice of giving Stakhanovites first preference in the allocation of living space." At the Stalin Automobile Factory, 100 Stakhanovites received new living quarters in October 1935; at the Stalingrad Tractor Factory, 60 Stakhanovites were so rewarded in mid-January 1936; and by the end of 1937, 800 Stakhanovite families had been installed in new homes especially built for them by the Molotov Automobile Works in Gor'kii. Elsewhere, Stakhanovites had their apartments repaired at the factory's expense or were allocated funds toward the same end.[23]

Other than apartments, Stakhanovites were rewarded with a wide range of goods including radios, bicycles, material from which suits and dresses could be made, or in rural areas, firewood, a sow, or a calf. In one case, a young female Stakhanovite was presented with the selected works of Lenin, prompting one old worker to remark, "That's what the whore deserves."[24] In many enterprises, all Stakhanovites were given priority in the distribution of certain deficit goods. According to a former section director of a canning factory, the system worked as follows: "Each plant had its supply section, and when supplies arrived,

[22] *Novatory, Sbornik* (Moscow: Molodaia gvardiia, 1972), 153.
[23] V. A. Sakharov, "Zarozhdenie i razvitie stakhanovskogo dvizheniia v avtotraktornoi promyshlennosti v gody vtoroi piatiletki" (kandidatskaia dissertatsiia, Moskovskii oblastnoi pedagogicheskii institut im. N. K. Krupskoi, 1979), 112–13. See also Harvard Interview Project on the Soviet Social System, Russian Research Center Library, Harvard University, interview no. 517, p. 36; no. 1497, p. 18.
[24] Harvard Project, no. 65, schedule B2, p. 30.

announcements were made for all Stakhanovites to come pick up their shoes or whatever may have arrived."[25]

Enterprise management was not the only agency that rewarded Stakhanovites. As indicated in Chapter 2, the party committee at Central Irmino mandated that the enterprise administration and the trade union organization provide Stakhanov with certain benefits. Administering a network of daycare facilities, workers' clubs, "palaces of culture," and sometimes literally palatial rest homes, the trade unions were very much involved in granting privileges to Stakhanovites. These consisted of passes to theatrical performances and the cinema, priority in the allocation of places in rest homes and sanatoria, and special excursions on days off and during vacations. Initiated on an ad hoc basis, this policy was formalized in a resolution of December 27, 1935, which also instructed trade unions to guarantee Stakhanovites first priority in subscriptions to new books and serial publications.[26] Finally, as we shall see in the next chapter, Stakhanovites and their families were the major beneficiaries of voluntarism among the wives of managerial and engineering personnel.

Thus, there were considerable advantages to being a Stakhanovite in the sphere of consumption and services. It is important to note, however, that not all Stakhanovites were dazzled by the blandishments associated with their status. There were some who, according to a former engineer, "felt unsure of themselves."

So if they were offered a better apartment, they would turn it down, because they know that they will never be a big shot, nor will they be a Stakhanovite for long, so they do not want to lose their contact with the workers, among whom they will soon find themselves again.[27]

Remaining a Stakhanovite usually required privileged treatment on the shop floor. Indeed, it would not be an exaggeration

[25] Ibid., no. 1486, pp. 13–14.
[26] N. Shvernik, "Stakhanovskoe dvizhenie i zadachi profsoiuzov," *Voprosy profdvizheniia*, no. 10 (1935):19; *Industrializatsiia severo-zapadnogo raiona v gody vtoroi i tret'ei piatiletok (1933–1941 gg.)* (Leningrad: LGU, 1969), 290, 350; *Sbornik vazhneishikh zakonov*, 235, 238.
[27] Harvard Project, no. 388, schedule B10, p. 80.

to say that to workers the wellspring of Stakhanovism was the opportunity it provided for working under improved conditions and, by these means, obtaining higher wages and the rewards that money could not buy. The account by the *Pravda* journalist Gershberg of an incident at Central Irmino one month after Stakhanov's record was set is extremely revealing in this respect:

Petrov arrived at the rostering point with a group of miners. From the conversation in which everyone used "ty" and "Kostia" when addressing Petrov, it was clear that the hewers from the night shift were upset because the preps had not arrived on time and the supply of compressed air was inadequate.

"Like Stakhanov, just like Stakhanov," cried a middle aged hewer who demanded that Petrov take up the matter with the party committee.

"We want to start work, Kostia," shouted another. "Or has all the air been pumped into Stakhanov's shelf?" ... "We all want to work like Stakhanov, Kostia, so either arrange it or don't banter at meetings."[28]

This scene was to be repeated with slight variations at other mines and industrial enterprises throughout the country. When workers' desire to work "like Stakhanov," that is, to be adequately supplied and serviced, was fulfilled, they stood a good chance of becoming Stakhanovites. Although in many cases temporary, that status gave them some leverage to demand continued attention from technical personnel and access to privileges that could well have made a difference in terms of their standard of living and hence their physical capacity to overfulfill their norms systematically.

II

We are now in a position to assess the nature and extent of worker antipathy to Stakhanovism. In Chapter 2 it was argued that the association of Stakhanovites' records with the possibility of norm increases and the attribution to individual Stakhanovites of achievements that involved several workers were significant causes of workers' opposition, especially during the first phase of Stakhanovism. It remains to determine what other sources of hostility existed and whether that hostility was directed primarily

[28] *Novatory*, 106.

against Stakhanovism as such, perceived distortions in the way it was organized, or individual Stakhanovites.

The consensus among Western scholars is that Stakhanovism was "unpopular" and Stakhanovites "were also anything but popular with rank and file workers."[29] Support for this view can be found among some of the Harvard Interview Project's respondents. For instance, a former carpenter described Stakhanovites as "usually...bootlickers, people who informed on their fellow workers." A packer claimed that "the result of their work was that everybody else had to work hard too." "The workers did not like them," asserted a bookkeeper, and a *kolkhoznik* called them "the biggest scoundrels."[30] Personal antipathy was part and parcel of regarding Stakhanovism as exploitative. Typical of this attitude was the remark of a former coal miner: "The whole movement was designed to increase norms and give people less of an opportunity to earn money."[31]

However, it almost goes without saying that these people did not represent a cross-section of attitudes within Soviet society and perhaps still less among Soviet workers. For the most part, they had lived under German occupation and either were sent as *Ostarbeiter* to work in German factories or had accompanied the German army as it retreated westward. Desperate to avoid repatriation and/or to become United States citizens after the war, many could easily have been disposed to give opinions that they thought would please their American interviewers.[32]

It is all the more significant, therefore, to find among the interview transcripts more balanced and even positive assessments of Stakhanovites and Stakhanovism. For example, one chief engineer distinguished between "phony" Stakhanovites

---

[29] Leonard Schapiro, *The Communist Party of the Soviet Union*, 2d ed. (London: Methuen, 1970), 466; Merle Fainsod, *How Russia Is Ruled*, rev. ed. (Cambridge, Mass.: Harvard University Press, 1965), 320. See also J. N. Westwood, *Endurance and Endeavour: Russian History 1812–1980*, 2d ed. (New York: Oxford University Press, 1981), 308.

[30] Harvard Project, no., 4, p. 8; no. 5, p. 8; no. 73, p. 5; no. 133, p. 17.

[31] Ibid., no. 456, p. 13. See also no. 279, schedule B3, p. 9; no. 492, p. 8.

[32] Problems associated with this sample are discussed in Alex Inkeles and Raymond A. Bauer, *The Soviet Citizen: Daily Life in a Totalitarian Society* (Cambridge, Mass.: Harvard University Press, 1961), 3–40.

who were "products of the *partorg*" and those who did "a real job," fulfilling their norms by as much as 200 percent under normal conditions. Another respondent, a former *kolkhoznik*, similarly noted that "there were real Stakhanovites who worked well, and then there were those who only joined at vodka with the brigadiers."[33] Several claimed that Stakhanovism actually reduced the burden of work for others. While acknowledging that Stakhanovites "made the norms higher, so that another worker, who could not work so well, was pushed lower," an armaments factory worker also pointed out that, in many cases, "they worked as rationalizers and made work easier." "The Stakhanov movement gave a push to these problems [of organization]," asserted another respondent. "The Stakhanov movement is essentially a movement of organizers. Interest in organization began to grow." And an ex-foreman, asked if Stakhanovism made his work harder, replied, "No, on the contrary. It made it easier. Once a worker is a Stakhanovite, he knows his job and the foreman can rely on him."[34]

Some of these comments can be read in different ways. By making work easier for the foreman, Stakhanovites did not necessarily improve conditions for other workers. Still, some respondents expressed outright sympathy and respect for Stakhanovites. "Men become Stakhanovites," remarked a former journalist with reference to *kolkhozniki*, "because it is the closest thing to improving their own property.... I have seen links on a *kolkhoz* work very hard, not because the party or Stalin wants them to, but because they want to improve their own section of the *kolkhoz* land." A construction foreman noted that "many of them in order to get ahead, to make a career, try to work hard and show what they have, and then when they have done well, they leave work and become instructors."[35]

Implied by these remarks was the belief that Stakhanovites deserved their rewards. One former *kolkhoznik* was explicit about this. Asked whether Stakhanovites received more for their work, he replied, "No. They received more than I did only according to the extra amount of work which they did. They got the same

[33] Harvard Project, no. 190, pp. 14–15; no. 640, p. 6.
[34] Ibid., no. 13, p. 10; no. 92, p. 5; no. 610, schedule B2, p. 3.
[35] Ibid., no. 67, p. 59; no. 611, p. 22.

"Broader the ranks of Stakhanovites of socialist fields!" From *Sputnik agitatora*, no. 8 (1936).

rate of pay."[36] Finally, among the very few respondents who admitted to having been Stakhanovites, there was one, a mining mechanic, who claimed: "Relations between these and the plain workers were good. The workers felt that if these Stakhanovites had to strain and could do so much work, they were welcome to produce more."[37]

There seems no more reason to accept the prevailing Western view than there is to agree with the Soviet contention that, among workers, only "backward" elements consisting of former kulaks or those harboring petty bourgeois attitudes opposed Stakhanovism. Precisely because Stakhanovism was manifested in different ways in different enterprises and at different phases of its development and because there was such a variety of Stakhanovites differentially motivated and rewarded, such sweeping generalizations and sociological stereotypes simply will not do. The Stakhanovite who had just arrived in a district of the West-

[36]　Ibid., no. 399, p. 8.
[37]　Ibid., no. 530, pp. 11–12. A search through the transcripts turned up only three former Stakhanovites.

ern *oblast'* to join a timber-cutting brigade of *kolkhozniki* was very different from the experienced hewers at Central Irmino mine who demanded that "Kostia" arrange conditions for them as in Stakhanov's case. Relations with their fellow workers were accordingly different.

In his brief monograph on Soviet trade unions, Isaac Deutscher advanced an argument that dissented from the prevalent Western view of workers' attitudes toward Stakhanovism, yet was almost exactly opposite to Soviet contentions. Deutscher included among those opposed to Stakhanovism "the cadre of industrial workers who had been brought up in class consciousness and class solidarity and taught to regard equality as the ultimate goal of socialism." This group, he claimed, "was strongly represented among the lower and middle officials of the trade unions." By contrast, he saw "an inherited peasant individualism ... still strong in the Soviet working class" as a critical factor in the effectiveness of Stakhanovism's appeal.[38]

This argument has two shortcomings. The first has to do with the question of equality. It is quite true that Stakhanovism represented another nail in the coffin of equality among workers. However, that coffin had been deliberately and relentlessly under construction at least since 1931, when Stalin attacked "petty bourgeois egalitarianism" (*uravnilovka*) and when the piece-rate scales were revised so as to expand the differentials between skilled and unskilled workers. What is more, equality as the ultimate aim of socialism surely was not to be restricted to manual workers, but was a vision that encompassed the entire social order. Why, then, did Deutscher's class-conscious workers and trade union officials fail to register any significant complaint against the striking inequalities between workers and the "commanders of production," which, at least in terms of wage and salary levels, reached an all-time high in 1933?[39]

The second shortcoming is Deutscher's identification of Stakhanovism's effectiveness with "an inherited peasant individualism." He notes, quite correctly, that workers with peasant

[38] Isaac Deutscher, *Soviet Trade Unions: Their Place in Soviet Labour Policy* (London: Royal Institute of International Affairs, 1950), 114–15.

[39] Such protest was fairly widespread in the years after the 1917 revolution and throughout the 1920s.

backgrounds were prominent among the outstanding Stakhanovites, but was this a function of those backgrounds? Collectivism in the form of the village commune and artels was alive and flourishing among Russian peasants before another form, the *kolkhoz*, was imposed on them during the First Five-Year Plan. It was not so much individualism in the villages as the waning and suppression of the traditional means by which peasants negotiated their passages into the industrial work force that may account for their susceptibility to Stakhanovism's appeal.

To take Stakhanov's by no means untypical case, he followed in the footsteps of his father and grandfather by journeying with other peasants from his native Orel village to the Donbass but, unlike his forebears, did not make the return trip. Again, like them, he initially boarded with *zemliaki* (people from the same village or district) but by 1928 had moved into a bachelors' dormitory and later married the dormitory's cook.[40] All the while, the traditional form of work organization, the artel, was under assault by party and union officials.[41] Although artels persisted well into the First Five-Year Plan period, there were only faint traces of their existence thereafter. It thus would be more accurate to say that peasant collectivism gave way to an individualism bred by the pulverization of Soviet society and the massive technological and material changes of the early 1930s.

Yet none of these processes was complete by 1935, and even if Deutscher misplaced the sources of workers' solidarity and its opposite, he was clearly onto something about the nature of workers' reactions to Stakhanovism. Sifting through the legal journals' reports of court cases, one comes across quite a few cadre workers and lower trade union personnel who were sentenced for anti-Stakhanovite activity. Indeed, incomplete statistics from *oblast'* courts show that, by March 1936, slightly more than half (50.8 percent) of such sentences were handed out to workers; 20 percent involved *brigadiry* and foremen; 11.5 percent, shop supervisors and employees; and 13.1 percent, *kolk-*

---

[40] Stakhanov, *Rasskaz*, 7–15.
[41] See Chapter 1, Section III. See also the reference to construction artels being "broken down" at Dneprostroi in E. H. Carr and R. W. Davies, *Foundations of a Planned Economy*, 3 vols. (Harmondsworth: Penguin, 1974–7), 1:490.

hozniki; the remaining 2.6 percent were classified as "others." Of all those sentenced, 11 percent were party members.[42]

What was judged by the authorities to be anti-Stakhanovite activity covered a multitude of acts ranging from the spreading of malicious rumors and verbal threats to intimidation, sabotage of Stakhanovites' work, and physical violence, occasionally resulting in death. Sentences ranged from probation to execution. The published reports of the investigations and charges provide fascinating glimpses into the day-to-day relations among workers both on and off the shop floor. They suggest numerous sources of tension, not all of which were necessarily associated with Stakhanovism.

For example, there was the case of two brothers, both railroad workers, who stole a tool from a Stakhanovite turner. After the latter had found the tool in the brothers' tool crib and threatened to report them, he was beaten. Whether the theft and subsequent beating represented a conscious attempt to sabotage the Stakhanovite's work as the court concluded or stemmed from a shortage of tools and fear of reprisals is not clear.[43] The beatings to which Komissarova was subjected by her alcoholic husband would seem to have had little to do with Stakhanovism except for the fact that she was the Leningrad Rabochii Textile Factory's outstanding Stakhanovite and a delegate to the All-Union conference in Moscow. Komissarov was consequently given a four-year sentence under article 73^1 of the Criminal Code, the article that was invoked in more than half of all sentences imposed for anti-Stakhanovite activity in Leningrad between December 1935 and March 1936.[44]

Then again, in many other cases there is little reason to doubt that antipathy toward Stakhanovism and its individual exemplars

---

[42] *SIu*, no. 8 (1936):4.

[43] Ibid., no. 4 (1936):7. The problem of tool pilferage was characterized by John Littlepage as "one of the most annoying and most disrupting occurrences in industry." For him, "the most useful principle in the Stakhanoff movement was the insistence that engineers and foremen should be held responsible for keeping workers constantly supplied with small tools and equipment." See John D. Littlepage and Demaree Bess, *In Search of Soviet Gold* (New York: Harcourt, Brace, 1939), 243–6.

[44] *SZ*, no. 6 (1936):27, 30.

was involved. Clearly, the woodworker who replaced the names of those on the factory's honor board with others – including his own – that had originally appeared on the board of disgrace was symbolically rejecting the official notion of what constituted an exemplary worker.[45] More often, however, the targets were less systemic and more personal. One worker at the Artem mine was reported to have told another who had just adopted a Stakhanovite method, "In the old days, we used to hang such Stakhanovites by the dozen."[46] A Nikolaev worker, Shtembers, described by investigators as a hooligan who had been repeatedly sentenced by the production-comrades court, went too far when he cursed the Stakhanovite Vlasova for overfulfilling her norm and then threw a spanner that injured her.[47] Other Stakhanovites were taunted with such names as self-seeker, careerist, and upstart, and one, also from Nikolaev, had to be confined to a psychiatric hospital after being continually mocked and abused.[48]

Often, more than one worker was involved in these actions. Shunning by the entire shop was reported in one case; in another, three workers convinced a party organizer to compose and other workers to sign a report alleging that a Stakhanovite stitcher had overfulfilled his norm by secretly taking home patterns and working there.[49] Then there was the case of four country lads who, having recently been hired by the Frezer Factory in Moscow, allegedly fell under the influence of a worker dismissed nine months earlier for drunkenness. The five of them "fell on" the Red'kin brothers, the first Stakhanovites in the factory, shouting, "Beat the Stakhanovites." Sentences of five and four years, respectively, were handed out by the people's court of the Stalin *raion*.[50]

Trade union officials and party organizers were occasionally mentioned as coconspirators, but more frequently the reports referred to their failure to take any action against the culprits.

[45] Ibid., no. 6 (1936):30.
[46] Ibid., no. 7 (1936):70.
[47] Ibid., no. 6 (1936):72.
[48] See Smolensk Party Archive, WKP-97, p. 40; *SZ*, no. 3, (1936):7; *SIu*, no. 15 (1936):11.
[49] *SZ*, no. 6 (1936):28, 70.
[50] *Vechernaia Moskva*, Jan. 5, 1936.

In one case that has already been cited, that in which the Stakhanovite turner Likhoradov was the victim, the chairman of the Briansk City Council of Trade Unions claimed no knowledge of the incident when questioned by a *Pravda* correspondent.[51] Moreover, after Likhoradov's antagonist had been sacked, an inspector from the Central Committee of the Union of Transportation Machinery Workers revoked the decision, and the matter was referred to the district court. Taking into account that Sviridov had worked for a number of years without reproof, the court considered his dismissal "harsh" and ordered that he be reinstated and paid for the period of his absence. Only then did the *oblast'* court intervene to correct what it considered a "grave political error."[52]

These reports by no means exhaust the record of anti-Stakhanovite actions and only hint at the motives behind them. Indeed, three common sources of tension between Stakhanovites and non-Stakhanovite workers hardly figure at all in the published version of court cases. One that seems to have been most widespread during the first phase of Stakhanovism was the deskilling or demotion of workers as a result of the application of Stakhanovite methods. Indicating that some eighty-two workers at three Leningrad factories had been transferred to subordinate positions, a report sent to the *obkom* party secretary, A. A. Zhdanov, in November 1935 asserted that the question of the rational use of "freed labor power" had caused fear among many other workers of possible demotions. The report went on to state that, at one breadmaking factory, "a number of workers had come to think that 'it was better to ask the director to be dismissed rather than wait to be discharged' " and that the same opinion could "especially be observed" among textile workers.[53]

The second source, which persisted so long as Stakhanovites were favored by foremen and other managerial-technical per-

[51] *Pravda*, Oct. 31, 1935.

[52] *SIu*, no. 3 (1936):5. It should also be mentioned that Likhoradov's coupons for purchasing additional foodstuffs were taken away by the trade union committee on the grounds that, according to an official quoted by Likhoradov, "You are earning a lot – 350 to 380 rubles – while workers with long service records are having trouble making 120 or 140 rubles." *ZI*, Oct. 24, 1935.

[53] *Industrializatsiia severo-zapadnogo raiona*, 350.

sonnel, was resentment against the inequality of service. Having already noted that the desire to be adequately serviced was the wellspring of the Stakhanovite movement, we must acknowledge that the frustration of this desire was a wellspring of opposition to Stakhanovism. The machinists who asked Gudov to "say that you will establish a record on our machines [so that]... they also will be carefully prepared" may, as Gudov recounts, have been concerned about not having "to stick our faces in the mud."[54] But in other cases, if not this one, more than honor was involved. It may well have been the fear of retaliation that prompted one Stakhanovite in the children's shoe section of Skorokhod to request the factory committee chairwoman to "see to it that enough work is found for everyone" and the latter to turn to *Trud* to inquire "what actually is the moral position of a Stakhanovite when he is fully occupied while his neighbor is idle?"[55]

Finally, while some skilled production workers feared demotion and others resented neglect, auxiliary workers had cause to feel alienated by Stakhanovism. Drafted to service Stakhanovites and their machines, these workers rarely shared the prestige or monetary rewards accorded to Stakhanovites. Along with unskilled production workers, they were generally ignored by the *partorgy* and the trade union organizations and reciprocated in kind. Although they were likely to express their disenchantment in informal "go-slows" that ate up the productivity increases of production workers, it is likely that some of those whom the reports of anti-Stakhanovite activity referred to as "hooligans" were in fact auxiliary workers.[56]

Summing up this analysis of anti-Stakhanovite behavior, we can say that its sources were varied and complex. As Deutscher asserted, solidarity was a key factor, although there is little evidence that opposition to Stakhanovites and Stakhanovism sprang from the kind of solidarity he posited. Rather, for *kolkhozniki*, it was the traditional solidarity of the village expressed against outsiders – often recent migrants – who did not share their work

[54] Quoted in O. A. Ermanskii, *Stakhanovskoe dvizhenie i stakhanovskie metody* (Moscow: Sotsekgiz, 1940), 313.
[55] *Trud*, Oct. 25, 1935.
[56] See Sakharov, "Zarozhdenie," 162–3, and for an interesting case of sabotage by an auxiliary worker at a copper smelting plant, *SIu*, no. 8 (1936):6.

culture;[57] for workers and not a few trade union and party officials, it was the solidarity forged by learning how to cope with
or "make out" in an industrial system that was vulnerable to
informal negotiation and output restriction. Insofar as Stakhanovism represented an attempt to eliminate this vulnerability, it
and the encouragement and protection it gave to "upstarts" and
"careerists" challenged that solidarity.

The extent to which antipathy toward Stakhanovism existed
among workers is even more difficult to assess than its sources.
On the one hand, it is clear that those charged with anti-
Stakhanovite activity represented only a fraction of workers who
for one reason or another resented Stakhanovism. On the other,
what the authorities considered anti-Stakhanovite acts often
stemmed from personal antagonisms in which the victim only
happened to be a Stakhanovite. Indeed, since Stakhanovite behavior was supposed to consist of punctuality, sobriety, cleanliness, mastery of technology, and other officially endorsed
qualities, any manifestation of lateness or absenteeism, drunkenness, slovenliness, and poor workmanship (*brakodel'stvo*) could be
interpreted as anti-Stakhanovite, especially when such behavior
impeded the work of Stakhanovites.

Further complicating the assessment is the impossibility of
knowing whether the accusations hurled against Stakhanovites
– that they were "phony," secretly worked at home, caused breakdowns, slept with the foreman, had been a Makhnoist bandit,
or hailed from socially alien elements – contained any truth.
Although the authorities tended to regard such accusations as
attempts to discredit the Stakhanovite movement, they may well
have stemmed from outrage that such workers could be rewarded as genuine Stakhanovites. Such was the case of a worker
of good standing as a spirits factory in Saratov, who wanted to
know why if "we all work the same, only one received a bonus."[58]

Nor is it possible to gauge accurately the extent and intensity
of anti-Stakhanovite activity over time. Figures from Sverdlovsk
oblast' indicate that the procurator's office was especially busy
between January and March 1936. Whereas in the last quarter

[57] For examples of such cases, see *SZ*, no. 1 (1936):49; no. 7 (1936):5.
[58] Ibid., no. 9 (1936):44. See also *SIu*, no. 8 (1936):5.

of 1935, the court processed 34 cases, handing out sentences to 47 people (13 of whom were workers), in the first quarter of 1936, there were 161 cases tried and 241 people sentenced.[59] Many if not most in the latter period were related to incidents occurring in December and January, that is, during the transition to Stakhanovite periods and before the new norms had been formulated. There are virtually no data on the number of court cases involving anti-Stakhanovite activity after March 1936 and, indeed, reports of individual cases are few and far between.

It could be surmised that, once it became clear that Stakhanovism was not merely one in a series of campaigns but a long-term component of Soviet industrial relations, workers' overt actions against Stakhanovites declined. Also, the severity of sentences imposed on those convicted of such actions may have had its intended deterrent effect. However, we know from other sources that neither anti-Stakhanovite sentiment nor its most obvious manifestations ceased.

The Smolensk Party Archive contains some interesting material testifying to their persistence. For instance, the minutes of the Tumanovo *raikom* party meeting for September 18, 1936, characterized the attitudes of ordinary workers toward Stakhanovites at a local brickmaking factory as "criminal." Several workers, for example, had laughed at and otherwise mocked a Komsomolite who had demonstrated a Stakhanovite technique. This was no isolated incident. Some fourteen months later, in December 1937, the *raikom* instructed the factory's director to investigate workers' collectives and dismiss those "alien" elements who had been violating labor discipline. The director, reprimanded earlier for his "bureaucratic relation to the Stakhanovite movement," was now threatened with expulsion from the party for the same reason.[60] Another report, this time by the industrial section of the *obkom*, noted that in Sychevka district, a number of Stakhanovite *kolkhozniki* had been beaten and the culprits had gone unpunished.[61] Later still, in 1938–9, the mobilization of Stakhanovites in connection with laws designed to tighten labor

---

[59] *SIu*, no. 4 (1936):1; no. 14 (1936):3.
[60] Smolensk Party Archive, WKP-97, pp. 40–1, 92.
[61] Ibid., 303.

discipline sparked occasional retaliation by workers labeled "disorganizers."[62] Finally, there is some evidence of a subculture of antipathy among workers expressed in black humor and the use of epithets such as "stakanovtsy" (literally, "drinking-glass ones") to refer to Stakhanovites who hobnobbed with the bosses, and "Stakhanovite goods" to designate defective articles or those of low quality.[63]

If the number of reported court cases is not a very accurate index of the extent of anti-Stakhanovite activity, it does suggest how the authorities chose to handle workers' dissidence. Initially, *oblast'* procurators were instructed to take the most severe view of crimes against Stakhanovites. The argument ran that, since Stalin had characterized the Stakhanovite movement as fundamentally revolutionary, any conscious attempt to undermine it should be regarded as a counterrevolutionary act, punishable by the appropriate article (article 58) of the Criminal Code. This was to be applied irrespective of social background or occupation.[64]

Soon, however, the RSFSR commissar of justice, Krylenko, was complaining that workers who merely had exhibited "backward" attitudes toward Stakhanovism or ignorance of its benefits had been tried as counterrevolutionaries and sentenced to long terms. He cited as an example the sentencing of a worker to five years because she had shouted to her workmate, "You just want to earn a bonus, you Parisian lady," after the latter had advocated the adoption of a Stakhanovite method.[65] Indeed, most of the articles that detailed the prosecution of crimes against the Stakhanovite movement were couched in terms of the importance of exercising class justice, that is, taking into account the social backgrounds, occupations, and past records of the accused. According to these criteria, workers of good standing were ipso facto incapable of consciously undermining Stakhanovism. Their

---

[62] A. Kirk to Secretary of State (March 1, 1939), U.S. State Department Decimal File, National Archives, 861.504/346, citing *Sovetskaia Ukraina*, Jan. 18, 1938, and *Izvestiia*, Feb. 16, 1939.

[63] Harvard Project, no. 5, p. 8; no. 309, p. 10; no. 1011, p. 55; no. 1497, p. 18; Inkeles and Bauer, *The Soviet Citizen*, 70.

[64] *SIu*, no. 1 (1936):5.

[65] Ibid., no. 5 (1936):2.

acts were to be interpreted as stemming from bad personal relations or misunderstandings with Stakhanovites. In those instances in which trade union or party officials had been implicated, primary responsibility was to be placed with the "hooligan" or "backward elements" who had deceived them by spreading malicious lies.

The central judicial authorities did more than instruct *oblast'* procurators. They reduced and reversed many of the sentences imposed on workers, particularly in Sverdlovsk *oblast'*, where the procurator had been especially zealous. As a result of the RSFSR Supreme Court's review carried out in February–March 1936, more than half of the sentences imposed in the *oblast'* were terminated or reduced.[66] Throughout the republic, the proportion of workers among those whose sentences were confirmed was only 17.5 percent, as compared with 50.8 percent before the review.[67] Criticism of judicial-investigative organs to the effect that they had failed "to show that the enemies of the Stakhanovite movement are class enemies and parasitical elements" persisted for some time, but there was otherwise little discussion in the legal journals of court cases involving anti-Stakhanovite activity.[68] As an ironic footnote, we might add that in September 1937, when the new party bureau of the Western *oblast'* passed judgment on the work of the procuracy and court, it condemned their leading officials for a number of "Right-Trotskyite practices," including "the closing, glossing over, and delaying of important political cases ... the beating and persecution of Stakhanovites, wrecking in the sovkhozes, kolkhozes, and MTS,

---

[66] Ibid., no. 11 (1936):8.

[67] Ibid., no. 8 (1936):5.

[68] Ibid., no. 30 (1936):7, see also no. 33, (1933):19. Only in 1940, when the courts became involved in trying workers who were accused of violating one or more of the recently passed laws against absenteeism and the unauthorized termination of employment, did the Supreme Court intervene again. An order issued on August 15 declared it "inadmissable and forbidden ... to include in the sentences references to favorable attestations in which the delinquents are characterized as Stakhanovites, exemplary workers, etc. Stubborn violators of labor discipline," the order continued, "can never be Stakhanovites or exemplary workers." *SIu*, no. 13 (1940):6–10, quoted in Schwarz, *Labor*, 113.

and plundering of socialist property."[69] Better to have been sorry than safe!

This is not to suggest, however, that workers who overtly opposed Stakhanovism or attacked individual Stakhanovites could count on getting off scot-free. For aside from the people's court system, there were the production-comrades courts (PTS). Created in accordance with a resolution of the Sixteenth Party Congress in 1930, these enterprise-based courts had powers to fine and to recommend the revocation of trade union membership, the regrading downward, and/or criminal prosecution of "violators of labor discipline."[70] Throughout 1936, judicial authorities pointed to these courts as appropriate mechanisms for dealing with cases involving backward workers who ridiculed Stakhanovites, undermined Stakhanovite periods, or were disruptive in other ways.[71]

Unfortunately, we do not know how many such cases these courts handled or how they handled them. In some districts of Moscow, at least as of the spring of 1936, the courts do not seem to have been used at all. This situation may have changed during 1937–8, when other administrative mechanisms were breaking down under the strain of the Great Purges. In any case, the legislation of 1938–9, which recriminalized infractions previously under the purview of the comrades courts, suggests that they were not functioning to the satisfaction of higher judicial authorities.

III

Production-comrades courts and other quasi-official public bodies are relevant to an analysis of relations between Stakhanovites and non-Stakhanovite workers for another reason. Stakhanovites figured prominently as members of these bodies, largely taking over the role originally assigned to shock workers. Indeed, although never prescribed as a formal obligation, Stakhanovites'

---

[69] Quoted in Merle Fainsod, *Smolensk under Soviet Rule* (New York: Vintage, 1958), 190.
[70] For the resolution defining the powers of the courts, see *SIu*, no. 10 (1931):14.
[71] Ibid., no. 13 (1936):11; no. 15 (1936):11.

participation in them constituted another dimension of what it meant to be a Stakhanovite, as well as of the politics of productivity.

According to the decree by which they were established, the courts were to consist of workers elected at general meetings for a term of six months. In practice, the standard procedure for elections involved the formation of a list of nominees by the trade union committee, usually in consultation with its party bureau, and with the expectation of unanimous approval by the meeting.[72] To workers who already regarded Stakhanovites as rate busters and self-seekers, their participation in the courts was yet another cause for resentment. For Stakhanovites, it was undoubtedly an onerous chore, but one that few who aspired to the maintenance of their status and privileges, party membership, and/or promotion to the ranks of the technical intelligentsia could refuse to perform. Then again, analogous with the *volost* courts of the post-Emancipation era or even their pre-Emancipation communal equivalents, the production-comrades courts could serve as a buffer between those under their jurisdiction and the regular police and judicial authorities.

The same could not be said, however, for the procurators' assistance groups and the campaigns surrounding the promulgation of the laws to tighten labor discipline in 1938–9.[73] In both cases, Stakhanovites acted as information gatherers and informers for the authorities. Their appeals to management and trade union organizations to deprive "shirkers," "loafers," and "flitters" of accommodation and social insurance appeared frequently in the press, as did their pronouncements in favor of the introduction of work books and the penalties for lateness prescribed by the new laws.[74]

Such public activity by Stakhanovites was similar to their denunciations in 1937–8 of "Trotskyite wreckers and saboteurs" and their approval of the death sentences handed down by the courts in the Show Trials.[75] Both were a measure of Stakhanovites' dependence on the central authorities for legitimating

[72] See Samuel Kucherov, *The Origins of Soviet Administration of Justice: Their History and Operation* (Leiden: Brill, 1970), 152–6.
[73] On the assistance groups, see *SIu*, no. 11 (1936):2.
[74] *Pravda*, Dec. 10, 12, 14, 15, 16, 17, 24, 1938; Jan. 7, 9, 1939.
[75] Ibid., Jan. 25, 27, Feb. 1, June 17, 1937; Stakhanov, *Rasskaz*, 124–6.

their role in Soviet society as loyal, patriotic workers. Though few could have been unaware of the irony of denouncing the likes of Piatakov, Sarkisov, and others who had done so much to promote Stakhanovism, there undoubtedly were other considerations that outweighed the return of favors.

During these years, the role of Stakhanovites in the factory became increasingly institutionalized. Aside from their participation in comrades courts and assistance groups, Stakhanovites were expected to take an active part in temporary control commissions, production conferences, conferences of production *aktivy*, and machine inspection brigades. These institutions, the latter two of which emerged in 1937 and 1938, were supposed to involve workers in administration in conformity with the Leninist principle of popular control of the organs of Soviet power.

Most Western historians have been skeptical about the degree of real control that such institutions could exercise, particularly under Stalin.[76] Even David Granick, who concluded in his study of industrial management that "Soviet leaders considered it to be of great importance and a significant weapon in their struggle to overcome political and economic difficulties," conceded that management's power to call conferences and recruit "appropriate" personnel to staff them constituted a "serious problem in the exercise of mass supervision over management."[77]

Nevertheless, some workers *were* more appropriate or better placed than others, and the central authorities made it clear whom they considered appropriate. Occasionally, Stakhanovites' participation was delineated by decree. For example, in January 1939, the Commissariat of Machine Construction specified that inspection brigades consist of designers, technicians, and Stak-

---

[76] For example, Fainsod does not even mention them in his discussion of "checks and restraints" on management in *How Russia Is Ruled*, 506–9. For a recent "revisionist" view, see David Christian, "The Supervisory Function in Russian and Soviet History," *Slavic Review* 41 (1982):73–90.

[77] David Granick, *Management of the Industrial Firm in the USSR* (New York: Columbia University Press, 1954), 235, 241. This is probably why *Pravda*, Mar. 11, 1937, took the editors of *Za industrializatsiiu* to task for referring to an *aktiv* conference at Moscow's Hammer and Sickle Factory as a "council of the factory's director." See the latter's self-criticism in *ZI*, Mar. 12, 1937.

hanovites.[78] All workers were encouraged to attend production conferences, but *aktiv* conferences, which were supposed to be held on a monthly basis, consisted of a more select group. According to G. M. Malenkov, then a rising star in the Soviet political firmament, these were junior management personnel, engineers, technicians, and Stakhanovite workers. They numbered about one thousand, or less than 3 percent of the 34,700 people employed by the Molotov Automobile Works in the first half of 1937.[79]

Obviously, then, not all Stakhanovites could be production *aktivy*. Yet it must have been difficult to avoid participation in at least one form of control, particularly during 1937, when the party leadership championed criticism from below as a means of rooting out "saboteurs" and "wreckers" in both the party organizations and industrial management. Can we therefore conclude that Stakhanovites were allies of the central authorities in their struggles with middle-echelon officaldom? There is much evidence to support such a conclusion. Aside from their participation in the above-mentioned control organs and sallies by outstanding Stakhanovites discussed in Chapter 3, there were the collectively signed open letters and conference resolutions that initiated special interenterprise or branch competitions.[80] Indeed, virtually whenever higher authorities felt that one aspect or another of production was being neglected, they could rely on Stakhanovites to testify to the urgency of the matter. So it was with "cyclicity" or the turnaround time in coal mining, and so it would be with the tightening of labor discipline.

However, being a Stakhanovite meant serving more than just one boss. Attendance at regional and branch conferences was one function that linked Stakhanovites with the party apparatus. In the case of the Western *oblast'*, a predominantly agricultural area, *obkom* party secretary Rumiantsev held *raikom* secretaries personally responsible for selecting appropriate delegates to attend a meeting of advanced *kolkhozniki*. Appropriate in this case

[78] Granick, *Management*, 97.
[79] Ibid., 241.
[80] See, e.g., the resolution of the Donets meeting of managers and Stakhanovites in the coal-mining industry of Dec. 30–1, 1937, in *Promyshlennost' i rabochii klass Ukrainskoi SSR, 1933–1941*, 2 vols. (Kiev: Naukova Dumka, 1977), 2:9–12.

meant "the best people, achieving good harvests, demonstrating Stakhanovite methods of work and mastery of agricultural machinery."[81] Similarly, the head of the *obkom's* industrial section wrote to *raikom* secretaries to request that they "ensure the careful selection" of Stakhanovites to participate in October Revolution celebrations and conversations with Rumiantsev and other party notables. According to the letter, dated October 26, 1935, the delegation should "consist of real Stakhanovites and not those 'elected' by procurement (*po svodke*)."[82] By the time the twentieth anniversary of the Revolution rolled around, Stakhanovites were included along with party and soviet activists, educational and cultural officials, doctors, agronomists, and employees of state and cooperative stores in preparation for the celebrations and were to figure among others honored at an "evening of heroes."[83]

If the central state and regional party apparatuses could make use of Stakhanovites, so too could enterprise management. Busygin's visits to *glavk* and commissariat headquarters to obtain steel were by no means unique phenomena.[84] Other, less well known Stakhanovites also served as expediters (*tolkachi*) for their respective enterprises. A letter to Ordzhonikidze from a group of Stakhanovites employed on the construction of a steelmaking plant in Nikopol' elicited four milling machines and 350 tons of cement.[85] After a meeting of Stakhanovite steelmakers had resolved to extend into 1937 the socialist competition campaign to produce 60,000 tons of steel per day, enterprise directors and the Trubostal' *glavk* dispatched several brigades of Stakhanovites to neighboring factories to obtain required materials.[86]

Stakhanovite status thus entailed having privileges, incurring risks, and assuming responsibilities. Privileges were gradated according to the prominence – local, sectional, or national – of Stakhanovites, that prominence being a function of the inno-

[81] Smolensk Party Archive, WKP-186, p. 238.
[82] Ibid., WKP-189, p. 148.
[83] Ibid., pp. 271, 286.
[84] See Chapter 3, Section IV; and *Tekhnicheskaia propaganda*, no. 19 (1935):47.
[85] *Promyshlennost'*, 1:404.
[86] Ibid., 418–20.

vativeness and occupation of the Stakhanovite as well as the strategic importance of the industry and enterprise in which he or she worked. The risks were not only alienation from the collective, but the possibility of retaliatory action. Although at least some outstanding Stakhanovites were subjected to the latter, the most vulnerable group would appear to have been those who remained at the bench and yet were integrated into the administrative structure through their participation in one or another form of public activity.

These responsibilities had other implications. They confirm that what higher authorities were asking of "advanced" workers was more than a good day's work. Aside from demonstrating productivity above the norm and working in an exemplary fashion, Stakhanovites were expected to contribute to the establishment of conditions that made increases in productivity and/or plan fulfillment possible. This was no easy task, especially in 1937–8, when the authority structure within industry was under assault, turnover among officials was extremely high as a consequence of the Great Purges, and indices of worker indiscipline, such as absenteeism and labor turnover, were on the rise.

Beyond this, Stakhanovites served a representational function, representing management in its negotiations with supply agencies, appearing to represent workers at various functions, and in some sense embodying the entire Soviet order and its achievements.[87] As we shall see in the next chapter, this last function extended beyond the work place. It cast Stakhanovites in the role of consumers as much as producers, making them archetypes of the New Soviet Man.

[87] That such demands on Stakhanovites' time could get out of hand is suggested by a letter from a Stakhanovite worker at the Moscow Caliber-Tool Factory in which he complained that his function as a representative was lowering his productivity. *ZI*, Apr. 9, 1937.

6

Stakhanovites in the cultural mythology of the 1930s

One cannot speak to Stakhanovites as a teacher, but as to equals. They discuss Tolstoy's style and how it resembles that of Homer.

P. Romanov, "Novye liudi,"

Traveling in the Donbass in the winter of 1936, Panteleimon Sergeevich Romanov, the author of numerous satirical sketches as well as the massive epic novel *Rus'*, looked out of his chauffer-driven car to see "sparkling gardens, beautiful stone houses decorated with wood filigree [and] a profusion of cherry, apple and acacia trees."

"What is this?" he asked the driver.

"Houses for the workers," was the laconic reply. "Each house has two apartments."

The car entered the grounds of the Petrovskii mine, and Romanov got out to visit the mine's Stakhanovite room. Inside, he found "each worker ... dressed in a good jacket and tie. There was no indication of the former disorder and lack of care in clothing," he wrote. In one corner of the room stood a piano, and flowers seemed to be everywhere. "Flowers," he noted, "have an important influence on the psyche. They now occupy an important place in life." So apparently did classical literature. It was here, in a room set aside for their use, that Stakhanovites were discussing Tolstoy and Homer.

It has been commonplace to dismiss such depictions of life in the Soviet Union of the 1930s as pure fantasy, more in the vein of mythology than reportage. And though it has long been recognized that myths play a significant role in the organization and synthesis of the main ideas of a culture, only recently has Soviet culture been examined from such a standpoint. For a previous generation of Sovietologists, ideology, formalized and

210

conveyed via indoctrination, was of paramount importance. Even while they concluded that many ordinary Soviet citizens responded apathetically and even cynically to such "ideological bombardment," most Sovietologists confined themselves to studying high politics and the instruments of Soviet power such as the coercive appatatus and agitprop.[1]

This concentration, long dominant in the field, has given way to other interests and approaches. Influenced by developments in anthropology, some scholars have begun to address Stalinist culture and, in particular, its generation of what could be called synthetic folklore. Hence, in recent years, books have appeared on the cult of Lenin, socialist realist novels as anthropological texts, post–Second World War middle-brow fiction, and the Soviet regime's "rituals of cultural management."[2] None of these, however, focuses on the 1930s, although Katerina Clark's study of the socialist realist novel treats that decade as central and somewhat special. As she points out, it was in the mid-1930s that Soviet officialdom, having abandoned the "little man" as the

cornerstone of the new society, gave full play to *homo extraordinarius*, of whom outstanding Stakhanovites were key examples. From this time on, there were in Stalinist culture . . . two orders of reality, ordinary and extraordinary, and correspondingly, two orders of human being, of time, place and so on. Ordinary reality was considered valuable only as it could be seen to reflect some form, or ideal essence, found in higher-order reality. The distinctions between ordinary reality and fiction lost the crucial importance they have in other philosophical systems.

At this time, as at no other, the boundaries between fiction and fact became blurred. In all areas of public life . . . the difference between

[1] See Raymond Bauer, Alex Inkeles, and Clyde Kluckhohn, *How the Soviet System Works* (Cambridge, Mass.: Harvard University Press, 1956), 96–113, 138–42; Alex Inkeles and Raymond Bauer, *The Soviet Citizen: Daily Life in a Totalitarian Society* (Cambridge, Mass.: Harvard University Press, 1961), 251–65, 269–72; Merle Fainsod, *How Russia Is Ruled* (Cambridge, Mass.: Harvard University Press, 1965), 594–5.
[2] Nina Tumarkin, *Lenin Lives! The Lenin Cult in Soviet Russia* (Cambridge, Mass.: Harvard University Press, 1983); Katerina Clark, *The Soviet Novel: History as Ritual* (University of Chicago Press, 1981); Vera Dunham, *In Stalin's Time: Middleclass Values in Soviet Fiction* (Cambridge University Press, 1976); and Christel Lane, *The Rites of Rulers: Ritual in Industrial Society – The Soviet Case* (Cambridge University Press, 1981).

fiction and fact, between theater and political event, between literary plot and factual reporting, all became somewhat hazy.[3]

Thus, it is not so much a question of whether the houses Romanov viewed from his car window were really so beautiful and inhabited by workers or whether the miners he encountered actually were comparing the aesthetics of Tolstoy and Homer.[4] Like the Potemkin villages of another age, the scenes described by the Soviet author were intended to portray an ideal or "higher reality." The closer, in terms of official ideology, Soviet society got to communism, the more important it became to stress the achievements of the present, soon to be consecrated socialist society.[5] As Stalin asserted at the All-Union conference of Stakhanovites, socialism was not to be construed as "a certain material equalization of people based on a poor man's standard of living." It required "a high productivity of labor, higher than under capitalism," and in this respect, the Stakhanovite movement represented a force for the "further consolidation of socialism in our country." At the same time, it was preparing the conditions for the transition from socialism to communism in that it "contains the first beginnings, still feeble it is true...of raising the cultural and technical level of the working class" to that of engineers, technicians, and other mental workers.[6]

However, none of this would have been possible, Stalin asserted, without certain preconditions that made Stakhanovism "absolutely ripe." "First and foremost" among these was "the radical improvement in the material welfare of the workers." In what was to become the most frequently cited statement from his speech and something of a motto for the Stakhanovite movement, Stalin proclaimed that "life has improved, comrades. Life

---

[3] Clark, *Soviet Novel*, 146–7.
[4] Of course, even before the advent of Stakhanovism, some (shock) workers had received separate homes such as those described by Romanov. See, e.g., the letter from such workers at the Chekist mine no. 10 in *Trud*, July 10, 1934.
[5] This necessity was not peculiar to the Stalin period. For a penetrating analysis of more recent formulations, see Alfred Evans, Jr., "The Decline of Developed Socialism? Some Trends in Recent Soviet Ideology," *Soviet Studies*, 38, no. 1 (1986):1–23.
[6] I. V. Stalin *Sochineniia*, ed. Robert H. McNeal (Stanford, Calif.: Hoover Institution, 1967), 1 (XIV), 90.

has become more joyous. And when life is joyous, work goes well."[7] Hence, not only had Stakhanovism opened up the vista of a society in which there would be "an abundance of products and articles of consumption of all kinds," but it was no less important to demonstrate that such a condition already existed for those workers who, as it were, had earned the right to live prosperously.

To understand this dimension of Soviet cultural mythology, it is therefore necessary to analyze Stakhanovites' role in the sphere of consumption; for as public-spirited as they were supposed to be, Stakhanovites did not live in the factories. As much as they claimed to love their work and as often as they cited the importance of arriving early for their shifts to check their machines, prepare their tools, and see that they had an adequate supply of raw materials, they were not supposed to sacrifice taking advantage of the abundance of goods and services available to them.

This part of their lives, though not directly connected with material production, grew out of and in turn reinforced the politics of productivity. Almost from the beginning, Stakhanovism contained instructions about how to live as well as how to work. In addition to providing a model for success on the shop floor, it conjured up images of the good life. Indeed, the nexus between work and rest, factory and home was inextricable. Many of the same qualities Stakhanovites were supposed to exhibit in the one sphere – cleanliness, neatness, preparedness, and a keenness for learning – were applicable to the other. Yet as we shall see, the ideal Stakhanovite home and family were not merely adjuncts of the work place. They were rather symbiotically related. It was not Stakhanovites but their wives who received instruction in home economics. The sexual division of labor in the household, a product of both traditional cultural attitudes and new precepts, thus provided an essential precondition for Stakhanovites' success on the job and the leisure time to pursue officially sanctioned cultural activities.

The idealized Stakhanovite, the purposeful, well-rounded individual, was a particularly well articulated example of the New Soviet Man. This ideological construct, which fundamentally re-

[7] Ibid., 91–2.

214   *Stakhanovism and the politics of productivity*

cast the role of the worker in Soviet society, was an important stabilizing factor in a period of great political and social instability. It was also one of the most enduring features of Stakhanovism. Exactly what it consisted of and what relation it bore to Soviet social and cultural reality are the questions to be pursued in this chapter.

I

Before dissecting the cultural mythology of Stakhanovites, we must descend to ordinary reality to assess the material and cultural standards of Soviet industrial workers. Given the paucity of the data and the tremendous variety of circumstances in which workers lived, only a rough approximation of certain general patterns is possible.

Contrary to what had been projected in the First Five-Year Plan, the real wages of Soviet workers fell dramatically after 1928. Estimates of the extent of the decline vary, depending on the indices used, the weight given to market prices as opposed to those of rationed goods, and the impact of the social wage (e.g., health care, pensions).[8] However, there is general agreement that the nadir was reached in 1932–3, after which there was a modest improvement, at least until 1937.

Of course, the composition of the industrial work force of the mid-1930s was very different from what it had been at the outset of rapid industrialization. As many workers were promoted to managerial and technical positions or became full-time party officials, an even larger number of working-class women and peasants of both sexes joined the ranks of industrial workers. The overall secular decline in wages was therefore not experienced as such by all or even a majority of workers throughout the entire period. Moreover, as individual wages dropped, so too did the birth rate among working-class families. Thus, the

[8] Abram Bergson, *The Structure of Soviet Wages* (Cambridge, Mass.: Harvard University Press, 1944); Janet Chapman, *Real Wages in Soviet Russia since 1928* (Cambridge, Mass.: Harvard University Press, 1963); Naum Jasny, *Soviet Industrialization, 1928–1952* (University of Chicago Press, 1961).

Table 6.1. *Changing composition of the Soviet working-class family*

	1927	1930	1932	1933	1934	1935
Size	4.36	4.02	3.93	3.83	3.77	3.80
Wage earners	1.25	1.32	1.45	1.44	1.44	1.47
Dependents	2.82	2.70	2.49	2.39	2.33	2.33
Ratio of earners to dependents	1:2.26	1:2.05	1:1.72	1:1.66	1:1.62	1:1.59

Sources: For 1927, *Statistika truda*, no. 5–6 (1928):16; for 1930–5, *Rabochii klass v upravlenii gosudarstvom (1926–1937 gg.)* (Moscow: Mysl', 1968), 49.

size of the working-class family shrank, as did the ratio of dependents to wage earners (Table 6.1).

There is no doubt, however, that the living standards of the average working-class family were lower at the end of the First Five-Year Plan than at its outset. Two indices, diet and living space, are revealing in this respect. In Leningrad, where workers' food rations were generally higher than in most other Soviet cities, the average consumption of meat between 1928 and 1933 fell by 72 percent, that of milk by 64 percent, fruit by 63 percent, and butter by 47· percent. In contrast, the consumption of potatoes rose by nearly 20 percent, rye bread by 44 percent, and vegetables by 8 percent.[9] The diet of Moscow workers was similarly altered during these years. Whereas their consumption of meat fell off by an estimated 60 percent and that of dairy products by 50 percent, there was an increase in the quantity of potatoes, cereals, and fish (usually dried) consumed.[10]

As pinched as were the diets of workers in these two cities, the situation in other industrial centers was generally worse. "No

[9] O. I. Shkaratan, "Material'noe blagosostoianie rabochego klassa SSSR v perekhodnyi period ot kapitalizma k sotsializmu (po materialam Leningrada)," *Istoriia SSSR*, no. 3 (1964): 40; *Rabochii klass v upravlenii gosudarstvom (1926–137 gg.)*, ed. K. V. Gusev and V. Z. Drobizhev (Moscow: Mysl' 1968), 50–1.

[10] John Barber, "The Standard of Living of Soviet Industrial Workers, 1928–1941," in *L'Industrialisation de l'URSS dans les années trente*, ed. Charles Bettelheim (Paris: Editions de l'Ecole des hautes études en sciences sociales, 1982), 111–12.

meat, no butter, and almost no sugar or milk . . . only bread and a little cereal grain" was the fare for the riggers of Magnitogorsk during 1932–3, according to John Scott.[11] "Nothing but black bread, dried fish and tea" was what an American engineer reported that the workers at several steel mills in the Donbass and northern Urals consumed.[12] Unlike a large number of peasants in the Ukraine, not many workers starved, but hunger was widespread.

By 1934, the food crisis had somewhat abated. However, whatever improvement was to occur over the next several years was not, *pace* Stalin, radical. Workers in 1937 were still consuming far fewer meat and dairy products and considerably more potatoes and black bread than in 1928, though the proportion of the diet consisting of the latter item began to fall.[13] Significantly, with the phasing out of rationing, the differentiation between workers receiving higher and lower pay increased. The ratios of per capita consumption of working-class families in the two extreme income categories for the last quarter of 1935 graphically reveal the spread. For meat it was 5.7 to 1; for fruit, 6.7 to 1; and for butter, an incredible 17 to 1.[14]

Housing was a more intractable problem. As with wages, the Five-Year Plan projections for improvements in per capita living space bore no relation to reality. Neither in 1932 nor in 1937 did housing construction reach the levels targeted in respective plans.[15] When one takes into account the unprecedented and largely unanticipated swelling of the urban population between 1928 and 1932 and, after a slight decline in 1933, the less spectacular but still prodigious increase during the Second Five-Year Plan, the full dimensions of the problem are revealed. Per capita living space, which was a modest 5.65 square meters in 1928, declined to 4.66 square meters in 1932 and by 1937 had reached

[11] John Scott, *Behind the Urals: An American Worker in Russia's City of Steel* (Bloomington: Indiana University Press, 1973), 112.

[12] Quoted in Barber, "Standard of Living," 112.

[13] *Rabochii klass v upravlenii*, 51. Workers' consumption of black bread in the first six months of 1936 reportedly declined 33% compared with the same period in 1935. See S. Kheinman, "Uroven' zhizni trudiashchikhsia SSR," *Planovoe khoziaistvo*, no. 8 (1936):114.

[14] Kheinman, "Uroven' zhizni," p. 116.

[15] See figures in Barber, "Standard of Living," 113–14.

a figure of 3.77. According to John Barber, who cites a variety of statistics to support his assertion, "All evidence suggests that workers' living space remained significantly lower than average as well as sharing in the general decline in size."[16]

The acute housing shortage produced such phenomena as workers sleeping in shifts on the same bed, a practice that was widespread in mining and construction enterprise barracks; railroad stations and even the factory floor serving as temporary living quarters; and workers' families being squeezed into corridors and corners, sharing bathrooms, kitchens, and no doubt much else with other tenants. These conditions were not particularly new, though they were probably more common in the 1930s. Still, given that most workers had migrated from the countryside, where living conditions were often more wretched, the absence of comforts and privacy was not necessarily experienced as deprivation.

Nor by the mid-1930s was it what the privileged stratum of workers experienced at all. The houses that Romanov described may have been figments of his imagination, but in many locales quarters were reserved for families of brigade leaders and leading Stakhanovites that resembled accommodation for managerial and engineering personnel. Such was the Busygin housing estate on the outskirts of Gor'kii. And at Magnitogorsk, according to John Scott, 15 percent of the population, composed of the families of foremen, brigade leaders, and skilled workers, lived in new apartments that were equipped with central heating, electricity, and running water.[17]

To this brief summary of workers' material standards must be added a consideration of their cultural activity and, more generally, the ways in which they spent their time. Here, the time-budget studies of working-class families that various Soviet economists periodically conducted are most useful. What they indicate is a gross disparity between male and female workers that,

---

[16] Ibid., 114. In Leningrad, where an additional 200,000 square meters of living space became available to workers in 1931 mainly because of the resettlement of "nonworking elements" of the population, the figure was 5.5 square meters per worker. Shkaratan, "Material'noe blagosostoianie," 42.

[17] *Behind the Urals*, 231–4.

Table 6.2. *Time budgets of male and female workers*

	1923–4		1930		1932		1936	
	M	F	M	F	M	F	M	F
Productive work	213.3	215.7	179.7	181.8	174	174	183	180
Housework	53.5	150	49.5	143.7	51	153	30	147
Cultural and educational activities	51.3	16.9	53.7	24.9	45	9	33	9
Public affairs	9.0	5.5	27.0	12.0	12	9	3	3
Total	327.1	388.1	309.9	362.4	282	345	249	339

Note: Data represent hours per month. M, male; F, female.
Source: John Barber, "Notes on the Soviet Working-class Family, 1928–1941" (paper presented at the Second World Congress for Soviet and East European Studies, Garmisch-Partenkirchen, West Germany, September–October, 1980), Tables 1–5.

far from diminishing, was greater by the mid-1930s than a decade earlier (Table 6.2).

Although the number of hours spent in productive work was roughly comparable for men and women throughout this period, the same cannot be said of time devoted to housework, cultural and educational activities, or, until 1936, public affairs. The greatest disparity was in housework, where the ratio of time spent by male and female workers was 1 to 2.8 in 1923–4, 1 to 2.9 in 1930, 1 to 3 in 1932, and 1 to 4.9 in 1936.[18] An examination of the content of this category suggests that the gap was even wider.

For working women, the preparation of food was by far the

[18] John Barber, "Notes on the Soviet Working-Class Family, 1928–1941" (paper presented at the Second World Congress for Soviet and East European Studies, Garmisch-Partenkirchen, W. Germany, September–October, 1980), Table 2. A time-budget study of more than one thousand working-class families in Leningrad in 1932 revealed that, for every hour that men devoted to housework, women spent 3.3 to 4.3 hours depending on the industry in which they worked and their level of skill. See V. Lebedev-Patreiko, G. Rabinovich, and D. Rodin, *Biudzhet vremeni rabochei sem'i (po materialam Leningradskogo obsledovaniia)* (Leningrad: LNIIKKh, 1933), 114.

most time-consuming household chore. In 1923–4, it comprised more than half of the 150 hours per month devoted to housework. By 1930, it had dropped to 66 hours (46 percent) but thereafter rose to 72 hours. Time spent looking after children ranked second, averaging between 11 and 15 percent of total housework time, followed by cleaning and repairing clothes, housekeeping, and personal hygiene.[19]

For male workers, personal hygiene ranked first. In 1923–4 it consumed 19 hours per month, or 34 percent of total housework time, rose to 24.6 hours (50 percent) in 1930, and 27 hours (53 percent) in 1932, before falling precipitously to 15 hours (50 percent) in 1936. Time spent on other household chores presents a variegated picture. In the cases of washing and repairing clothes and cleaning and repairing house, the trend was downward; in that of looking after children, it rose between 1923–4 and 1930, only to fall thereafter; and in the preparation of food, it dropped sharply from 14.4 hours in 1923–4 to only 6 hours by 1930 and then rose less steeply, comprising 9 hours per month in both 1932 and 1936.[20] Thus, if one excludes personal hygiene (which, arguably, should not be considered part of housework), the ratios given above are altered as follows: 1 to 3.7 in 1923–4, 1 to 4.5 in 1930, 1 to 5.6 in 1932, and 1 to 8.6 in the Stakhanovite year of 1936.

Why this was so is a question that can be approached from two directions, namely from above and from below. To the extent that the early Bolshevik leadership was committed to the emancipation of women from the narrow confines of the household, that commitment was informed by both normative and instrumental considerations.[21] The former was inherited from the humanistic and egalitarian strains within Europe socialist movements as well as the nineteenth-century Russian intelligentsia's fitful attempts to grapple with the Woman Question. The latter was shaped more by the recognition that any far-

[19] Barber, "Soviet Working-Class Family," Table 2.
[20] Ibid.
[21] This distinction is made by Gail W. Lapidus, *Women in Soviet Society* (Berkeley and Los Angeles: University of California Press, 1978), 73–82. Lapidus contrasts both with a third orientation, typified in the writings of Stalin, where utilitarian considerations were paramount.

reaching reorganization of Soviet society along socialist lines
would necessarily involve the transformation of the traditional
household and family structures. If the Women's Department
(Zhenotdel) of the Central Committee embodied the party's mis-
sionary zeal toward women, then Lenin's condemnation of "the
backwardness of women, their lack of understanding for the
revolutionary ideals of the man," and early Soviet economists'
emphasis on rationalizing the expenditure of human labor and
channeling it into social production reflected the second
orientation.[22]

Both were much in evidence in the 1920s, inspiring educational theories and policy, literacy and antireligious campaigns,
and experimentation in communal living. However, the impe-
diments to achieving equality both within the working-class family and outside it remained formidable. They included the
wavering commitment of party leaders, lack of enthusiasm and
even hostility among rank-and-file members, the inadequacy of
social services, the weight of tradition among workers themselves, and, so long as NEP was extant, limited employment
opportunities. Of these, only the last was to be overcome, as was
NEP itself, by the First Five-Year Plan. But being out of the
household for seven hours of wage work did not relieve women
of the burdens of housework. Rather, it intensified them. As Gail
Lapidus explains:

> The exploitation of agriculture to serve industrial expansion, the rel-
> ative neglect of light industry and consumer goods, the under-devel-
> opment of the service sector, and the subordination of welfare to
> productivity ... had far reaching consequences for the role of the house-
> hold in Soviet economic development and for the role of women within
> it. The effects of these patterns was to require the household to supply
> for itself a wide range of services that in other societies at comparable
> levels of development were usually provided by the market.[23]

Far reaching though the consequences would be, they were
not necessarily immediate. The fact that men and especially
women spent less time on housework in 1930 than in 1923–4

---

[22] Quoted in Lapidus, *Women*, 74. This is not to imply that Lenin was
unconcerned with the plight of women as such or that Zhenotdel
activists ignored the general social and economic benefits to be derived from female emancipation.
[23] Ibid., 103–4.

may signify that there was less food to prepare. But it could also be correlated with the proliferation of public catering facilities, laundries, and childcare facilities and the extension of electrical service in the course of the late 1920s. Inadequate as they were, and as low a priority as they had, the provision of these services went some way toward reducing the burdens of housework.

No less significant is the increase in time that both women and men devoted to cultural and educational activities as well as public affairs. This may well have been the result of the campaigns the party sponsored in the 1920s as part of its commitment to overcome women's "backwardness," as well as a symptom of the Cultural Revolution, then at its height. Much of the participation in public affairs consisted of passive attendance at meetings usually held in the work place and often during working hours. But approximately one-third of the time working men devoted to this activity was taken up by active party, Komsomol, and trade union responsibilities.[24]

By 1932, however, time devoted to political activities had fallen and was to decline still further by 1936. John Barber is almost certainly correct to see this as a consequence of both the emphasis on production rather than politics in the work place and the "peasantization" of the work force.[25] Particularly as far as women were concerned, it may also be connected with the increase in time devoted to housework, itself a reflection of social services failing to keep pace with the swelling of the industrial work force.

The downward trend in male participation in cultural and educational activities is slightly more puzzling. To be sure, the lower degree of literacy among peasant migrants and their relative unfamiliarity with cultural outlets such as the theater, the cinema, libraries, and bookstores could account for part of the drop. According to one Soviet study, whereas workers in large cities devoted 5.6 hours per week to reading and attending the theater in 1923–4, such pursuits took up only 4.5 hours in 1936.[26]

---

[24] *Trud v SSSR, 1931g.* (Moscow: Gosekgiz, 1932), 173.
[25] Barber, "Soviet Working-Class Family," 8.
[26] L. A. Gordon, E. V. Kropov, and L. A. Onikov, *Cherty sotsialisticheskogo obraza zhizni: Byt gorodskikh rabochikh vchera, segodnia, zavtra* (Moscow: Znanie, 1977), 149. The different cultural background and attitudes of peasant migrants may also explain the sharp drop in the amount of time devoted to personal hygiene between 1932 and 1936.

Nevertheless, one would have expected the expansion of adult education and vocational training courses to have compensated at the least. The solution to the puzzle may lie in the reduction in the number of formal class hours in apprentice school (FZU) courses and the increase after 1933 in the on-the-job component of technical training at the expense of formal classroom instruction.[27] In other words, it is possible that more workers were being trained even while the time required to complete such training was reduced.

It is also possible that the number of workers actually engaged in some form of study under the new scheme has been exaggerated. One writer, commenting on the state of technical minimum courses in Leningrad as of 1936, claimed that enterprise management allocated only half of the ten days per month recommended by Narkomtiazhprom. It was also noted that because of overtime work, "there is hardly an enterprise where study is not sacrificed." Average attendance among Leningrad workers in May 1936 was put at 65 percent.[28]

In summary, even as the sexual division of labor was narrowed in industry between the mid-1920s and mid-1930s, it widened in the household. For women, this meant the "double shift," which left little time and energy for other pursuits. For male workers, the most striking change was their depoliticization and, conversely, an increase in unstructured leisure time. The absence of any systematic data makes it impossible to analyze how such

[27] According to a joint Central Committee–Sovnarkom decree of September 1933, beginning in 1934 FZU courses were to be reduced from three to four years to six to twelve months, and 80% of study time was to be devoted to production. For the impact of the decree on technical training, see A. I. Vdovin and V. Z. Drobizhev, *Rost rabochego klassa SSSR, 1917–1940gg.* (Moscow: Mysl', 1976), 198; L. Al'ter, "Kul'turno-tekhnicheskii pod"em trudiashchikhsia SSSR," *Planovoe khoziaistvo*, no. 12 (1938): 25–7; I. I. Kuz'minov, *Stakhanovskoe dvizhenie – vysshii etap sotsialisticheskogo sorevnovaniia* (Moscow: Sotsekgiz, 1940), 50; and Sheila Fitzpatrick, *Education and Social Mobility in the Soviet Union, 1921–34* (Cambridge University Press, 1979), 226.

[28] V. Kokshin, "Tehknicheskuiu uchebu na vysshuiu stepen'," *NFI*, no. 6 (1936): 12–14. This was the case at the Pervomaisk coal trust, where attendance at technical minimum courses was reported to be 23% and master of socialist labor courses to be 41% for the first six months of 1936. *Sotsialisticheskii Donbass (hereafter SD)* July 27, 1936.

time was spent.[29] Nor is it possible to calculate the amount of leisure time enjoyed by male workers in terms of their skills, occupations, and location or whether they were Stakhanovites. We can, however, explore the ideal-typical dimensions of this question by asking how those whose lives were characterized as joyous were supposed to occupy their nonworking hours.

II

Stalinist Russia, no less than other societies, contained codes of behavior or precepts according to which individual success was judged and rewarded. There were, of course, many paths to success and numerous yardsticks by which it could be measured depending on circumstances and what the authorities considered behavior appropriate to them. During the First Five-Year Plan, the most rewarding path for workers was that taken by outstanding shock workers, many of whom were selected for promotion to the ranks of officialdom.

In subsequent years, these *vydvizhentsy* continued to be the beneficiaries of the regime's solicitude. However, they were not the only ones "to express an identification with Soviet power, pride in its achievements and the desire that these achievements should be celebrated in an appropriately cultural way."[30] Many former peasants who had been tempered by the rough-and-tumble conditions in the factories took pride in their achievements, whether such achievements consisted of mere survival, learning a skill, or becoming a relatively privileged shock worker.[31] Having learned how to work according to instructions,

---

[29] The study cited in note 26 shows that, for workers of both sexes, leisure activities (taking walks, visiting or being visited by friends, engaging in sport, etc.) took up 6.4 hours per week in 1923–4 but 7.9 hours in 1936. No breakdown by sex is given.

[30] Fitzpatrick, *Education and Social Mobility*, 253.

[31] The intrinsic satisfactions of work, of a job well done, should not be underestimated. As Eric Hobsbawm has written with respect to an earlier transition in Europe and North America, "The workers themselves provided their employers with a solution to the problem of labour management: by and large, they liked to work and their expectations were remarkably modest. The unskilled or raw immigrants from the countryside were proud of their strength, and came from

they needed instructions on how to live. In less traumatic circumstances, this need could have been fulfilled by the existing core of urbanized proletarians (as, indeed, had been the case in the 1890s and again in the years just before the First World War). But at least in proportional terms, the core had shrunk, and its social weight had diminished. Moreover, the militant class outlook that had been a vital part of the proletariat's revolutionary tradition and identity was distinctly out of favor with the authorities, in both the domestic and, from 1934, the international contexts.

It was not, therefore, proletarian or working-class culture to which uprooted peasants and new workers adapted, but an urban culture that was itself undergoing profound changes.[32] Sensitive foreigners, such as Klaus Mehnert, noticed the differences as early as the winter of 1932. Domestic (*bytovye*) and production communes were no longer sanctioned, their egalitarian practices having become anathema to party leaders. "The commune,... that's a great and beautiful idea," he was told by a former member who had since become "the first engineer in our works." "One day we'll certainly realize it. But everything at the right time.... At the moment,... the commune is a Utopia, the sum total of petit bourgeois, left-deviation, Trotzki-ist levelling mania." Asked to justify "this state of differentiation and the tendency towards egoism which it doubtless inspires," another former communard asserted:

By unfolding all productive energies, we are coming by way of the principle of output to such an immense increase in production, that one day, this state of shortage of everything, in which we are at present, will be overcome.... When once the abundance has been achieved, then ... things will evolve into Communism quite of their own accord.[33]

This obviously would be a long-term process. In the meantime, the overturning of many revolutionary shibboleths, what N. S. Timasheff referred to as the Great Retreat, continued apace. The Old Bolsheviks and their tradition of self-sacrifice ceased to have

an environment where hard labour was the criterion of a person's worth." E. J. Hobsbawm, *The Age of Capital, 1848–1875*. (London: Abacus, 1977), 260–1.

[32] I am indebted to Diane Koenker for this insight.

[33] Klaus Mehnert, *Youth in Soviet Russia*, trans. Michael Davidson (New York: Harcourt, Brace, 1933), 253, 264–5.

validity, their society eventually was disbanded, as was the Society of Former Political Prisoners and Exiles. Rankings, badges, and ratings of all kinds, but especially in the military and in sport, proliferated. "Higher, farther, and faster" became the new incantations.[34] The cult of the individual hero assumed huge proportions and was crowned by that of the Father of the Peoples, Stalin.

All the while, the image of the heroic worker was undergoing a change. Working to exhaustion and storming in general came to be associated not with communist zeal but with backwardness. Working in a rhythmic manner, studying but also engaging in other pursuits were the characteristics that higher authorities claimed to admire most. As the director of a Urals machine-tool enterprise put it in September 1934:

> Many of us consider that the shock worker is one who works day and night in the shop or factory, who does not crawl out of the shop, and who does not live for other interests except those of production.
>
> It seems to me that it would be more correct to consider a shock worker as someone who works at the factory exactly seven hours, since Soviet power does not permit anyone to work more, who regularly goes to the cinema, visits others, engages in sport and at the same time fulfills all production tasks. Our Soviet shock worker must live in a cultured manner and take advantage of all the good things of life that Soviet power offers him.

To this, Piatakov, presiding over the meeting at which the director spoke, uttered, "Correct."[35]

But what were "the good things of life" and what did living in a cultured manner mean? So long as workers lived on rations in crowded barracks or corners and their leisure time was minimal, these questions were almost irrelevant. Indeed, insofar as being cultured (*kul'turnost'*) was associated with the bourgeoisie

---

[34] See the table of the number of people who scaled the five highest peaks in the USSR in 1934 (452) and 1935 (4,263), in *Sotsialisticheskoe stroitel'stvo SSSR* (Moscow: TsUNKhU, 1936), 554. For the substitution of "physical culture" by "sport" in the Soviet lexicon and the rapid development of sports clubs and individual athletic competition during these years, see James Riordan, *Sport in Soviet Society* (Cambridge University Press, 1977), 120–52.

[35] *Soveshchanie khoziaistvennikov, inzhenerov, tekhnikov, partiinykh i profsoiuznykh rabotnikov tiazheloi promyshlennosti, 20–22 sentiabria, 1934 g. Stenograficheskii otchet* (Moscow: ONTI NKTP SSSR, 1935), 48–9.

"Life is joyous, comrades" – Busygin, his wife, and daughter. From *Stakhanovets*, no. 1 (1938).

and its standards, even to pose such questions was unthinkable. By the mid–1930s, however, the standards had changed, leisure time had expanded for at least some (male) workers, and, as a result of productivity increases and the expanded application of the progressive piece-rate system, so had their pay packets.

Although we have no firm basis for asertaining what the material and cultural expectations of these workers were – except that they were probably greater than they had been four or five years earlier – we do have some idea of what they were encouraged to seek in these respects. This is because there exists an array of sources relating to the lives of outstanding Stakhanovites, or rather the idealized versions of those lives in the form of speeches, newspaper profiles, and autobiographical accounts published in book and pamphlet format.

Built around the "Life is joyous" theme, these sources typically contrast an arduous and dismal past – sometimes that of tsarist times but also no more remote than the First Five-Year Plan years – with a brilliant present and prospects for an even brighter future. They thus constitute a kind of cultural agenda, one that was shot through with optimism. It bears repeating that the mythology presented in these accounts bore little relation to the lives of most Soviet workers, Stakhanovites included. Neverthe-

glass – these were the building materials of the new cultured life.[40]

So, too, was the possession of scarce consumer goods. "Now that we have begun to earn decent wages," remarked Diukanov to the All-Union conference of Stakhanovites, "we want to lead a cultured life. We want bicycles, pianos, phonographs, records, radio sets, and many other articles of culture. But these things are still not to be had in the Donbass. If the party and the government help us, the Donbass will live still better, in a more cultured way."[41]

The party and government were not slow to respond to this demand, which was also articulated by Central Irmino's party organizer, K. G. Petrov. In early January 1936, when more than 900 Stakhanovite coal miners, engineers, managers, and party officials gathered for a meeting in Stalino, Ordzhonikidze ordered that more than a thousand prizes be distributed to the delegates. The prizes included 50 automobiles (only 12 of which went to Stakhanovites), 25 motorcycles, 500 bicycles, 150 phonographs, 200 hunting rifles, and 150 pocket watches.[42] Individual Stakhanovites in other parts of the country were also favored with gifts. Reference has already been made to the cornucopia of food products presented to the Busygin family. But even more obscure Stakhanovites such as E. M. Fedorova, a garment worker at Leningrad's Red Banner Factory, could suddenly be deluged. From her enterprise, she received a watch; from the district soviet and party *raikom*, a vase, clock, tablecloth, electric samovar, clothes iron, phonograph, and records; from the enterprise party committee, the works of Lenin and Stalin; and from the Leningrad soviet, 122 books.[43]

[40] In his autobiography, Stakhanov refers to the paved thoroughfares of the Donbass cities and towns he visited with almost comical repetitiveness. See A. G. Stakhanov, *Rasskaz o moei zhizni* (Moscow: Gossotsizd., 1937), 88, 89, 95, 133.

[41] *Pervoe Vsesoiuznoe soveshchanie rabochikh i rabotnits-stakhanovtsev, 14–17 noiabria 1935 g., Stenograficheskii otchet* (Moscow: Partizdat, 1935), 30.

[42] *Pravda*, Jan. 11, 1936. For the list of gifts and recipients see *Pervyi vsedonetskii slet stakhanovtsev-masterov uglia, 7–10 ianvaria 1936 g. Stalino, Stenograficheskii otchet* (Kiev: Partizdat TsK KP(b)U, 1936), 291–6.

[43] *Rabotnitsa*, no. 5 (1936): 2.

less, it would be foolish to ignore them for this reason or [
the possibility that they had some bearing on ordinary w
cultural orientations and aspirations.

To begin with, the acquisition of a room of one's owr
one were married and had a family, an apartment was
complishment of which the recipient could be proud. F
spent his first few years in Gor'kii living in a makeshift w
barracks, S. A. Faustov, Busygin's rival for top honors .
Molotov Automobile Works, boasted of his "beautiful apar
with all the comforts." "If someone had told me that I wou
living in a multi-story stone building, constructed accordi
the latest word in technology, . . . I would have laughed i
face," he wrote.[36] The contrast between the corner wher
Moscow Frunze textile worker, M. Lysakova, had previ
lived and the "large, airy, warm apartment" she occupied
becoming a Stakhanovite was at least as great. Another !
hanovite textile worker, E. G. Illarionova, confessed to b
"embarrassed" by her apartment, which she described as b
than the one in which the director lived.[37] Where the desire
proper accommodation went unfulfilled, as in the case of a l
ingrad textile mill's best Stakhanovite, the press reminded n
agement of its responsibility.[38]

Personal rewards and the satisfaction derived therefrom w
matched by the celebration of what the nation could now o
its citizens. In place of ramshackle, jerry-built wooden structu
stood "real palaces" of brick, stone, and concrete; in place
dark, muddy streets ruled by hooligans, there were well-light
paved thoroughfares filled with automobiles and trams. Hous
was still abysmally scarce, but in Gor'kii there was a Busy;
quarter that was a showplace of worker accommodation, and
Stalingrad new apartments with flower-bedecked balconies lin
the newly asphalted boulevards. Most basic consumer goods we
still in short supply, but at least Gor'kii had its three story c
partment store, "shimmering with glass."[39] Brick, asphalt, ai

[36] S. A. Faustov, *Moi rost* (Gor'kii: Gor'kovskoe oblastnoe izdatel'stv
1938), 8, 24.
[37] *Pravda*, Jan. 11, 1936; *Rabotnitsa*, no. 3 (1936): 9.
[38] *LP*, Oct. 21, 1935.
[39] Faustov, *Moi rost* 8; D. N. Vasil'ev, *Moia mechta* (Stalingrad: Kraevc
knigoizd., 1936), 5.

Most Stakhanovites, however, did not rely solely on the munificence of state, party, and enterprise organizations. With their "decent" wages, they found themselves able to purchase a range of consumer goods, especially clothing. In this respect no less than in their productivity, they seemed anxious to catch up to and surpass Western norms. As one trade union journal put it, "Just as they smash the old production norms, so the Stakhanovites surpass the limits of the possibilities of daily life."[44] To the turner Likhoradov, it was simply a matter of taking advantage of the opportunities provided by the Soviet government to "live in a cultured way." "Why," he asked rhetorically, "should I not wear a good serge suit [and] smoke good cigarettes?"[45] Were such aspirations compatible with socialist principles? Of course they were. According to one commentator:

The transition from socialism to communism does not at all mean the gradual (or even any) liquidation of articles of personal consumption. . . . Yesterday's peasant, sleeping on sackcloth draped over the plankings above the stove, now acquires a bed with springs, good furniture, sheets, tule blankets, curtains, etc.

"This is why," the commentator added, "Stakhanovites announce with pride their growing prosperity."[46]

The problem was that not all Stakhanovites knew how to spend their money wisely. This seemed to be particularly the case with young Stakhanovites, whose "surplus of means often is wasted on dandyism if not on drink."[47] Thus, the itemization in the press of goods presented to or purchased by model Stakhanovites served an instructional purpose and, in the latter case, illustrated what money could now buy. For example, when a cutting machinist from a mine in Chistiakovo went on a buying spree in November 1935, *Pravda* listed his acquisitions: coats for himself and his wife, several suits, shoes, slippers, and bolts of cloth, as well as a phonograph and records. Another machinist, from the Il'ich mine, was reported to have spent more than 1,300 rubles on coats, trousers, boots, a chest of drawers and other items. For Ivan Antonov, a fitter at Leningrad's Stalin Factory,

---

[44] *Profsoiuznyi rabotnik*, no. 1 (1936): 12
[45] *Pervoe Vsesoiuznoe soveshchanie*, 179.
[46] *LP*, June 6, 1936.
[47] *Klub*, no. 3 (1936): 8.

increased wages were exchanged for a piano, a sofa, a sewing machine, firewood, and felt boots for his two children.[48] Then there was N. I. Slavnikova, a young boring-machine operator who had earned so much that she could not decide what to buy first. As she recounted to the All-Union conference, she turned for advice to her friend Marusia, who had actually earned 500 rubles more than Slavnikova in October 1935. "What shall we do with all this money?" asked Nina. "I will buy myself beige shoes for 180 rubles, a silk dress for 200 rubles, and a coat for 700 rubles," was Marusia's reply.[49]

Clothes were not considered articles of culture as such, but they did help to create a cultured appearance. The following description of two young Stakhanovites celebrating the New Year could have come from the society page, were there such an institution in the Soviet press:

The *brigadir*-welder Vl. Baranov (28, the best Stakhanovite at Elektro-zavod) glided across the floor in a slow tango with Shura Ovchinnikova (20, the best Stakhanovite at TsAGI). He was dressed in a black Boston suit that fully accentuated his solidly built figure; she was in a crepe de chine dress and black shoes with white trimming.[50]

Such sophisticates were a long way from the *kolkhozniki*, but even in the villages Stakhanovites could cut a relatively "advanced" figure, as evidenced by the following *chastushka* recited by Pasha Angelina:

> Oh, thank you dear Lenin,
> Oh, thank you dear Stalin,
> Oh, thank you and thank you again
> For Soviet power.
>
> Knit for me, dear mama
> A dress of fine red calico.

[48] *Pravda*, Mar. 2, 1936; *Profsoiuznyi rabotnik*, no. 1 (1936):12. See also *Izvestiia*, Nov. 14, 1936, for an account of a Leningrad Stakhanovite family that spent 1,500 rubles on clothes and linens in one month. For other itemizations, see *Pravda*, Apr. 26, 1936; Mar. 30, 1938.

[49] *Pervoe Vsesoiuznoe soveshchanie*, 42–3.

[50] *Vechernaia Moskva*, Jan. 2, 1936. On changing styles in clothes among Urals workers during these years, see V. Iu. Krupianskaia, I. R. Budina, N. S. Polishchuk, and N. V. Iukhneva, *Kul'tura i byt gorniakov i metallurgov Nizhnego Tagila* (1917–1970) (Moscow: Nauka, 1974), 236–9.

With a Stakhanovite I will go strolling,
With a backward one I don't want to.[51]

Clothes, no less than decent accommodation, were important
to A. D. Generalova, an automobile worker at the Molotov factory in Gor'kii. In her brief autobiography, which was written
"above all for women to tell them about . . . how I found the path
to happiness," she relates how "several years ago, I lived in barracks and had nothing to wear to go out for a stroll." All that
changed after she became a Stakhanovite and was given a bicycle,
a phonograph, and a furnished apartment by the director. "Now
I live in a good apartment, have all the clothes I need, and am
a respectable, marriageable girl."[52] It must have been with such
girls in mind that various trusts advertised in the journal *Stakhanovets* for Lilac, Crimean Rose, and Sweet Pea eau de cologne,
toothpaste, and patterns of the latest styles in clothing from
Moscow, Leningrad, Paris, London, and Vienna.[53]

A cultured appearance was important, however, not only for
marriageable girls and not only during leisure hours. Shura Martynova, the outstanding female Stakhanovite at Skorokhod, was
on her way to work with her husband when she was photographed wearing a fur coat, a feathered hat, and overshoes. A
Stakhanovite textile worker, Milovanova, wrote in her factory's
newspaper that before leaving for work she made it a practice
to clean her shoes, look into the mirror, and carefully arrange
her dress. Cleanliness extended to her use of language as well.
"Now I no longer swear," she remarked, "because I know that
for Stakhanovites it is not in character" (*nam stakhanovtsam eto ne
k litsu*).[54]

---

[51] *SD*, Nov. 23, 1936. The occasion was the third congress of Donetsk
oblast' soviets.
[52] A. D. Generalova, *Kak ia stala stakhanovkoi* (Gor'kii: Gor'kovskoe oblastnoe izdatel'stvo, 1938), 3, 14–15.
[53] *Stakhanovets*, no. 2 (1937); nos. 1 and 2 (1938).
[54] *Rabsel'kor*, no. 1 (1936):30; no. 11 (1936):12–13. What a contrast with
1932, when, at the party's Seventeenth Conference, the commissar
of light industry was at pains to point out that the outward appearance of Western workers was deceiving. Many did dress neatly, he
conceded, but this was at the expense of going hungry. "Workers
abroad take great care about their wardrobe," Liubimov noted, "in
order to conform to the requirements of bourgeois circles. . . . The

Making Stakhanovites cultured. An advertisement in *Stakhanovets*, no. 1 (1938).

These positive examples were supplemented by criticisms of low standards of dress and organizational efforts to improve the situation. In April 1936, E. Fadeeva, a medal-winning Stakhanovite textile worker, wrote to *Pravda* complaining about the "untidiness, slovenliness, and lack of culture" exhibited by her fellow workers on the job. This, in her view, displayed a lack of respect toward themselves and their work.[55] The letter sparked a number of meetings at Moscow factories.[56] At the Paris Commune Shoe Factory, the slovenly appearance of many workers, including Stakhanovites, was decried. Gorshkov, a young bachelor, was

old jacket is cleaned and pressed every week." *XVII konferentsiia VKP(b). Ianv.–fev. 1932 g. Stenograficheskii otchet* (Moscow: Partizdat, 1932), 39.
[55] *Pravda*, Apr. 20, 1936.
[56] And not just in Moscow. See the report of a meeting at the First of May Factory in Leningrad in *Rabsel'kor*, no. 11 (1936):13, and the remarks of the Stakhanovite turner Matiunin at a meeting of Stakhanovites and managerial-technical personnel in Khabarovsk in *Tikhookeanskaia zvezda*, July 22, 1936.

described by one of his workmates as coming to work unshaven, in torn pants, and with his belt open ("And he is a Stakhanovite!"). Another worker, Naryshkina, was seen shuffling into her shop dirty and disheveled.

This was very much in contrast to the appearance of those attending the meeting at which such denunciations were made. As described by the *Pravda* correspondent, the men were wearing starched white collars and jackets; the female workers were dressed in clean blouses and good skirts, and some were even lightly powdered. "This too," the correspondent noted, "is a necessary instrument of the workers that can influence fulfillment of the plan and the quality of production."[57]

However, managers and engineers had to cooperate and set a good example. One speaker at the meeting criticized management for a shortage of towels, soap, and mirrors in the lavatories. At the Red October Confectionary Factory, female workers resolved to press for an additional restroom so that they could have a manicure every other day.[58] Later that year, turners at the Nevskii Machine Construction Factory in Leningrad lodged a complaint about not having anywhere to change into work clothes. Moreover, they claimed that, far from setting a good example, the engineers were coming to work unshaven and in greasy clothing, "in the style of workers" (*po rabochemu*). Such behavior smacked of the misguided petty bourgeois egalitarianism that Stalin had long ago condemned as having nothing to do with socialism. In any case, it was an insult to the "genuine Stakhanovite," who was characterized as a "model of cleanliness, tidiness, and culture."[59]

Finally, the most obvious manifestation of being cultured was partaking in cultural activities. As with production, quantity was very important. To demonstrate that in the year since Stakhanov's record life really had become more joyous, *Izvestiia* found a plane operator from a Moscow instruments factory who had been to three performances of *Evgenii Onegin*, two each of *Boris Godunov* and *The Demon*, and one each of *Carmen* and *Rigoletto*. This same Stakhanovite, Kondrat'ev, also read – everything from

[57] *Pravda*, Apr. 24, 1936.
[58] Ibid., Apr. 26, 1936.
[59] *LP*, Oct. 26, 1936.

Gor'kii's *Mother* and *War and Peace* to several of Sholokhov's works. O. P. Chapygina, a Frunze factory worker, also enjoyed the opera and theater. But what was particularly noteworthy was her personal library, which contained 282 books.[60] No less cultured was Aleksandr Ponomarev, the experienced Leningrad fitter who was the subject of a photodisplay that appeared in the Soviet pavilion at the 1937 Paris Exhibition. The camera caught him in several "characteristic moments" of his "everyday life," such as reading at home (with a portrait of Stalin gazing down at him from the wall), visiting the Hermitage with his family, and attending the ballet at the Kirov Theater, accompanied by his wife.[61]

These, however, were unusual cases, even in the realm of higher reality. Many Stakhanovites, including those among the outstanding elite, were barely literate. For Stakhanov, Busygin, and others, acquiring culture initially meant being tutored in the Russian language and other subjects before entering one of the industrial academies. D. Kontsedalov, Stakhanov's workmate at Central Irmino, learned how to read together with his wife. "Every day I learn something new," he wrote to the local Komsomol newspaper. "This pleases me as much as the first day when I established a record in productivity."[62]

Thus, if some Stakhanovites were models of cultured individuals, others could be advertised as examples of individuals who had learned to acquire culture. Yet the actual diffusion of culture among Stakhanovites entailed more than finding exemplary individuals. It required bringing culture to workers in the form of new cinemas, libraries, parks, reading circles, group excursions, and so forth.[63] Much of this effort devolved onto the trade unions. Responsible for organizing and operating workers' clubs

[60] *Izvestiia*, Aug. 30, 1936.
[61] *Stakhanovets*, no. 12 (1937):54–6. See also the account of Ivan Antonov, who as a rule did not go to the theater or think about purchasing a summer suit until he became a Stakhanovite, in *Profsoiuznyi rabotnik*, no. 1 (1936):12.
[62] *Marsh udarnykh brigad. Molodezh v gody vosstanovleniia narodnogo khoziaistva i sostialisticheskogo stroitel'stva, 1921–1941 gg. Sbornik dokumentov* (Moscow: Molodaia gvardiia, 1965), 340–1.
[63] For increases in the number of such cultural outlets in these years, see *Kul'turnoe stroitel'stvo, SSSR, Statisticheskii sbornik* (Moscow–Leningrad: Gosplanizdat, 1940), 141–204.

and "palaces of culture," the unions' factory committees began
to orient their activities especially toward Stakhanovites. Special
Stakhanovite rooms, such as the one visited by Romanov, were
set up in these establishments. Literacy classes and lectures on
such subjects as "what Stakhanovites should read," personal hygiene, and gardening were organized.[64]

The educational functions of the clubs were supplemented
and reinforced by the press. *Stakhanovets*, a journal published by
VTsSPS, interspersed reports on Stakhanovites' techniques and
the obstacles they faced on the shop floor with pages devoted to
history and the natural sciences. Nor were the recreational needs
of Stakhanovites ignored. In addition to an informational series
on "noteworthy dates" and a contest that tested readers' knowledge of inventors and inventions, the journal ran a series that
told Stakhanovites what to see when they visited Moscow.[65] *Oblast'*
newspapers were particularly well placed to guide their readers
toward the most appropriate forms of entertainment and recreation. Thus, in its May Day issue, *Magnitogorskii rabochii* published the responses of seventy Stakhanovites to the question of
what they intended to do on the holiday. Fifty were going to
attend the theater, the cinema, or the circus, twenty-five would
be preparing lessons or engaging in various forms of public
activity, three were working on "inventions," and almost all
would be reading newspapers and books.[66] It was just such articles that one Stakhanovite asked *Sotsialisticheskii Donbass* (whose
coverage of Stakhanovism was otherwise extensive) to print so
that "we can better orient ourselves toward the theater, the cinema and literature."[67]

Cultured individuals dressing and working in a cultured manner, earning "decent" wages that enabled them to buy articles
of culture, and acquiring a knowledge of culture – this was the
idealized picture of Stakhanovites. The picture, however, is in-

[64] *Klub*, no. 2 (1936):8, 10–11, 14–15; no. 3 (1936): 8, 21. Note, incidentally, the term "palace," which replaced the more humble "house"
of culture around this time.
[65] *Stakhanovets*, no. 1 (1937):56, 60–1; no. 3 (1937):63; no. 4 (1937):52–
5; no. 6 (1937):53–6.
[66] *Magnitogorskii rabochii*, May 1, 1936. Obviously, each worker was in-
tending to engage in more than one activity.
[67] *SD*, May 5, 1936.

complete. It excludes the home life of Stakhanovites and the roles that other members of the Stakhanovite family were to play. As international tensions mounted and as struggles within the party and state exploded into the Ezhovshchina, the idealized Stakhanovite family came to assume an importance that could not have been foreseen and that was to endure long after Stakhanovism in the factories had lost much of its significance.

III

The proportional increase in the burden borne by women in the working-class household during the first half of the 1930s coincided with, and was reinforced by, a shift in official Soviet policy toward the family. This shift was neither sudden nor entirely the result of state voluntarism. It occurred as part of a larger process of social integration and stabilization that followed upon the massive social and economic upheavals of the late 1920s and early 1930s.

Although in the course of the First Five-Year Plan, controversies over the proper role of women in a socialist society diminished, the party remained committed, at least in theory, to achieving more than the formal equality of the sexes provided by legislation. Even after the notion of the withering away of the family had been condemned as a leftist deviation and despite the lack of substantial progress in reducing the burdens of housework for women (or educating men to its importance), this ideal persisted in party rhetoric. As an International Women's Day editorial of 1933 put it, "Our party strives to emancipate women from the material burdens of backward housework by replacing it with communal households, public dining, central washhouses, childcare, etc."[68]

Thereafter, the emancipatory goal was replaced by an emphasis on the responsibilities of women to the family and the joys derived therefrom. Having been mobilized for production, women would henceforth be mobilized for reproduction. To quote Lapidus again:

[68] *ZI*, Mar. 8, 1933.

The new orientation, far from devaluing the role of the family, now treated it as a pivotal social institution performing vital functions. It was to serve above all as a model of social order, and for this purpose marital stability was essential. The independence, autonomy and mobility encouraged by earlier legislation were henceforth to be restricted in the interests of preserving a stable and monogamous partnership.[69]

Commenting from enforced exile on the emergent "cult of the family," Trotsky pointed out that responsibility for maintaining a stable and monogamous partnership varied not only according to sex, but among women of different social strata. In contrast to the "5 percent, maybe 10," who "build their 'hearthstone' " by relying on "a cook, a telephone for giving orders to the stores [and] an automobile for errands," working women were "compelled to run to the shops, prepare dinner . . . and carry [their] children on foot from the kindergarten – if, indeed, a kindergarten is available." "No socialist labels," he added, "can conceal the social contrast, which is no less striking than the contrast between the bourgeois lady and the proletarian woman in any country of the West."[70]

Where, then, did Stakhanovism fit into this picture of "hypocritical respectability"? There is curiously little information about female Stakhanovites building their hearthstones or raising families. Far from projecting an image of domesticity, female Stakhanovites were impatient to advance in their careers, even if they did so at the expense of homemaking and child rearing. The Skorokhod shoe laster Martynova turned her dining table into a time and motion study base. Using knives and spoons, she went through the production motions while her husband, also a laster, timed her.[71] For Marfa Fomina, the best Stakhanovite at Leningrad's Dzerzhinskii Textile Mill, marriage and raising a family were incompatible with the ambitions of finishing school, increasing the number of machines she tended, and developing her skills as a parachutist. An illiterate country girl until 1932, she now lived in a "beautiful room," studied, engaged in sport,

[69] Lapidus, *Women*, 112.
[70] Leon Trotsky, *The Revolution Betrayed* (New York: Merit, 1965), 156–7.
[71] *Pravda*, Oct. 12, 1935; *LP*, Nov. 14, 1936.

and did "interesting things" in the evening. "Could anyone be as happy as me?" she exulted.[72]

Stakhanovites were noticeably scarce among the working women who testified to the wisdom of the draft decree banning abortions. This was despite the intense propaganda about the advantages Soviet women enjoyed compared with their counterparts in other countries.[73] Indeed, not long before the draft was published, two items appeared in the press underlining the hardships endured by Stakhanovite women who were single parents. One reported the suicide of a *brigadir* at a Kiev spirits factory. According to *Pravda*, her suicide note blamed the enterprise administration for the death of her chronically ill son because it had repeatedly turned down her requests for decent accommodation.[74] Less grim but no less revealing was the self-portrait written by a *brigadir* from the Ordzhonikidze Machine Construction Factory in Moscow. She not only was a Stakhanovite, but as a member of the shop's cultural section helped to arrange for newspaper readings and discussions during rest periods, played the accordian, had recently attended the opera, visited the Tretiakov Gallery and the Lenin Museum, and had ambitions of studying music and pursuing some kind of literary work. All this, however, left her little time to be with her son. Her account of dragging him to her friends on days off or to the baby sitter contrasts strikingly with the ideal family situation of other accounts.[75]

The wives of Stakhanovites led very different lives, and it is with respect to them that we find Stakhanovism and the inculcation of family values intersecting with and reinforcing one another. Initially, these fortunate women were assigned the role of competent helpmates whose example could be emulated by the wives of other workers. "To your lot," read the assistant director's letter that accompanied the food parcel sent to the Busygins' apartment, "has fallen the great fortune to be the wife of a man about whom the entire factory is talking. Greeting you,... I send a small present and ask you to care for your

[72] *LP*, Oct. 21, 1935; *Profsoiuznyi rabotnik*, no. 2 (1936):9.
[73] For a few exceptions, see *LP*, May 28, June 1, July 30, 1936.
[74] *Pravda*, Mar. 6, 1936. See also *Izvestiia*, Mar. 6, 1936.
[75] *ZI*, Mar. 8, 1937.

husband so that he has sufficient rest to repeat his shock work every day." The good woman replied in kind that she would "assume responsibility to create conditions at home so that coming from work, he can eat well and rest well and with fresh energy go to the factory to achieve new victories."[76]

Other Stakhanovites' wives were no less helpful. They closely followed the work of their husbands, inquiring about their results. They promised to create cultured conditions in the home, which meant preparing tasty, nourishing dishes and correctly educating their children.[77] One woman was described by her Stakhanovite husband, a Donbass miner, as "a real Mikoian" because of her talent at managing the family's food budget. Another was a regular customer at a Leningrad store from which she ordered for home delivery butter, eggs, sardines, and sweet wine. These were all products that, according to *Leningradskaia pravda*, "count among the ordinary, everyday menus of any worker-Stakhanovite."[78] And even in the far north, *kolkhoz* women were boasting that, with the earnings of their timber-cutting Stakhanovite husbands, they could afford to place orders with the local ORS to feed and clothe their families properly.[79]

The obvious point was to emphasize to other women that they, too, could lead happy, secure, and comfortable lives if their husbands became Stakhanovites.[80] This image of domestic bliss eventually came to constitute an important theme of the Stakhanovite movement. Stakhanov's description of one of his days off in July 1936 fairly reeks of it. Arising at 9:00 A.M., he had breakfast. While the children went to play and Klavdia, his wife, visited with neighbors, he listened to the radio and read the newspaper. Later, the family decided to drive in their M–1 to the banks of the Donets River. There, they had lunch, went

---

[76] Quoted in V. Lel'chuk, "Aleksei Busygin," in *Novatory, Sbornik* (Moscow: Molodaia gvardiia, 1972), 154. See also *Rabotnitsa*, no. 3 (1936):3, where housewives were urged "to help husbands and children become Stakhanovites."

[77] *PS*, no. 13 (1936):76; *LP*, Oct. 18, 1935. See also the letter from the wives of three Baku Stakhanovites in *Pravda*, Nov. 3, 1935.

[78] *Pervyi vsedonetskii slet*, 127; *LP*, Nov. 5, 1936.

[79] *Za sotsialisticheskii sever* (Kotlas), Feb. 17, 1936.

[80] In case anyone missed the point, however, the far northern women asked, "Why can't your husbands be Stakhanovites, have high wages and purchase new goods?" Ibid.

boating, and played volleyball with other miners' families. At home again, Stakhanov wrote out his Russian lessons. Diukanov and his wife dropped by for a visit. After tea, the women "occupied themselves with their affairs," while the two men played checkers. Then they all went to the local workers' club, where they saw a performance of Pogodin's play *The Aristocrats*.[81]

We should note here a number of attributes of the archetypal Stakhanovite family. Popularity was one. Wherever Stakhanov went – the riverside, the park, the theater, his native village – he reported being surrounded by admiring people. Busygin was so popular that he had a problem deciding where to spend New Year's Eve. So many invitations![82] Sobriety is also evident. The Stakhanovs and Diukanovs drank tea, and the samovar figured prominently in photographs of the apartments of other Stakhanovite families.[83] Finally, the forms of entertainment and recreation, if not exactly elevated, were at least secular and modern – listening to the radio, reading the newspaper, playing volleyball and checkers, going to the theater.

No less interesting is what is left out of Stakhanov's account. We are told that he arose and had breakfast, but not who prepared this or the other meals of the day. While Stakhanov read the newspaper to learn about the new records of cutting-machine operators and the international situation, in which he expressed "especial interest," Klavdia visited neighbors. Was she also interested in international affairs? What did she read? Could she read? And what were the "affairs" that she and Diukanova pursued while the men played checkers?

---

[81] Stakhanov, *Rasskaz*, 86. *The Aristocrats*, first performed in January 1935, concerned criminals who were reformed through their labor on the Belomor Canal. *Teatral'naia entsiklopediia*, 5 vols. (Moscow: Sovetskaia Entsiklopediia, 1961), 1:275.

[82] *Izvestiia*, Jan. 1, 1936.

[83] For such photographs, see *Stakhanovets*, no. 12 (1937):37, 41, 52–4. The theme of alcoholics being cured through instruction in Stakhanovite work techniques and the provision of articles of culture (musical instruments, dominoes, books, newspapers, and flowers) appeared in a number of testimonials. See the speech by I. A. Makarov in *Pervoe Vsesoiuznoe soveshchanie*, 68–9, and *Vsesoiuznoe soveshchanie zhen khoziaistvennikov i inzhenerno-tekhnicheskikh rabotnikov tiazheloi promyshlennosti. Stenograficheskii otchet* (Moscow: NKTP, 1936), 237.

These questions arise because they were raised at the time, not about Stakhanov's wife in particular, but about the wives of other Stakhanovites. They emerged in the rather bizarre but revealing – probably unintentionally revealing – context of an All-Union conference of the wives of commanders of production, that is, heavy-industrial enterprise directors and engineers. More than 1,300 of these worthy ladies – "housewife-activists" is the way they were described and identified themselves – convened in the Kremlin in May 1936. For three days, they informed one another about and celebrated the good works they had been doing at their respective enterprises. As if to underline the significance of the occasion, all of the highest Soviet dignitaries attended, or at least were photographed on the podium. Forty of the women went away with medals awarded for their initiative in organizing the movement to raise the cultural and living standards of workers and employees in heavy industry.[84]

This movement actually had begun in 1934. Its earliest forms were the beautification of the factory environs (flowers again!) and the improvement of food and service in enterprise cafeterias and conditions in enterprise barracks and dormitories. Though these activities continued to animate the women, it is clear that, with the rise of Stakhanovism, their philanthropy took a new turn. Now Stakhanovites' families would be the main, indeed in many instances the sole, beneficiaries. Evgeniia Vesnik, one of the movement's founders, proudly announced that at the Krivoi Rog metallurgical enterprise she and other women had arranged for a model dormitory for Stakhanovites to be opened. It contained bathrooms, showers, an "American" laundry, a beauty parlor, and a reading room.[85] Another lady, from Dzerzhinsk, intended while in Moscow to purchase tulle curtains, mirrors, and oil cloth for thirty Stakhanovite rooms in the enterprise dormitory.[86] Others inspected Stakhanovites' apartments and read literary works over tea.[87]

It was the wives and children of Stakhanovites, however, who received the greatest attention. Having in many cases only re-

---

[84] *Pravda*, May 14, 1936.
[85] *Vsesoiuznoe soveshchanie zhen*, 17.
[86] Ibid., 58.
[87] Ibid., 189, 232.

cently acquired culture themselves, the public-spirited wives of commanders sought to create in their own image cultured women from among Stakhanovite families. They taught them how to read and how to dance, how to crochet, and what to buy. One woman came up with the ingenious idea of giving prizes to the Stakhanovite's wife who kept her house in the best order.[88]

In vain had Nadezhda Krupskaia, a speaker at the conference, worried about these women cutting themselves off from the working class. "We have found a common language with the wives of Stakhanovites," proclaimed a woman from Tagil in the Urals.[89] No doubt, the recipients of such instruction were glad to speak the same language as the wives of their husbands' bosses. As one woman stated in response to an inquiry from the editor of the Skorokhod factory newspaper, "We don't want to be left behind. We will work and study to help our husbands build a still brighter future."[90] The fear of being left behind was probably quite genuine. If, as Trotsky contended, "one of the very dramatic chapters in the great book of Soviets" will be about ambitious Soviet bureaucrats who abandoned their uncultured spouses, then at least a few pages might be devoted to the fickleness of advanced workers.[91]

IV

Stakhanovites and their wives were thus favored for a number of reasons when it came to receiving instruction. Yet however advanced they were on the shop floor and however quickly they mastered middle-class etiquette, they were still, after all, manual workers. Charity, far from overcoming the inequality between donor and recipient, tended to justify and therefore perpetuate such a relationship.

One wonders, however, about the children. Could it be that

[88] Ibid., 106–7.
[89] Ibid., 72.
[90] *LP*, July 4, 1936.
[91] Trotsky, *Revolution Betrayed*, 156. The phenomenon was already quite well known in the mid–1920s. See the testimony in *The Family in the U.S.S.R.*, ed. Rudolf Schlesinger (London: Routledge & Kegan Paul, 1949), 106–7, 109.

a quite different fate was being prepared for them? The evidence is slight but suggestive. In the kindergartens and excursions organized by the charitable wives, Stakhanovites' children were grouped together with those of engineers and technicians.[92] Then there were the children of outstanding Stakhanovites. If little Alesha Martekhov was told by his teacher that as the son of the famous Leningrad Stakhanovite forge operator he had a great responsibility to do well in school, then other Stakhanovites' children eventually could set their sights higher.[93] Take, for instance, the two sons of Aleksandr Ponomarev, who in 1937 were sixteen and ten years old. While the older one was studying to become the captain of oceangoing vessels, little Lev expressed his desire to be a pilot flying polar routes. "Before the youth of our country, all paths are open!" read the caption beneath their photograph.[94]

Did this mean not only that life would still be more joyous for one's children, but that it would be so because one's children did not have to be workers? Why did the wives of commanders of production consider it appropriate to isolate Stakhanovites' children from those of other workers? And why at the meeting of Stakhanovite miners in Stalino did Sarkisov mention that several of their children were in the process of becoming – or had already become – engineers?[95] Could it have been that, despite claims that Stakhanovites had overcome the gap between mental and manual labor, the instances of role reversal in which they engaged, the privileges they acquired, and the precariousness of being a production engineer or an *intelligent* of whatever specialty, there was no getting around the fact that the standards of status and culture remained largely unchanged?

It is true that at least some Stakhanovites exercised considerable discretionary power in their work and the organization of labor. They could demand the delivery of certain materials and power and order about subordinate and auxiliary workers.

[92] *Vsesoiuznoe soveshchanie zhen*, 65, 154. See also the reference to special schools attended by Stakhanovites' children in Harvard Interview Project on the Soviet Social System, Russian Research Center Library, Harvard University, interview no. 1106, p. 21.

[93] *LP*, Oct. 18, 1935.

[94] *Stakhanovets*, no. 12 (1937):53.

[95] *Pervyi vsedonetskii slet*, 40–1.

However, as Michael Burawoy has pointed out, one can – and in our case, must – distinguish the unification of conception and execution on an individual level from that at the collective or societal level.[96] The former, which does afford a degree of job control, could just as well signify a return to artisanal methods as a harbinger of communism. In any case, status and standards within an individual enterprise or even within the general arena of material production do not necessarily prevail in other spheres of activity. Indeed, it could be argued that so long as material production takes place in certain delimited institutions (industrial enterprises, collective and state farms) and involves only a proportion of the entire able-bodied adult population, cultural standards will be established elsewhere, by those engaged primarily in mental labor.

Role reversal, the idea that Stakhanovites knew more than the professors, may have irked some professors but was nonetheless a phenomenon in which certain astute academicians could take part without sacrificing their positions and could probably even enhance them. Stakhanov and his emulators did not become professors, but were rather in the first instance instructors of their work techniques. In the complex hierarchy of Soviet industry, this put them somewhere between workers of the higher skill grades and low-level technical personnel, or roughly where subforemen and adjusters stood. This was higher than they had been before, but a long way from a shift engineer, factory director, or *glavk* official.

The cultural mythology of this period did not and was not supposed to transform the values of society as a whole. Rather, it was to encourage workers and, in the first instance, Stakhanovites to identify their personal ambitions with those of the nation. Stakhanovites may have helped to revolutionize technique as Stalin claimed, but evidently not relations of production. They had neither risen to the top nor redefined who deserved to be there.

Even in terms of privileges, most Stakhanovites rated no higher than ordinary engineering-technical personnel. The fact that their wages were frequently higher than foremen's salaries,

[96] Michael Burawoy, *The Politics of Production* (London: Verso, 1985), 54, 82.

excluding bonuses, was regarded as an anomaly that had to be corrected and eventually was. Scarce consumer goods, tickets to the theater, and trips to their unions' sanatoria were not perquisites that could be obtained for the asking, but came irregularly like the ideal conditions on the shop floor that were conducive to the setting of records. With the exception of complaints by several former engineers who were interviewed as part of the Harvard Interview Project, the evidence overwhelmingly points to the fact that such employees generally enjoyed a higher standard of living than Stakhanovites.[97]

Although that standard was higher, it was not more secure. Even while a niche was being created for Stakhanovites, room was being made farther up the industrial hierarchy. Parallel with and temporarily eclipsing the image of the Stakhanovite worker as the New Soviet Man was the phenomenon of Stakhanovites being promoted to the ranks of lower and even middle management. Like the *vydvizhenchestvo* of the First Five-Year Plan period, this phenomenon was the result of both the prodigious expansion of the white-collar sector and party policy designed to create more accountable white-collar cadres. Such a policy might well have been implicit in the Stakhanovite movement from the outset, but it is apparent neither in the rhetoric nor in the reality of 1935–6. That the promotion of Stakhanovites occurred to the extent that it did can be attributed in large part to the arrests and shake-ups that marked the next two years. It was thus overdetermined.

While many Stakhanovite mothers and fathers looked forward to their children making the leap, others had the opportunity to do it themselves. These two developments – of some workers improving their material and cultural standards but remaining workers, and others ceasing to be such – were not peculiar to the late 1930s. Nor were they limited to Soviet society. There was something peculiar, however, about the culture of this period and the behavior it sanctioned that is captured in the following recollection of a former naval officer:

I would go to the theater . . . and take a seat from where I could watch people coming in. And I could tell by the way they came in who these

---

[97] Harvard Project, no. 114, p. 11; no. 388, schedule B10, p. 81; no. 1497, p. 18.

people were.... Now, a Stakhanovite comes in.... He is in a curious position. He doesn't really know whether he belongs here. He's been thrown to the top suddenly. But he has an invitation from his plant he carries in his hand and he walks with a self-assured step.[98]

We may therefore conclude by endorsing Jerry Hough's observation that the "Big Deal" about which Vera Dunham has written so persuasively "really originated in the 1930s rather than in the 1940s."[99] That is, beginning in the middle of the Second Five-Year Plan and extending into the years of the Great Purges, the political authorities needed to produce and found "contented citizens who, in turn, would be eager to pass on the contentment to their children."[100] We must add, however, that this earlier manifestation of the deal was more democratic than its postwar successor. Far from being restricted to the professional groups – Dunham's "middle class" – its main targets were industrial workers and, by extension, the more ambitious and accommodating elements among *kolkhoz* peasants.

Nevertheless, both earlier and later manifestations had two things in common. First, the cultural mythology of the latter half of the 1930s was decidedly domestic in orientation and integrative in function. It stressed material acquisitions, thereby stimulating acquisitiveness; it fetishized cleanliness and order; and it virtually banished struggle in favor of "apolitical conformism." In all these respects, it prefigured the Big Deal of the late 1940s and early 1950s. Second, although pitched at a lower level of society, the deal of the 1930s involved many of the same people who would be part of the Big Deal of the postwar era. As just indicated, the acquisition of *kul'turnost'* by Stakhanovites prepared them and their children for social advancement, even if higher reality taught them to be content where they were. Dreaming about raising their technical and cultural standards to the level of engineers, some Stakhanovites actually would move into technical positions even before the outbreak of the Great Patriotic War. It is to this process and the cataclysm that made it possible that we now turn.

[98]   Ibid., no. 105, schedule B2, pp. 39–40.
[99]   Jerry Hough, "Introduction," in Dunham, *In Stalin's Time*, xiii.
[100] Dunham, *In Stalin's Time*, 17.

7

From the Great Purges to the Great Patriotic War: the decline of Stakhanovism

The years 1936–8 are inextricably connected in Soviet history with the Great Purges, and rightly so. Although police terror was not as indiscriminate as some have claimed and although many estimates of the number of its victims have erred on the side of exaggeration, virtually no element of Soviet society was unaffected. Aside from relatives and friends of those who disappeared into the GULAG, there were many others – how many can never be calculated – who feared denunciation and dreaded the knock on the door. To them, we should add those who were making the arrests, prosecuting, and incarcerating, as well as those who inherited the possessions and positions of victims of the purges. Nor should we exclude those who testified against the accused, shied away from them, or publicly approved of their prosecutions in signed letters to the press and at factorywide meetings.

The very pervasiveness of the Great Purges and their important place in Soviet history have tended to obscure other contemporaneous developments, among them Stakhanovism. It has already been suggested that police terror largely replaced Stakhanovism as a device for bringing pressure upon industrial cadres. This is not to say, however, that Stakhanovism ceased to be of any use to the political authorities. Although it would never again be hailed as the panacea for the nation's industrial ills, it continued to be invoked as a powerful movement for organizational and technical innovation. Moreover, as was argued in the preceding chapter, its association with *kultur'nost'* served to orient workers toward certain values that had a stabilizing effect. This was of critical importance given the profound instability within the state and the evident danger of such instability spilling over into, or being exploited by, elements within society.

Stakhanovism therefore survived the Great Purges, but not unchanged. The ways in which it changed or, more precisely, was circumscribed will be discussed later in this chapter. First, however, we must consider the fate of Stakhanovites and their bosses in those dark years.

I

The Great Purges swept most professions in 1936–8, but neither simultaneously nor to the same extent. Treating the purges as a unitary phenomenon has certain advantages, but here we shall proceed along the lines of recent studies that have concentrated on specific arenas and/or localities and have relied for the most part on official Soviet sources.[1] The arena that most concerns us is industry, particularly at the enterprise level. There, the purges began earlier and lasted longer than the assault on the party apparatus, though the two processes obviously had much in common.

As already indicated, the Novosibirsk trial in November 1936 marked a turning point in the relationship between the political leadership and industrial cadres. Since the Metro–Vickers Trial of 1933, denunciation of managerial and technical personnel had not included accusations of wrecking at the behest of foreign enemies or because of Trotskyist sympathies. These were, how-

---

[1] See, e.g., Gabor T. Rittersporn, "Soviet Officialdom and Political Evolution, Judiciary Apparatus and Penal Policy in the 1930s," *Theory and Society*, 13 (1984):211–37; and his "L'Etat en lutte contre lui-même: Tensions sociales et conflits politiques en URSS, 1936–1938," *Libre*, no. 4 (1978):3–38; Roberta T. Manning, "Government in the Soviet Countryside in the Stalinist Thirties: The Case of Belyi Raion in 1937," *The Carl Beck Papers in Russian and East European Studies*, no. 301 (Russian and East European Studies Program, University of Pittsburgh, n.d.); and J. Arch Getty, *Origins of the Great Purges: The Communist Party Reconsidered, 1933–1938* (Cambridge University Press, 1985).

ever, the charges leveled at Novosibirsk against the Kemerovo engineers, who by implicating Piatakov in their wrecking activities set the stage for further judicial proceedings.

The trial of Piatakov and other alleged members of the Anti-Soviet Trotskyite Center in January 1937 represented a decisive blow against Narkomtiazhprom and has been linked to Ordzhonikidze's untimely death some three weeks later. It was also the occasion for the massive mobilization of public opinion against the accused. From factories across the land came an avalanche of resolutions expressing outrage at the crimes that were confessed and promises to liquidate the consequences of wrecking and compensate the nation "with harmonious Stakhanovite labor."[2] This was not all, for not all the wreckers had been caught. Even while the trial was still in progress, *Pravda* reported that Trotsky's son, Sergei Sedov, and a man named Zaks, who happened to be Zinoviev's nephew, had been carrying out wrecking activities under the benevolent eye of the director of the Serebrovskii Machine Construction Factory in Krasnoiarsk. Thanks to the "many facts about wrecking" brought to the attention of the authorities by the Stakhanovite Dmitrieva and others, the culprits were apprehended. The "facts" included poor ventilation, a lack of repairs to valuable equipment, and idleness of capital investments.[3]

Although far less spectacular than the Piatakov trial, the case of Sedov was more ominous for industrial management and production specialists. Whereas in the context of the anti-Trotskyist hysteria the arrest of Sedov was no surprise, the indictment of the factory's director and the extension of the charge of wrecking to include poor maintenance and other problems common to industrial enterprises presaged a transformation and lethal escalation of struggles that Stakhanovism had initiated but failed to resolve.

Still, Narkomtiazhprom sought to limit the damage to its subordinates, pointing out through its organ, *Za industrializatsiiu*, that "only a few individuals can be counted as Trotskyite wreck-

[2] *Pravda*, Jan. 25, 27, 28, 29, 31, Feb. 1, 1937.
[3] Ibid., Jan. 27, 1937.

ers" as opposed to "the millions and millions of workers, Stakhanovites, engineers, and managerial personnel" who would deal
a "lethal blow" to the wreckers' plans. The newspaper also gave
space to enterprise directors to explain how they were liquidating
the consequences of wrecking.[4] While a fatal accident at the
Shakhtantratsit mine no. 13 could bring an indictment for wrecking against the chief engineer and several subordinates, *Pravda*
saw fit to chastise party and managerial organs in the Donbass
for interpreting "every mistake, every failure as the work of the
enemy." True vigilance, it was stated, should not be confused
with "mindlessly enter[ing] on a list of saboteurs people who
want to keep pace with Stakhanovites but do not know how to
do so."[5]

Further evidence suggests that what was taking place at this
time was a scramble, or rather a series of scrambles, within industry, as different groups in different parts of the country
sought to stave off the heavy hand of the police or seek some
advantage from those who were most vulnerable to it. In what
must have been an act of desperation, Stepan Birman, the normally outspoken director of the Petrovskii metallurgical complex, turned to Ordzhonikidze "as an old comrade and Politburo
member." He complained that the central authorities' call for
criticism and self-criticism was being interpreted – by whom?
one wonders – as an excuse "to heap all kinds of mud on each
other, but in the first instance, on leading managerial officials."[6]
Partial corroboration of Birman's complaint can be found in *Za
industrializatsiiu*. In late February, it reported that shock workers
and Stakhanovites had criticized "with great feeling" Dnepropetrovsk's shop supervisors and managers, some of whom lacked
the courage to attend shop meetings.[7] This was not the only
place where mud was being heaped. At a Stalingrad Tractor
production conference, a Stakhanovite fitter none too subtly referred to "the abominations of the Trotskyite bandit wreckers"

---

[4] *ZI*, Feb. 1, 1937.
[5] Ibid., Feb. 8, 1937; *Pravda*, Feb. 17, 1937.
[6] Birman's letter was quoted extensively and critically by Molotov in his
speech to the Central Committee's plenum. The speech was published
after an inexplicable six-week delay. See *ZI*, April 21, 1937.
[7] *ZI*, Feb. 28, 1937.

that he had read about before launching into specific criticisms of his own factory's management.[8]

It would appear that the death of Ordzhonikidze removed a major obstacle to the unleashing of the NKVD against industrial cadres whom Sergo had been able to protect. One of them was Victor Kravchenko, then director of the Nikopol Metallurgical Combinat's pipe-rolling plant. The day after he was informed of his patron's death, Kravchenko reported receiving an invitation for "a little chat" from an officer in charge of the NKVD's Economic Division in Nikopol. The chat turned into an all-night interrogation, one of many he was to endure over the next several months.[9]

The publication of Stalin's and Molotov's speeches to the Central Committee's plenum and the convening of economic-administrative *aktiv* and primary party organization meetings made life infinitely more precarious for industrial executives. Whatever maneuverability had remained for management after Ordzhonikidze's death now disappeared. On March 1, *Za industrializatsiiu* repeated the message of its editorial a month earlier, namely that "the Stakhanovites had broken through the dam that the Trotskyite scoundrels had tried to construct" and that "new Stakhanovite élan will help to quickly liquidate the consequences of wrecking." However, even before being excoriated by *Pravda*, the editors had to admit that this was a "rotten theory" that served only to weaken the struggle against wreckers and discredit Stakhanovism.[10]

This was in fact one of several "rotten theories" that Stalin denounced in the first of his two speeches to the party plenum. He referred to the Trotskyites who had "systematically operated under the noses of Stakhanovites" in the Kuzbass and Donbass, causing preparatory work to lag behind output. "What can one Stakhanovite do if wrecking activity proceeds?" he asked rhetorically. Even the "theory that... the systematic fulfillment of economic plans reduces wrecking and its consequences" had to be destroyed. In short, the old slogan of mastering technology

---

[8] Ibid., Feb. 12, 1937.
[9] Victor Kravchenko, *I Chose Freedom* (New York: Scribner's, 1946), 237, 242–3, 263–4.
[10] *Pravda*, March 19, 1937; *ZI*, March 4, 1937.

was now to be subordinated to "a new slogan about mastering Bolshevism, about the political education of cadres and the liquidation of our political carelessness."[11]

Molotov made essentially the same point. It was a "huge mistake" to assume that because of economic successes wrecking was not a serious problem. Even if the chemicals *glavk* had overfulfilled its plans for 1935 and 1936, "does this mean that Rataichek wasn't Rataichek, that a wrecker isn't a wrecker, that a Trotskyite isn't a Trotskyite? Of course not. It means that in order to survive, wreckers cannot occupy themselves solely with wrecking."

It also obviously meant that economic successes would not guarantee the security or survival of industrial officials, that, in effect, the politics of productivity was being subordinated to that of cat and mouse. Officials who claimed success on the basis of plan fulfillment were merely covering up wrecking activity, since "many of our plans are artificially low." However, those who blamed all their "sins" on wreckers were no better. They were attempting to cover up for their own incompetence.[12]

Thus cornered from above, enterprise management became easy prey for rank-and-file activists, prominent among whom were Stakhanovites. Three years earlier, in 1934, the deputy commissar of heavy industry had told directors that "the ground must shake" when they walked onto the shop floor and that workers did not want directors who were "liberal." How wrong he was – or how much the tables had turned – can be measured by the nature and intensity of *aktiv* meetings. Rudeness and unapproachability were precisely the terms used to condemn the Cheliabinsk Tractor Factory's director. *Aktivy* accused him of displaying a scornful attitude toward Stakhanovites, ordinary workers, and technical personnel, of firing pregnant women rather than granting them maternity leave, and of hurling curses at and dismissing Stakhanovites rather than acquiescing to their requests for assistance.[13] The director of the Red Proletarian Factory in Moscow reputedly considered himself an "independent prince," and his counterpart at the Kirov Metalworks Factory in Makeevka had his portrait hung at the entrance to the plant

[11] *Pravda*, March 29, 1937.
[12] *ZI*, April 21, 1937.
[13] Ibid., April 4, 1937.

and carried at the head of parades marking revolutionary holidays.[14]

When it came to reelecting party committees, this time with secret ballots and without prepared lists, plant directors, at least in Moscow, were often passed over. "What is this," asked a bewildered *raikom* official, "a campaign against directors or something that has adequate grounds and justification?"[15] What it was, was a vicious cycle. Having fallen under suspicion as a group, individual factory directors became targets of workers' wrath. Having thus lost their authority or, in the parlance of the time, their ability to command, they became that much more expendable.

Of course, in many instances, directors were so remote from their workers that the latter's wrath inevitably fell on production specialists and lower managerial and administrative personnel. "The organization of work is such," complained one Drozhin, identified as the best Stakhanovite at the Kaganovich Brake Factory, "that until the twentieth of each month ... neither the shop head nor the foreman will tell us what to do. We are forced to seek work ourselves. After the twentieth, feverish haste takes over."[16] "Enough of being liberal with those who do not lead and assist the Stakhanovite movement," wrote a Stakhanovite from the Ordzhonikidze Machine Construction Factory in Moscow. "If a person obviously undermines or sabotages the movement, then we are accustomed to bringing him to justice."[17] Who were such people? At the Luboretskii factory, according to one of its Stakhanovites, it was the director, the chairman of the factory committee, and engineering-technical personnel, from shop supervisors down to the foremen. At the Stalin Automobile

---

[14] Ibid., April 8, 1937; see also April 10, 12, 1937. Such forms of behavior did not require injunctions from above but were absolutely typical of directors in the First Five-Year Plan. They conformed to the traditional Russian notions of how a *nachal'nik* should behave and perhaps also reflected the incredible strain under which these individuals operated. For the characterization of Gvakhariia, the director at Makeevka, as "a fanatical supporter of industrialization for the sake of industrialization," see Alexander Weissberg, *The Accused*, trans. Edward Fitzgerald (New York: Simon & Schuster, 1951), 366.

[15] *Pravda*, April 25, 1937.

[16] *ZI*, April 12, 1937. See also *Stakhanovets*, no. 8 (1937):7.

[17] *Stakhanovets*, no. 7 (1937):10–11.

Factory, according to four Stakhanovites, it was the shop super-visor, Kogan. Their complaints against him appeared under the title "Carelessness or Wrecking?"[18]

In the Donbass, party and trade union organs engaged in "indiscriminate repression" of mining employees, despite *Pravda*'s earlier injunction. According to a joint Central Com-mittee–Sovnarkom resolution of April 28, 1937, management did nothing to defend engineers and technicians, but "on the contrary, in order to protect themselves, many managers dismiss from work people whose culpability is not only unproven but not even investigated."[19] It is unlikely that such repression could have occurred without the complicity of local NKVD officers, but at least at this stage, the NKVD was above public rebuke.

Elsewhere, excessively close ties between managers and pro-duction specialists proved to be the undoing of both. Among the charges leveled at G. V. Gvakhariia, the director whose por-trait was carried in parades, was that he had brought along with him to the enterprise a long "tail" that included the Trotskyite wrecker Mamishvili. Similarly, I. I. Melamed, the factory direc-tor singled out for praise by Ordzhonikidze, found that his days were numbered when it was revealed that he had approved the distribution of sizable bonuses to engineering-technical person-nel who had been excluded from the party for Trotskyism.[20] The fact that Melamed's generosity had extended to leading Stakhanovites not only did not help him, but was cited by *Pravda* as evidence of his squandering of state funds.

If specialists could be dragged down with managers and vice versa, what about Stakhanovites? Were, for example, the out-standing Stakhanovites of the Kaganovich factory compromised because Melamed had allocated "tens of thousands of rubles" toward banquets celebrating their achievements? Did Busygin, Faustov, and others at the Molotov Automobile Works need to

---

[18] Ibid., no. 8 (1937):20.
[19] *KPSS v rezoliutsiiakh i resheniiakh*, 9th ed. (Moscow: Politizdat, 1984–), 6:388–91.
[20] *Pravda*, April 8, 13, 1937. Of course, there were other factors. Gvak-hariia apparently had been a Left Oppositionist and was the nephew of Ordzhonikidze. For a brief biographical sketch by an Austrian engineer who had occasion to meet him, see Weissberg, *The Accused*, 365–9.

worry because they had received apartments and other gifts from a director who subsequently disappeared? Probably not. A thorough search through the available sources failed to unearth a single instance of a Stakhanovite running afoul of the NKVD.[21] This is not to say that all Stakhanovites were immune from threats and persecution, but that despite the intricate web of connections with their bosses, they were no more vulnerable than ordinary workers, and apparently even less so.

Nor is it to suggest that Stakhanovites emerged unscathed from the struggles already described. According to an investigation by the party Control Commission, many primary party organizations (PPOs) in Moscow had been expelling conscientious workers, including Stakhanovites, on the grounds of their passivity. Whether intended to demonstrate compliance with the terms of earlier party purges or to weed out troublesome elements, the maneuver backfired. When the commission discovered that among the "passives" were Stakhanovite women who had sacrificed public and production work to look after their infant children, it looked very much as if the PPOs had engaged in a "groundless administrative-prosecutional campaign."[22]

As Arch Getty has argued, such campaigns had become the stock in trade of regional party leaders desperate to deflect the heat from above onto rank-and-file members. This struggle between center and periphery took a new turn in June 1937. After the arrest and execution of Soviet territorial army commanders, many of whom sat on party *obkomy*, the regional party organizations were decimated by arrests.[23] Among those who disappeared and were subsequently denounced as enemies of the people was S. Sarkisov, Donetsk *obkom* secretary and the patron of the Stakhanovite movement in the coal-mining industry.

[21] A Harvard interview project interviewee claimed that her husband, a railroad worker who often overfulfilled his norm, had been denied Stakhanovite status by the NKVD's special section on the grounds that he was the son of a kulak. Even if this was not an isolated case, it merely suggests that the police could prevent someone from being recognized as a Stakhanovite and reaping the benefits derived therefrom. Harvard Interview Project on the Soviet Social System, Russian Research Center Library, Harvard University, Interview no. 1398, p. 11.

[22] *Pravda*, April 18, 1937.

[23] Getty, *Origins of the Great Purges*, 48–91, 145–71.

Another patron, indeed the man whom we have already identified as the organizer of Stakhanov's record, was more fortunate. K. G. Petrov, former party organizer at the Central Irmino mine, had become secretary of the Kadievka party *gorkom* by 1937. The kind of leadership he exercised in this capacity was vividly portrayed in a "Letter from the Donbass," published in September of that year. Preceded by martial music, replete with drum rolls, Petrov arrived at Central Irmino to address a five-minute preshift meeting. "Pat, boring phrases pour[ed] forth":

> The mine is working disgracefully. Several commanders are working so badly that it is criminal (*prestupno plokho*).... The secretary of the Donetsk party *obkom*, comrade Pramnek, is closely following the work of the mine, and had sent a telegram to the mine's leadership. Comrade Pramnek is convinced.... A turnaround must be achieved in three days so that we can send a reply to comrade Pramnek.

Then, "in an instant, the shiny automobile carrying comrade Petrov sped away trailing a cloud of dust."[24] Despite the strong implication of Petrov's bossism, he survived.[25]

So, too, did Stepan Shcherbinskii, but it was a close call. What might be described as the Shcherbinskii affair well illustrates how the Great Purges could impinge on Stakhanovites and how because of their peculiar status they could survive. Shcherbinskii was a master iron roller at the Stalin Works in Stalino, a party member, and an outstanding Stakhanovite. In September 1937, he was admitted to one of the industrial academies in Moscow but, before departing, wrote an article blaming the shop administration for his failure to maintain previous levels of output in the months before his departure.[26] He also denounced the enterprise's trade union chairman in a meeting of the party *aktiv*.

The shop's party committee thereupon mounted a counterattack. In a character reference sent to the industrial academy's party secretary, it accused Shcherbinskii of demanding to be paid in gold and of hiding the personal effects of his brother-in-law, who had been arrested as an enemy of the people. These claims

---

[24] *Stakhanovets*, no. 9 (1937):15.

[25] Pramnek was shifted from the Gor'kii to Donetsk *obkom* to replace Sarkisov. He was soon to disappear. Petrov survived not only the purges but a great deal else. For his feisty speech to the Twenty-Seventh Party Congress, see *Pravda*, March 3, 1986.

[26] *SD*, Sept. 18, 1937.

were supported by a letter from the trade union chairman whom Shcherbinskii had denounced. On January 23, 1938, in the presence of Shcherbinskii, who had returned to Stalino to clear his name, the shop's party organization discussed his case. Further allegations, apparently aimed at stripping Shcherbinskii of his Stakhanovite status, were made. One shop employee admitted that he had created especially favorable conditions for Shcherbinskii's shift. Another recalled that the "enemy of the people," Sarkisov, has visited the shop while Shcherbinskii was working, though how this bore on his case is not clear. When a worker dared to speak on Shcherbinskii's behalf, he was shouted down with cries of "You're only defending your buddy."

Shcherbinskii's fate appeared grim. Although apprised of his case, neither the *raikom* nor *gorkom* secretaries saw fit to intervene. Only on February 1, 1938, did the former order the retraction of the defamatory character reference and write to the industrial academy to clear Shcherbinskii's name. According to *Sostialisticheskii Donbass*, he did so on instructions "from above."[27]

This little affair was only one of thousands of similar cases that consumed party organizations during the purges. What made it unusual was the publicity it received, and for this there is an obvious explanation. Shcherbinskii was not an ordinary worker. Though it is conceivable that he would have been exonerated in any case, his Stakhanovite status was undoubtedly a factor in Moscow's decision to intervene and publicly condemn his "defamers." Had he been an ordinary worker, however, it is unlikely that he would have been "defamed" in the first place. Though it was by no means unique for individuals to be implicated in the alleged crimes of distant relations, the other charge against him smacks of managerial resentment against an upstart. The comment about arranging favorable conditions was probably true, however disingenuous the motive for making it. As noted in Chapter 4 the favoritism of foremen and technicians was a precondition for many workers to become Stakhanovites. Shcherbinskii's "crime" was that he had turned on management, acting on the assumption, which he may well have articulated, that he was worth his weight in gold.

It is difficult to judge who was the most unsavory character

[27] Ibid., Feb. 9, 1938. See also *Pravda*, Feb. 8, 1938.

in this affair. All were operating in circumstances that were not of their own making. In such circumstances, yesterday's allies could easily become today's enemies, particularly if one or the other was in danger of becoming an "enemy of the people." The power of the police to define individuals as such, the strong antibossist sentiment of *aktiv* meetings, and the frenetic scrambling among industrial cadres – all this and more were characteristic of the industrial arena during the Great Purges. In short, the Great Purge in industry was not solely an assault on industrial cadres nor a series of affairs like that of Shcherbinskii, but a combination of both. It was both "the state against itself" [28] and workers against their bosses, higher state authorities not only failing to mediate and moderate the latter struggle, but actually aiding and abetting it.

Neither the dimensions nor the terminal date of the terror that swept nearly all levels of the industrial hierarchy can be determined with any precision.[29] As stated above, all industrial cadres were affected, though not to the same extent or in the same way. Not all officials were subjected to criticism at *aktiv* meetings or interrogation by the NKVD, and among those who were, not all were arrested. Many engineers were able to return to production work after short periods of incarceration, which was generally not the case with enterprise directors.[30] Other specialists, particularly, one assumes, those who cooperated with the police, received promotions or took up positions within the NKVD's Economic Divisions.[31] Nevertheless, Kaganovich was not exaggerating when he reported to the Eighteenth Party Con-

---

[28] The phrase is taken from the title of Rittersporn's article. See note 1.

[29] In his analysis of enterprise directors' tenure David Granick gives June 1938 as the cutoff date but admits to having done so "more or less arbitrarily . . . for the reduction in the rate of removals by purging does not seem to have been sudden." This would also have been the case with other managerial and technical personnel. See *Management of the Industrial Firm in the USSR* (New York: Columbia University Press, 1954), 50–1.

[30] This point is emphasized in Kendall E. Bailes, *Technology and Society under Lenin and Stalin* (Princeton, N.J.: Princeton University Press, 1978), 287.

[31] Ibid., 330–1. Bailes considers this part of engineers' "flight from production."

gress that, "over the period 1937–38, a huge renewal of administrative cadres occurred" in heavy industry.[32]

II

Most of the evidence cited thus far dates from the first half of 1937. It is clear, however, that what Kaganovich euphemistically referred to as "renewal" continued well into the following year. The removal of industrial cadres on the grounds of alleged wrecking activities continued to occur in connection with specific industrial accidents. This was the case with a so-called Right-Trotskyite group of four officials from a Budennyi trust coal mine, where a fire had killed one miner and injured sixteen others. In a fashion reminiscent of the earlier Show Trials, *Sotsialisticheskii Donbass* devoted two full pages to the proceedings.[33] Three days later, the newspaper announced the discovery of another group working in the Artem and Makeevka coal trusts. This time, the charges included the organization of cave-ins as well as the disruption of synchronized production, the reduction in the length of galleries, the curvature of drifts, and the destruction of underground transport.[34] These were offenses not only against proper mining operations but against the Stakhanovite movement. As the newspaper noted: "The Stakhanovite movement opened the path to the unprecedented growth of labor productivity.... This was well understood by the Trotskyite–Bukharinite agents of fascist intelligence services in the Donbass. In their attempts to weaken the USSR, they did everything possible to undermine the Stakhanovite movement."[35]

By the autumn of 1938, coincidental with, and probably connected to, the replacement of N. I. Ezhov as commissar of internal affairs, wrecking no longer figured among accusations leveled against industrial officials. The Soviet press and the resolutions of party and state organs ceased to blame industrial

---

[32] *Industriia*, Mar. 18, 1939.
[33] *SD*, Aug. 1, 1938.
[34] Ibid., Aug. 4, 1938.
[35] Ibid., Aug. 21, 1938.

accidents and the poor performance of particular enterprises on agents and spies of foreign powers or internal enemies of the people. Other causes were cited. Chief among them was the failure of management to assert leadership in the struggle for labor discipline, a struggle that took on new meaning after the passage of the laws of December 20 and 28, 1938.

In this there was a great irony. Nothing seems to have undermined or even wrecked labor discipline as much as the campaign against wreckers. References to the paralysis of industrial cadres and the fact that "backward" and "unconscious" elements among the workers were taking advantage of it appeared throughout 1937, in the joint resolution on the Donbass coal-mining industry, in a *Pravda* editorial in June, and in accounts of party and industrial *aktiv* meetings.[36]

Aggregate figures on absenteeism provide only a dim reflection of the problem, no doubt because managers were reluctant to record the absence of workers. Still, the recorded rate in 1937 was higher than that for any year since 1932.[37] The situation seems to have been particularly serious in the mining industry. Charged with enforcing the law of November 15, 1932, mining officials claimed that, if they dismissed workers for lateness and unexcused absences, workers would find employment at neighboring mines. It was an old excuse, but probably a valid one.[38] By early 1938, L. M. Kaganovich, recently appointed commissar of heavy industry, proposed five-year contracts with bonuses for continuous work at the same mine as a means of combating turnover among miners.[39]

Even when workers were on the job, they were not necessarily at work. If, as was claimed in 1939, Krivoi Rog iron ore miners had become accustomed to working three or four hours per day and no more, we should not be surprised that figures for the

---

[36] *Pravda*, June 24, 1937; *ZI*, May 5, 9. According to four Stakhanovites from the Stalin Automobile Works, their shop supervisor "adheres to the strange policy of refusing nothing and at the same time doing nothing." See *Stakhanovets*, no. 8 (1937):20.

[37] John Barber, "Labour Discipline in Soviet Industry, 1928–1941" (paper presented at the Twelfth AAASS Convention, Philadelphia, November 1980), Table B.

[38] *Pravda*, May 23, 1937.

[39] Ibid., Jan. 4, 1938.

first half of 1938 show them spending only half of their nominal work time productively.[40] Elsewhere, the situation was only marginally better. In the rolling mills of the nation's steel industry, downtime accounted for 23 percent of work time in the last six months of 1937.[41] And at Moscow's premier electrical goods factory, the following situation was said to exist in August 1937:

Throughout the day, an unending stream of people spills over into the corridors of the factory, throughout the shops and onto the stairwells. This is the best indication of the level of discipline and organization of production. In the corridor of Elektrozavod, books are traded and ice cream is sold. Half a factory, and half a department store![42]

Further evidence of the erosion of managerial authority came from the sensitive area of output norms and wages. In the spring of 1937, the *glavki* within Narkomtiazhprom reviewed and upwardly revised existing output norms on the basis of enterprise submissions. The revisions appear to have been of a lower order than those of the previous year. As had been the case in 1936, the increase often fell short of the average rate of overfulfillment of existing norms. For example, in ferrous metallurgy, workers overfulfilled their norms by a reported average of 33 percent in 1936, but their norms were raised by only 13 percent; in transport machine construction, the corresponding figures were 41 and 17 percent.[43] The overall increase in heavy industry was reported to be somewhat less than 20 percent.[44]

The fact that no general increase in output norms occurred in 1938 – possibly a result of the chaotic state of industrial administration – meant that eventually most workers were able to ov-

---

[40] Donald Filtzer, *Soviet Workers and Stalinist Industrialization* (Armonk, N.Y.: Sharpe, 1986), 168; P. Kuznetsov, "Normirovanie truda – na sluzhbu stakhanovskomu dvizheniiu," *Planovoe khoziaistvo*, no. 1 (1939):136.

[41] E. Lokshin, "Stakhanovskoe dvizhenie v tiazheloi promyshlennosti," *Planovoe khoziaistvo*, no. 2 (1938):63.

[42] Quoted from *ZI* in O. A. Ermanskii, *Stakhanovskoe dvizhenie i stakhanovskie metody* (Moscow: Sotsekgiz, 1940), 327.

[43] Ibid., 251.

[44] *Moscow Daily News*, April 24, 1937, cited in Albert Pasquier, *Le Stakhanovisme: L'Organisation du travail en URSS* (Caen: Robert, 1937), 71.

Table 7.1. *Average fulfillment of output norms*

Industry	June 1937		June 1938	
	Average fulfillment	% Workers not fulfilling norms	Average fulfillment	% Workers not fulfilling norms
Coal	137.5	12.0	144.8	6.5
Electrical power	147.6	2.4	172.9	0.7
Iron ore	144.3	9.0	156.4	4.8
Chemicals	125.4	25.2	150.2	11.0
Metallurgy	131.2	17.6	150.5	10.4
Metalworks	130.1	21.7	158.3	9.9
Paper	112.6	30.2	121.2	27.9
Leather	121.8	17.5	140.2	9.8

Source: A. Grigor'ev, "Uporiadochit' zarplatu, ukrepit' tekhnicheskoe normirovanie," *Planovoe khoziaistvo*, no. 10 (1938):78.

erfulfill their quotas (Table 7.1).[45] However, this did not ensure that enterprises were fulfilling their plans. For one thing, norm fulfillment was frequently expressed as a function of time actually worked, thereby excluding stoppage time; for another, averages could be the expression of the high overfulfillment rates of a small number of workers and more modest results among most others, as well as occasional nearly record performances and ordinary results by the same worker.

Finally, citing unexpected delays in supplies and other hitches in the production process but no doubt also worried about losing scarce workers, many enterprise officials exercised their prerogative of downwardly adjusting norms. This seems to have been particularly the case in the mining industry, where conditions were notoriously unpredictable and competition for workers among neighboring enterprises could be fierce. Whatever the circumstances at Kapital'naia no. 6, the chief engineer lowered

[45] The absence of the textile industry from Table 7.1 somewhat distorts the picture, because the proportion of textile workers failing to reach their norms remained quite high. The table also fails to distinguish between auxiliary workers, whose rate of norm fulfillment was relatively high, and production workers.

its wagon loaders' norms to the extent that all automatically became "masters of coal," that is, were able to fulfill their norms by 200 percent.[46] Successive lowering of norms by section heads and mine administrators was said to be systematic in the Krivoi Rog.[47] So, too, was attributing to workers output for which they were not responsible or that had never taken place. In this manner, 4,370 phantom tons of iron ore were extracted in just one section of the Rosa Luxemburg mine in June 1938.[48]

The result was often glaring disparities between output norms and enterprise targets. The example of the Red Miner colliery is illustrative. According to a *Pravda* article of July 1938, fulfillment of the mine's monthly plan required each worker to fullfill his output norm by 140 to 150 percent. In actuality, the shift target of 225 tons was never reached, though almost all workers were overfulfilling their individual norms.[49]

If, as was alleged, trust officials were unconcerned about these phenomena, the political authorities were becoming increasingly alarmed. By 1938, it had become clear that the industrialization drive was stalling. Output of key industrial goods such as coal, oil, iron ore, and steel increased only slightly in 1937, indeed, less so than for any year since the beginning of the First Five-Year Plan.[50] The two indices of efficiency in steelmaking, the coefficient of utilization of available blast furnace capacity and output per square meter of open-hearth volume, actually declined, as did output of coal in the Donbass.[51]

As the "renewal" of cadres continued into 1938, at least some of the authorities presiding over it came to recognize the necessity for a shift of strategy. Precisely who within the party

---

[46] *Industriia*, Feb. 14, 1938; see also Feb. 5, 1939. These revelations tended to be made on the eve of norm revisions.

[47] *Planovoe khoziaistvo*, no. 2 (1938):78.

[48] *Pravda*, July 24, 1938.

[49] Ibid.

[50] Roger A. Clarke, *Soviet Economic Facts, 1917–1970* (New York: Macmillan, 1972), 53, 54, 58, 60.

[51] M. Gardner Clark, *The Economics of Soviet Steel* (Cambridge, Mass.: Harvard University Press, 1956), 251–4; *Gornyi zhurnal*, no. 2 (1938):10. To some extent, the declines were the result of cyclical fluctuations in investment and construction, as discussed by Mark Harrison, *Soviet Planning in Peace and War*, 1938–1945 (Cambridge University Press, 1985), 7.

leadership pushed for such a shift and at what point they succeeded is unclear, though the resignation of Ezhov undoubtedly
marks a significant milestone.[52]

The shift was toward what one scholar has termed "the re-
covery of the state apparatus' fundamental cohesion."[53] That is,
in the face of widespread labor indiscipline, the "flight from
production" by engineering graduates, and a number of other
challenges to be detailed below, the central political authorities
closed ranks with industrial administrative and technical personnel.[54] In effect, they reconstructed the status quo ante. In
return for greater security of tenure, to be achieved by limiting
the arbitrary powers of the police and curbing the antibossist
rhetoric so prominent during 1935–8, industrial cadres were to
exercise the full plenitude of their authority. This process was
marked not only by a series of decrees designed to restore labor
discipline, but by a rise in the status of the cadres expected to
carry out such measures.

The new orientation was implicit in the praise that the press
began to heap on the new crop of directors, engineers, and
technicians. Articles promoting experiments with joint engineer–Stakhanovite brigades emphasized the importance of co-
operation and mutual respect between the two groups. Indeed,
experimentation in general emerged as a prominent theme in
articles by and about successful "commanders of production."[55]
Under the title "On Technical Risks, Cowardice and Bolshevik
Responsibility," one recently appointed director extolled those
who "bravely innovate, rationalize, experiment, and do not fear
production and technical risks," while castigating those who

---

[52] For some speculative scenarios, see Getty, *Origins of the Great Purges*,
182–95, and Gabor T. Rittersporn, "Staline en 1938: Apogée du
verbe et defaute politique," *Libre*, no. 6 (1979):99–164.

[53] Rittersporn, "L'Etat en lutte," 29.

[54] On the "flight from production," see Bailes, *Technology and Society*,
320–36. Bailes argues that this problem was endemic to the "pressure
cooker system" of Soviet industry but was exacerbated by the purges.

[55] *Mashinostroenie* (hereafter *Mash.*), Oct. 9, Nov. 16, 1938; Jan. 26, 1939.
The inspiration for these so-called complex brigades supposedly
came from N. S. Khrushchev, then secretary of the Moscow party
obkom.

sought to live peacefully, avoiding responsibility.[56] The latter included line managers who readily agreed to every subordinate's request as well as engineers who sought safer positions outside of production.

Another means of encouraging industrial cadres to assert their leadership was to combat the anti-intelligentsia sentiment that rank-and-file activists had exhibited during the Great Purges. Despite *Pravda*'s evident satisfaction that in Leningrad "the party masses are unanimously electing to party organs engineers who have recently entered into party work," not everyone in the party caught on so quickly.[57] When A. A. Zhdanov addressed a plenum of the Komsomol's Central Committee in October 1938, it was to attack the "widely distributed old, anti-Leninist, and fundamentally erroneous attitude towards the intelligentsia according to which directors of enterprises and engineers are regarded as people 'removed' from the workers." Such an attitude, Zhdanov asserted, was "barbaric and hooligan" and moreover "dangerous to the Soviet state."[58]

The renewed respect for authority was now to extend down to the positions of foreman and brigade leader. Negotiation between section heads and workers over the appointment and dismissal of brigade leaders, a procedure that was common in the mining and construction industries, consequently became intolerable. "There are cases," *Industriia* reported with some alarm, "when the section head insists on dismissing a *brigadir* and some backward workers have tried to block it." This was a violation of the principle of managerial authority (*edinonachalie*) and had to cease. The supervisor could seek the advice of foremen and individual Stakhanovites, but the appointment had to be a command (*prikaz*) in order to give the brigade leader the authority of a junior administrator.[59]

Beginning in the autumn of 1938 and continuing into 1939, the effort to establish a strict sense of hierarchy and discipline on the shop floor intensified. Previously eclipsed by the attention

---

[56] *Pravda*, Sept. 22, 1938. See also *Pravda*, June 11, July 19, Nov. 18, 1938, and *SD*, April 17, 1938.

[57] *Pravda*, April 27, 1938; see also June 3, 1938.

[58] Ibid., Nov. 4, 1938.

[59] *Industriia*, June 23, 1938; see also June 10 and Sept. 2, 1938.

devoted to Stakhanovites and their achievements, foremen were now proclaimed the "central figures in production."[60] Raising the status of foremen entailed adjusting their pay upward. Although for years many Stakhanovites had been earning more than foremen, this situation rarely received critical comment. By 1939, however, numerous press articles characterized it as anomalous and unacceptable.[61] Eventually, in May 1940, a joint Sovnarkom–Central Committee decree stipulated that foremen's base pay be higher than that of skilled workers and that they should receive bonuses for overfulfillment of their section's monthly targets as well as for economizing on wage fund expenditures.[62]

The closing of ranks between the political leadership and industrial cadres inevitably led to a diminution of the status of Stakhanovites and the importance of Stakhanovism. Yet a large number of Stakhanovites were the direct beneficiaries of this development. This apparent paradox is to be explained by the fact that, in the course of the Great Purge in industry, many Stakhanovites were promoted to the ranks of enterprise management or, having received specialized training, took up positions in the technical apparatus. As Zhdanov reminded the Komsomol's Central Committee, the managers and engineers supposedly removed from the workers were none other than "yesterday's Stakhanovites who came from the people."[63]

Whereas upward social mobility has been extensively studied in the context of the First Five-Year Plan, that which occurred during 1936–8 has received much less scholarly attention.[64] This

---

[60] *Mash.*, Nov. 2, 1938.

[61] See, e.g., ibid., Jan. 15, 26, April 15, June 10, 1939. For an earlier complaint, see *ZI*, Oct. 4, 1936.

[62] *Industrializatsiia SSSR, 1938–1941 gg., Dokumenty i materialy* (Moscow: Nauka, 1973), 121–3.

[63] See note 58.

[64] On First Five-Year Plan mobility, see Sheila Fitzpatrick, *Education and Social Mobility in the Soviet Union, 1921–1934* (Cambridge University Press, 1979) and her "Stalin and the Making of a New Elite, 1928–1939," *Slavic Review*, 38 (1979):377–402. Fitzpatrick notes: "The end of the First Five-Year Plan *vydvizhenie* . . . was by no means the end of large-scale upward mobility through education, promotion on the job and training programmes. . . . [What followed] was a less dramatic pattern than that of the First Five-Year Plan period, less

may be because, unlike the earlier *vydvizhentsy*, none of the promoted Stakhanovites ever achieved high political office. Nevertheless, if we are to comprehend the social dynamics of Soviet society and the social underpinnings of industrial administration during the Great Patriotic War and beyond, an analysis of this process is in order.

III

The promotion of Stakhanovites commenced before the Great Purge in industry got underway. As early as the spring of 1936, Stakhanov and scores of other Stakhanovite miners were attached to various coal trusts as instructors. This position appears to have been created on instructions from the Donetsk party *obkom* for the purpose of demonstrating and popularizing Stakhanovites' techniques.[65] Eventually, Busygin, Gudov, and other outstanding Stakhanovites served in this capacity.

We have very little information on the experiences of Stakhanovite instructors. Judging by his "diary" entries, Stakhanov's were successful, notwithstanding the noncooperation of certain low-ranking technical personnel.[66] Still, all could not have been well with this institution. By April 1937, Stakhanov was publicly complaining that the coal trusts and Narkomtiazhprom had forgotten about instructors.[67] Whether this meant that no new instructors were being appointed or that the original cohort was not being assigned to new work sites is not clear.

In any case, many instructors, including Stakhanov, required

politically significant in terms of abrupt elite transformation, but in no sense restrictive of upward social mobility" (*Education and Social Mobility*, 239).

[65] Z. G. Likholoboda, *Rabochie Donbassa v gody pervykh piatiletok (1928–1937 gg.)* (Donetsk: Donetskii gosudarstvennyi universitet, 1973), 148. Sarkisov claimed that 50 were serving in this capacity and that the number would soon rise to 100. See *Pravda*, April 29, 1936, and *SD*, May 4, 1936.

[66] A. G. Stakhanov, *Rasskaz o moei zhizni* (Moscow: Gossotzizd., 1937), 68–87.

[67] *ZI*, April 29, 1937; see also June 15, 1937, for an account of the chilly reception given to an instructional brigade of bricklayers in Sverdlovsk.

a good deal of instruction themselves. This they were to obtain in the industrial academies. The academies were one of many adult educational institutions founded in the 1920s. Since the opening of the first in 1927, they had accommodated a small student body consisting mostly of former workers who had been promoted to managerial positions. By 1933, there were eleven academies, most of them situated in Moscow, with a total enrollment of 3,507 students.[68] The number of academies (and presumably students) thereafter declined, and before the advent of Stakhanovism, the institution seemed destined for extinction.

In 1936, apparently for the first time, the entering class included a sizable contingent of students who had come directly from the bench or who had served as instructors. There were 40 such students among the 500 taken into the academies run by Narkomtiazhprom and 20 of the 100 in the academies for light industry.[69] All were Stakhanovites. Some, like Stakhanov, had already received special instruction from tutors before beginning their formal studies. Even so, as Busygin and others were later to admit, they found academic work trying.[70] The curriculum consisted of general education courses with special emphasis on the sciences and technology. It was therefore the rough equivalent of the education received by youths in the technicums or vocational secondary schools (FZUs). Graduates of the academy were supposed to be qualified for middle-level managerial and technical positions.

The guiding principle here was that to supervise and manage required skills that could best be learned through formal education. More than salary or security, it was the recognition of this principle that imparted to managers a higher status than

[68] V. Z. Drobizhev, "Rol' rabochego klassa v formirovanii komandnykh kadrov sotsialisticheskoi promyshlennosti (1917–1936 gg.)," *Istoriia SSSR*, no. 4 (1961):63; V. M. Kulagina, *Leningradskie kommunisty v bor'be za osvoenie novoi tekhniki (1933–1935 gg.)* (Leningrad: LGU, 1962), 54–5.

[69] *Pravda*, Sept. 9, 1936.

[70] A. Kh. Busygin, *Zhizn' moia i moikh druzei* (Moscow: Profizdat, 1939), 67–8. See also *Stakhanovets*, no. 8 (1937):9; and M. I. Vinogradova, "Riadom s legendoi," in *Vzgliad skvoz' gody: Zapiski stakhanovtsev* (Moscow: Sovremennik, 1984), 313–14. Some of their difficulties may have been due to the rather primitive pedagogical practices as described by S. Iashin in *Stakhanovets*, no. 8 (1937):43.

workers and, within management, favored degree holders over *praktiki*. Thus, enrollment in one of the academies in itself constituted promotion for even the most outstanding Stakhanovites.

We can therefore appreciate, if not approve of, the audacity of A. A. Ermolaeva, one of the leading Stakhanovites at the Nogin Mill in Smolensk. In October 1936, this semiliterate worker with only four years of schooling wrote to I. P. Rumiantsev, first secretary of the Western District's party *obkom*, to seek his "advice" about how she could complete her education. Couched in the most obsequious language, the letter reminded Rumiantsev about her promise at a meeting of Stakhanovites to master the new output and technical norms and reported that "I have kept my word that I gave you, Ivan Petrovich." It also indicated that she had applied for party membership. The letter was passed on to the appropriate trust official by one of Rumiantsev's assistants, who requested that funds be allocated for Ermolaeva to attend the seven-year school. The trust went one better by offering Ermolaeva her choice of institutions, and seizing the opportunity, she selected the Industrial Academy of Light Industry in Moscow. The mill's director thereupon agreed to arrange for individual preparatory instruction.[71]

The number of academies and their student body continued to grow at a moderate pace. By 1939, more than eight thousand students were enrolled in 22 academies.[72] However, academy graduates never comprised more than a small fraction of the total number of Stakhanovite-promotees. As had been the case in the First Five-Year Plan, but for different reasons, the overwhelming majority of workers appointed to managerial and technical posts in the late 1930s lacked any formal specialized education.[73]

They did not necessarily lack the requisite skills. In January 1936, Narkomtiazhprom introduced two vocational training programs to supplement the technical minimum course. These were the Stakhanovite courses for workers who had passed their tech-

[71] Smolensk Party Archive, WKP-195, pp. 186–90.
[72] *Stakhanovets*, no. 9 (1939):17.
[73] "In numerical terms, the *praktiki* benefited *more* from the purges than did graduates of Soviet higher educational institutions." Kendall E. Bailes, "Stalin and the Making of a New Elite: A Comment," *Slavic Review*, 39 (1980):287.

nical minimum examinations and courses for masters of socialist labor, designed for more advanced workers. Of the two, the latter was the more demanding, calling for 1,200 hours of study in the Russian language, mathematics, and the physical sciences over a period of two years.[74] In their first year of operation, the Stakhanovite courses enrolled 386,800 workers, of whom 241,700 successfully completed their studies. Enrollments in the master of socialist labor courses increased from 120,000 in 1936 to 500,000 the following year and was expected to reach 1.5 million by the end of the Third Five-Year Plan.[75]

The explicit aim of the master of socialist labor course, as expressed by Gosplan's Department of Labor and Cadres, was to provide "the basic contingent of workers from leading occupations with skills that draw the worker nearer to the level of technology [and] secure an advance of the worker's cultural-technical level." This cultural-technical level was said to approximate that of engineering-technical personnel.[76] Did this mean that masters of socialist labor qualified for promotion? That is, indeed, what was claimed. Yet because of the narrow scope and poor quality of the courses, graduates were not eligible for entry into technicums, which remained the chief educational institution for the training of lower- and middle-level industrial cadres. Thus, in the normal course of events, masters of socialist labor should have had to undergo further study to reach a level equivalent to that provided by the seven-year general education schools, and only then qualify for entry into technicums. The technicum degree, not a master of socialist labor certificate, signified the successful completion of a specialized secondary education course.

But the events of the late 1930s were anything but normal. Worker promotion during these years conformed neither to educational policy nor to Gosplan's projections, but rather was

---

[74] N. B. Lebedev and O. I. Shkaratan, *Ocherki istorii sotsialisticheskogo sorevnovaniia* (Leningrad: Lenizdat, 1966), 151. For equivalent arrangements in the construction industry, see *Industrializatiia SSSR, 1933–1937 gg. Dokumenty i materialy* (Moscow: Nauka, 1971), 214–15.

[75] B. L. Markus, *Trud v sotsialisticheskom obshchestve* (Moscow: Gospollit, 1939), 224; *Industrializatsiia SSSR, 1933–1937*, 480, 503–4, 608–9.

[76] *Industrializatsiia SSSR, 1933–1937*, 504.

shaped by the Great Purges. Whatever the original function of the master of socialist labor course, tens of thousands who had completed it and perhaps an equal number who had not were promoted to positions as brigade leaders, foremen, shift and section supervisors, and technicians. The overwhelming majority of these promotees were Stakhanovites.

The transformation of Stakhanovites into low-level managers (*malye komandiry*) began to assume major proportions by the middle of 1937. A *Pravda* editorial of June 9 signaled the intensification of this process. "Often, in our factories," it stated,

> when section heads or foremen are promoted to more responsible positions, or when the necessity to replace them by more competent people arises, the whining begins: "We lack people." The commissariats are asked to provide them or they are sought from neighboring enterprises and even in other cities, while youthful forces, raised in the enterprise itself and ready for promotion are held back.[77]

The editorial urged enterprise officials and party committees to take note of those outstanding Stakhanovites – Krivonos, Iusim, and Smetanin were mentioned by name – who were performing well as shop or section supervisors and to promote other Stakhanovites.

By August, *Pravda* was claiming that where Stakhanovites had been promoted they brought "a new brisk order to factory administration" but that elsewhere "wreckers and fascist agents are intentionally blocking the promotion of Stakhanovites."[78] Many such "wreckers" in the Donbass were "decisively purged" by L. M. Kaganovich after he took over as commissar of heavy industry. In their place, Kaganovich appointed "from the very bottom hundreds of Stakhanovites."[79] This renewal of cadres immediately preceded and provides a clue for making sense of Stalin's extraordinary tribute to low-level and middle-echelon managers. Speaking in the Kremlin before a gathering of four hundred managers and Stakhanovites from the mining

---

[77] *Pravda*, June 9, 1937. For some earlier instances of Stakhanovites' promotion, see *Pravda*, April 29, 1936, and *Magnitogorskii rabochii*, April 21, 1936.

[78] *Pravda*, Aug. 30, 1937.

[79] Ibid., Oct. 7, 1937. See Kaganovich's remarks quoted in I.I. Kuz'minov, *Stakhanovskoe dvizhenie – vysshii etap sotsialisticheskogo sorevnovaniia* (Moscow: Sotsekgiz, 1940), 139.

Table 7.2. *Promotion of Stakhanovites at the Molotov Automobile Works (Gor'kii)*

	1937	1938	1939
Number of Stakhanovites as of Jan. 1	4,675	6,792	14,008
Number of Stakhanovites promoted	523	307	416
Percentage of Stakhanovites promoted	11.2	4.5	3.0

Source: V. A. Sakharov, *Zarozhdenie i razvitie stakhanovskogo dvizheniia (na materialakh avtotraktornoi promyshlennosti)* (Moscow: MGU, 1985), 115–16; *Stakhanovets*, no. 8 (1938):15; and *Istoriia industrializatsii nizhegorodskogo-Gor'kovskogo kraia (1926–1941 gg.)* (Gor'kii: Volgo-Viatskoe knizhnoe izdatel'stvo, 1968), 443.

and metallurgical industries, Stalin characterized his audience as "modest people [who] do not leap forward, and are almost unnoticed. But," he continued, "it would be blindness not to notice them, since the fate of production in our economy depends on these people."[80]

How many Stakhanovites joined the ranks of lower and middle management during the late 1930s cannot be determined with any precision. Certainly it was in the order of tens of thousands. At the Molotov Automobile Works alone, 523 Stakhanovites were promoted in 1937, 162 becoming foremen, 128 brigade leaders, 123 technicians and norm setters, 102 adjusters, and 8 section heads.[81] Proportional to the number of Stakhanovites registered as of January 1, this was the banner year for promotions (Table 7.2). Detailed figures for other enterprises are not available, but occasional references in the press and elsewhere suggest that what occurred at the Molotov plant was not unusual.[82]

A number of points must be made to put the promotion of Stakhanovites in general perspective. First, although it appears that Stakhanovite or at least shock worker status was a precondition for promotion from the bench, upward mobility was not

[80] *Pravda*, Oct. 31, 1937.
[81] *Stakhanovets*, no. 8 (1938):15.
[82] See, e.g., *Pravda*, April 25, 1938; *PS*, no. 11, 1939: Ermanskii, *Stakhanovskoe dvizhenie*, 342; and Kuz'minov, *Stakhanovskoe dvizhenie*, 139.

restricted to such workers. Foremen, section heads, and other low- and middle-echelon personnel moved up the industrial hierarchy, and there was a continual influx of technical and higher school graduates.[83] Some assumed positions vacated by victims of the Great Purges. However, these years also witnessed an expansion in the number of engineering-technical positions, such that the proportion of engineering-technical personnel to workers rose from 70.5 per 1,000 workers in 1936 to 110 per 1,000 workers in 1940.[84]

Then again, Stakhanovites were promoted not only to industrial management, but also to full- and part-time trade union and party work. For example, most of the new trade union committee elected at the Leningrad Elektrosila plant in July 1937 consisted of Stakhanovites, including the chairman.[85] Other Stakhanovites became enterprise party committee secretaries, district soviet chairmen, and Komsomol and trade union officials.[86]

Finally, as we have seen with respect to the acquisition of culture, the publicity surrounding the promotion of Stakhanovites was no less significant than its reality. Here, the experiences of the outstanding Stakhanovites is most revealing. As *Pravda* proclaimed, "The broad vital path open to every honest toiler in the USSR is best illustrated by the experience of the pioneers of the Stakhanovite movement."[87] Examples followed. Some, such as Stakhanov, Busygin, Odintseva, and the Vinogradovas, studied in the industrial academies; others had already

---

[83] A. F. Khavin, "Razvitie tiazheloi promyshlennosti v tret'ei piatiletke (1938–iiun' 1941 gg.)," *Istoriia SSSR*, no. 1 (1959):26–8; Fitzpatrick, "Stalin and the Making of a New Elite," 396–400.

[84] Bailes, *Technology and Society*, 289.

[85] *LP*, July 21, 1937.

[86] *Mash.*, June 5, 18, 1937; Sept. 4, 1938. *Pravda*, Jan. 11, 1938; *Profsoiuzy SSSR*, no. 1 (1938):76–7; no. 8–9 (1939):55–6. After the trade union committee elections of 1938 and 1939, Stakhanovites comprised 26 and 29% of committee members. David Granick considered this surprisingly low in view of the higher proportion of Stakhanovites among the industrial work force (see Table 7.3). However, he failed to note that some 15 to 20% of committee members consisted of engineering-technical personnel. See Granick, *Management*, 250, and *Stakhanovets*, no. 8 (1939):23.

[87] *Pravda*, Nov. 14, 1937.

assumed responsible positions in industry. Nikita Izotov, the Stakhanovite *avant le mot*, had become director of a coal-mining trust. He was also a delegate at the party's Eighteenth Congress in March 1939; Krivonos headed a railroad depot that employed 1,700 workers. In May 1938, he was appointed commander of the South Donetsk Railway. Also a delegate to the Eighteenth Congress, Krivonos was elected to the Central Revision Commission and served as well on the Central Committee of the Ukrainian party organization; Iakov Iusim, the former line engineer and section supervisor, found himself director of the Kaganovich Ball Bearings Factory after the removal of Melamed. "Who would be able to imagine this three or four years ago?" wrote A. Ognev after his appointment as commander of the Tula Locomotive Depot.[88] Who indeed? By May 1938 he was commander of the important Moscow-Circuit Railway. No Stakhanovite, however, would rise as high in the industrial hierarchy as the former shoe stitcher Nikolai Smetanin. In July 1938 Smetanin was appointed director of the Skorokhod factory, where he had worked since 1918. But the following year he joined the party and was elevated to deputy commissar of light industry. He would serve in this commissariat (later, ministry) until his retirement in 1962.[89]

These and other outstanding Stakhanovites were valuable resources for demonstrating the triumph of Soviet democracy as enshrined in the new constitution. Ten of them – Stakhanov, Diukanov, Busygin, Krivonos, Ognev, Smetanin, M. N. Mazai, N. Russkikh, V. D. Bogdanov, and F. K. Sil'chenko – were members of the editorial commission that drafted the constitution's final version. In December 1936, this version was presented to the Extraordinary Eighth All-Union Congress of Soviets, which unanimously approved it. Among the more than 2,000 delegates at the congress were 317 listed as workers, of whom 307 (97 percent) were Stakhanovites.[90] Subsequently, many Stakhanovites served as deputies to the All-Union and Republican Supreme Soviets as well as major *oblast'* and city soviets. For example, as of January 1940, the Leningrad *oblast'* soviet contained 1,080

[88] Ibid., Nov. 21, 1937.
[89] *Bol'shaia Sovetskaia entsiklopediia*, 3rd ed. (Moscow, 1970–8), 23:606.
[90] *LP*, Dec. 2, 1936.

deputies, of whom 342 (31 percent) were reported to be Stakhanovites.[91] There may well have been former Stakhanovites
among the 721 "employees" (*rabotniki*) as well.

How did these "authentic representatives of the new Soviet
intelligentsia" fare in their new positions? Some clearly were in
over their heads. Iusim is perhaps an extreme example. Not
long after he took over as director, things started going badly
at the ball bearings factory. Output declined from month to
month, and many workers began to seek employment elsewhere.
The *Pravda* article detailing these and other problems was generous toward the new director. He had been given bad advice
by the *raikom* secretary and assistant secretary; many recently
appointed (former Stakhanovite?) section heads were incompetent; and the head of the supply department turned out to
be an enemy of the people.[92] However, soon afterward, the same
newspaper cited Iusim as an example of recently appointed commanders who "do not want to spoil relations with disorganizers
of production." There followed other criticisms pertaining to
the high percentage of defective goods and, ironically, the lack
of support to Stakhanovite initiatives.[93]

The problem with the unfortunately named Gonobobleva, a
former Stakhanovite weaver who became director of the Kirov
Mill in Ivanovo, was that she could not get along with the party
obkom secretary. After a special brigade, dispatched by the *obkom*,
found her work unsatisfactory – this, after she had been director
for only three weeks – she complained of persecution.[94] Other
less prominent former Stakhanovites experienced difficulties of
another sort. As one promotee at a machine construction factory
put it: "When I . . . was a Stakhanovite, I received a lot of attention, but as a promoted foreman, I was ignored. For a long time
I tried to get a pass to the rest home, while Stakhanovites working
at my old job received passes without any difficulty."[95] The complaint was no less genuine for the fact that it was published as
part of the campaign to raise foremen's status. Nor were, for

[91] Ibid., Jan. 4, 1940.
[92] *Pravda*, Dec. 4, 1938.
[93] Ibid., Dec. 13, 1938.
[94] Ibid., Nov. 1, 1938.
[95] *Mash.*, Aug. 20, 1938.

that matter, the complaints of other foremen about having to take sizable pay cuts after being promoted.

In contrast, many former Stakhanovites adapted well to their new positions. Krivonos reported that some of his fellow drivers assumed he would take a liberal view of their tardiness after he had been promoted to depot head. This was why he wore a tie. It not only made him feel important, but "compel[led] people to relate to me with respect."[96] More typical, perhaps, was one of the "new people" that John Scott encountered at Magnitogorsk. This was a man named Atiasov, a twenty-six-year-old Stakhanovite crane operator who had been appointed chairman of the coke plant's trade union committee. Lacking any formal education and having a hazy idea of his responsibilities, Atiasov

knew enough to realize vaguely that the factory committee exists for the purpose of aiding the administration to cut costs, improve quality, maintain labor discipline and so forth. He probably also knew... that there are certain laws and regulations relating to working conditions which should be abided by, but when violated flagrantly might result in public criticism, a lot of talk with no after effects and eventual silence on the subject....

His handwriting is childish and he adds with great difficulty. I have seen his office and it is such a mess that Saltikov [recently appointed head of the plant] can never find anything. But he is delighted with his job and he goes to the Secretary of the Shop Party Committee for help. He has not reached the questioning stage and perhaps never will. No questions, qualms or heretical thoughts plague him; he is as faithful as a dog.[97]

Scott predicted that, unless he fell in with bad company or were made a scapegoat for some accident, Atiasov would "rise fairly high in the Stalinist hierarchy." Unfortunately, it is not possible to follow the career of Atiasov or other Stakhanovite promotees beyond 1941. Those who survived the war were seemingly well placed for further advancement, and undoubtedly many rose within the industrial hierarchy. However, overtaken for the most part by younger and better educated postwar graduates of engineering schools, most remained in the capacity of lower- and middle-echelon managers. As such, they did not so much preside over postwar reconstruction as serve as a reason-

[96] *Pravda*, Aug. 30, 1937.
[97] National Archives, U.S. State Department Decimal File, 861.5048/107, "Memorandum Setting forth Examples of Wrecking Activities at Magnitogorsk," March 10, 1938, pp. 18–19.

ably reliable cohort for the implementation of policies emanating from above.

IV

During the Great Purges, the politics of productivity took second place to other considerations. For higher political and police authorities, it was no longer a question of getting the most out of existing cadres but of replacing them with more pliable ones under the pretext of suppressing wrecking; for industrial cadres and lower party functionaries who were often linked with them in "family circles," the avoidance of accusations of wrecking and political unreliability assumed primary importance; and for workers, getting back at their immediate bosses, bending rules to their advantage, and rising within the industrial hierarchy were all possibilities worth pursuing.

The intrusion of these considerations into industrial relations was reflected in a corresponding diminution of the importance of Stakhanovism. Production records by individual Stakhanovites continued to be arranged and celebrated, though it is significant that no record holder received the acclaim of the pioneers of the movement. Stakhanovite periods continued to punctuate the Soviet calendar, but their *raison d'être* increasingly had less to do with systematizing innovations than commemorating events external to industry itself. Finally, the most widely publicized innovations in the late 1930s were not attributed to Stakhanovites at all, and earlier innovations that had been identified as Stakhanovite techniques were not sustained. Each of these developments deserves closer attention.

After the rapture that greeted Stakhanovites' initial records, the official attitude toward such individual feats was more ambivalent. On the one hand, records provided some measure of what was possible given available technology and played a useful role in the review of output norms. On the other, they were an all too convenient means by which management and lower party functionaries paraded their support for Stakhanovism while otherwise carrying on as normal or, as the standard expression had it, failing to consolidate the achievements of individual Stakhanovites. This ambivalence appears to have intensified in 1937, leading to a rather curious sequence of events just as the Second Five-Year Plan was ending.

During the summer of 1937, the pursuit of records came under unusually strong criticism in the Soviet press.[98] A typical
example was the commentary on a report from the Stalin (formerly Central Irmino) mine that Diukanov had fulfilled his shift
norm by 1,157 percent. The commentary revealed that the report had failed to factor in the norms of Diukanov's assistants
and obscured the fact that the mine as a whole was fulfilling its
program by only 70 percent. Moreover, the day after the record
had been set, Diukanov's rate of fulfillment dropped to 137
percent, and neither of his assistants fulfilled their norms.[99]

Still, the authorities did not discourage the setting of records
entirely. The twentieth anniversaries of the October Revolution
and the founding of the Cheka were accompanied by a spate of
production records, and a "Stalinist *dekada* of Stakhanovite records" greeted the elections to the Supreme Soviet. No sooner
had this ten-day period elapsed than a meeting of Moscow Stakhanovites called on workers throughout the country to prepare
for the Stalinist month of Stakhanovite records, which was to
coincide with the beginning of the Third Five-Year Plan. The
call evoked a tremendous public response from Stakhanovites
meeting elsewhere. New production records were established in
Leningrad, Ivanovo, Kuibyshev, and Makeevka. At one enterprise in Perm, 150 records were set in one day alone, the day
being the second anniversary of the naming of the enterprise
after Stalin.[100]

One is struck by the contrast between these reports, published
in *Pravda*, and national figures for daily output of pig iron, steel,
and rolled iron printed directly below them. In each case, actual
output was well below the plan. The contrast may have jolted
higher authorities, for in a matter of days, *Pravda* published an
article by Ivan Gudov under the title "Several Problems of the
Stakhanovite Movement." "The basic problem," according to Gudov, was that the high productivity of individual Stakhanovites
had not been generalized. For example, Gudov cited his own
feat of producing 1,152 cams in a single shift. This represented
not only 4,582 percent of his norm, but one and a half months'
supply of cams according to the enterprise's program. Since,

[98] See, e.g., *Stakhanovets*, no. 7 (1937):16; *Industriia*, Sept. 28, 1937.
[99] *Stakhanovets*, no. 9 (1937):15.
[100] *Pravda*, Dec. 19, 21, 1937.

however, the production of other machine parts lagged behind, most of the cams had to be sent to the enterprise's warehouse, where they would gather dust. Indeed, as an editorial soon revealed, Gudov's shop was not fulfilling its program, nor was the shop where a milling machine operator, Nestorov, produced enough parts for the DIP-500 machine to last for two years.[101]

Recordism clearly had gotten out of hand, or so the Central Committee regarded the situation. On December 28, 1937, it revoked the call for a Stalinist month of records, incidentally revealing that the initiative for this effort had come from the Moscow party committee. Never again would there be such an initiative. Records continued to mark certain occasions such as the first session of the Supreme Soviet, the Eighteenth Party Congress, or the anniversary of Stakhanov's record. But they ceased to qualify those who made them as the best in their field or to have the mobilizing function they once had in the politics of productivity.[102]

Instead of preparing records, the Central Committee urged management to expand the ranks of Stakhanovites. This had already been happening in 1937, and it continued over the next two years (Table 7.3).

Several comments should be made about this trend. First, it would appear that the criteria for designating workers as Stakhanovites became less restrictive and were no longer tied to the rate of norm fulfillment. According to one Soviet historian, trade union functionaries in Leningrad automatically included workers who occasionally applied Stakhanovite methods, graduates of Stakhanovite courses and even informal training circles, and those who otherwise demonstrated competence in a skill.[103] If this were the case in Leningrad, it doubtlessly occurred in other parts of the country.

Second, despite such liberality, the figures mask frequent fluctuations at the enterprise level. For example, the number of

---

[101] Ibid., Dec. 25, 28, 1937.
[102] See the article entitled "Who Is the Best Steelworker in the USSR?" *Pravda*, Aug. 30, 1938, which concluded that it was not the record holder, Chaikovskii, but rather the worker who *averaged* a high rate of productivity.
[103] A. R. Dzeniskevich, *Rabochie Leningrada nakanune Velikoi Otechestvennoi voiny, 1938–iiun' 1941, g.* (Leningrad: Nauka, 1983), 156.

Table 7.3. *Stakhanovites and shock workers in industry*

Date	Stakhanovites		Shock workers		Combined	
	No.	%[a]	No.	%[a]	No.	%[a]
Sept. 1936	992,600	22.0	1,037,700	23.0	2,030,300	45.0
Jan. 1, 1938	1,593,100	24.9	1,219,300	18.9	2,812,400	43.8
July 1, 1938	1,810,800	34.4	1,116,100	18.5	2,971,800	47.6
Oct. 1, 1939	2,001,000	34.4	1,082,800	18.6	3,083,800	53.0
July 1, 1940	1,952,500	33.7	1,005,700	17.4	2,958,200	51.1

Note: Data are for trade union members only.
[a]Percentage of all trade union members.
Source: S. L. Seniavskii and V. B. Tel'pukhovskii, *Rabochii klass SSSR, 1938–1965* (Moscow: Mysl', 1971), 384. For a slightly different set of figures, see *Industrializatsiia SSSR, 1938–1941 gg. Dokumenty i materialy* (Moscow: Nauka, 1973), 366–73. Both sets are derived from VTsSPS computations!

Stakhanovites at the Stalingrad Tractor Factory plummeted from 4,290 as of May 1937 to 2,785 a month later, presumably because of the difficulty workers experienced in fulfilling the new norms. By October there were fewer Stakhanovites than there had been at any time since December 1935. Similar declines occurred at the Khar'kov and Cheliabinsk Tractor Factories.[104] Even in the absence of norm increases, numbers could fluctuate because of shifting production schedules and mixes. This evidently was the case in the rolling mill shop of Elektrostal' where the number of Stakhanovites was put at 619 in January 1938, 488 in February, 524 in March, 118 in April, and 420 in May.[105] Such ups and downs were sufficient to produce a large number of former Stakhanovites, so large in fact that in March 1938 a conference consisting of Stakhanovites who had lost their title was convened in the Donbass. According to the speakers, frequent transfers from one job to another, the deterioration of

[104] V. A. Sakharov, *Zarozhdenie i razvitie stakhanovskogo dvizheniia (na materialakh avtotraktornoi promyshlennosti)* (Moscow: MGU, 1985), 115–16.
[105] *Industriia*, July 2, 1938.

equipment, and the sudden stoppage of supplies were responsible for their loss of Stakhanovite status.[106]

Still, until 1940 the trend was up, and as had been the case with shock workers before 1935, the expansion in the number of Stakhanovites inevitably led to the debasement of the category. It also led to the proliferation of subcategories. What had been an informal distinction between outstanding or the best and ordinary Stakhanovites eventually became formalized and extended. By November 1938, the coal-mining industry contained first-class masters of coal, masters of coal, and Stakhanovites as well as that pool of potential Stakhanovites, the shock workers.[107] Other branches of industry had their *otlichniki* of socialist competition, two hundred percenters, recipients of the Order of Lenin, the Red Banner of Labor, and the Badge of Honor, and numerous other celebrated (*znatnye*) and esteemed (*pochetnye*) individuals.

The need to distinguish among Stakhanovites in this manner reflected the increasingly hierarchical character of Soviet society in the late 1930s. It was also to some extent compensation for the closing of ranks between management and the political authorities that not only excluded workers, but entailed a demotion in their status. Most of these terms would eventually become detached from the macrocategory of Stakhanovite and outlive the phenomenon of Stakhanovism.

Even while the number of Stakhanovites increased, some of the movement's most characteristic innovations were being abandoned. This included Stakhanov's method of dividing labor between hewers and timberers. The high point of the application of this method was reached in late 1936, when approximately half of all hewers could concentrate exclusively on cutting and breaking coal. By March 1937, the proportion had dropped to 43 percent and in April it was reported that fewer hewers were

---

[106] Ibid., Mar. 30, 1938.
[107] *SD*, Nov. 15, 1938. See also P. Liubavin, "V bor'be za ugol'," *PS*, no. 16 (1939):42; E. E. Kazakov, "Deiatel'nost' profsoiuzov Kuzbassa po razvitiiu stakhanovskogo dvizheniia v gody vtoroi piatiletki," in *Ocherki sotsial'no-ekonomicheskoi i kul'turnoi zhizni Sibiri*, chast' 2 (Novosibirsk: OTsPES AN SSSR, 1972), 230.

working according to Stakhanov's method than a year earlier.[108] By October 1937, not a single hewer at the Stalin mine, the birthplace of Stakhanovism, was employing the method.[109]

What had been the first and most widely publicized innovation of the Stakhanovite movement was thus quietly shelved. By 1939, a noted economist, speaking before a section of the Academy of Sciences, could advocate the recombination of the occupations of hewing and timbering, albeit as one of the "new forms of the Stakhanovite movement" and with the claim that the recombination was "on the basis of a new organization of labor that had not existed when Stakhanov divided these occupations."[110]

The story of Stakhanov's method, however, does not end here. In the spring of 1947, at the height of the postwar reconstruction of the Donbass mining industry, Pantelei Ryndin, a pneumatic pick operator, rediscovered the method. By increasing the length of the ledge in the coal face at Artem mine no. 10 and dividing the labor of his brigade in the same manner as Stakhanov had, Ryndin produced 128 tons of coal during his shift. This was reported as fifteen times his norm, which is to say that the output norm for hewers in 1947 was only slightly more than it had been twelve years earlier before the advent of Stakhanovism.[111]

Much the same thing happened to a method of ore drilling introduced by Aleksei Semivolos in July 1940. It, too, involved a finer division of labor such that the mechanical device, in this case, the boring drill, could be used more or less continually by one worker. Employing this method, Semivolos was able to advance the ore face by more than twenty-five meters and fulfill his shift norm by thirteen times.[112] But the application of this method lapsed even before the Nazi invasion and occupation. In 1947 another Krivoi Rog miner, L. Boriskin, was credited with reviving it.[113]

---

[108] Ermanskii, *Stakhanovskoe dvizhenie*, 321; *Gornyi zhurnal*, no. 9 (1937):4; *Pravda*, April 10, 1937.

[109] *SD*, May 10, 20, 1938. For evidence of further decline in 1938, see *SD*, Sept. 27, 1938.

[110] M. Rubinshtein, *Novye formy stakhanovskogo dvizheniia* (Moscow: AN SSSR, 1940), 24–6.

[111] *Trud*, April 3, 1947; see also Sept. 26, 1947.

[112] Ibid., Mar. 20, 1941.

[113] Ibid., Jan. 12, April 16, 1947.

Analogous trends could be observed in other industries such as metalworks and metallurgy.[114] However, we would do well to stay with coal mining, for it was in this industry, where workers' control over the production process was most difficult to break, that struggles over the organization of production assumed their most transparent character. As discussed in Chapter 1, miners were traditionally assigned their places and tasks in the mine by rostering, which occurred before each shift entered the mine. In the early 1930s, several mining engineers came up with alternatives to this arrangement in the form of schedules that were designed to maintain proportionality among the different phases of mining and reduce idle time. Although backed by the party, scheduling proved enormously difficult to apply, owing to the impossibility of accurately predicting thicknesses and curvatures in coal seams, not to mention the problems of absenteeism, turnover, and noncooperation among miners. Thus, at most mines in the Donbass, the power of the foreman to adjust rosters on a daily basis survived these attempts at rationalization.

Stakhanov's method did not impinge on foremen's responsibilities, except perhaps to complicate rostering. But in the summer of 1936, scheduling was revived, this time in the guise of an innovation that would assist the Stakhanovite movement. For S. Sarkisov, Donetsk party secretary, it was also a matter of prestige. "The mines must work like factories," he declared, echoing the words of mine owners and engineers in the capitalist world.[115] Scheduling figured prominently in the deliberations of Narkomtiazhprom's council, where Stakhanov, Diukanov, and other Stakhanovites warmly endorsed it.

In early July, both the commissariat and the Donetsk party *obkom* resolved to replace rosters with monthly schedules by the end of the year "at all or the vast majority of mines."[116] Official enthusiasm for this objective bore striking similarities to other Stalinist campaigns such as the collectivization of agriculture. As in that case, only with less disastrous consequences, the lack of adequate preparation and the resultant chaos produced reac-

---

[114] For some examples see Ermanskii, *Stakhanovskoe dvizhenie*, 321–2.
[115] *SD*, June 11, 1936; see also *SD*, July 5, 1936; *Pravda*, July 11, 1936; *Gornyi zhurnal*, no. 8–9 (1936):5–6.
[116] For the resolutions see *SD*, July 12, 1936.

tions in kind. By the end of August 1936, it was reported that the roster system had been abandoned by more than half the mines in the Donbass, but only formally, for foremen would frequently assemble workers on the street or elsewhere and give instructions as previously. Two months later, the results of the campaign were judged "very poor" because mining management was supposedly treating it as an end in itself, that is, was compelling workers to conform to schedules that were inappropriate to the shifting needs of mining work.[117]

As hastily as the campaign had been promoted, it was abandoned. The joint resolution of April 1937 that dealt with the Donbass coal-mining industry (see Section I) did not mention it. The resolution blamed the failure to fulfill plans for preparatory work and mining construction neither on rosters nor (more appropriately) on Stakhanovism's pressure for immediate results in terms of coal output. Rather, the "theory of concentration" of mining and the failure of Glavugol' and Donbassugol' to recognize it as "dangerous" and "crudely mistaken" were held responsible. The technical journals continued to promote scheduling for a while longer, but on November 21, 1938, Glavugol' published instructions entitled "The Organization of the Roster System in the Mines," which effectively put an end to attempts to rationalize job assignments.[118]

The checkered history of innovations that were labeled Stakhanovite or conducive to the Stakhanovite movement does not in itself indicate the waxing and waning of Stakhanovism in the late 1930s and beyond. It does suggest the contingent quality of innovations and the extent to which the Soviet leadership was willing to jettison them if they proved to be too difficult to implement or counterproductive. The contingency was based on a combination of circumstances and considerations. In the mid-1930s, Stakhanovism was an effective means of popularizing innovations of a certain kind, namely those that freed workers in the leading occupations from auxiliary tasks and speeded up

[117] *Pravda*, Aug. 29, 1936; *SD*, Oct. 17, 1936.

[118] Bailes considers the campaign against the "theory of concentration" to have been "wrong-headed political intervention [which] inhibited the modernization of the coal industry." *Technology and Society*, 357–8. See also *Gornyi zhurnal*, no. 8–9 (1936):12–13; no. 17 (1937):6–19. Glavugol's instructions were published in *SD*, Nov. 21, 1938.

production processes. The main disadvantages of these innovations were the piecemeal nature of their application and the fact that spurts in the output of certain items were incompatible with the coordination of production and the principle of central allocation of resources on the basis of forward planning.

Both enterprise personnel and industrial administrators at higher levels had to pay for these contradictions, many of them with their lives. Many workers suffered, too, inasmuch as increased norms led to the intensification of competition for receiving adequate supplies and machines that worked properly. But by 1938 circumstances were beginning to change. The new cohort of cadres that had risen as a result of both Stakhanovism and the Great Purges was deemed by central authorities to be worthy of both material and ideological support. It was not that they had necessarily earned it or were any less prone to engage in the evasive actions of their predecessors. Rather, it was that they had become an essential ingredient of a new strategy to meet new challenges. The challenges were an industrial work force that had grown accustomed to disobeying vulnerable bosses, declining or at best stagnating productivity, increased international tensions, and the fact that the latter exacerbated the labor shortage (at least in nondefense industries) as the USSR geared itself for war.

Whether the chaotic effects of the Great Purges or the impending world war was responsible for the reinforcement of managerial authority and the near militarization of labor in the years 1938–41 is an issue that cannot be resolved here. Undoubtedly, both contributed, though it would probably take another monograph to determine how and to what degree.[119] It should be noted, however, that the introduction of workbooks, legislation extending work time and providing for severe punishment even for the slightest lateness, and the State Labor Reserve system for drafting teenagers into vocational schools did not exhaust the leadership's response to the challenges just cited. These years also saw innovations in the organization of production that were qualitatively different from those that preceded them. Although Stakhanovism remained the idiom for their dis-

---

[119] For a recent interpretation that stresses the military buildup and consequential labor shortage, see Filtzer, *Soviet Workers*, 233–53.

semination, they contradicted in several respects the earlier thrust of that movement. Three such innovations became the subjects of intense campaigns. One was the synchronization (*tsik-lichnost'*) of production in the mining industry. The other two were related primarily to metalworks and machine construction and entailed the combination of occupations and the simultaneous operation of several machines by a single worker.

Synchronization, as distinct from scheduling, referred to the staggering of the different phases of mining rather than the assignment of miners to particular tasks. It was therefore compatible with rostering and indeed may have hastened official acquiescence to the reintroduction of the latter. The main principle was that, the sooner the nonproductive phases of mining were accomplished, the greater the time for excavation – cutting and breaking – and therefore the greater the amount of coal produced. In this respect alone, synchronization represented a shift in emphasis away from the leading occupations toward auxiliary and repair work and from output per se toward factors conducive to greater efficiency. The appropriate unit of measurement, therefore, was not the amount of coal dug or brought to the surface, but the number of cycles within a given period as measured by the time elapsed between successive incisions. As stipulated in the directive issued by Narkomtiazhprom in January 1938, each pit was assigned a norm of a certain number of cycles per month. In the Donbass, where the average for mines employing cutting machines had been 17.5 cycles in December, the norm was set at 21; for the mining of ledges on steeply sloping seams where pneumatic picks were used, the norm was 40.[120]

Synchronization soon dwarfed all other priorities in coal mining. As in the case of previous initiatives, it developed into a campaign that was centrally organized and centrally assessed. It also had its individual exemplars who received extensive publicity. Significantly, however, they were not workers but engineer-*praktiki*, who were only occasionally referred to as Stakhanovites.[121] Moreover, their achievement of two, three, and

[120] *Gornyi zhurnal*, no. 2 (1938):5–7.
[121] The two most prominent "innovators" were N. G. Gvozdyr'kov of

even five cycles per day was ascribed not to the initiative and dedication of workers, but to the "correct organization" instituted by the engineers themselves.[122] As Kaganovich had indicated in his directive, "sportsman-like records of individual workers" were incompatible with the successful implementation of synchronized production.

We have here, then, a campaign in the Stakhanovite mold but missing some of its characteristic ingredients and above all identifiable worker-Stakhanovites. What it did not lack was management's manipulation of the new criterion of its performance. Some section heads achieved more than thirty cycles per month by ordering their machinists to reduce the depth of their cuts into the coal face; others simply added more workers or reduced the length of the face to be cut. The result was that, while the number of cycles increased from one month to the next, the output of coal dropped.[123]

Such distortions effectively undermined the campaign and led to the abandonment of synchronization as a top priority. According to the Commissariat of Coal's figures, the average number of cycles per month in the Donbass was only 14.8 in 1939 and dropped to 14.6 in 1940.[124] After the reintroduction of three 8-hour shifts in 1940, coal mines reverted to a system of two shifts for production and one for repair and preparatory work. Every third shift was to commence a new cycle, theoretically giving an average of one per day. The fact that twelve years later the Voroshilovgrad party *obkom* secretary was calling for this result suggests that its achievement was a long time in coming.[125]

This process by which certain distortions in the organization of production induced a shift in priorities, which themselves generated distortions in their implementation, will be recognized by students of Soviet economic history as absolutely typical. Whether involving heavy nails, too many high-wattage light

the Kirovugol' trust and Shashitskii of Snezhniantratsit. See *SD*, Feb. 3, 12, June 8, 1938; and *Industriia*, July 28, 1938.

[122] *Stakhanovets*, no. 4 (1938):44–5.

[123] *Pravda*, Nov. 21, 1938.

[124] *Industrializatsiia SSSR, 1938–1941*, 172–4.

[125] *Trud*, Jan. 10, 1952.

bulbs, or "false" cycles, the "success indicator problem" was and remains a sore point in the Soviet planning system. As Alec Nove put it:

> In every case, the essence of the problem is that the centre is trying to set up an incentive system designed to achieve more efficiency, but, because it does not *and cannot* know the specific circumstances, its instructions can frequently contradict what those on the spot know to be the sensible thing to do.[126]

Yet acting on their sense of the sensible thing to do can get those on the spot in a great deal of trouble. What has varied over time has been the center's assessment of responsibility for the distortions, irrationalities, and wastage resulting from this problem and the severity of the sanctions it has imposed.

Turning to the other two organizational innovations referred to above, the simultaneous operation of several machines by a single worker had been at the heart of the Stakhanovite movement in the textile industry and was the basis of Gudov's prodigious overfulfillment of his norms. The multiple-machine movement that commenced in 1939 differed not only in the scope of its application, but in its endorsement of the acquisition of skills by workers to enable them to operate *different* kinds of machines that performed different functions.

This was testimony to the increased level of skill of the Soviet working class, particularly in machine construction. However, other factors were involved as well. As we have seen in the case of coal mining, the conventional wisdom among Soviet economists favored an extreme division of labor in industry. This was due partly to the pragmatic consideration that it was easier to train workers to carry out a narrow spectrum of operations and partly to an ideological predisposition that owed as much to Taylor and Ford as it did to Marx and Engels. Notwithstanding occasional challenges to this wisdom, such as the attack on the application of the functional principle (*funktsionalka*) in textile production, problems arising from the division of labor were thought to be solvable by the proper organization of production. This was essentially the responsibility of management. Its failure to synchronize production and thereby reduce idle labor time

---

[126] Alec Nove, *The Soviet Economic System* (London: Allen & Unwin, 1977), 85–108. Quote from 107–8; emphasis in original.

thus proved to be a major source of disappointment for higher authorities.

Another drain on productivity was the relatively high proportion of auxiliary and maintenance workers compared with those on production lines. Thus, whereas Soviet blast and open-hearth furnaces outperformed on average those in the United States in terms of coefficients of available capacity, this advantage was negated by the fact that Soviet furnaces were operated by three to five times as many workers. According to a Gosplan memorandum of 1937, furnaces of identical capacities produced 800 kilograms of steel per worker-hour in the United States but at best 559 kilograms in the Soviet Union. Gosplan explained this disparity by pointing to the "excessive detailing of labor," which prevented production workers from making even the smallest repairs and divided maintenance brigades according to the type of equipment to be repaired.[127]

Such a case could not have been made a few years earlier. Its articulation suggests that the division of labor as a panacea to the problems of labor productivity was losing its luster as far as industrial officials were concerned and that they were eager to proceed with recombining certain occupations.

An indication of such eagerness as well as the persistence of ideologically based resistance to it can be found in O. A. Ermanskii's book on Stakhanovite methods. The book essentially elaborated the critique that had appeared in his *Theory and Practice of Rationalization*. It characterized the idea of combining several occupations as a "peculiar survival of handicraft mentality in the consciousness of people" that "throws overboard the division of labor for which Stakhanov and his comrades have been fighting." In Ermanskii's view, only when a task needed to be performed occasionally or in cases where several identical operations were being combined was the approach permissible.[128]

Between October 1938, when Ermanskii's book was ready for publication, and its actual appearance, more than a year had

---

[127] *Industrializatsiia SSSR, 1938–1941*, p. 317–18. See also Clark, *Economics of Soviet Steel*, 247. For other unflattering comparisons, see *Pravda*, Aug. 30, 1937.

[128] Ermanskii, *Stakhanovskoe dvizhenie*, 51, 57–8, 71. For his earlier critique see *Teoriia i praktika ratsionalizatsii*, 5th ed. (Moscow: ONTI, 1933), 305–8.

elapsed, during which the entire question of the division and combination of labor was reconsidered. What undoubtedly tipped the balance against the position defended by Ermanskii was a factor external to industry but having a direct bearing on it. This was the intensification of military recruitment as part of the Soviet Union's preparations for war. More than anything else, the resultant pressure on labor resources explains why the initiatives taken in the summer of 1939 at the Ordzhonikidze Machine Factory in Sverdlovsk and the Khar'kov Machine Construction Factory resonated throughout the country as earlier ones had not.[129]

These initiatives involved individual Stakhanovites operating several nonautomatic lathes and, at Khar'kov, both grinding and milling machines. In Leningrad, where the initiatives probably received their widest application, some metalworkers mastered as many as five different specialties – milling, planing, lathe operating, mortising, and drill-press operating. Simultaneously, auxiliary and maintenance workers combined occupations, performing the work of electricians and locksmiths, greasers and fitters.[130] This was also the case in other industries, such as metallurgy, where furnace operators also took over the pouring of coke, and in coal mining, where electric-drill operators also fired the shots and conveyor operators loaded coal onto the conveyors. And in railroad transport, the organization of maintenance work by a brigade of locomotive machinists earned the brigade leader, N. A. Lunin, fame equal to that of earlier outstanding Stakhanovites.

There are at least three reasons for considering these movements to be departures from Stakhanovism. First, as David Granick noted, official support for the initiatives was equivocal.[131] Even while urging their widespread adoption, the commissar of heavy machine construction mandated rather modest wage in-

---

[129]   Similarly, the publicity surrounding the entry of women into almost exclusively male occupations and the campaign to curb seasonal migration of miners date from this time. See *Industriia*, April 11, 1939.

[130]   *Industrializatsiia severo-zapadnogo raiona v gody vtoroi i tret'ei piatiletok, 1933–1941 gg. Dokumenty i materialy* (Leningrad: LGU, 1969), 396–7; Dzeniskevich, *Rabochie Leningrada*, 150–5.

[131]   Granick, *Management*, 86.

centives that were to apply only after output norms on all machines had been fulfilled for three months.[132] Ambivalence concerning whether it was permissible to lower output norms and/or cut the rates at which multiple-machine operators were paid remained for some time. While criticizing the management of general machine construction and aviation factories for cutting rates, the assistant director of VTsSPS's Department of Wages indicated that expenses incurred in repositioning machines and introducing new appurtenances and workers could be covered by doing just that.[133]

Second, partly because of official cautiousness, neither initiative developed into a mass phenomenon. According to a Leningrad party *gorkom* report of April 1940, the city's multiple-machine operators and workers combining trades numbered 19,276. This may well have been the peak, for several months later the party secretary reported that there had been no overall increase in the interim. Indeed, the number declined at several major plants.[134] Within enterprises of the Commissariat of Heavy Machine Construction, the number of multiple-machine operators was 4,015 at the beginning of 1940 and 4,436 by the end of the year. This represented roughly 3 percent of all workers employed in such enterprises and only 5 to 6 percent of production workers.[135]

The limited extent of these movements also reflected technical and organizational considerations. Since in most cases the engaging and disengaging of machines had to be performed manually, a worker operating several machines had to stagger these operations, thus cutting into machine time and making it more difficult to fulfill the assigned technical and output norms. The alternatives were to assign additional workers, which defeated the purpose of the innovation, or to operate at least some machines on an overtime basis.

Finally, it is significant that the main advantage of these in-

[132] *Mash.*, Aug. 5, 21, 1939.
[133] *Stakhanovets*, no. 2 (1940):20–1.
[134] *Industrializatsiia severo-zapadnogo raiona*, 400; *Pokoleniia udarnikov. Sbornik dokumentov i materialov o sotsialisticheskom sorevnovanii na predpriiatiiakh Leningrada v 1928–1961 gg.* (Leningrad: Lenizdat, 1963), 117.
[135] *Industrializatsiia SSSR, 1938–1941*, 159, 162–3.

292   *Stakhanovism and the politics of productivity*

novations was expressed not in terms of productivity, but rather as reducing the labor requirements of enterprises. When the head of the Baltic Shipbuilding Works' Technical Norm Bureau praised the movement for combining trades, he did so by claiming that it "gives us the possibility of *fulfilling* our program for 1940 with fewer workers."[136] Such statements were as common as the public rejection of management's requests for additional workers.[137] Together they suggest that the supply of labor was taking over from productivity as the generator of economic politics before the war.

In short, several forces were working in the late 1930s and early 1940s to blur the specificity and erode the importance of Stakhanovism. The Great Purges largely replaced it as a means of applying pressure to middle-level management. Before the purges, Stakhanovism had been associated with worker innovation and generous rewards for those who mastered new techniques. After the purges, innovations were apt to be attributed to engineering-technical personnel and tended to involve coordinated collective organization rather than individual prowess. Many Stakhanovites benefited indirectly from the purges by being promoted at an accelerated rate. But Stakhanovism ceased to have much significance for those who remained at the bench even while an increasing proportion of them were designated as Stakhanovites.

The change reflected official disenchantment with previous Stakhanovite methods and the closing of ranks with managerial and technical personnel in the face of widespread lack of discipline among workers and stagnating productivity. The increasing prospect of war intensified these processes. Stakhanovites were still useful to higher authorities, but not in the same way as previously. Their production records and participation in socialist competition no longer brought them the accolades of heroes. They no longer necessarily paid off in terms of material benefits either. Beginning in 1939, progressive piece-rate payment was curtailed, first in machine construction, then in coal mining, textiles, and other industries.[138]

[136] *LP*, Jan. 17, 1940. Emphasis mine.
[137] See, e.g., *PS*, no. 14 (1939):32–5; no. 16 (1939):41–2; no. 19 (1939):12–16; *Problemy ekonomiki*, no. 11–12 (1940):107–21.
[138] *Mash.*, Jan. 16, 1939; *Planovoe khoziaistvo*, no. 6 (1939):79–80; *Industrializatsiia SSSR, 1938–41*, 175–6.

Ultimately, the usefulness of Stakhanovites lay less in how much they produced or in what methods they used than in their roles as models of punctuality and discipline on the shop floor. They were relied upon to echo official concern about lateness and absenteeism, to affirm the necessity for legislation to curb these scourges, and to act as the eyes and ears of higher authorities in the implementation of those laws. More than the degree of norm overfulfillment, it was probably the extent to which Stakhanovites carried out these unenviable tasks that distinguished the increasing proportion of nominal Stakhanovites from active ones in the years immediately preceding the Great Patriotic War.

In those years, which saw border clashes with Japanese forces, the Winter War against Finland, and the Soviet annexation of eastern Poland, the Baltic States, and Bessarabia, the Stakhanovite movement and individual Stakhanovites were frequently referred to as patriotic. After the Nazis launched their invasion of the USSR, patriotism became a much more prominent theme in Soviet discourse and Stakhanovism a much less prominent one.

Conclusion

Stakhanovism arose exactly midway between the Bolsheviks' sei-
zure of power and Stalin's death in 1953. Its emergence also
stood at the midpoint between the beginning of the force-paced
industrialization drive and the onset of the Great Patriotic War.
These temporal parameters are worth bearing in mind, for they
help to situate Stakhanovism within the broad contours of Soviet
history.

By the middle of the 1930s, what has been referred to as the
extensive period in the development of the Soviet planned economy was drawing to a close.[1] During this period, peasants had
been separated from their means of production through collectivization and absorption into the rapidly growing industrial sector as wage and semislave prisoner-laborers. Accumulation for
investment was achieved essentially by the administrative manipulation of prices and the depression of the living standards
of working people. Industrial output expanded largely through
increased inputs of labor and mechanical power. Breakdowns,
spoilage, and accidents were frequent, as mainly unskilled workers confronted equipment for which they had little or no
training.

Sooner or later, the factors of production on which this
method of industrial expansion depended would become exhausted, and that is what began to happen toward the end of
the First Five-Year Plan. Already in 1932, it was estimated that,

---

[1] Michael Burawoy, *The Politics of Production* (London: Verso, 1985),
164–5. For a brilliant conceptualization and assessment of the resultant crisis, see R. W. Davies, "The Soviet Economic Crisis of 1931–
1933 "(CREES discussion paper, Soviet Industrialisation Project Series [SIPS], University of Birmingham, no. 4, 1976).

to achieve the rate of growth then being projected for the Second Five-Year Plan, an additional 8 million workers would be required.[2] That is, the industrial work force would have to double once again. This was clearly unreasonable and was understood to be so at the time. Even while cutting back the rate of growth, the central authorities recognized the necessity of achieving increased productivity through more intensive methods of production. The effective implementation of such methods in turn required that enterprises be given greater control over the allocation of resources, investment strategy, wage policy, and other aspects of economic administration.[3]

However, such increased autonomy for individual enterprises was incompatible with the still nascent Stalinist command economy. Soviet authorities, in other words, found themselves in something of a bind. Because of both economies of scale and considerations of national prestige, they had presided over the creation of enormous enterprises that supplied not only employment but living space, food, and recreation to their large heterogeneous labor forces. They had also encouraged a strict hierarchical relationship between management and labor, referring to managers and technical specialists as "commanders of production." But they were clearly unwilling to reinforce the responsibilities of these commanders with actual decision-making power, because to do so would have undermined their own claim to leadership and jeopardized the institutional framework that they had assiduously constructed. Instead, they imposed numerous (and often mutually contradictory) criteria by which to judge enterprise performance and a dense network of supervisors – party organizers, control commission plenipotentiaries, and police officials – who ironically often found themselves championing the cause of those whom they were supposed to be supervising.

From this perspective, Stakhanovism represented a way of intensifying production but without succumbing to the managerialist or autonomist implications of this emphasis. In the ab-

---

[2] V. S. Lel'chuk, *Industrializatsiia SSSR: Istoriia, opyt, problemy* (Moscow: Politizdat, 1984), 205.

[3] This is, of course, exactly what has been recognized and to a degree implemented in the post-Stalin era, notably in Hungary and China and more fitfully in Czechoslovakia, Poland, and the USSR itself.

sence of any automatically operating means of compelling management to lower costs or otherwise "sell" products at competitive prices, Stakhanovism provided such compulsion. Such at least was the thrust of the terms laid down by the commissar of heavy industry, G. K. Ordzhonikidze, and pursued by other industrial commissars as well. Demands from above for the application of prescribed methods of production would be supplemented by pressure from below, that is, from Stakhanovites, to be provided with the means of fulfilling their norms. Moreover, it was not enough for management to respond to demands. It had to head up the Stakhanovite movement.

The state's investment in Stakhanovism had yet another objective. This was to orient workers toward the mastery of technology. The theme of mastering technology predated Stakhanovism and has certainly survived to the present. It was evident in the 1920s in the Central Institute of Labor's experimentation with and popularization of production technique under the Taylorist-inspired concept of the Scientific Organization of Labor (NOT), and it has figured in the revival and elaboration of that concept since the early 1960s. But neither before nor since the heyday of Stakhanovism has mastering technology occupied such a central place in Soviet discourse. This was not the result of some whim of Stalin and his associates. It followed from certain historically specific factors, among which the emergence of a new industrial work force during the First Five-Year Plan, its political inertness, and cultural disorientation were perhaps the most important.

Precursors of Stakhanovism can be found in several shock worker and socialist competition campaigns, particularly Izotovism and the movement for excellence in production (*otlichnichestvo*). What those party-invented phenomena lacked was a systematic linkage between labor activism and advanced technique. Stakhanovism provided such a link, recapitulating and combining the thrust of NOT with individual overfulfillment of output norms. As for the innovations attributed to Stakhanovites, most were qualitatively indistinct from the thousands of "inventions" that flooded enterprise rationalization bureaus in previous years. Many, including Stakhanov's own, essentially repeated production methods that had been proposed by engineers but were shelved for one reason or another.

Thus, it was not so much the methods themselves that distinguished Stakhanovism as the manner in which they were treated. The fact that Stakhanovites' production records were typically expressed as a function of their individual output norms is critical in this connection. Without the mechanisms of capitalism whereby inefficient workers are compelled to sell their labor power at a lower rate or face unemployment, Stakhanovism could get workers to compete with themselves as well as other workers.

The politics of productivity essentially involved the manner in which these state-sponsored initiatives were handled by the two groups on whom this study has focused – industrial cadres (and their allies in enterprise-based party and trade union organs) and workers. By demonstrating that both these groups were able to maneuver within the determinate social relations of production, this study concurs with several others in emphasizing the difficulties of the political dictatorship in accomplishing its goals. Even in the absence of any autonomous space in which civil society could function or rather, to switch metaphors, because the state had swallowed civil society, the exercise of state power was profoundly affected by what was being digested.

The administration of the Stakhanovite movement provided ample opportunities for maneuvering. The manipulation of criteria for determining who qualified as a Stakhanovite, the assignment of workers to tasks or machines with "soft" norms, the distribution of bonuses and gifts, the arrangement of production records and storming during Stakhanovite days, *dekady*, and months, the use of Stakhanovites as expediters and propagandists for their enterprises, and the resort to supplementary payments and crediting workers with fictitious work to insulate them from disruptions of the production process were just some of the ways that industrial cadres coped with the pressures imposed on them. Workers also maneuvered. Stakhanovites mitigated the arbitrariness of their immediate bosses by demanding opportunities to remain Stakhanovites. They frequently made public their complaints about sabotage of the movement; they pressed for improvements in sanitary and living conditions; and they sought and in many instances achieved promotion both through their production work and by policing the shop floor. Non-Stakhanovites both resisted and adjusted to Stakhanovism. Some deliberately sabotaged the work of Stakhanovites because they either anticipated higher norms or resented speedups; others demanded the opportunities provided to Stakhanovites for fulfilling their norms.

Ultimately, however, the greatest degree of maneuverability was at the top. Higher authorities could and did define priorities with respect to Stakhanovism, sometimes putting the stress on qualitative changes in work organization, then emphasizing immediate results in terms of output, alternatively blaming production specialists, enterprise directors, or backward workers for sabotaging Stakhanovism and eventually abandoning Stakhanovism as the vehicle through which to discipline industrial cadres and workers.

They also crucially set the ideological tone for Stakhanovism, constructing the ideal reality and behavioral norms that were no less important in teaching Soviet workers how to live than output norms were in shaping the way they worked. In a culture that revered labor, often more in the abstract than in actuality, the celebration of Stakhanovites' achievements could be as genuine as it was crude. Such bread and circuses were in stark, perhaps even intentional contrast to the turbulent political climate. For that very reason, this aspect of Stalinist popular culture deserves far more attention from historians than it has received.

What, then, was the impact of Stakhanovism on Soviet production relations? Here, it must be stressed that much of the maneuvering by both industrial cadres and workers had a fundamentally *conservative* effect, namely to ward off changes that both groups considered threatening. This is not to say that Stakhanovism had no impact at all.[4] It did shake up what some scholars have termed the internal labor market within enterprises, that is, the administrative rules governing wage rates, job assignments, and promotion possibilities. It thus limited, if only temporarily, the authority of foremen, shop and section heads, and the norm-determining apparatus. Some workers, namely the locally and nationally prominent Stakhanovites, were able to

---

[4] On this point, I disagree with Donald Filtzer, *Soviet Workers and Stalinist Industrialization* (Armonk, N.Y.: Sharpe, 1986), 197: "Stakhanovism had done nothing to shake up the fundamental set of relations between managers and workers on the shop-floor." Of course, much depends on the definition of "fundamental."

take advantage of this situation or, to put it another way, increase their bargaining power. However, they made their gain at the expense of other workers – brigade leaders who were not Stakhanovites, production workers whose job profiles were narrowed and whose work consequently became more tedious, and auxiliary and service workers in general.

Stakhanovism thus intensified antagonisms within an already fractionalized work force. It fed upon the individualistic consciousness among workers that was a product of their overwhelmingly recent origins as workers, the predominance of piece rates, the absence of truly representative institutions, and other severe constraints on worker solidarity. These factors, dating back to the First Five-Year Plan period, militated against the most rudimentary articulation of the Soviet industrial work force as a class. It is for this reason that the term "class" generally has not been used in this study.[5]

Even Stakhanovites lacked internal cohesion and stability. Except for the relatively small stratum of pioneer and outstanding Stakhanovites, their privileges were meager, contingent, and often ephemeral. Divisions among them were in many cases no less great than those between Stakhanovites and non-Stakhanovite workers. Most important perhaps, their bargaining power was not collective, but rather individual, and depended critically on the threat of intervention from above. For all the officially sponsored rhetoric about Stakhanovites closing the gap between mental and manual labor, they were in no greater position to make the rules governing their employment than were other workers. This is perhaps why they so readily joined in the persecution of their immediate bosses during the Great Purges.

Ironically, the purges ultimately led to a reinforcement of managerial authority down to the level of foreman and brigade leader. What was done with that authority is far from clear. It appears that instructions from above continued to be circum-

---

[5] This is an enormously complex question. The distinction being made here is between a demographic agglomeration of industrial workers (Marx's "class in itself") and the collective behavior of that agglomeration directed in response to and against another class ("class for itself"). The point is that opportunities for such behavior were severely restricted.

vented and that accommodations with workers, if not the norm, were frequent, but this question, too, requires further research.[6]

Finally, the impact of Stakhanovism on labor productivity must be addressed. Until recently, this question attracted more attention from Western scholars than any other having to do with Stakhanovism. Writing in the 1940s, Maurice Dobb asserted that, although short-term accelerations of tempo were occasionally undertaken at the expense of long-term results, "once pioneered, [Stakhanovites'] methods could easily be copied even by much less enterprising or well-trained workers, thereby raising the whole level of productivity." Dobb concluded that even if one cannot separate changes in working methods from the introduction of new machinery, the amount by which the increase in labor productivity in the period 1935–7 exceeded the plan "can be attributed in the main to Stakhanovism."[7]

But can it? Solomon Schwarz contended that the internal organization of industrial plants during 1936–7 was in a state of "virtual crisis" as a result of Stakhanovism and in the assessment of Albert Pasquier, there was "veritable disarray in the Soviet economy," because "the generalization of Stakhanovite methods requires a minute execution of preparatory work and imposes a rigorous coordination as difficult to achieve as it is impossible to predict."[8] Yet on the basis of his experience at Magnitogorsk, John Scott wrote that "by and large, 1936, the Stakhanovite year, was a great success," and in his study of the entire Soviet steel industry, M. Gardner Clark attributed to Stakhanovism two key technical innovations that eventually raised the productivity of open-hearth furnaces.[9]

Is it possible that, despite the "crisis" and "disarray" brought on by Stakhanovism, it nonetheless caused labor productivity to

[6] A good start has been made by Filtzer, *Soviet Workers*, 233–53.
[7] Maurice Dobb, *Soviet Economic Development Since 1917* (London: Routledge & Kegan Paul, 1966), 468.
[8] Solomon Schwarz, *Labor in the Soviet Union* (New York: Praeger, 1952), 197; Albert Pasquier, *Le Stakhanovisme: L'Organisation du travail en URSS* (Caen: Robert, 1937), 79, 82.
[9] John Scott, *Behind the Urals: An American Worker in Russia's City of Steel* (Bloomington: Indiana University Press, 1973), 162; M. Gardner Clark, *The Economics of Soviet Steel* (Cambridge, Mass: Harvard University Press, 1956), 251.

rise? After all, Stakhanovism did impart to workers a sense of the importance of proper technique to a degree unparalleled by any other state-sponsored initiative in the USSR. It also offered to those who introduced Stakhanovite methods rewards that were, and remain, unmatched in Soviet experience. These two kinds of incentives – the intrinsic satisfaction derived from the mastery of a skill and extrinsic material rewards and social prestige – comprised the constituent elements of a work ethic that was relatively new in the Soviet context.

However, the motivation and skills of workers do not in themselves guarantee high labor productivity. Particularly in the case of large-scale factory production, the integration and coordination of supply schedules, a high standard of machinery, semifinished products, and maintenance work, a safe working environment, and the provision of nourishing diets, adequate living space, recreation, and intellectual stimulation all contribute as well. In this sense, Stalin and Molotov were absolutely correct when they asserted that Stakhanovism by itself could not overcome the absence of these factors of productivity. They were certainly wrong, however, to identify wrecking as the main cause of the absence.

It was rather a function of what one scholar has called the tension between mobilization and balance;[10] of the impossibility, especially in a situation of chronic shortage, of calculating and simultaneously fulfilling all planning requirements; of the necessity of managers' cutting corners to meet those requirements that central authorities assigned the highest priorities; of one productive unit stealing resources and personnel from others to ensure adequate supplies of both; and of the deliberate falsification of information that the center relied upon for drawing up its plans. This is not to suggest that national economic planning is inherently futile or incompatible with increases in productivity, for the Soviet record amply disproves such a notion. It is to assert that the sort of centralized planning that emerged under Stalin and has survived with modifications to the present

---

[10] Mark Harrison, *Soviet Planning in Peace and War, 1938–1945* (Cambridge University Press, 1985), 3–11. "Tension" rather than "contradiction," because as Harrison notes, "there was a sense in which they needed each other."

has achieved increases in labor productivity largely by increasing the constant capital content of production and not without enormous wastage.[11]

It follows from this that an extremely important distinction must be made between labor productivity as measured by labor expenditure per unit and the effective use to which gains in productivity are put. Thus, to refer to a typical example cited earlier in the text, if a machine operator suddenly increases his or her productivity and turns out a prodigious quantity of machine parts but, because of a lack of complementarity with whatever else is being produced (or the rate at which other parts are being turned out), these parts must be stored for a lengthy period of time, much of that increase is wasted. Or, again, if increases in machine time and intensity are not matched by corresponding improvements in maintenance and the provision of supplies, then such increases will lead to greater depreciation than anticipated and consequently shortages and stoppages.

Stakhanovism can thus be seen to have played both a positive and a negative role in labor productivity. It enhanced the adaptation of workers to technological changes that were enormous and far reaching. But by making a fetish of individual performance and achievement, particularly in circumstances where there was growing interdependence among producers and production processes, it exacerbated the difficulties of achieving proportionality. This in turn complicated the provisioning of workers with the necessary means of production and making effective use of what they produced.

Ultimately, therefore, Stakhanovism undermined its own effectiveness. To the extent that it gave workers incentives to raise their productivity, it presupposed that conditions outside the control of workers would be satisfied so that they could concentrate on achieving and overfulfilling their norms. Yet by increasing the likelihood of distortions and bottlenecks and in other ways intensifying competition among workers for favorable con-

---

[11] This is written at a time when the USSR is engaged in a national reassessment of its economic system. One of the most radical of such reassessments argues that "the rejection of the Leninist New Economic Policy complicated in the most serious way socialist construction in the USSR." See Nikolai Shmelev, "Avansy i Dolgi," *Novyi mir* no. 6 (1987):142–58.

ditions, it may well have sapped the enthusiasm that it initially inspired.

Over and above this ironic effect are two other factors that undoubtedly contributed to Stakhanovism's loss of potency among workers and its eventual marginalization as an instrument for raising productivity. One was the peculiar combination of bureaucratized administration of the movement with the high degree of arbitrariness – the very antithesis of bureaucracy in Weberian terms – exercised by the enterprise-based administrators. The vagaries of calculating what an individual worker produced and under what conditions and the frequently changing criteria for distinguishing Stakhanovites must have produced a sense of helplessness and indifference among many workers. Paradoxically, compensating or bribing workers who threatened to quit or make a fuss would have had the same effect of delegitimizing Stakhanovism. The other factor was the historical circumstances that arose in the aftermath of the Great Purges. In closing ranks with industrial management and technical personnel, higher authorities were exercising their capacity to shift the grounds of the politics of productivity and provide for the introduction of less spectacular but also less disruptive changes in the organization of production. Stakhanovism thus reverted to a sometimes convenient idiom and soporific with which to compensate individual workers. Thus did it survive until the Great Patriotic War – and for years afterward up to the death of Stalin.

During the Great Patriotic War, the state could offer workers little in the way of material incentives except relative insulation from deprivation. The disciplinary measures introduced in 1938–40 were reinforced at the outset of the war. Ration cards for foodstuffs and manufactured goods, gradated according to the type of work performed, reappeared in Moscow and Leningrad in July 1941 and subsequently in other cities and towns. In this respect as well as many others – the extreme dearth of clothing, living space, medicines, household appliances, and many other rationed goods, the reliance on factory canteens and kitchen gardens, the running down of transportation services – wartime conditions in the rear resembled those of the First Five-Year Plan period. Wages in industry rose, from an average of 375 rubles per month in 1940 to 573 rubles in 1944, but then the number of hours worked rose as well. Prices (except that for vodka) remained fairly stable in normal state outlets but rose by ten and twenty times in peasant markets. "Commercial" stores selling rationed goods at prices close to those in the peasant markets opened in 1944.[12]

A rough-and-ready hierarchy of consumption thus emerged. Unskilled workers in defense-related industries and most workers and junior employees in other sectors were compelled to rely mainly on their rations and the factory canteens. Engineering-technical personnel, whose average pay increased from 768 rubles per month in 1940 to 1,209 rubles in 1944, and defense workers could afford to supplement their rations with goods purchased in peasant markets or commercial stores.[13]

Industrial workers continued to overfulfill their norms by stupendous margins and especially in defense-related industries received notoriety as two hundred and three hundred percenters. Some even managed (occasionally) to fulfill the shift norms of as many as ten other workers, thus becoming known as one thousanders. The most prominent of such workers was D. F. Bosyi, a Leningrad milling machine operator whom the party had assigned to a Nizhnii Tagil armaments factory in the Urals. On February 14, 1942, the anniversary of the founding of the Red Army, Bosyi increased the cutting speed of his machine and made other adjustments that enabled him to fulfill his shift norm by 1,450 percent.[14] Thanks to the alertness of the party *raikom*, Bosyi's feat was immediately publicized in the district press and not long thereafter throughout the USSR. The following month, Bosyi, the railroad depot worker, Lunin, and two ore drillers, Semivolos and Iankin, became the first workers since the beginning of the war to receive the state prize awarded by Sovnarkom.[15]

The similarities with what had occurred seven years earlier at

[12] Alec Nove, *An Economic History of the USSR* (London: Lane, 1969), 278–81, 306–7.
[13] Ibid.
[14] L. S. Rogachevskaia, *Sotsialisticheskoe sorevnovanie v SSSR: Istoricheskie ocherki 1917–1970 gg.* (Moscow: Nauka, 1977), 187–9; T. Dmitrenko, "Dmitrii Bosyi," in *Novatory, Sbornik* (Moscow: Molodaia gvardiia, 1972), 270–80.
[15] *Pravda*, March 24, 1942.

the Central Irmino mine are obvious. The differences were no less significant. Bosyi's innovation led not to a shake-up in industry, but rather to a modest display of labor activism limited to a few hundred skilled machinists. It received far less publicity than did other forms of labor activism, such as Komsomol youth front brigades and All-Union socialist competition drives that were derivatives of First Five-Year Plan techniques. Finally, it was not translated into higher output norms, nor, so far as can be determined, did it provoke overt resistance by workers.

In general, among the arsenal of techniques employed to popularize achievements on the "labor front" during the war, what was distinctly Stakhanovite represented only a small cache. The fact that front brigade members, who numbered more than a million by 1945, skilled workers who "patronized" (i.e., taught) recent recruits, and those distinguishing themselves in socialist competition were referred to as Stakhanovites merely obscured the historical specificity of Stakhanovism.[16]

The postwar reconstruction phase of Soviet economic development essentially recapitulated and combined prewar techniques for popularizing innovations and new priorities. Experimentation with technical improvements, some of which had been developed previously in capitalist countries, preceded the discovery of Soviet innovators and subsequently led to campaigns to apply what was claimed to be the innovators' methods. Thus, increasing the speed at which certain metal-cutting machines could be operated became associated with the metalworkers P. B. Bykov and G. S. Bortkevich; and disseminating technical knowledge among unskilled workers and improving the quality of output were linked with two foremen, N. A. Rossiiskii and A. S. Chutkikh.[17]

The campaigns to promote these "innovations" did not stop at the Soviet borders. As part and parcel of the Soviet domination of central and eastern Europe after the war, Stakhanovism was exported. Bykov, Rossiiskii, and other prominent Stakhanovites

[16] Rogachevskaia, *Sotsialisticheskoe sorevnovanie*, 212; G. I. Shigalin, *Narodnoe khoziaistvo SSSR v period Velikoi Otechestvennoi voiny* (Moscow: Sotsekgiz, 1960), 116–18; A. V. Mitrofanova, *Rabochii klass SSSR v gody Velikoi Otechestvennoi voiny* (Moscow: Nauka, 1971), 153–69; 296–315.

[17] Rogachevskaia, *Sotsialisticheskoe sorevnovanie*, 227–33.

from the USSR traveled to the People's Democracies to exhibit their techniques.[18] At the same time, eastern European analogues of the original core of outstanding Stakhanovites were discovered. In Bulgaria, Maria Todorova was the first to adopt the Vinogradovas' technique for operating Northrupp weaving machines; in Poland, the first Stakhanovite was a coal miner; in Czechoslovakia, a machine operator; and in the Soviet zone of occupied Germany, where Stakhanovites were known as "activists," it was Adolf Hennecke, a coal miner whose production record of October 13, 1948, was achieved in circumstances remarkably similar to those that existed at Central Irmino on the night of August 30–1, 1935.[19]

Both in the Soviet Union and in eastern Europe, the campaigns organized to promote the adoption of advanced techniques of production took the form of agreements to engage in socialist competition. Juries composed of trade union officials, engineering-technical personnel, and prominent Stakhanovites periodically awarded prizes or symbolic banners to individuals, brigades, shops, and enterprises that distinguished themselves. This routinization of labor activism under the rubric of socialist competition has continued more or less uninterruptedly in the USSR since the late 1940s. Not the death of Stalin, nor the reformism of the Khrushchev years, nor the more cautious policies of his successors fundamentally altered this practice. Socialist competition, defined as an inextricable component of socialist production relations that serves to speed along socioeconomic progress, has been and remains a constant feature of Soviet economic life.[20]

What has changed are the terms under which socialist competition has occurred. "Stakhanovism," as a term too closely as-

[18] *Trud*, Jan. 6, 1952; P. Bykov, *Put' k schast'iu* (Moscow: Profizdat, 1951).

[19] S. R. Gershberg, *Rukovodstvo kommunisticheskoi partii dvizheniem novatorov v promyshlennosti (1935–1941)* (Moscow: Gospolitizdat, 1956), 236–8. On the Hennecke movement, probably the most extensively developed of such postwar phenomena, see Benno Sarel, *La classe ouvrière d'Allemagne Orientale* (Paris: Les editions ouvrières, 1958), 61–84; and Reinhard Bendix, *Work and Authority in Industry: Ideologies of Management in the Course of Industrialization* (Berkeley and Los Angeles: University of Calif. Press, 1974), 417–33.

[20] *Sotsialisticheskoe sorevnovanie, Voprosy teorii, praktiki i organizatsii* (Moscow: Nauka, 1978), 31, 36.

sociated with the "cult of personality," went out of use in the mid-1950s, to be replaced by the "communist attitude toward labor" as displayed by shock workers and collectives of communist labor. For a time, even historical treatments of Stakhanovism were apt to avoid using the term, preferring the more innocuous "movement of innovators" (*dvizhenie novatorov*).[21]

This trend was reversed by the late 1960s. In the following decade, veteran Stakhanovites appeared, bemedaled, at commemorative meetings, their achievements were popularized in biographies and autobiographies, and Stakhanovism became firmly established in Soviet historiography as the characteristic mode of labor activism in the era of the Second and Third Five-Year Plans.[22] When Stakhanov died in 1977, his adopted town of Kadievka was renamed in his honor, making it the only such place in the Soviet Union to bear the name of an industrial worker.[23]

More recently, the fiftieth anniversary of Stakhanovism was celebrated by a massive outpouring of popular literature, lectures, museum displays, and special exhibitions.[24] Scholarly pub-

[21] The supreme example was Gershberg, *Rukovodstvo*. Others included A. L. Oprishchenko, "Dvizhenie novatorov proizvodstva v predvoennye gody," *Istoriia KPSS*, no. 6 (1966):106–9; A. V. Volchenko, "O dvizhenii novatorov promyshlennogo proizvodstva v Kuzbasse (1935–1941 gg.)," in *Iz istorii rabochego klassa v Kuzbasse (1917–1967 gg.), Sbornik statei*, (Kemerovo, 1968), 3:61–71.

[22] For the proceedings of a conference marking the fortieth anniversary of Stakhanovism, see *Sotsialisticheskoe sorevnovanie i ego rol' v usloviiakh razvitogo sotsializma* (Moscow: Mysl', 1977). Biographies published in the 1970s included V. K. Diunin and V. Proskura, *Shagni pervym (o A. G. Stakhanove)* (Moscow: Gospolit 1972); *Novatory* (1972); and K. G. Petrov, *Zhivye sily* (Donetsk: Donbass, 1971); among the autobiographies were A. Kh. Busygin, *Sversheniia* (Moscow: Profizdat, 1972), and the revised edition of I. I. Gudov, *Sud'ba rabochego* (Moscow: Politizdat, 1970).

[23] Actually, in 1938, Otdykh ("Rest"), a new residential settlement in the Moscow *oblast'*, was renamed Stakhanovo. Nine years later, the name was changed again, this time to commemorate the centenary of the birth of the Russian physicist N. E. Zhukovskii. This was consistent with the late Stalinist appropriation of tsarist Russia's scientific and cultural achievements. See G. R. F. Bursa, "Political Changes of Names of Soviet Towns," *Slavonic and East European Review*, 63 (1985):173, 178.

[24] *Voroshilovgradshchina – rodina stakhanovskogo dvizheniia (k 50–letiiu slav-*

lications featured articles on Stakhanovism that, either ignoring
or explicitly denying its conflictual aspects, emphasized the co-
operation it supposedly fostered between workers and engineering-technical personnel.[25] Thus was a tradition invented
from which advanced workers, the "Stakhanovites of the 1980s,"
could draw inspiration. One wonders how many actually do.

*nogo pochina), metodologicheskie rekomendatsii v pomoshch' propagandistam,
lektoram, politinformatoram* (Voroshilovgrad, 1985); *50 stakhanovskikh
let: Stati, vospominaniia, ocherki, interv'iu, khronika* (Donetsk: Donbass,
1985); and *50 let stakhanovskomu dvizheniiu: Iubeleinaia vystavka. Pu-
tovoditel' po iubeleinoi vystavke VDNKh SSSR* (Moscow, 1985).

[25] For example, V. S. Lel'chuk, "VKP(b) vo glave tvorcheskogo pochina
rabochego klassa," *Voprosy istorii KPSS*, no. 8 (1985):83–95; and A. V.
Mitrofanova and L. S. Rogachevskaia, "Stakhanovskoe dvizhenie: Istoriia i istoriografiia," *Voprosy istorii*, no. 8 (1985):3–20.

Selected bibliography

Archival materials

Harvard Interview Project on the Soviet Social System. Russian Research Center, Harvard University, Cambridge, Mass., 1949–51.
Smolensk Party Archive, 1917–1941. National Archives, Washington, D.C. Microfilm copy.
State Department Decimal File, 1928–1941. National Archives, Washington, D.C.

Dissertations and unpublished papers

Barber, John. "Labour Discipline in Soviet Industry, 1928–1941." Paper presented at the Twelfth AAASS Convention, Philadelphia, November 1980.
  "Notes on the Soviet Working-Class Family, 1928–1941." Paper presented at the Second World Congress for Soviet and East European Studies, Garmisch-Partenkirchen, W. Germany, September–October 1980.
Davies, R. W. "The Soviet Economic Crisis of 1931–1933." CREES discussion paper, Soviet Industrialisation Project Series (SIPS), University of Birmingham, no. 4, 1976.
Glicksman, Jerzy. "Conditions of Industrial Labor in the USSR: A Study of the Incentive System in Soviet Industry." Manuscript, Harvard Interview Project on the Soviet Social System. Russian Research Center, Harvard University, Cambridge, Mass., 1954.
Kuromiya, Hiroaki. "The Artel and Social Relations in Soviet Industry in the 1920s." Paper presented at a colloquium, The Social History of the Soviet Union in the NEP Period, Bloomington, Ind., October 1986.
Rittersporn, Gabor T. "Rethinking Stalinism." Paper presented at the Annual Conference of the British National Association for Soviet and East European Studies, Cambridge, England, March 1983.
Sakharov, V. A. "Zarozhdenie i razvitie stakhanovskogo dvizheniia v

310   *Selected bibliography*

avtotraktornoi promyshlennosti v gody vtoroi piatiletki." Kandidatskaia dissertatsiia, Moskovskii oblastnoi pedagogicheskii institut,
im. N. K. Krupskoi, 1979.

Newspapers

Izvestiia
Komsomol'skaia pravda
Leningradskaia pravda
Magnitogorskii rabochii
Mashinostroenie
New York Times
Pravda

Sotsialisticheskii Donbass
Tikhookeanskaia zvezda (Khabarovsk)
Trud
Vechernaia Moskva
Za industrializatsiiu; after September 1937,
Industriia
Za sotsialisticheskii sever (Kotlas)

Journals

Biulleten' Oppozitsii, emigré Trotskyist journal
Bol'shevik, semimonthly organ of Communist Party Central Committee
Gornyi zhurnal, monthly journal of Society of Mining Engineers (1934–
    6)
Klub, journal of VTsSPS
Molodaia gvardiia, organ of VLKSM Central Committee
Na fronte industrializatsii (Leningrad), organ of Leningrad Soviet Exec-
    utive Committee
Na trudovom fronte, journal of People's Commissariat of Labor (1931–2)
Novyi gorniak (Stalino), journal of Glavugol' and Central Committee of
    Union of Coal Miners of Donbass
Novyi mir, journal of Union of Writers
Organizatsii truda, organ of Central Institute of Labor
Organizatsiia upravleniia, organ of Central Scientific-Investigative Insti-
    tute of Narkomtiazhprom (1931–8)
Partiinoe stroitel'stvo, organ of Communist Party Central Committee
Plan, journal of Gosplan USSR and Central Administration of National
    Economic Accounting (1933–7)
Planovoe khoziaistvo, journal of Gosplan USSR
Problemy ekonomiki, journal of Institute of Economics of Academy of
    Sciences, USSR
Profsoiuznyi rabotnik (Leningrad), organ of Leningrad Council of Trade
    Unions (1936–7)
Profsoiuzy SSSR, journal of VTsSPS (1938–41)
Puti industrializatsii, journal of Presidium of Vesenkha (1928–31)
Rabsel'kor (Leningrad)
Sovetskaia iiustitsiia, organ of People's Commissariat of Justice
Sovetskoe gosudarstvo i pravo, organ of Institute of Government and Law
    of Academy of Sciences, USSR
Sotsialisticheskaia zakonnost', organ of Procuracy of the USSR

Sotsialisticheskii vestnik, journal of Menshevik emigration
Stakhanovets, journal of VTsSPS (1936–40)
Statistika truda, organ of Central Bureau of Labor Statistics (1922–9)
Tekhnicheskaia propaganda, organ of Narkomtiazhprom (1932–6)
Udarnik, journal of VTsSPS (1931–2)
Voprosy profdvizheniia, journal of VTsSPS (1933–7)
Voprosy truda, monthly journal of People's Commissariat of Labor (1928–33)
Za promyshlennye kadry, journal of Vesenkha and, from, 1932, of Narkomtiazhprom

Collections of laws, resolutions, and other documents

Dokumenty trudovoi slavy Moskvichei, 1919–1965. Moscow, 1967.
Industrializatsiia severo-zapadnogo raiona v gody vtoroi i tret'ei piatiletok, 1933–1941 gg. Dokumenty i materialy. Leningrad, 1969.
Industrializatsiia SSSR, 1929–1932 gg. Dokumenty i materialy. Moscow, 1970.
Industrializatsiia SSSR, 1933–1937 gg. Dokumenty i materialy. Moscow, 1971.
Industrializatsiia SSSR, 1938–1941 gg. Dokumenty i materialy. Moscow, 1973.
Istoriia industrializatsii nizhegorodskogo–Gor'kovskogo kraia (1926–1941 gg.). Gor'kii, 1968.
Istoriia industrializatsii tsentral'no-chernozemnogo raiona (1933–1941 gg.). Kursk, 1972.
Komsomol'tsy i molodezh Ivanovskoi oblasti v gody stroitel'stva sotsializma (1921–1940 gg.). Sbornik dokumentov i materialov. Ivanovo, 1967.
KPSS v rezoliutsiiakh i resheniiakh s"ezdov, konferentsii i plenumov TsK, 10 vols., 8th ed. Moscow, 1971; 9th ed., Moscow, 1984– .
Marsh udarnykh brigad. Molodezh v gody vosstanovleniia narodnogo khoziaistva i sotsialisticheskogo stroitel'stva, 1921–1941 gg Sbornik dokumentov. Moscow, 1965.
Pokolenie udarnikov. Sbornik dokumentov i materialov o sotsialisticheskom sorevnovanii na predpriiatiiakh Leningrada v 1928–1961 gg. Leningrad, 1963.
Politicheskii i trudovoi pod"em rabochego klassa SSSR (1928–1929 gg.). Sbornik dokumentov. Moscow, 1956.
Profsoiuzy SSSR. Dokumenty i materialy, 5 vols. Moscow 1963–73.
Promyshlennost' i rabochii klass Ukrainskoi SSR, 1933–1941 gg., 2 vols. Kiev, 1977.
Resheniia II plenuma Tsentral'nogo komiteta soiuza gornorabochikh SSSR. Shestogo sozyva (20–26 sentiabria 1928 goda). Moscow, 1928.
Rezoliutsiia IX s"ezda profsoiuzov. Moscow, 1932.
Sbornik vazhneishikh zakonov i postanovlenii o trude. Moscow, 1958.

Sobranie zakonov i rasporiazhenii raboche-krest'ianskogo pravitel'stva SSSR.
Moscow, 1924–37.
Sotsialisticheskoe sorevnovanie v SSSR, 1918–1964 gg. Dokumenty i materialy Profsoiuzov. Moscow, 1965

Statistical compilations

Beilin, A. E. *Kadry spetsialistov SSSR, ikh formirovanie i rost.* Moscow, 1935.
Itogi vypolneniia pervogo piatiletnogo plana razvitiia narodnogo khoziaistva soiuza SSR, 2d ed. Moscow, 1934.
Kul'turnoe stroitel'stvo SSSR. Statisticheskii sbornik. Moscow–Leningrad, 1940.
Molodezh' SSSR. Statisticheskii sbornik. Moscow, TsUNKhU and TsK VLKSM, 1936.
Profsoiuznaia perepis', 1932–1933 g. Moscow, VTsSPS Statotdel, 1934.
Sotsialisticheskoe stroitel'stvo SSSR, Moscow, TsUNKhU, 1936.
Trud v SSSR, 1931 g. Moscow, 1932.
Trud v SSSR. Statisticheskii sbornik. Moscow, TsUNKhU, 1936.

Stenographic reports of congresses and conferences

XVII konferentsiia VKP(b), ianv.–fev. 1932 g. Stenograficheskii otchet. Moscow, 1932.
XVII s"ezd Vsesoiuznoi kommunisticheskoi partii (bol'shevikov) 27 ianvaria – 10 fevralia 1934 g. Stenograficheskii otchet. Moscow, 1934.
VII Vsesoiuznaia konferentsiia VLKSM. Stenograficheskii otchet. Moscow, 1933.
IX Vsesoiuznyi s"ezd VLKSM, Ianvar' 1931 g. Stenograficheskii otchet. Moscow, 1931.
X S"ezd VLKSM. Stenograficheskii otchet, 2 vols. Moscow, 1936.
Pervoe Vsesoiuznoe soveshchanie rabochikh i rabotnits-stakhanovtsev, 14–17 noiabria, 1935. Stenograficheskii otchet. Moscow, 1935.
Pervyi vsedonetskii slet stakhanovtsev-masterov uglia, 7–10 ianvaria 1936 g., Stalino. Stenograficheskii otchet. Kiev, 1936.
Report of the Court Proceedings in the Case of the Anti-Soviet Trotskyite Centre. Moscow, 1937.
Soveshchanie khoziaistvennikov, inzhenerov, tekhnikov, partiinykh i profsoiuznykh rabotnikov tiazheloi promyshlennosti, 20–22 sentiabria 1934 g., Stenograficheskii otchet. Moscow–Leningrad, 1935.
Sovet pri narodnom komissare tiazheloi promyshlennosti SSSR. Pervyi plenum, 10–12 maia 1935 g. Moscow–Leningrad, 1935.
Trudy pervoi Vsesoiuznoi konferentsii po mekhanizatsii kamennougol'noi promyshlennosti. Khar'kov, 1931.
Vsesoiuznoe soveshchanie zhen khoziaistvennikov i inzhenerno-tekhnicheskikh rabotnikov tiazheloi promyshlennosti. Stenograficheskii otchet. Moscow, 1936.

Selected bibliography   313

Books and articles (Russian)

Bakunin, A. V. *Vozniknovenie i razvitie stakhanovskogo dvizheniia na Urale.* Sverdlovsk, 1985.
Beilin, L. A. *Ekonomicheskie osnovy sotsialisticheskogo sorevnovaniia.* Moscow, 1970.
Berdnikova, D. "Ot kommunisticheskikh subbotnikov k stakhanovskomu dvizheniiu." *Uchenye zapiski Leningradskogo instituta istorii VKP(b),* no. 1 (1940):137–67.
Busygin, A. Kh. *Sversheniia.* Moscow, 1972.
Zhizn' moia i moikh druzei. Moscow, 1939.
Bykov, P. *Put' k schast'iu.* Moscow, 1951.
Byli industrial'nye. Ocherki i vospominaniia. Moscow, 1970.
Diunin, V. K., and Proskura, V. *Shagni pervym.* Moscow, 1972.
Drobizhev, V. Z. "Rol' rabochego klassa v formirovanii komandnykh kadrov sotsialisticheskoi promyshlennosti (1917–1936 gg.)." *Istoriia SSSR,* no. 4 (1961):55–75.
Dubner, P.M., and Kozyrev, M. *Kollektivy i kommuny v bor'be za kommunisticheskoi formy truda.* Moscow–Leningrad, 1930.
Dzeniskevich, A. R. *Rabochie Leningrada nakanune Velikoi Otechestvennoi voiny, 1938 – iiun' 1941 g.* Leningrad, 1983.
Ermanskii, O. A. *Stakhanovskoe dvizhenie i stakhanovskie metody.* Moscow, 1940.
Teoriia i praktika ratsionalizatsii, 5th ed. Moscow, 1933.
Ershova, E. A., et al. *Istoriia Leningradskoi Gosudarstvennoi Ordena Lenina i Ordena Trudovogo Krasnogo Znameni obuvnoi fabriki Skorokhod imeni Ia. Kalinina.* Leningrad, 1969.
Eskin, M. *Osnovnye puti razvitiia sotsialisticheskikh form truda,* 2d ed. Leningrad, 1936.
Evstaf'ev, G. N. *Sotsialisticheskoe sorevnovanie – zakonnost' i dvizhushchia sila ekonomicheskogo razvitiia sovetskogo obshchestva.* Moscow, 1952.
Faustov, S. A. *Moi rost.* Gor'kii, 1938.
Generalova, A. D. *Kak ia stala stakhanovkoi.* Gor'kii, 1938.
Gershberg, S. R. *Rabota u nas takaia: Zapisi zhurnalista-pravdista tridtsatykh godov.* Moscow, 1971.
Rukovodstvo kommunisticheskoi partii dvizheniem novatorov v promyshlennosti (1935–1941). Moscow, 1956.
Gordon, L. A., Kropov, E. V., and Onikov, L. A. *Cherty sotsialisticheskogo obraza zhizni: Byt gorodskikh rabochikh vchera, segodnia i zavtra.* Moscow, 1977.
Kalistratov, Iu. A. *Za udarnyi proizvodstvennyi kollektiv,* 2d ed. Moscow, 1931.
Kapustin, A., and Trifonov, N. *Sotsialistichecheskoe sorevnovanie v massy.* Moscow–Leningrad, 1929.
Karpinskii, V. A. *Stakhanovskoe dvizhenie.* Moscow, 1936.
Kazakov, E. E. "Deiatel'nost' profsoiuzov Kuzbassa po razvitiiu stak-

hanovskogo dvizheniia v gody piatiletki." In *Ocherki sotsial'no-ekonomicheskoi i kul'turnoi zhizni Sibiri,* chast' 2. Novosibirsk, 1972.

K godovshchine I vsesoiuznogo soveshchanii stakhanovtsev. Sbornik statei direktorov Leningradskikh predpriiatii legkoi promyshlennosti. Moscow–Leningrad, 1936.

Khabibulina, R. Ia. *Leningradskie kommunisty-organizatory stakhanovskogo dvizheniia (1935–1937 gg.).* Leningrad, 1961.

"Opyt sravnitel'nogo analiza sostava stakhanovtsev i uchastnikov dvizheniia za kommunisticheskoe otnoshenie k trudu." In *Rabochii klass SSSR na sovremennom etape.* Leningrad, 1982.

Khavin, A. F. "Razvitie tiazheloi promyshlennosti v tret'ei piatiletke (1938–iiun' 1941 gg.)." *Istoriia SSSR,* no. 1 (1959):10–35.

Khronika stakhanovskogo dvizheniia v tiazheloi promyshlennosti, 2 vols. Moscow, 1935.

Krupianskaia, V. Iu., Budina, I. R., Polishchuk, N. S., and Iukhneva, N. V. *Kul'tura i byt gorniakov i metallurgov Nizhego Tagila (1917–1970).* Moscow, 1974.

Kulagina, V. M. *Leningradskie kommunisty v bor'be za osvoenie novoi tekhniki (1933–1935 gg.).* Leningrad, 1962.

Kuz'minov, I. I. *Stakhanovskoe dvizhenie – vysshii etap sotsialisticheskogo sorevnovaniia.* Moscow, 1940.

Lebedeva, N. B., and Shkaratan, O. I. *Ocherki istorii sotsialisticheskogo sorevnovaniia.* Leningrad, 1966.

Lebedev-Patreiko, V., Rabinovich, G., and Rodin, D. *Biudzhet vremeni rabochei sem'i (po materialam Leningradskogo obsledovaniia).* Leningrad, 1933.

Lel'chuk, V. S. *Industrializatsiia SSSR: Istoriia, opyt, problemy.* Moscow, 1984.

"VKP(b) vo glave tvorcheskogo pochina rabochego klassa." *Voprosy istorii KPSS,* no. 8 (1985):83–95.

Lenin, V. I. *Polnoe sobranie sochinenii,* 55 vols., 5th ed. Moscow, 1959–65.

Likholoboda, Z. G. *Rabochie Donbassa v gody pervykh piatiletok (1928–1937 gg.).* Donetsk, 1973.

Malafeev, A. N. *Istoriia tsenoobrazovaniia v SSSR.* Moscow, 1964.

Markus, B. L. *Trud v sotsialistichekom obshchestve.* Moscow, 1939.

Mikhailovskii, I. N. *Komsomol Ukrainy v bor'be za postroenie sotsializma v SSSR (1925–1937 gg.).* L'vov, 1966.

Mitrofanova, A. V. *Rabochii klass SSSR v gody Velikoi Otechestvennoi voiny.* Moscow, 1971.

Mitrofanova, A. V., and Rogachevskaia, L. S. "Stakhanovskoe dvizhenie: Istoriia i istoriografiia." *Voprosy istorii,* no. 8 (1985):3–20.

Nemchinov, V. P. *Razvitie tekhniki dobychi uglia.* Moscow, 1965.

"Neopublikovannoe vystuplenie G. K. Ordzhonikidze." *Voprosy istorii,* no. 8 (1978):94–7.

Novatory, Sbornik. Moscow, 1972.

Okuneva, I. O. *O rezervakh povysheniia proizvoditel'nosti truda.* Moscow, 1940.

Ol'khov, V. *Za zhivoe rukovodstvo sotssorevnovaniem.* Moscow, 1930.

O novykh normakh i stakhanovskoi rabote. Po materialam otraslevykh konferentsii. Leningrad, 1936.

Oprishchenko, A. L. "Dvizhenie novatorov proizvodstva v predvoennye gody." *Istoriia KPSS*, no. 6 (1966):106–9.

Ordzhonikidze, G. K. *Stat'i i rechi,* 2 vols. Moscow, 1956–7.

Organizatsiia truda v stakhanovskom dvizhenii. Sbornik TsIT. Moscow–Leningrad, 1936.

Ostapenko, I. P. *Uchastie rabochego klassa SSSR v upravlenii proizvodstvom (Proizvodstvennye soveshchaniia v promyshlennosti v 1921–1932 gg.).* Moscow, 1964.

Petrov, K. G. *Zhivye sily.* Donetsk, 1971.

50 stakhanovskikh let: Stati, vospominaniia, ocherki, interv'iu, khronika. Donetsk, 1985.

Ponomarenko, G. Ia. *Vo glave trudovogo pod"ema. Kommunisty Donbassa-organizatory sotsialisticheskogo sorevnovaniia rabochego klassa v pervoi piatiletki.* Kiev, 1971.

Rabochii klass v upravlenii gosudarstvom (1926–1937 gg.). Edited by K. V. Gusev and V. Z. Drobizhev. Moscow, 1968.

Rashin, A. G. "Rost kul'turno-technicheskogo urovnia rabochego klassa SSSR v 1917–1958 gg." *Istoriia SSSR*, no. 2 (1961):10–24.

Rogachevskaia, L. S. *Sotsialisticheskoe sorevnovanie v SSSR, istoricheskie ocherki, 1917–1970 gg.* Moscow, 1977.

Romanov, P. "Novye liudi," *Novyi mir*, no. 3 (1936):157–64.

Rotshtein, A. I. *Problemy promyshlennoi statistiki,* 3 vols. Leningrad, 1936–47.

Rubinshtein, M. *Novye formy stakhanovskogo dvizheniia.* Moscow, 1940.

Sakharov, V. A. *Zarozhdenie i razvitie stakhanovskogo dvizheniia (na materialakh po avtotraktornoi promyshlennosti).* Moscow, 1985.

Seniavskii, S. L., and Tel'pukhovskii, V. B., *Rabochii klass SSSR, 1938–1965.* Moscow, 1971.

Shigalin, G. I. *Narodnoe khoziaistvo SSSR v period Velikoi Otechestvennoi voiny.* Moscow, 1960.

Shkaratan, O. I. "Material'noe blagosostoianie rabochego klassa SSSR v perekhodnyi period ot kapitalizma k sotsializmu (po materialam Leningrada)," *Istoriia SSSR*, no. 3 (1964):17–44.

Slutskii, A. B. *Rabochii klass Ukrainy v bor'be za sozdanie fundamenta sotsialisticheskoi ekonomiki (1926–1932 gg.).* Kiev, 1963.

Sorevnovanie i ego rol' v usloviiakh razvitogo sotsializma. Moscow, 1977.

Sotsialisticheskoe sorevnovanie v promyshlennosti SSSR, Sbornik statei. Edited by Ia. M. Bineman. Moscow, 1930.

Sotsialisticheskoe sorevnovanie. Voprosy teorii, praktiki i organizatsii. Moscow, 1978.

Stakhanov, A. G. *Rasskaz o moei zhizni.* Moscow, 1937.

Zhizn' shakhterskaia. Kiev, 1975.

Stalin, I. V. *Sochineniia,* 3 vols. (14–16). Edited by Robert H. McNeal. Stanford, Calif., 1967.

Tekhnika gornogo dela i metallurgi. Moscow, 1968.

Vainshtein, A. *Voprosy stakhanovskogo dvizheniia v leningradskoi promysh-lennosti.* Leningrad, 1937.
Vasil'ev, D. N. *Moia mechta.* Stalingrad, 1936.
Vdovin, A. I., and Drobizhev, V. Z. *Rost rabochego klassa SSSR, 1917–1940 gg.* Moscow, 1976.
Volchenko, A. V. "O dvizhenii novatorov promyshlennogo proizvodstva v Kuzbasse (1935–1941 gg.)." In *Iz istorii rabochego klassa v Kuzbasse (1917–1967 gg.). Sbornik statei.* vol. 3. Kemerovo, 1968.
Voroshilovgradshchina – rodina stakhanovskogo dvizheniia (K 50-letiiu slav-nogo pochina), metologicheskie rekomendatsii v pomoshch' propagandistam, lektoram, politinformatoram. Voroshilovgrad, 1985.
Vzgliad skvoz' gody: Zapiski stakhanovstev. Moscow, 1984.
Zarkhii, S. *Kommuna v tsekhe.* Moscow–Leningrad, 1930.
Zelenko, G. I. "Podgotovka kvalifitsirovannoi rabochei sily." In *Voprosy truda v SSSR.* Edited by G. A. Prudenskii. Moscow, 1958.
Zil'bergleit, P. B. *Proizvoditel'nost' truda v kamennougol'noi promyshlennosti.* Khar'kov, 1930.
Zvorykin, A. *Ocherki po istorii sovetskoi gornoi tekhniki.* Moscow, 1950.

Books and articles (Western)

Anstett, Marcel. *La formation de la main d'oeuvre qualifée en Union Sovietique de 1917 à 1954.* Paris, 1958.
Bailes, Kendall E. "Stalin and the Making of a New Elite: A Comment." *Slavic Review,* 39 (1980):286–9.
   Technology and Society under Lenin and Stalin: Origins of the Soviet Technical Intelligentsia, 1917–1941. Princeton, N.J., 1978.
Barber, John. "The Standard of Living of Soviet Industrial Workers, 1928–1941." In *L'Industrialisation de l'URSS dans les années trente.* Edited by Charles Bettelheim. Paris, 1982.
Barker, G. R. *Some Problems of Incentives and Labour Productivity in Soviet Industry.* Oxford, n.d.
Bauer, Raymond; Inkeles, Alex; and Kluckhohn, Clyde. *How the Soviet System Works.* Cambridge, Mass., 1956.
Baykov, Alexander. *The Development of the Soviet Economic System.* Cambridge, England, 1948.
Beattie, Robert. "A 'Great Turn' That Never Happened? A Reconsideration of the Soviet Decree on Labor Discipline of November 1932." *Russian History/Histoire russe* (forthcoming).
Behrend, Hilde. "The Effort Bargain." *Industrial and Labour Relations Review,* 10 (1957):503–15.
Bendix, Reinhard. *Work and Authority in Industry: Ideologies of Management in the Course of Industrialization,* New York, 1963.
Berger, Harold, and Shurr, S. H. *The Mining Industries, 1899–1939: A Study of Output, Employment and Productivity.* New York, 1944.
Bergson, Abram. *The Structure of Soviet Wages.* Cambridge, Mass., 1944.

Berliner, Joseph. *Factory and Manager in the USSR*. Cambridge, Mass., 1957.

Brady, Robert. *The Rationalization Movement in Germany Industry*. New York, 1974.

Braverman, Harry. *Labor and Monopoly Capital: The Degradation of Work in the Twentieth Century*. New York, 1974.

Burawoy, Michael. *Manufacturing Consent: Changes in the Labor Process under Monopoly Capitalism*. Chicago, 1979.

"Piece Rates, Hungarian Style," *Socialist Review*, no. 79 (1985):43–85.

The Politics of Production. London, 1985.

Bursa, G. R. F. "Political Changes of Names of Soviet Towns," *Slavonic and East European Review*, 62 (1985):161–93.

Carr, E. H., and Davies, R. W. *Foundations of a Planned Economy, 1926–1929*, 3 vols. Harmondsworth, 1971–4.

Citrine, Sir Walter. *I Search for Truth in Russia*, London, 1936.

Clark, Katerina. *The Soviet Novel: History as Ritual*. Chicago, 1981.

"Utopian Anthropology as a Context for Stalinist Literature." In *Stalinism: Essays in Historical Interpretation*. Edited by Robert C. Tucker. New York, 1977.

Clark, M. Gardner. *The Economics of Soviet Steel*. Cambridge, Mass., 1956.

Clarke, Roger A. *Soviet Economic Facts, 1917–1970*. New York, 1972.

Cohen, Stephen. "Bolshevism and Stalinism." In *Stalinism: Essays in Historical Interpretation*. Edited by Robert C. Tucker. New York, 1977. Reprinted in Stephen Cohen, *Rethinking the Soviet Experience: Politics and History Since 1917*. New York, 1985.

Conquest, Robert. *The Great Terror: Stalin's Purge of the Thirties*. New York, 1973.

Industrial Workers in the USSR. London, 1967.

Corrigan, Phillip; Ramsay, Harvie; and Sayer, Derek. *Socialist Construction and Marxist Theory: Bolshevism and Its Critique*. New York, 1978.

Depretto, J. P. "Le record de Stakhanov." In *L'Industrialisation de l'URSS dans les années trente*. Edited by Charles Bettelheim. Paris, 1982.

Deustcher, Isaac. "Socialist Competition." In *Heretics and Renegades and Other Essays*. London, 1969.

Soviet Trade Unions: Their Place in Soviet Labour Policy. London, 1950.

Dobb, Maurice. *Soviet Economic Development since 1917*. London, 1966.

Dunham, Vera. *In Stalin's Time: Middleclass Values in Soviet Fiction*. Cambridge, England, 1976.

Eley, Geoff. "History with the Politics Left Out – Again? *Russian Review* 45 (1986): 385–94.

Fainsod, Merle. *How Russia Is Ruled*, rev. ed. Cambridge, Mass., 1965.

Smolensk under Soviet Rule. New York, 1958.

Filtzer, Donald. *Soviet Workers and Stalinist Industrialization: The Formation of Modern Soviet Production Relations, 1928–1941*. Armonk, N.Y., 1986.

Fitzpatrick, Sheila. *Education and Social Mobility in the Soviet Union, 1921–1934*. Cambridge, England, 1978.

"Politics of Soviet Industrialization: Vesenkha and Its Relationship with Rabkrin, 1929–1930." Kennan Insitute Occasional Paper no. 167. Washington, D.C., 1983.

"Stalin and the Making of a New Elite, 1928–1939," *Slavic Review*, 38 (1979):377–402.

Fitzpatrick, Sheila, ed. *Cultural Revolution in Russia, 1928–1931*. Bloomington, Ind., 1978.

Friedmann, Georges. *De la Sainte Russie a l'URSS*, 2d ed. Paris, 1938.

Getty, J. Arch. *Origins of the Great Purges: The Soviet Communist Party Reconsidered, 1933–1938*. Cambridge, England, 1985.

"Party and Purge in Smolensk: 1933–1937," *Slavic Review*, 42 (1983):60–79.

Goodrich, Carter. *The Miner's Freedom: Study of the Working Life in a Changing Industry*. Boston, 1925.

Granick, David. *Management of the Industrial Firm in the USSR: A Study in Soviet Economic Planning*. New York, 1954.

Hanfmann, Eugenia, and Getzels, Jacob W. "Interpersonal Attitudes of Former Soviet Citizens, as Studied by a Semi-Projective Method." *Psychological Monographs, General and Applied*. 69 (1955)): 1–37.

Haraszti, Miklos. *A Worker in a Worker's State*. Translated by Michael Wright, Harmondsworth, 1977.

Harrison, Mark. *Soviet Planning in Peace and War. 1938–1945*. Cambridge, England, 1985.

Hobsbawm, Eric. *The Age of Capital, 1848–1875*. London, 1977.

Workers: World of Labor. New York, 1984.

Inkeles, Alex, and Bauer, Raymond A. *The Soviet Citizen: Daily Life in a Totalitarian Society*. Cambridge, Mass., 1961.

Jasny, Naum. *Soviet Industrialization, 1928–1952*. Chicago, 1961.

Kingsbury, Susan M., and Fairchild, Mildred. *Factory, Family and Women in the Soviet Union*. New York, 1935.

Körber, Lili. *Life in a Soviet Factory*. Translated by Claud W. Sykes, London, 1933.

Kravchenko, Victor. *I Chose Freedom*. New York, 1946.

Kucherov, Samuel. *The Origins of Soviet Administration of Justice: Their History and Operation*. Leiden, 1970.

Kuromiya, Hiroaki. "Edinonachalie and the Soviet Industrial Manager, 1928–1937." *Soviet Studies*, 36 (1984):185–204.

Lampert, Nicholas. *The Technical Intelligentsia and the Soviet State: A Study of Soviet Managers and Technicians, 1928–1935*. New York, 1979.

Lapidus, Gail. *Women in Soviet Society*. Berkeley and Los Angeles, 1978.

Lewin, Moshe. *The Making of the Soviet System: Essays in the Social History of Interwar Russia*. New York, 1985.

Political Undercurrents in Soviet Economic Debates. Princeton, N.J., 1974.

Russian Peasants and Soviet Power: A Study of Collectivization. Evanston, Ill., 1968.

Littlepage, John, and Bess, Demeree. *In Search of Soviet Gold*. New York, 1938.

Maignien, Yannick. *La division du travail manuel et intellectuel et sa suppres-*

sion dans le passage au communisme chez Marx et ses successeurs. Paris, 1975.

Mehnert, Klaus. *Youth in Soviet Russia.* Translated by Michael Davidson. New York, 1933.

Noble, David. *America by Design, Science, Technology and the Rise of Corporate Capitalism.* New York, 1982.

Nove, Alec. *An Economic History of the USSR.* London, 1969.

The Soviet Economic System. London, 1977.

Offe, Claus. *Industry and Inequality: The Achievement Principle in Work and Social Status.* London, 1976.

Pasquier, Albert. *Le Stakhanovisme: L'Organisation du travail en URSS.* Caen, 1937.

Rigby, T. H. *Communist Party Membership in the USSR. 1917–1967* Princeton, N.J., 1968.

Riordan, James. *Sport in Soviet Society.* Cambridge, England, 1977.

Rittersporn, Gabor T. "L'Etat en lutte contre lui-même: Tensions sociales et conflicts politiques en URSS, 1936–1938." *Libre,* no. 4 (1978): 3–38.

"The 1930s in the Longue Durée of Soviet History." *Telos,* no. 53 (1982):107–16.

"Société et appareil d'état sovietiques (1936–1938): Contradictions et interferences." *Annales E.S.C.,* 34 (1979):843–67.

"Staline en 1938: Apogée du verbe et defaute politique." *Libre,* no. 6 (1979):99–164.

Roy, Donald. "Efficiency and 'the Fix': Informal Intergroup Relations in a Piecework Machine Shop," *American Journal of Sociology* 60 (1955): 255–66.

Sarel, Benno. *La classe ouvrière d'Allemagne Orientale.* Paris, 1958.

Schwarz, Solomon. "The Continuous Work Week in Soviet Russia," *International Labour Review,* no. 2 (1931): 157–80.

Labor in the Soviet Union. New York, 1952.

Scott, John. *Behind the Urals: An American Worker in Russia's City of Steel.* Bloomington, Ind., 1973.

Shiokawa, Nobuaki. "Labor Turnover in the USSR, 1928–33: A Sectoral Analysis." *Annals of the Institute of Social Science* (Tokyo), no. 23 (1982):65–94.

Siegelbaum, Lewis H. "Productive Collectives and Communes and the 'Imperatives' of Soviet Industrialization, 1929–1931." *Slavic Review,* 45 (1986):65–84.

"Shock Work." In *The Modern Encyclopedia of Russian and Soviet History.* Edited by Joseph L. Wieczynski, vol. 35. Gulf Breeze, Fla., 1983.

"Socialist Competition and Socialist Construction in the USSR: The Experience of the First Five-year Plan (1928–1932)," *Thesis Eleven,* no. 4 (1982):48–67.

"Soviet Norm Determination in Theory and Practice, 1917–1941." *Soviet Studies,* 36 (1984):45–68.

Sirianni, Carmen. *Workers Control and Socialist Democracy: The Soviet Experience.* London, 1982.

Smith, Andrew. *I Was a Soviet Worker*. London, 1938.

Stalin, J. V. *Works*, 13 vols. Moscow, 1952–5.

Stearns, Peter. *Lives of Labour: Work in a Maturing Industrial Society*. London, 1975.

Sutton, Anthony C. *Western Technology and Soviet Economic Development, 1930–1945*. Stanford, Calif., 1971.

Taylor, Frederick W. *The Principles of Scientific Management*. New York, 1967.

Timasheff, Nicholas. *The Great Retreat: The Growth and Decline of Communism in Russia*. New York, 1946.

Trotsky, Leon. *The Revolution Betrayed*. New York, 1965.

Weissberg, Alexander. *The Accused*. New York, 1951.

Yanowitch, Murray. "Trends in Differentials between Salaried Personnel and Wage Workers in Soviet Industry." *Soviet Studies*, 11 (1960): 229–46.

Zaleski, Eugene. *Planning for Economic Growth in the Soviet Union, 1918–1932*. Chapel Hill, N.C., 1971.

Index

321

SOVIET AND EAST EUROPEAN STUDIES

Books in the series

Rudolf Bićanić *Economic Policy in Socialist Yugoslavia*
Galia Golan *Yom Kippur and After: The Soviet Union and the
Middle East Crisis*
Maureen Perrie *The Agrarian Policy of the Russian Socialist-Revolutionary
Party from Its Origins through the Revolution of 1905–1907*
Paul Vyšný *Neo-Slavism and the Czechs 1898–1914*
Gabriel Gorodetsky *The Precarious Truce: Anglo-Soviet Relations
1924–1927*
James Riordan *Sport in Soviet Society: Development of Sport and Physical
Education in Russia and the USSR*
Gregory Walker *Soviet Book Publishing Policy*
Felicity Ann O'Dell *Socialisation through Children's Literature:
The Soviet Example*
T. H. Rigby *Lenin's Government: Sovnarkom 1917–1922*
Stella Alexander *Church and State in Yugoslavia since 1945*
M. Cave *Computers and Economic Planning: The Soviet Experience*
Jozef M. van Brabant *Socialist Economic Integration: Aspects of
Contemporary Economic Problems in Eastern Europe*
R. F. Leslie, ed. *The History of Poland since 1863*
M. R. Myant *Socialism and Democracy in Czechoslovakia 1945–1948*
Blair A. Ruble *Soviet Trade Unions: Their Development in the 1970s*
Angela Stent *From Embargo to Ostpolitik: The Political Economy of West
German–Soviet Relations 1955–1980*
William J. Conyngham *The Modernisation of Soviet
Industrial Management*
Jean Woodall *The Socialist Corporation and Technocratic Power*
Israel Getzler *Kronstadt 1917–1921: The Fate of a Soviet Democracy*
David A. Dyker *The Process of Investment in the Soviet Union*
S. A. Smith *Red Petrograd: Revolution in the Factories 1917–1918*
Saul Estrin *Self-Management: Economic Theory and Yugoslav Practice*
Ray Taras *Ideology in a Socialist State: Poland 1956–1983*
Silvana Malle *The Economic Organization of War Communism 1918–1921*
S. G. Wheatcroft and R. W. Davies *Materials for a Balance of the Soviet
National Economy 1928–1930*
Mark Harrison *Soviet Planning in Peace and War 1938–1945*
James McAdams *East Germany and Détente*
J. Arch Getty *Origins of the Great Purges: The Soviet Communist Party
Reconsidered 1933–1938*
Tadeusz Swietochowski *Russian Azerbaijan 1905–1920: The Shaping of
National Identity*
David S. Mason *Public Opinion and Political Change in Poland
1980–1982*
Stephen White *The Origins of Détente: The Genoa Conference and Soviet–
Western Relations 1921–1922*
Catherine Andreyev *Vlasov and the Russian Liberation Movement*

326